The Art of Translation in Light of Bakhtin's Re-accentuation

Literatures, Cultures, Translation

Literatures, Cultures, Translation presents books that engage central issues in translation studies such as history, politics, and gender in and of literary translation, as well as books that open new avenues for study. Volumes in the series follow two main strands of inquiry: one strand brings a wider context to translation through an interdisciplinary interrogation, while the other hones in on the history and politics of the translation of seminal works in literary and intellectual history.

Series Editors
Brian James Baer, Kent State University, USA
Michelle Woods, The State University of New York, New Paltz, USA

Editorial Board
Paul Bandia, Professeur titulaire, Concordia University, Canada, and Senior Fellow, the W.E.B. Du Bois Institute for African American Research, Harvard University, USA
Susan Bassnett, Professor of Comparative Literature, Warwick University, UK.
Leo Tak-hung Chan, Guangxi University, Hong Kong, China
Michael Cronin, Dublin City University, Republic of Ireland
Edwin Gentzler, University of Massachusetts Amherst, USA
Carol Maier, Kent State University, USA
Denise Merkle, Moncton University, Canada
Michaela Wolf, University of Graz, Austria

Volumes in the Series

Translation and the Making of Modern Russian Literature
Brian James Baer

Interpreting in Nazi Concentration Camps
Edited by Michaela Wolf

Exorcising Translation: Towards an Intercivilizational Turn
Douglas Robinson

Literary Translation and the Making of Originals
Karen Emmerich

The Translator on Stage
Geraldine Brodie

Transgender, Translation, Translingual Address
Douglas Robinson

Western Theory in East Asian Contexts: Translation and Translingual Writing
Leo Tak-hung Chan

The Translator's Visibility: Scenes from Contemporary Latin American Fiction
Heather Cleary

The Relocation of Culture: Translations, Migrations, Borders
Simona Bertacco and Nicoletta Vallorani

The Art of Translation in Light of Bakhtin's Re-accentuation
Edited by Slav Gratchev and Margarita Marinova

Migration and Mutation: New Perspectives on the Sonnet in Translation
Edited by Carole Birkan-Berz, Oriane Monthéard,
and Erin Cunningham (forthcoming)

World Literature in Soviet Contexts: Socialist Realities and Imaginary Worlds
Edited by Emily Finer and Peter Budrin (forthcoming)

The Art of Translation in Light of Bakhtin's Re-accentuation

Edited by
Slav Gratchev and Margarita Marinova

Afterword by
Galin Tihanov

BLOOMSBURY ACADEMIC
LONDON • NEW YORK • OXFORD • NEW DELHI • SYDNEY

BLOOMSBURY ACADEMIC
Bloomsbury Publishing Inc
1385 Broadway, New York, NY 10018, USA
50 Bedford Square, London, WC1B 3DP, UK
29 Earlsfort Terrace, Dublin 2, Ireland

BLOOMSBURY, BLOOMSBURY ACADEMIC and the Diana logo are trademarks of Bloomsbury Publishing Plc

First published in the United States of America 2022
Paperback edition published 2024

Copyright © Slav Gratchev and Margarita Marinova, 2022

Each chapter copyright © by the contributor, 2022

Cover design by Daniel Benneworth-Gray
Cover images © Moscow State University Science Library

All rights reserved. No part of this publication may be reproduced or transmitted in any form or by any means, electronic or mechanical, including photocopying, recording, or any information storage or retrieval system, without prior permission in writing from the publishers.

Bloomsbury Publishing Inc does not have any control over, or responsibility for, any third-party websites referred to or in this book. All internet addresses given in this book were correct at the time of going to press. The author and publisher regret any inconvenience caused if addresses have changed or sites have ceased to exist, but can accept no responsibility for any such changes.

Whilst every effort has been made to locate copyright holders the publishers would be grateful to hear from any person(s) not here acknowledged.

A catalog record for this book is available from the Library of Congress.

ISBN: HB: 978-1-5013-9023-4
PB: 978-1-5013-9027-2
ePDF: 978-1-5013-9025-8
eBook: 978-1-5013-9024-1

Series: Literatures, Cultures, Translation

Typeset by Newgen KnowledgeWorks Pvt. Ltd., Chennai, India

To find out more about our authors and books visit www.bloomsbury.com and sign up for our newsletters.

Contents

List of Figures		ix
Notes on Contributors		xi
Introduction		1
	Slav Gratchev	
1	*Dubliners* Retranslated: Re-accentuating Multivoicedness	9
	Kris Peeters, Guillermo Sanz Gallego, and Monica Paulis	
2	Bakhtin's Dialogism and Language Interpretation	45
	Ida Day	
3	Heteroglossia, Liminality, and Literary Translation	57
	Bo Li	
4	What Is an "Original"?: Creation, Translation, "Re-accentuation," and the Question of Primacy	79
	Michael Eskin	
5	A Study of Three Scarletts: The Homeopathic Effect of Role Language	93
	Yumi Tanaka	
6	The Master-Stylizer and the Creative Act: Mikhail Bakhtin on Translation	113
	Margarita Marinova	
7	Eduardo Mendoza, Lost and Found in Translation	129
	Melissa Garr	
8	Dialogue Disrupted	147
	Victor Fet	
9	Accentuation and Re-accentuation in Language, Literature, and Translation	161
	Susan Petrilli and Augusto Ponzio	
10	Sifting through Dialogic Ashes: Translating Complex Meanings in Muñoz Molina's *Beatus Ille*	189
	Steven Mills	

11	The Many Faces of Alice in Carnival: From Intersemiotic to Intervisual Translation *Riitta Oittinen*	207
12	Juvenile *Quixotes* in Eighteenth-Century England *Scott Pollard*	253
	Afterword: Translating (with) Bakhtin *Galin Tihanov*	275
	Index	283

Figures

11.1	"… for this curious child was very fond of pretending to be two people"	208
11.2	Dialogics, heteroglossia, and carnival	209
11.3	Cheshirecats	213
11.4	Alice's eyes	216
11.5	Doublefold Alice	217
11.6	"… once or twice she had peeped into the book her sister was reading, but it had no pictures or conversations …"	218
11.7	"… for the hot day made her feel very sleepy and stupid …"	219
11.8	The pool of tears 1	220
11.9	The pool of tears 2	220
11.10	The Mouse and Alice in the pool of tears	221
11.11	The Mouse and Alice under the tree	221
11.12	"… the next moment she felt a blow on her chin: it had struck her foot!"	222
11.13	"The first thing I've got to do," said Alice to herself, as she wandered about in the wood," is to grow to my right size again; …"	223
11.14	"'Who are you?' said the Caterpillar"	224
11.15	"'Who are you?' said the Caterpillar"	225
11.16	Father William	226
11.17	Father William	227
11.18	"… so I'll see what this bottle does"	227
11.19	"The top of what? The stalk of what?" thought Alice	228
11.20	"'Come! my head's free at last!' said Alice in a tone of delight, which changed into alarm in another moment, when she found that her shoulders were nowhere to be seen …"	229

11.21	"… was going to dive in among the leaves … when a sharp hiss made her draw back: a large pigeon had flown into her face, and was violently beating her with its wings. 'Serpent!' screamed the pigeon"	230
11.22	"'Serpent!' screamed the pigeon"	231
11.23	Big Alice in the White Rabbit's house	232
11.24	Alice escaping from the White Rabbit's house	232
11.25	Alice's monstruous feet	233
11.26	Poor Bill the Lizard	234
11.27	The mischievous crowd and Bill the Lizard	234
11.28	The Gryphon	235
11.29	The Gryphon	236
11.30	The Gryphon, the Mockturtle, and Alice 1	237
11.31	The Gryphon, the Mockturtle, and Alice 2	238
11.32	The Gryphon, the Mockturtle, and Alice 3	238
11.33	The Gryphon, the Mockturtle, and Alice 4	239
11.34	"The chief difficulty which Alice found at first was to manage her ostrich …"	239
11.35	"The chief difficulty which Alice found at first was to manage her ostrich …"	240
11.36	The embarrassed, smiling Queen	240
11.37	"'Nonsense!' cried Alice, so loudly that everybody jumped, 'the idea of having the sentence first!'"	241
11.38	"'I won't', said Alice, 'you're nothing but a pack of cards! Who cares for you?'"	242

Contributors

Ida Day is Assistant Professor of Spanish at Marshall University and a Spanish interpreter for CyraCom International. Her recent publications include four book chapters in *Global Issues in Contemporary Hispanic Women's Writing* (2012); *Ecological Crisis and Cultural Representation in Latin America* (2016); *Ecofictions, Ecorealities and Slow Violence in Latin America and the Latinx World* (2019); and *The Poetics of Avant-Garde in Literature, Arts and Philosophy* (2020). Her articles on ecocriticism and Latin American studies have appeared in academic journals such as *Revista de Crítica Literaria Latinoamericana*, *IXQUIC Revista Hispánica Internacional de Análisis Literario y Cultural*, *Indigenous Knowledge: Other Ways of Knowing*, and *Mountain Interstate Foreign Language Review*.

Michael Eskin is an award-winning author, translator, publisher, and cofounder of Upper West Side Philosophers, Inc. He has taught at Rutgers, Cambridge, and Columbia Universities. His many publications on cultural, literary, and philosophical subjects include *Nabokov's Version of Pushkin's Eugene Onegin* (1994); *Ethics and Dialogue in the Works of Levinas, Bakhtin, Mandel'shtam, and Celan* (2000); *Poetic Affairs: Celan, Grünbein, Brodsky* (2008); *The Bars of Atlantis: Selected Essays by Durs Grünbein* (as editor, 2010); *The Wisdom of Parenthood: An Essay* (2013); and, most recently, "Schwerer werden. Leichter sein." *Gespräche um Paul Celan* (2020). His translations have appeared in *The New Yorker*, *Sport 40*, and *World Literature Today*, among other venues.

Victor Fet is Professor of Biology at Marshall University. He teaches genetics, evolution, biogeography, and general biology and has over hundred publications on animal systematics and evolution. Fet has edited and translated several books on biology from Russian. He has published five books of poetry in his native Russian, as well as literary reviews and essays; he is especially interested in the work of Vladimir Nabokov and Lewis Carroll. He has also published translations of poetry by Lewis Carroll and Roald Hoffmann. His poetry has appeared in many expatriate Russian journals and almanacs in Europe and the United States.

Guillermo Sanz Gallego is a lecturer at the Vrije Universiteit Brussel (VUB), where he teaches literary translation, translation studies, and research methodology, among other subjects. He has coedited journal issues and has also published numerous articles and book chapters on the translation and retranslation of literature and historic texts, as well as on the influence of censorship on translation.

Melissa Garr is Associate Professor of Spanish at Florida Southern College. Her interests are in genre fiction, twentieth- and twenty-first-century Spanish literature, and the work of Mikhail Bakhtin. Her book chapters appeared in *Mikhail Bakhtin's Heritage in Literature, Arts, and Psychology* (2018) and *Shklovsky's Heritage in Literature, Arts and Philosophy* (2019). Her current research involves digital humanities and the pedagogy of digital exhibits.

Slav Gratchev is Professor of Spanish at Marshall University and recipient of Distinguished Artist and Scholar Award (2019). He is author/editor of nine books: *The Polyphonic World of Cervantes and Dostoevsky* (2017); *Don Quixote: The Re-accentuation of the World's Greatest Literary Hero* (2017); *Bakhtin's Heritage in Literature, Arts, and Psychology* (2018); *Dialogues with Shklovsky: The Duvakin Interviews, 1967–68* (2019); *Viktor Shklovsky's Heritage in Literature, Arts and Philosophy* (2019); *Mikhail Bakhtin: The Duvakin Interviews, 1973* (2019); *Don Quixote Around the Globe: Perceptions and Interpretations* (2020); *The Poetics of Avant-garde in Literature, Arts and Philosophy* (2020); and *Russian Modernism in the Memories of the Survivors* (2021). In addition, he has published numerous articles and essays on Cervantes, Dostoevsky, Bakhtin, and other subjects in a variety of journals such as *Cervantes, College Literature, The South Atlantic Review, Comparative Literature and Culture, The Russian Review,* and *The Nabokovian*.

Bo Li is Assistant Professor of Translation Studies at Lingnan University in Hong Kong. He is the author of *The Dialogical Approach to Translation Studies: Bakhtinian Thoughts and Translation Studies* (in Chinese, 2017). He has published articles on gender and translation, translation history, and subtitle translation in various journals including *Translation and Interpreting Studies, Comparative Literature Studies, Perspectives: Studies in Translation Theory and Practice, Media History,* and *Chinese Translators Journal*. He is currently Executive Associate Editor of *Translation Quarterly* by the Hong Kong Translation Society, and he has edited a special issue of translation of Hong Kong literature in 2017.

Margarita Marinova is Professor of English and Comparative Literature at Christopher Newport University. She has published four books: *Transnational Russian-American Travel Writing* (2011); *Mikhail Bulgakov's Don Quixote* (2014); and *Mikhail Bakhtin: The Duvakin Interviews, 1973* (2019), and *Russian Modernism in the Memory of Survivors* (2021). She has also published articles about Russian and Soviet literature and culture, Cervantes in Russia, contemporary Bulgarian literature, and travel studies in scholarly collections (most recently, *Don Quixote: The Re-accentuation of the World's Greatest Literary Hero* [2017]; *Mikhail Bakhtin's Heritage in Literature, Arts, and Psychology: Art and Answerability* [2018]); and in journals such as the *Slavic and East European Journal*, *Studies in Travel Writing*, *The Comparatist*, and *Tulsa Studies in Women's Literature*.

Steven Mills is Associate Professor of Spanish at Buena Vista University. He has recently authored two book chapters: on Bakhtin and Cartesian dualism in *Bakhtin's Heritage in Literature, Arts and Psychology* (2018) and on Spanish author Rosa Montero's treatment of racism in her science fiction in *Viktor Shklovsky's Heritage in Literature, Arts, and Philosophy* (2019). As well, he published a number of articles on Antonio Machado, Miguel de Unamuno, and empathy in language learning, in addition to a book review on Eduardo del Campo in different scholarly journals, including *Hispania* and *Language Experience Forum*.

Riitta Oittinen is Adjunct Professor at Tampere University. She is also an artist and prolific academician who has over 200 publications. Among her monographs are *I Am Me—I Am Other: On the Dialogics of Translating for Children* (1993); *Translator's Carnival* (1995); *Translating for Children* (2000); *The Verbal, the Visual, the Translator* (2008); *Whose Story? Translating the Verbal and the Visual in Literature for Young Readers* (2009); and *Translating Picturebooks. The Verbal, the Visual, and the Aural for a Child Audience* (2018). Recently she has re-illustrated the Lewis Carroll's *Alice's Adventures in Wonderland* as well as *Through the Looking-Glass, and What Alice Found There*.

Monica Paulis is a PhD candidate at the University of Antwerp. She is a certified translator for Italian, English, German, and French, and speaks fluent Dutch. Her research focuses on translation studies. More specifically, she is working on the comparative analysis of five translations of James Joyce's *Ulysses* within the conceptual framework of Bakhtin's Dialogism into Italian.

Kris Peeters is Professor and Chair of the Department of Translation and Interpreting at the University of Antwerp. He is the author of a history of

French early modern literature entitled *Parcours littéraires du moyen âge aux Lumières* (2007), and the coeditor of nine books on early modern French literature. In addition, he has published numerous book chapters and articles on French literature, Bakhtinian poetics of the novel, and Bakhtinian poetics of translation in various journals including *Texte, RHLF, SVEC, Meta, Parallèles,* and *European Joyce Studies*.

Susan Petrilli is Professor of Philosophy and Theory of Languages, Bari University, Visiting Research Fellow, Adelaide University, Vice-President of International Association for Semiotic Studies, and 7th Sebeok Fellow of the Semiotic Society of America. She has authored, translated, and edited numerous essays, book chapters, and volumes. Her publications in philosophy of language, semiotics, and translation theory include *Signifying and Understanding* (2009); *Sign Crossroads in Global Perspective* (2010); *Sign Studies and Semioethics* (2014); *The Global World and Its Manifold Faces* (2016); *Signs, Language and Listening* (2019); as well as recent essays in *Semiotica* (IASS), *International Journal for the Semiotics of Law, Philology,* and *Calumet*.

Scott Pollard is Professor of English at Christopher Newport University. He has coauthored/coedited two books, *Table Lands: Food in Children's Literature* (2020) and *Critical Approaches to Food in Children's Literature* (2009), with Kara Keeling. He also coedited, with Margarita Marinova, the translation of Mikhail Bulgakov's dramatic adaptation of *Don Quixote* (2014). His articles and essays have appeared in various academic journals, such as *Children's Literature, College Literature, The Comparatist, Literature Film Quarterly, Latin American Literary Review,* and *The Lion and Unicorn,* as well as in *Don Quixote: The Reaccentuation of the World's Greatest Literary Hero* (2017).

Augusto Ponzio, Professor Emeritus of Philosophy and Theory of Languages, Bari University, is a renowned philosopher of language and is also a semiotician. He directs several book series including "Athanor" (1990 onwards). As editor of scholarly publications, translator, and author, he has disseminated ideas of Petrus Hispanus, Mikhail Bakhtin, Emmanuel Levinas, Karl Marx, Ferruccio Rossi-Landi, Adam Schaff, Thomas Sebeok, and Roland Barthes. With Susan Petrilli, he has coauthored *Semiotics Unbounded* (2005); *Fundamentos da Filosofia da linguagem* (2007); *Dizionario, Enciclopedia, Traduzione* (2019); and *Identità e alterità* (2019). His recent books include *Rencontres de parole* (2010); *Semiotica e letteratura* (2015); *La coda dell'occhio* (2016); *Emmanuel Levinas* (2019); and *A Ligereiza da palavra* (2019).

Yumi Tanaka is Associate Professor in the Department of Humanities and Cultures at Japan Women's University. She earned her PhD in comparative literature at the University of Tokyo in 2014. Her research focuses on readings and adaptations of *Don Quixote* in Japanese and American literature and on the relationship between Japanese literature and world literature. She is the author of *Ikiteyuku don kihote: Nichi bei gendai shosetsu ni okeru hi-romanshugiteki juyou* (The Survival of Don Quixote: Anti-Romantic Receptions of Don Quixote in American and Japanese Contemporary Novels) (2019), and she is a coauthor of *Mikhail Bakhtin's Heritage in Literature, Arts, and Psychology* (2018).

Galin Tihanov is the George Steiner Professor of Comparative Literature at Queen Mary University of London. He has held visiting appointments at universities in Europe, North and South America, and Asia. He is the author of five books, including *The Birth and Death of Literary Theory: Regimes of Relevance in Russia and Beyond* (2019). Tihanov's research interests range from Russian, German, and Central European intellectual history to world literature, cultural theory, cosmopolitanism, and exile. He is elected member of Academia Europaea, past president of the ICLA Committee on Literary Theory, and member of the Executive Board of the Institute for World Literature at Harvard University; he is also honorary scientific advisor to the Institute of Foreign Literatures, CASS (Beijing). He is currently writing *Cosmopolitanism: A Very Short Introduction*, commissioned by Oxford University Press.

Introduction

Slav Gratchev

Although Bakhtin's theory of novelistic discourse rarely touches upon the subject of translation, when it does appear in his work, it suggests that he thought translation played an important role in the constitution and dissemination of literature. This is hardly surprising. After all, as a repository of multivoicedness and dialogistic practices, which are driving forces of cultural development and change, translation has to be viewed as both needed and highly valuable. Yet Bakhtin's thoughts about it are often vague and hardly unambiguous. On several occasions, he shares his distrust of translatability as a practical possibility, while at the same time exalting the importance of "free (that is, reformulating) translation of others' works"[1] to the birth of European novel prose. But what, exactly, does this "free translation" entail, and to what extent does it allow for the original authorial voice to be preserved? Does it also acknowledge the significance of the translator's own historical time and voice? Bakhtin's concept of *re-accentuation* is especially useful as we attempt to answer these questions and make sense of his theoretical ideas about translation in the context of the very practical work translators around the globe engage in on a daily basis.

We invited interpreters of both the oral and the written word to share their thoughts about the difficulties and discoveries they dealt with in their work. We also asked philosophers of language and cultural studies critics to join the conversation with their insights about the nature of the artistic process of translation. What aspects of the original do we chose to convey in the target language of choice? How much of the literal should be preserved, especially as we deal with poetry, such as that of masters like Robert Burns or Lewis Carroll, or the stylistically marked, highly recognizable and multilayered prose of writers like Dostoevsky or Gogol? How much freedom do we have to change the source text so that its voice becomes better suited to the realities (linguistic and cultural) of our own times? What can we learn from the history of translating and retranslating classics into different languages? The contributors to this volume—scholars from the United States, Hong Kong, Finland, Japan, Spain, Italy, Bangladesh, and Belgium—bring their own polyphonic experiences with the theory and practice of translation to address such questions with the help of Bakhtin's ideas about this topic in order to illuminate their relevance to translation studies today. Each essay offers a specific case study as an opportunity to ruminate on the subject of rendering the words of an other, yet they are all connected by the individual author(s)' understanding of the art of translation as the practice of cultural *re-accentuation* (a transferal of the original text and its characters to the novel soil of a different language and culture, which inevitably leads to the proliferation of multivalent meanings), and exploration of the various re-accentuation devices employed over the span of the past 100 years in translating modern texts from one language to another.

In Chapter 1, Kris Peeters, Guillermo Sanz Gallego, and Monica Paulis investigate how in Joyce's *Dubliners*, heteroglossia often takes the appearance of multivoicedness, as the narrator adopts stylistic choices that reproduce characters' inner voices. In early translations into Dutch, French, German, Spanish and Italian, such instances of multivoiced discourse are indeed reduced to conventionalized monological discourse. In more recent retranslations in those languages, however, Joyce's multivoicedness leads to a stylistic re-accentuation of the earlier translations, and those retranslators, because they can react to the earlier translators' choices while relying on scholarship and annotated editions, develop a more profound responsive understanding of the source text that brings them to de-explicitate and deconventionalize their predecessors.

In Chapter 2, Ida Day examines the process of interpretation, specifically Spanish/English over-the-phone medical interpretation, in the context of the dialogic principles of Bakhtinian theory. She places the focus on the author's practical experience as an interpreter for CyraCom International, the leading provider of language interpretation and translation services to health care in the United States. Day wants to problematize the role of an interpreter as a neutral and unobtrusive linguistic "message conveyer" on one hand and a cross-cultural facilitator of communication on the other. In accordance with Bakhtin's notion of dialogism, the essay aims to demonstrate that the linguistic aspect is just one element of communication, since any utterance is affected by other factors, such as context, background, mood, and point of view. Day argues that for the message to be transmitted accurately, the interpreter needs to be sensitive to the cultural context of the patient in order to provide not only a linguistic but also a cultural bridge between a provider and a patient who do not have a common worldview. Such dialogue is viewed as a "double-voiced discourse," which contains two voices, two expressions, and two worldviews. Those are, however, "dialogically interrelated," and affect one another; the role of the interpreter is to re-accentuate these verbal exchanges—to transfer the original meaning to a different language and culture.

Bo Li, in Chapter 3, examines what happens to literary texts when the author writes from a position of liminality, and considers the question, already raised by other scholars, of the place of the translator in the process of rendering such liminal writing into another language. Does the translator inhabit a third space, or should he/she strive to enter and work from the same position the liminal author originally occupied? Li focuses on Chinese American author Maxine H. Kingston's *Tripmaster Monkey: His Fake Book* and its Chinese translation, and he argues that the heteroglossic construction of discourse in the novel reveals the living situations of Chinese communities in the United States. The novel's heteroglossic features, like Pidgin English and code-switching, are crucial to the character identity construction, as the erasure of such features would surely damage the integrity of the work and its understanding. Therefore, Li's investigation of the Chinese translation of Kingston's novel focuses on how these heteroglossic features, loaded with textual and social meaning, are dealt with.

Michael Eskin's purely philosophical essay, which appears here as Chapter 4, suggests that, even at its best, translation is habitually presented as second-best as it can be seen only in comparison with the original, which, presumably, holds some higher "truth": one of original intent, of the "spirit" of the original's language, and of tradition.

But what if original and translation emerge side by side, in constant mutual dialogue, critiquing each other in the process of their mutual creation and, thus, forming by way of ever adjusting to each other, such that at the end of the process it no longer makes sense to speak of original and translation as clearly demarcated ontological entities (even though the original's author may be a native speaker of only one of the two languages)?

To answer this complicated question, Eskin analyzes one particular case of such literary-processual destabilization: a case in which both translation and original ought to be considered of equal status—merely *re-accentuating* each another rather than marking the metamorphosis of a presumably *primary* text into its *secondary* or *derivative* avatar. More specifically, Eskin looks at the award-winning book *November-Rose: A Speech on Death* by Kathrin Stengel, which was published simultaneously in two languages. The theoretical problems which this case opens up take us into the heart of current debates about the relationship between a translation and an original, and authentic speech and merely re-accentuated speech, among other topics.

In Chapter 5, Yumi Tanaka analyzes reinterpretations of Margaret Mitchell's *Gone with the Wind* in three new Japanese translations. In 2015, Konomi Ara, a scholar of African American culture, published a translation which emphasized each character's class position. That same year, Yukiko Konosu, a professional literary translator, deployed role languages to modernize the characters' voices in her own translation of Mitchell's work. In 2018, Mariko Hayashi, a popular writer, began serializing her own creative translation of the novel in a literary magazine. Tanaka suggests that these three texts should be viewed as productive re-accentuations of *Gone with the Wind*, and that they deepen and broaden the artistic and ideological understanding of the original in some very important ways.

Margarita Marinova in Chapter 6 moves from a discussion of Bakhtin's earlier ideas about translation practices (mostly referenced in texts from the 1930s and 1940s) to his final thoughts on the topic recorded in the last of the Duvakin interviews from 1973. Among the questions she grapples with, especially in connection with her own experiences of translating Bakhtin's voice for English audiences, are the following: Does one need to bring a completely different set of skills to the translation of poetry than to the translation of prose? Can both poetic and prosaic translations be viewed as variants of a live speech act, and if so, would that preclude a text's translatability? She is especially intrigued by the "translator-stylizers," whose work is deemed to be incredibly valuable yet also somewhat mysterious in Bakhtin's interpretation, and explores the connection between the practices of those early translators to our experiences with translating today.

Chapter 7, written by Melissa Garr, puts forward the idea that literary translation can result in the creation of beautiful, more nuanced texts, or conversely, may cause a peculiar "flattening" effect whereby much of the texture of the original text is lost. The task is rendered more difficult in the case of parodic novels and polyphonic novels, particularly if the author of the original work is a translator himself. Garr then engages in an investigation of Eduardo Mendoza's work, which provides excellent illustrations of these challenges. Although he is a multiple prize-winning and bestselling author, few of his humorous or parodic novels have been translated into English, compared to other European languages. Garr examines English translations of Eduardo Mendoza's parodic novels to determine how the re-accentuation inherent in the translation of their humor demonstrates changes in the texts' polyphony, double-voicedness, and heteroglossia. She shows how these translated re-accentuations avoid the "flattening" effect that may not create as rich a reading experience for English-language readers. In addition, Garr surveys possible ways through which translators can avoid committing what Bakhtin calls a "crude violation of the author's will" as they re-accentuate Mendoza's parodic novels in the language of the target audience.

Victor Fet in Chapter 8 explores translation as dialogic re-accentuation limited by cultural and temporal factors. What happens if the target language is not open or ready for such a dialogue? How would translatability suffer? Lewis Carroll, possibly the most translated Anglophone author ever, presents an interesting case study. Fet grounds his investigations in the translations of Carroll's iconic surrealist poem *The Hunting of the Snark* (1876) into Russian, and explores the vocabulary and style choices used in the domestication/foreignization of the original in nearly forty Russian translations published since 1991. The author insists that while this attention is remarkable, and even cult-like, most translations suffer from a severe disengagement from the original text. Based on a careful text analysis, Fet uncovers numerous cases when the translator's own agenda is deployed well beyond the reasonable limits of re-accentuation, or even parody. Fet's observations show that often this replacement is justified by references to the "eccentric" nature of the Victorian author, whose identity suffers as a result. The observed patterns could indicate that the dialogue between Victorian English and post-Soviet Russian has suffered tremendous setbacks recently. It appears that the target language (both the translators' and readers') is neither able to nor interested in taking the source seriously. The Bakhtinian dialogue is disrupted; the re-accentuation process is damaged; and translation becomes a disappointing travesty.

In Chapter 9, Susan Petrilli and Augusto Ponzio argue that the processes of translation are never neutral by nature; instead, they concern the sense that renders the utterance significant, that motivates it, that confers a precise intentionality upon it.

As the authors argue, in interlinguistic translation, the translated text is not "almost the same thing," but "the same other." Their chapter focuses on the word whose essential characteristic, based on its inevitable accentuation/intonation, is nothing less but interaction and dialogue between one's own word and the other's word.

Steven Mills in Chapter 10 aims to show that by adding the voice of the translator to the novel *Beatus Ille* by Antonio Muñoz Molina, a fundamental message in the original Spanish is lost in the English translation. The original title, according to Mills, was one of Muñoz Molina's major tools to derive new hope from tragedies as a commentary on the possibility for progress toward a brighter Spanish future in the midst of a transition from dictatorship to democracy. The author is concerned that Edith Grossman, who translated the novel, changed its title to *Manuscript of Ashes*, inserting symbols of decay and ephemeral memories into the conversation and, by doing so, she dramatically re-accentuated the original message away from its original meaning. Mills thus aims to reveal Muñoz Molina's original subtle message of hope following the despair, lost in *Manuscript of Ashes*, as well as to analyze from a new angle the new meaning that emerges from the intermingling of Muñoz Molina's and Grossman's voices.

Riitta Oittinen, in Chapter 11, puts forward that neither language, culture, nor even the literary work itself can dictate what will happen in the translation process and its ultimate result. The translator is always in a dialogic interaction with all participants in the act—the author, the illustrator, an anticipated and real audience, and so on. Oittinen looks at Lewis Carroll's first Alice story in *Alice's Adventures in Wonderland* through a carnivalistic magnifying glass. As she has illustrated the book twice, she has had the opportunity to return to the story more recently adding to it another layer of re-accentuation. Her project can be seen as an example of an intersemiotic translation (a translation from words into images), and the chapter provides us with the opportunity to witness this process in action.

Finally, in Chapter 12, Scott Pollard explores connections between *Don Quixote* and the new genre of British children's literature. The translated *Quixote* is also embedded in the beginnings of British children's literature in 1744, when the printer John Newbery inaugurated the children's book trade. Newbery and his competitors discovered *Don Quixote,* and three juvenile editions of it were published by Woodgate (1768), Turpin (1776), and Newbery (1778). These three are the beginnings of a tradition of juvenile *Quixote* adaptations that extends to the present. Bakhtin's theory of re-accentuation provides Pollard with the critical framework to investigate how a Spanish novel finds itself reworked in eighteenth-century British children's books. Through the analysis of the three above-mentioned adaptations, Pollard's essay analyzes how the embedded potentialities of *Don Quixote* manifest the distinct functions of eighteenth-century children's literature as an outgrowth of Enlightenment education.

These essays, taken together and drawn from different cultural contexts and disciplines (such as literature, literary theory, the visual arts, translation studies, and philosophy) demonstrate clearly the continued international relevance of Bakhtin's ideas to the study of creative practices, and further the current scholarly conversations about translation as an intercultural phenomenon.

Note

1. Mikhail M. Bakhtin, *The Dialogic Imagination: Four Essays*, ed. Michael Holquist and Caryl Emerson (Austin: University of Texas Press, 1984), 378.

Bibliography

Bakhtin, Mikhail M. *The Dialogic Imagination: Four Essays*. Edited by Michael Holquist and Caryl Emerson. Austin: University of Texas Press, 1984.

1

Dubliners Retranslated: Re-accentuating Multivoicedness

Kris Peeters, Guillermo Sanz Gallego, and Monica Paulis

Introduction

"Re-accentuation" is one of the key concepts of Bakhtin's epistemology of discourse in the novel (Section 1). It is related to the way in which the novel and its readers deal with heteroglossia (Section 2). It also is, as we will argue, a key concept for the study of literary translations (Section 3), even more so for the diachronous study of subsequent translations (Section 4). The text upon which we will center our argumentation is Joyce's *Dubliners* (Section 5). The corpus of translations analyzed is composed of thirty-six translations of *Dubliners* into the five languages we collectively read: Dutch, French, German, Spanish and Italian (Section 6). We shall analyze a sample of twelve excerpts, according to a three-dimensional comparative approach that considers translations to be (a) subsequent events in the re-accentuation process over time, (b) yet also in space, and (c) through re-dialogizing translation strategies (Section 7). The excerpts analyzed are taken from five early translations and five retranslations, that is, subsequent translations into the same languages (Sections 8.1 to 8.5). The final section of our paper (Section 9) is devoted to conclusions regarding retranslation as a means of re-dialogizing re-accentuation of both the source text material and the earlier translations.

1. Re-accentuation, Heteroglossia, Multivoicedness

Re-accentuation is a key concept of Bakhtin's long essay on "Discourse in the Novel,"[1] but is not an easy one to grasp. As is often the case with Bakhtin, it is related to many other concepts and lacks the "closed," clear-cut definition that would be adverse to his dialogical understanding of the Self, language, and reality.

Re-accentuation involves the changing dialogizing background against which fiction is understood. It is a way of conceptualizing how classic texts travel through time while being continuously reinterpreted and reused.[2] Time provides changing social and ideological contexts and, thus, brings new understandings of the text's "responsiveness" or "answerability,"[3] new dialogical answers to its open-ended meaning potential. To put it bluntly: the text itself does not change, but reception contexts do; therefore, the text's dialogical understanding changes with time. Bakhtin himself puts it as follows: "the historical life of classic works is in fact the uninterrupted process of their social and ideological re-accentuation."[4] Re-accentuation, then, is the long-term process in which a classic text's social-historical specificity meets an uninterrupted chain of dialogical responses, "in which, in short, one historical specificity speaks to another."[5] In Bakhtin's essay, which describes the history of the European novel as a series of representations in, and of, language, this process is very much a matter of discourse: a novel's social-historical specificity is related to the way in which it uses and represents contemporary social contexts and languages. Re-accentuation therefore is related to historical and social context, but also to heteroglossia present in that context.

Language as it is used in society is a rather chaotic affair, for which Bakhtin has coined several concepts by infusing existing prefixes and words in Russian with new meanings.[6] Heteroglossia—*raznojazychie* (diverse-languageness), or *inojazychie* (other-languageness)[7]—refers to the idea that living language always shows traces of Otherness, of complex historical and social processes of influence between, and diversification of, languages. Heterology on the other hand—*raznorechie* (contra-diction, or diverse-discourseness)[8]—refers to the coexistence (*sobytie*)[9] and diversity of speech types and genres within a language that arise spontaneously from time and social diversity and spaces. Finally, multivoicedness, or double-voicedness—*raznogolosie* (discord, diverse-voiceness)[10]—is concerned with how individual voices embody heterology and heteroglossia, by showing previously uttered speech reused— the "other's voice" or "word"[11]—in (free) indirect speech, stylization, parody, hidden polemic, and so on.[12] For the purposes of our analysis, we shall use "heteroglossia" as an umbrella term for the wealth of social-linguistic diversity in society, and for the idea that the language available to the novel as a material, as a "given" (*dannoe*),[13] is always a language "borrowed from others."[14] "Multivoicedness" shall refer to the phenomenon that occurs when that heteroglossic "given" is incorporated in what is "created" (*sozdannoe*) in the novel, that is, when narrators' and characters' voices embody heteroglossia, thus allowing for the variety of language materials and social voices to attain the novel's narrative and linguistic form.

2. Heteroglossia and Its Representation in the Novel

Indeed, novelists deal with and react to heteroglossia in society. They have to, because language is the novel's raw material, much in the same way as a painter uses oil and pigments. Some novelists organize the chaos of languages according to a hierarchical principle, subduing the "centrifugal forces" of heteroglossia to the "centripetal forces" of linguistic hierarchy and correctness.[15] Such novels belong to what Bakhtin calls the "First Stylistic Line" in the novel's history.[16] Their form is single-voiced: characters and narrators share one and the same language, that of "general literariness."[17] Novels of the First Line are authoritarian in their attitude toward "the realities of heteroglossia,"[18] exclude these realities from verbal art in the name of reputedly correct language, and resort to the allegedly (morally and aesthetically) superior language of epic grandeur.[19] Novels of the "Second Stylistic Line," on the other hand, reveal the social and stylistic variety of heteroglossia and allow narrators and characters to develop their own speeches by embodying socially specific ways of expression, thus turning the novel into a dialogue of voices. Such novels are multivoiced and relativize the authoritarian "general literariness" of the First Line. They bring conventionalized literary language back, through processes of "carnivalization,"[20] to what they believe to be its legitimate place. That place is not above, but amid all languages of the public space. Literary language, then, becomes *a* instead of *the* language of literature: it is confronted, in the novel, with the centrifugal forces of language that show "the present [contemporary society] in all its openendedness."[21] That Second Line goes all the way back to the *fabliau* and Rabelais and includes Cervantes's *Don Quixote*,[22] Dickens's *Bleakhouse* and *Little Dorrit*,[23] and Dostoevsky's *Brothers Karamazov* that Bakhtin has written about. It also includes, as we shall see, the work of James Joyce: *Ulysses*, quite famously,[24] but also *Dubliners*, the collection of short stories written in 1905-7 and published in 1914, in which Joyce's experimentation with voices and multivoicedness started.

Heteroglossia and its novelistic counterpart, multivoicedness, are at the center of the concept of re-accentuation: novelists in their time and social context, as well as readers in their own social-historical contexts, react to heteroglossia in society and to the place they see for it in literature. All great prose is rooted in heteroglossia. Therefore, how a classic is re-accented involves the process of subsequent dialogical understandings of its attitude toward heteroglossia, along the two Stylistic Lines in the history of prose fiction.

3. Translation as Complex Re-accentuation

Re-accentuation, however, can occur in many ways: a literary text may be revered, imitated, quoted, adapted, parodied, censured, and so on. But re-accentuation not only occurs when a classic is used or reused in a certain way and in a certain context. It also occurs, with no less variety,[25] when that work is translated. Translations play a key part in the afterlife of the classics: without translations, there would be no world literature.[26] However, literary translation is no marvelous machine of perfectly transparent transcoding.[27] It is foremost an example of human understanding, which is why each translation represents an event (*sobytie*) in the historical process of re-accentuation. Every age re-accents the works of the past; that is the essential condition of the historical afterlife of the classics. That afterlife equally implies that "each generation has its own translation."[28]

Any literary translation is, indeed, a reading, an interpretation of the source text (hereafter ST), and therefore a dialogical understanding that can occur only in its own context, that is, the target context (hereafter TC). Translation, put otherwise, is an example of re-accentuation that is more complex because it implies a twofold change of context. Translating a classic involves a change of historical context (in time, from past to present), but also of social and linguistic-cultural context (in space, from source to target context). Translators are both interpreters of the ST and gatekeepers to the TC, who decide how to cast the ST material into another linguistic form that they believe to be a rendering of the ST which is culturally acceptable in the TC. The question when it comes to translation as re-accentuation, therefore, is: how do translators formulate a dialogical response to the other's voice (the author's voice) that they believe to be both adequate in its rendering of the ST material and acceptable in its form for the TC readership, in its own social-historical and linguistic-cultural context?[29] How do translators perform the delicate balancing act of responding to that dialogical divide of both source- and target-orientedness? How do they cross contextual barriers in both time and space? And how do such complex forms of re-accentuation evolve over time?

4. Explicitation, Conventionalization, Retranslation

In translation studies, some theories can be found with regard to those questions. On the one hand, it has been suggested that translated texts show explicitation, that is, a more explicit and unambiguous rendering of the ST content or meaning: translations avoid ambiguity and smoothen interpretation, in order to achieve their prime goal which is TC readability. This theory is known as the Explicitation Hypothesis.[30] Another theory, the Conventionalization (or Normalization) Hypothesis,[31] suggests that translations also tend to flatten linguistic differences present in the ST. In Bakhtinian terms, this would mean that translations tend to transform heteroglossia and multivoicedness into more conventional literary language, in order to perform a re-accentuation that moves away from the Second and into the First Line of conventionalized literariness. Translators, in other words, tend to resolve the dialogical divide of both source- and target-orientedness by resorting to a monological re-accentuation of the ST: they prioritize TC readability and the beauty of well-constructed literariness over ST complexity and ambiguity, and the chaos of everyday heteroglossia.

Yet, although the Explicitation and Conventionalization Hypotheses may hold for some types of translation, they are no "translation universals"[32] when it comes to literary translation, especially in the case of subsequent translations of the same ST into the same language, that is, retranslation.[33] And that is where a third theory comes in, namely the Retranslation Hypothesis.[34] This theory claims that retranslations remain "closer" to the original and are more "faithful" to the ST content and style. Therefore, they are said to be more source-oriented than first (or early) translations, which are reputedly more target-oriented. First translations struggle with the not yet classic text's linguistic and cultural Otherness and flatten the author's voice in order to assure a smooth integration into the TC. Retranslations occur at a moment when the ST is already a classic—otherwise it would not be retranslated—and therefore is already known in the TC. This is why retranslators no longer need to assure such a smooth integration and can restore the ST material in a richer way. In Bakhtinian terms, this hypothesis would imply that retranslations, contrary to first or early translations, tend to be multivoiced, showing ST ambiguity and heteroglossia instead of explicitation and conventionalization, thus allowing the TC reader to perceive ST Otherness. In retranslation, put otherwise, the dialogical divide we discussed results in a dialogical translation strategy, which is not to explain, but to show, not to make more readable, but to include more of the ST meaning potential rather than privilege a single meaning. In previous research,[35] we were able to show that such practices do indeed occur in retranslations, as we shall explain in Section 5.

Nevertheless, the Retranslation Hypothesis is open to criticism as well: things are more complicated than what this dichotomic hypothesis seems to suggest. As we have seen before, re-accentuation involves the dialogue between two historical and social-linguistic contexts. In the case of translation, those would be the source and target contexts. In the case of *re*translation, however, earlier translations are already part of the TC. Therefore, retranslations not only engage in dialogue with the ST. Rather, while re-accenting the ST, they also re-accent the earlier translations which had already re-accented the same ST, and are already present in the TC. This is why retranslators also engage in dialogical polemic, either overt or "hidden,"[36] with the earlier translators' work, upon which they can rely but which they also alter. This is why retranslations are not simply more "source-oriented" as the Retranslation Hypothesis suggests. Rather, as retranslations are a *double* dialogical response, to the ST material but also to the TC presence of earlier translations, they are in fact more both source-*and*-target-oriented, or one might say, more source-*through*-target-oriented. Whereas translations are re-accentuations, *re*translations are re-accentuations *to the second degree*: retranslations re-accent the ST (as any translation does), but they do so while also re-accenting the earlier re-accentuations (earlier translations, that is), already present in the TC, of that same ST.

The above discussion urges us to now put forward what we would like to call the "Re-dialogization Hypothesis": first or early translations tend to explicitate meaning, and to conventionalize style by reducing heteroglossia. Retranslations, on the other hand, reintroduce the ST's dialogical open-endedness in the TC because they re-accent not only the ST, but also the earlier re-accentuations already present in the TC. They do so by de-explicitating what was explicitated in earlier translations, and by de-conventionalizing, that is, reintroducing ST heteroglossia where it had been overlooked by former translators and replaced by instances of conventionalization. Rather than being *either* source- *or* target-oriented, retranslations therefore achieve a deeper *both-and* logic, that is, a deeper dialogical incorporation of the ST material in the target text form.

This "Re-dialogization Hypothesis" is what we shall now put to the test of a corpus of translations of Joyce's *Dubliners* into Dutch, French, German, Italian, and Spanish. Before doing so, we will provide a short introduction on *Dubliners* and our reasons for choosing that text for the analysis.

5. Ambiguity and Multivoicedness in Joyce's *Dubliners*

This paper can be seen as a continuation of a study we published in 2020.[37] In that article, we tested our theory as explained in Section 4 on the "Oxen of the Sun" episode of Joyce's *Ulysses*, while comparing three Dutch and three Spanish translations. We selected that chapter because it has traditionally been claimed to be "untranslatable," and because it contains an important number of cases of heteroglossia and multivoicedness.

In this study, we aim to explore whether the conclusions of that former research—that is, that first translations explicitate meaning and standardize or conventionalize language more than retranslations do, and that retranslations show a broader range of interpretations (ambiguity, as opposed to explicitation) and language variety (heteroglossia, as opposed to conventional literary style) than first translations do—are also valid for one of Joyce's first works, *Dubliners*. At the same time, we are broadening our view by exploring whether the same tendencies can be observed across five languages instead of two, that is, whether our hypothesis makes sense for other languages and TCs as well.

Dubliners is a collection of fifteen short stories in which Joyce depicts Dublin and its society in the early twentieth century. The main characters are lower middle-class citizens, some of whom will reappear in *Ulysses*, such as Lenehan and Corley (from "Two Gallants"). Joyce portrays a disenchanted stratum of Irish society with neither hopes nor ambition to thrive. In this sense, the economic decline of Dublin plays an important role in the general mood of the characters and their stories. One example is the story of "Eveline," a young girl who is struggling to decide whether to emigrate to Buenos Aires with a sailor or stay in Dublin. A similar case can be found in "The Boarding House," in which Mrs. Mooney, concerned with the more than likely consequences of a love affair between one of her tenants and her 19-year-old daughter, manages to force the man to marry the young lady.

Although *Dubliners* was published eight years before *Ulysses*, Joyce's characteristic narrative resources, including multivoicedness, can be observed in different short stories, in the form of free indirect speech and in cases of Hugh Kenner's "Uncle Charles Principle"[38] in particular. This is one of the main reasons why we selected this collection of short stories for our analysis. Yet, *Dubliners* also provides an interesting test field of ambiguity. Indeed, the short stories are also characterized by open-endedness, "powerfully suggestive in [their] terseness, evocative rather than explicative, allusive rather than descriptive."[39] The evocative and elusive nature of the stories creates ambiguity, as they lack "the structural shape of an ending [that] creates a deeper sense."[40]

For our analysis, we selected as ST the Penguin annotated edition of *Dubliners*,[41] which has proven to be very useful for our purposes. Considering that the choice of instances of ambiguity is not only complex but can even be controversial, we have selected the passages we will discuss by taking into consideration Terence Brown's notes in this edition. The excerpts we selected are signaled as ambiguous, by means of annotations such as "possible allusion to," "may also suggest," "interpretative possibilities ... are many," "presumably ...," "Joyce may intend ...," "possibly a reference to ...," "also with the implication of ...," "perhaps ...," "may be ...," "a possible allusion to ...," "suggests possible reference to ... but it may also refer to ..." In addition, we also selected passages that show heteroglossia, for instance in the form of Dublin slang.

6. *Dubliners*' Translated Afterlife: Nearly Forty Shades of Sway

Dubliners has been widely translated into a large number of languages. Our corpus comprises two translations into Dutch, six into German, six into French, eight into Spanish, and no less than fourteen into Italian. The first (yet partial) translation into any of these languages appears to have been the French translation of "Eveline" by Hélène du Pasquier, published in 1921 by the Parisian editor Les Écrits nouveaux, which was followed in 1922—the year in which *Ulysses* was published—by the translations of "Araby" (also by Pasquier), "A Painful Case" and "A Little Cloud" by Yva Fernandez and "The Sisters" by Jacques-Paul Reynaud. In 1926, these three translators were jointly published by Plon in what would become the first complete translation of the stories,[42] which remained unchallenged in France until 1974.

The second language into which *Dubliners* was (partially) translated, is Italian: "Araby" was translated by Carlo Linati in 1924, "Eveline" and "The Dead" were published in 1931 in a translation by Amalia Popper. The first complete edition of *Gente di Dublino* was published in 1933, in a translation by Annie and Adriano Lami. By that time Joyce's work had gained popularity in Italy thanks to the French translations that circulated in the country. Actually, Italian critics were among the first in Europe to take interest in the Irish writer; by the time *Gente di Dublino* was published, Joyce's position in the Italian literary world was already well established.[43]

The German-speaking world made its acquaintance with the then lesser-known James Joyce in 1919 through the translation of the play *Exiles* (*Verbannte*, by Hannah von Mettal), published not in Germany but in Zurich where Joyce was living at the time. *Verbannte* is the first Joyce translation to have appeared in any language. However, it was not until 1928 that *Dubliners* was translated into German, shortly after *A Portrait of the Artist as a Young Man* (1926) and *Ulysses* (1927), all in translations by Georg Goyert.[44]

In Spain, on the other hand, the first translation of Joyce's work consisted of a few excerpts from *Ulysses* translated by Antonio Marichalar in 1924. In 1926, the first translation of one of *Dubliners*' stories ("Eveline") appeared, notably not in Spanish but in Catalan. It was not until 1942 that *Dubliners* was translated into Spanish by Ignacio Abelló, who had already translated "The Dead" the year before.[45]

Among the languages selected, Dutch represents the latest addition to an impressive catalogue of translations. The Dutch and Flemish readers had in fact to wait until 1962, when *A Portrait of the Artist as a Young Man* was translated by Max Schuchart, and even longer to be able to hold a copy of the first Dutch translation of *Dubliners*, made by Rein Bloem in 1967, that is, just over forty years after the first complete translation into French.

In recent years, there has been an important increase in the number of translations in most of these languages (see Bibliography). This growth is due to the influence of two recent and interrelated phenomena: the expiring of copyright on Joyce's works in 2011 and the increasing success of, and fierce competition in, the world of e-publishing, which enabled small independent editors to release their own translations thanks to the limited costs of digital publishing. This evolution noticeably concerns the Italian, but also German and Spanish language, more than French or Dutch. This can be explained by the fact that the French and Dutch literary systems are very concentrated in a single dominating publishing center (Paris and Amsterdam, respectively), from where distribution all over the French- or Dutch-speaking world is organized. The Italian and German publishing industries, on the contrary, gravitate around several centers (Rome, Milan, Torino, Bologna, Florence; Zurich, Berlin, Mainz, Cologne, Munich, to name the larger ones), and this increases commercial and intellectual competition among editors, who have to fight each other to get a grip on the national market. As a result, editors publish their own translation in order to compete with extant translations published by others. This is also the case in the Spanish-speaking world, which comprises not only Spain (where Madrid and Barcelona play the leading roles), but also Latin-America. Finally, the commercial viability of a new translation also hinges on the size of a literary market, that is, its potential readership. This may explain the small number of translations into

Dutch, whose linguistic realm is limited to the Netherlands, the northern part of Belgium (Flanders), and a few small former Dutch colonies, totalizing a potential readership of some twenty-five million.

7. A Three-Dimensional Approach

Taking into account that we cannot possibly discuss all of the selected passages from thirty-six translations, we have chosen one early translation (hereafter ET) and one retranslation (hereafter RT) for every language discussed (hereafter /D, /F, /G, /S, and /I). For each language, we shall focus on a few passages to exemplify our argumentation, while ensuring that by the end of our analysis all twelve passages will have been covered. The ETs that we have selected are not necessarily first translations: while this is true for the Dutch, French, and Spanish literary systems in which the first translations have remained unchallenged for decades, we have chosen the first widely commercialized translation in German and in Italian. As far as the RTs are concerned, we have made a selection of translations based on completeness and editorial success, while observing a comparable time span of approximately thirty-five years between ET and RT (twenty-six to forty-six, depending on availability). For each of the languages discussed in the following sections, we shall briefly introduce the translations analyzed. But before doing so, let us shortly resume the rationale of our study, that is, the way in which the analysis relates to the theoretical parts of our paper as explained in Sections 1 to 5. According to those sections, the method applied will be three-dimensional:

(a) We consider subsequent translations to be a series of steps in the historical process of re-accentuation. Translations, whether ET or RT, are dialogical re-accentuations of the ST, in the TC. Yet RTs are re-accentuations to the second degree, that is, they also re-accent the way in which the ET(s) had already re-accented the ST in the TC. Therefore, we shall analyze how RTs re-accent the ST, but also whether, how, and to what extent, RTs re-accent ETs.
(b) Re-accentuation occurs within the social-historical context of the translations, that is, the TC. Therefore, our analysis will be comparative in nature, with regard to the contexts of the Dutch, French, German, Italian, and Spanish translations.
(c) At the same time, we shall also be examining whether our Re-dialogization Hypothesis holds regardless of differences in TC. Therefore, we shall examine whether explicitation and

conventionalization occur mostly in ETs, and less in RTs and whether this holds for all five TCs. As we consider RT to be a re-accentuation to the second degree, we shall also investigate whether RTs show re-dialogization strategies with regard to ETs, that is, whether RTs re-introduce implicitness and ambiguity in instances where ETs had opted for explicitation. Similarly, we will also examine whether RTs reintroduce, as we hypothesize, the ST's heteroglossia and multivoicedness, by de-conventionalizing what was conventionalized in ETs.

8. *Dubliners* across Time and Space: Retranslation as De-explicitating, De-conventionalizing Re-accentuation

8.1. *Dubliners* in Dutch

Dubliners has been translated into Dutch only twice: first in 1968 by Rein Bloem, and then in 2016 as *Dublinezen*,[46] by Erik Bindervoet and Robbert-Jan Henkes, who had previously translated *Finnegan's Wake* and *Ulysses*.

The early translation in Dutch (ET/D) shows many instances of explicitation. This is the beginning of "The Sisters," the first of Joyce's stories:

Excerpt 1

There was no hope for him this time: it was the third stroke. Night after night I had passed the house (it was vacation time) and studied the lighted square of window: and night after night I had found it lighted in the same way, faintly and evenly. If he was dead, I thought, I would see the reflection of candles on the darkened blind for I knew that two candles must be set at the head of a corpse. He had often said to me: "I am not long for this world," and I had thought his words idle. Now I knew they were true. (ST 1)

<u>Dit keer was er voor hem geen hoop meer</u>: het was zijn derde *beroerte*. Avond aan avond was ik langs het huis gelopen (het was in de vakantie) en had ik naar <u>het verlichte vlak van het raam</u> gekeken <u>en elke avond</u> was het op dezelfde wijze verlicht, zwak en gelijkmatig. Als hij dood was, dacht ik, zou ik de weerschijn van kaarsen op *het donkere gordijn* zien, want ik wist dat er bij het hoofd van een lijk twee kaarsen geplaatst moeten worden. Hij had me vaak gezegd: "*Ik zal er niet lang meer zijn*"

en <u>ik had zijn woorden hol vinden klinken</u>. Nu wist ik <u>dat ze uitgekomen waren</u>. (ET/D 7; our italics and underlining)

<u>Er was geen hoop meer voor hem dit keer</u>: het was de derde **klap**. Avond aan avond was ik langs het huis gelopen (het was vakantie**tijd**) en had ik aandachtig naar <u>het verlichte venstervierkant</u> gekeken<u>: en avond aan avond</u> zag ik dat het op dezelfde manier was verlicht, zwak en gelijkmatig. Als hij dood was, dacht ik, dan zou ik de weerschijn van de kaarsen op **het verduisterende rolgordijn** zien want ik wist dat er twee kaarsen moeten worden neergezet bij het hoofd van een lijk. Hij had vaak tegen mij gezegd: *ik maak het niet lang meer* **op deze wereld** en ik <u>had zijn woorden ijdel gevonden</u>. Nu wist ik <u>dat ze waar waren</u>. (RT/D 9; our bold face and underlining; translators' italics)

ET/D explicitates ST meaning on occasions that we have italicized. For instance, "it was the third stroke"—which is ambiguous, as it can mean a seizure, but also a violent blow, including figuratively—was rendered unambiguously as a "seizure."[47] Similarly, "I am not long for this world" was translated with "I won't be here for long anymore," while "the darkened blind" was misinterpreted, becoming a "dark curtain." Second, ET/D also shows conventionalizations that we have underlined. Whereas the ST narrator adopts the colloquial voice of a teenager, ET/D regularly resorts to conventionalized literary style. The first sentence is smoothened by anteposition of "this time," the colon in the second sentence has disappeared, and the repetition of "night after night" is avoided. Also, the unconventional "lighted square of window" is conventionalized, becoming "the lighted surface of the window." The final sentences are conventionalized as well: "I had thought his words idle"—which alludes to Matthew 12:36[48]—becomes "I had found his words to sound hollow" and "Now I knew they were true" is rendered as "Now I knew they had come true."

RT/D is quite different and these differences coincide with the instances in which ET/D had resorted to explicitation or conventionalization. Ambiguity and the biblical allusion are reintroduced,[49] and the misrendering of the "darkened blind" is amended. On each of these occasions that we have highlighted using underlining for heteroglossia (de-conventionalization) and bold face for changes related to ambiguity (de-explicitation), RT/D corrects ET/D while restoring the ST material. Consequently, RT/D retains word order in the first sentence as well as the colon and the repetition in the second sentence. The "stroke" now is an equally ambiguous "klap" (blow), and the "lighted square of window" is translated by means of a heterological neologism, "venstervierkant" (window square). Interestingly, RT/D also reuses ET/D, even verbatim, yet not in instances in which ET/D explicitates or conventionalizes.

Our second example is taken from "Eveline":

Excerpt 2

She was about to explore another life with Frank. Frank was very kind, manly, open-hearted. She was to go away with him by the night-boat to be his wife and to live with him in Buenos Ayres where he had a home waiting for her. (ST 31)

<u>Ze zou nu</u> een ander leven *leren kennen* met Frank. Frank was <u>erg</u> aardig, mannelijk, openhartig. Ze zou *met hem mee gaan* met de nachtboot, om zijn vrouw te *worden* en met hem in Buenos Aires te gaan wonen, waar hij een huis had dat op waar wachtte. (ET/D 38; our italics and underlining)

<u>Ze stond op het punt om</u> een ander leven **te gaan ontdekken** met Frank. Frank was <u>heel</u> aardig, mannelijk, openhartig. Ze zou met hem **weggaan** op de nachtboot om zijn vrouw te **zijn** en met hem in Buenos Aires te gaan wonen waar hij een huis had dat op haar wachtte. (RT/D 42; our bold face and underlining)

As shown by our underlining, ET/D resorts to a more conventional literary style: "She was about to" becomes "She would now," the colloquial "very kind" is translated with the formal "erg aardig." Similarly, several words are explicitated, as we have highlighted by italics: "to explore" is rendered with "learn to know" and Eveline is not about to "go away" to "be," but to "go with him" to "become" Frank's wife. These changes, although they may seem minimal, are in fact very important, because explicitation and conventionalization result in ET/D rendering ST multivoicedness by single-voiced narratorial discourse. Indeed, Joyce's narrator uses Eveline's inner voice, her thoughts and words, to tell her story, by means of Kenner's "Uncle Charles Principle." This reveals the psychology of a woman unsettled at the perspective of being "about to" "go away" and leave Dublin—there are three "with Frank" or "with him" in just three sentences, and one more "with him" on the same page (see Excerpt 7 below). In her mind, Eveline is not going *to* Argentina, but "away with"; not to *become*, but, statically, "to be" her lover's wife; not to experience an amorous adventure, but "to explore another life." In ET/D, however, Eveline is a third-person character who, in the hands of the narrator, has become voiceless, and far less disconcerted and passive.

In this excerpt, too, RT/D de-explicitates what was explicitated in ET/D, and reintroduces heteroglossia where ET/D was conventionalizing. This results in the re-dialogizing reintroduction of multivoicedness: Eveline is again an inert character, someone who "*was about to*" leave Dublin behind, to "*explore another life*," to "*go away*" with Frank to "*be*" his wife. In the end (but actually from the beginning of the story, as our analysis shows), Eveline, "passive, like a helpless animal" (ST 34), is incapable of leaving.

The Dutch translations, in brief, conform to our Re-dialogization Hypothesis. In the excerpts discussed, and in many other instances, ET/D explicitates content or meaning and conventionalizes language. This also results, in Excerpt 2 (as well as in Excerpts 3, 4, 7, 10, and 12 discussed below), in a change of narratorial voice and character psychology, as multivoicedness is lost as a consequence of explicitation and conventionalization. RT/D, on the other hand, de-explicitates ET/D, and reintroduces heteroglossia and multivoicedness, thus demonstrating re-dialogization strategies in the same instances in which ET/D had explicitated and/or conventionalized ST material. This confirms that retranslation is indeed a re-accentuation to the second degree.

8.2. *Dubliners* in French

In the French context, the situation is somewhat different. We have found six translations: three of which are in paperback editions issued nearly at the same time (1993–4), and three of which are partial translations in bilingual editions intended for students. The first translation we discussed in Section 6 has been regularly republished, by Plon and by Garnier Flammarion and Presses Pocket in paperback editions. It is still on the market, in paperbacks by Presses Pocket (2018) or independent publishers such as Createspace (2014) or Les Editions du Cénacle (2018). Unchallenged until 1974, this is ET/F we shall use, in the 1969 Plon edition. Our RT/F is the 1993 retranslation by the professor of English and American literature Benoît Tadié, which is the last complete French translation to date.

The French translations are comparable to the Dutch ones: re-dialogization strategies—de-explicitation, de-conventionalization, and the resulting reintroduction of multivoicedness—occur in RT/F, where ET/F had opted for explicitation and/or conventionalization. The "lighted square of window" from Excerpt 1, for instance, reads as "le carré de lumière de la fenêtre" (the square of light of the window) in ET/F (37); RT/F (39) de-explicitates in "le carré de fenêtre éclairé" (the lighted square of window). Similarly, "She was about to explore another life" (Excerpt 2) is rendered as "Elle allait tâter d'une autre vie" (ET/F 93; "She was going to taste of another life"); and "Elle allait explorer une nouvelle vie" (RT/F 69; "She was going to explore a new life"), respectively.

As the latter example shows, however, the re-dialogizing re-accentuation of ET/F in RT/F, although present, is less absolute than in RT/D. RT/F still shows traces of explicitation and conventionalization: RT/F translates "She was about to" with "going to," and "another life" with "a new life," which is still explicitating and still alters Eveline's psychology. Conventionalization has not completely disappeared either: "There was no hope for him this time" (Excerpt 1) was rendered with "Il n'y avait plus d'espoir pour lui désormais" (ET/F 37; "henceforth"); then "Cette fois, il n'y avait plus d'espoir pour lui" (RT/F 39; "This time"). RT/F thus still conventionalizes, although substantially less than ET/F does, by anteposition of the adverbial clause.

Notwithstanding this important nuance, RT/F does show re-dialogization strategies, as we will illustrate with an example taken from "A Mother":

Excerpt 3

Mrs. Kearney's anger began to flutter in her cheek and she had all she could do to keep from asking:

"And who is the Cometty pray?" (ST 139)

La colère de Mrs. Kearney commençait à lui monter au visage et elle eut toutes les peines du monde à s'empêcher de demander:

—Et qui est le comité, je vous prie? (ET/F 282; our underlining)

La colère de Mrs. Kearney commençait à lui palpiter dans les joues et elle dut faire l'impossible pour se retenir de demander:

—Et qui est-ce au juste ce Cometty,[10] je vous prie? (RT/F 180; our underlining; translator's italics)

[10]Déformation de « committee » (comité): Mrs. Kearney imite (intérieurement) l'accent « grossier » de Mr. Fitzpatrick. (RT/F endnote, 283)

Mrs. Kearney parodies, in her inner voice, Mr. Fitzpatrick's accent. In ET/F, this heteroglossic multivoicedness disappears, sacrificed to conventional correctness; in RT/F, both heteroglossia and multivoicedness are restored and underlined by means of italics and an endnote explaining that "Cometty"—however spelled with two m's instead of one in ST—is a "Deformation of 'committee'": Mrs. Kearney is imitating (internally) the 'coarse' accent of "Mr. Fitzpatrick."

Re-dialogization, although present, is often less complete in RT/F than was the case in Dutch. These are the sentences following the "Eveline" passage cited before, in Excerpt 2:

Excerpt 4

How well she remembered the first time she had seen him; he was lodging in a house on the main road where she used to visit. It seemed a few weeks ago. He was standing at the gate, his peaked cap pushed back on his head and his hair tumbled forward over a face of bronze. (ST 31)

Comme elle se souvenait très bien de la première fois où elle l'avait vu ! Il logeait dans une maison de la grand-rue, où elle avait pris l'habitude d'aller le voir. Il semblait qu'il <u>n'y eût que quelques semaines de cela</u>. Il se tenait à la grille, sa casquette à visière <u>était</u> repoussée en arrière, et ses cheveux retombaient en avant sur <u>son visage bronzé</u>. (ET/F 94; our underlining)

Elle se souvenait si bien de la première fois qu'elle l'avait vu!_Il logeait dans une maison de la grand-rue où elle se rendait autrefois en visite. Il **lui** semblait **que c'était il y a quelques semaines**. Il était debout près du portail, la casquette à visière rejetée en arrière, les cheveux tombant en désordre sur **un visage de bronze**. (RT/F 69–70; our bold face and underlining)

As compared to ET/F, RT/F often de-explicitates and de-conventionalizes: "a few weeks ago" is simply "a few weeks ago" instead of the outdated, formal, and literary "il n'y eût que quelques semaines de cela," which is a very long way from Eveline's colloquial inner voice. Comparably, the explicitation of "a face of bronze" in "son visage bronzé" in ET/F (his bronzed face) is de-explicitated in RT/F, which thus restores Eveline's admiring gaze on the sailor. However, conventionalization has not disappeared entirely: as in ET/F, RT/F replaces the ST colon with an exclamation mark, thus underlining the presence of free indirect speech, by a discourse marker that is conventional in French literature since Flaubert, the founding father of realism whom Joyce admired.[50] Nonetheless, although punctuation is conventionalized, multivoicedness is reconstructed, and, as was the case in Excerpt 3, emphasized by typography. This is not the case, though, where RT/F renders "It seemed a few weeks ago" as "Il **lui** semblait que c'était il y a quelques semaines." By adding the third-person pronoun "lui" (to her), RT/F turns Eveline's free indirect speech into a third-person single-voiced narratorial comment.

In brief, the French translations correspond to what we hypothesized, but in a less pronounced way. RT/F does de-explicitate and de-conventionalize ET/F, but it also shows traces of explicitation and conventionalization, which result in heteroglossia and multivoicedness being only partially restored. This twofold picture is probably related to institutional context: in the longstanding, single-centered, and conservative French literary system, the centripetal forces of conventional literary style are particularly powerful.

8.3. *Dubliners* in German

The German-speaking world has seen at least six translations, published in Germany (including the former DDR), Austria, and Switzerland. Dieter Zimmer's translation (ET/G) is not the first one, but it is the one that entered the canon: we have found at least nine editions, from 1969 to 1996. Jan Strümpel's 2014 retranslation (RT/G) is the last one to date.

Our fifth example is taken from "Two Gallants":

Excerpt 5

She's on the turf now. I saw her driving down Earl Street one night with two fellows with her on a car. (ST 47)

Jetzt geht sie auf den Strich. Ich hab sie abends mal mit zwei Mackern auf einem Wagen **die Earl Street** runterfahren sehen. (ET/G 53; our italics and bold face)

Sie geht wieder anschaffen. Ich habe sie eines Abends **die Earl Street** runterfahren sehen, auf einem Wagen mit zwei Kerlen dabei. (RT/G 47; our italics and bold face)

Both ET/G and RT/G replace the first sentence, which is slang for "She is engaged in prostitution now,"[51] with common, informal euphemisms. The expression used in ET/G literally means "to walk on the line" and is signaled by *Duden*[52] as a "casual" expression for street prostitution. RT/G uses "anschaffen" which is vaguer and therefore even more euphemistic: "anschaffen" means to buy something, or to earn money. Used in a casual register it can refer to prostitution, but also to theft (*Duden*). In both cases, Dublin slang is rendered with colloquial, yet standard German expressions, resulting in the loss of heteroglossia by means of conventionalization. Nonetheless, heteroglossia is also recreated, as is the case in most of the translations across the five languages, by keeping

"Earl street," which was situated in the red light district of the time, in English, and without further explicitation. Further, RT/G translates "now" with "wieder" (again), thus distorting meaning. On the other hand, a mistranslation found in ET/I, /D, and /S, which is that "on a car" was translated by "in a car/automobile" is absent in German, in which both translations correctly render this with "auf einem Wagen." Finally, RT/G restores a syntactical structure which is closer to the ST, when compared to ET/G.

Our sixth example is taken from "The Dead":

Excerpt 6

I suppose you were in love with this Michael Furey, Gretta, he said. I was great with him at that time, she said. (ST 221)

—*Du warst wohl* in diesen Michael Furey verliebt, Gretta, sagte er.
—Ich hab mir damals *viel aus ihm gemacht*, sagte sie. (ET/G 225; our italics)

—**Ich nehme an**, du warst in diesen Michael Furey verliebt, Gretta, sagte er.
—Ich war damals *sehr gut mit ihm befreundet*, sagte sie. (RT/G 210; our bold face and italics)

An instance of explicitation present in ET/G is found in the beginning of the first sentence: "You were surely." In RT/G, this explicitation is de-explicitated by means of a word-for-word translation recreating ST syntactical structure, although not entirely: a comma was added, which is a mild form of conventionalization. In this example as well, there is a typical Irish expression that has proven to be a difficulty for both translators: neither ET/G nor RT/G manage to render "I was great with him"—meaning "I was his girl," possibly implying a serious relationship without sexual connotations according to Terence Brown,[53] or implying on the contrary a possible pregnancy according to Marie-Dominique Garnier[54]—without explicitating and conventionalizing. ET/G can be glossed "he was a big deal to me" while RT/G translates with "I was a good friend of his," which is less explicitating, yet presents the relationship in a disambiguated way as platonic. RT/S as well as RT/D, as we shall explain in Section 8.5, fully recreates ambiguity and multivoicedness.

For our final example on the German translations, we go back one last time to "Eveline"; this is how the page we already saw in Excerpts 2 and 4 continues:

Excerpt 7

Then they had come to know each other. He used to meet her outside the Stores every evening and see her home. He took her to see The Bohemian Girl and she felt elated as she sat in an unaccustomed part of the theatre with him. He was awfully fond of music and sang a little. People knew that they were courting. (ST 31)

Dann hatten sie sich kennengelernt. Jeden Abend holte er sie vor dem Laden ab und brachte sie nach Hause. Er ging mit ihr in Die Zigeunerin, und sie war *in gehobener Stimmung*, als sie mit ihm zusammen in einem ungewohnten Teil des Theaters saß. Er hatte Musik schrecklich gern und sang <u>selber</u> ein wenig. Die Leute wußten, daß sie miteinander gingen. (ET/G 37–8; our italics)

<u>Dann lernten sie sich kennen</u>. *Jeden Abend wartete er vor dem Geschäft* und *ging mit zu ihr*. Er nahm sie mit in Die Zigeunerin, und sie war *begeistert*, als sie in einem ungewohnten Bereich des Theaters mit ihm saß. Er mochte Musik furchtbar gern und sang ein wenig. Die Leute wussten, dass sie einander umwarben. (RT/G 32; our italics and underlining)

This passage presents some examples of explicitation in both ET/G and RT/G. For example, "every evening he picked her up in front of the store" (ET/G) and "every evening he waited for her in front of the store" (RT/G) are both explicitating. RT/G also explicitates on an occasion where ET/G does not explicitate, by translating "and see her home" with "und ging mit zu ihr." This suggests what remains implicit in the ST, that is, that he may have entered the house on these occasions. Similarly, "Sie war in gehobener Stimmung," (she was in an uplifted mood) (ET/G), is an explicitating and downplaying translation of "she felt elated." Instead of focusing on Eveline's own perception of the situation in her inner voice, ET/G portrays her general mood, thus distorting the Uncle Charles Principle, much in the same way as was the case with ET/D in Excerpt 2 or ET/F in Excerpt 4. Similarly, however, the RT/G rendering "begeistert" as "enthusiastic" also downplays Eveline's "elated" feeling. Both ET/G and RT/G render, therefore, the multivoicedness of the ST passage with a single-voiced narratorial comment on how Eveline feels.

There are also instances of conventionalization, and these occur in both ET/G and RT/G as well. The first sentence, for instance, is conventionalized in RT/G by resorting to a simple past tense where the ST shows a past perfect. Simple past is the conventional preterite in German, but is again closer to a single-voiced narration than it is to Eveline's inner voice. On the other hand, the conventionalization (by adding a pronoun) in "sang *selber* ein wenig" (sang a little himself) (ET/G)—which however does not distort voices, as the reader can still imagine Eveline thinking and reformulating in free indirect speech what Frank may have told her—is de-conventionalized in RT/G. As for the rendering of *The Bohemian girl*, an 1843 romantic opera in English by the Dublin-born composer Michael William Balfe, both translations resort to the existing German translation made in 1846 and not, as is the case in ET/D, RT/D, ET/I, and RT/I, to free translations, either because the libretto was never translated (which is the case for Dutch) or because the translators did not know that it had been translated, as has occurred in Italian.[55]

In brief, although the German translations, both ET/G and RT/G, show evidence of a less frequency of translational inaccuracies as compared to other languages, for instance in Excerpt 5, the image we get is somewhat fuzzier. RT/G does indeed sometimes de-explicitate ET/G, and it does sometimes reproduce syntactical structures with less conventionalization. However, neither explicitation nor conventionalization has disappeared entirely from RT/G, as was the case in RT/D: heteroglossia is still downplayed, although partially reproduced, as it also is in RT/F. But especially multivoicedness seems to have been challenging for both German translators. Whereas the French translations struggled with heteroglossia and multivoicedness because of conventionalizing strategies, in the German translations the loss of multivoicedness seems to be due primarily to explicitations.

8.4. *Dubliners* in Italian

In Italy, at least fourteen different translations of *Dubliners* were published, among which two recent retranslations in 2018. In the Italian context, there is an interesting trend to be observed, which is that several retranslations appear at very small intervals: between 1987 and 1989, four translations were published, three of which with the major players Feltrinelli, Mondadori, and Garzanti (the latter being a revision, by Emilio Tadini, of the 1976 Papi translation). At the same time, Dall'Oglio and Mondadori stopped distributing the 1933 Lami and 1949 Cancogni translations, whereas Einaudi, also a big player but without a new translation in its portfolio, continued to distribute the latter—our ET/I—until 2012. By that time, two additional translations were already on the market, to be followed by two more. This accelerated production of "active retranslations"[56] in direct competition with one another certainly challenges the tenacious cliché that retranslations supposedly occur when earlier translations have "aged" and become outdated.

Franca Cancogni's translation (ET/I) was the first to become a classic. First published in 1949 by Einaudi (who reprinted it until 2012), the text was also printed by Mondadori until 1987 when it was replaced by a new translation by Attilio Brilli. As Einaudi and Mondadori are two of the most influential publishing houses in the country, this guaranteed Cancogni's translation a longstanding and large distribution. As for RT/I, Marina Emo Capodilista's translation was regularly reprinted between 1974 and 2017 by the low-cost publisher Newton Compton. Furthermore, it was republished in 2017 together with Enrico Terrinoni's 2012 retranslation of *Ulysses*, in the popular, low-priced "I capolavori" (masterworks) series, which is the edition we used.

ET/I shows several instances of explicitation, as well as conventionalization. This is an example from "A Mother":

Excerpt 8

Mrs Kearney said that she didn't know anything about Mr Fitzpatrick. (ST 142)

<u>Ma</u> la signora Kearney <u>ribatté</u> che lei *non conosceva nessun* signor Fitzpatrick. (ET/I 139; our underlining and italics)

La signora Kearney **disse** che <u>non sapeva niente del</u> signor Fitzpatrick. (RT/I 2056; our bold face and italics)

ET/I explicitates ST in the segment rendered in italics as "she didn't know any Mr Fitzpatrick" (this also occurs in ET/D and /S), whereas conventionalization can be observed in the addition of "Ma" (But) and the use of a declarative verb that means "retorted" rather than "said." RT/I translates word-for-word, thus avoiding both explicitation and conventionalization. Similar translation strategies occur in Excerpt 6 discussed above: ET/I translates "I was great with him at that time" with "Andavamo molto d'accordo" (We got along very well), which is, although in this case only partially, de-explicitated and de-conventionalized in RT/I, into "Stavamo molto insieme, allora" (We were often together, then). In Excerpt 8, heteroglossia, however, suffers from the conversion of "Mrs." and "Mr." to the conventional Italian "signora" and "signor," contrary to what we saw in ET/D and /G and in RT/G (and also /S) that reproduce the heteroglossia of English addresses.

A further example can be found in "A Painful Case":

Excerpt 9

She, witness, had often tried to reason with her mother and had induced her to join a league. (ST 111)

... piú volte ella aveva cercato *di ricondurla alla ragione consigliandola a farsi socia di una lega antialcol.* (ET/I 113; our italics)

La testimone aveva **spesso** cercato *di fare ragionare* **la madre** e *l'aveva persuasa a diventare socia di una lega antialcolica.* (RT/I 1638; our bold face and italics)

Similarly to what can be observed in all ETs across the five languages, ET/I is explicitating in this passage: "to reason with her" becomes "to bring her back to reason," thus pointing to one specific meaning of the verb which, in ST, is ambiguous. In the same vein, the ambiguity of "a league"—which however is unambiguous to the characters within the story, whose voices are being used by the narrator—is explicitated in all ETs, into an "anti-alcohol league." ET/D, /F, /G, and /S also explicitate that the mother has effectively joined the league, while this remains in fact unclear in the ST. ET/I is the only ET that does not explicitate on this occasion: "consigliandola" (advising her) does not reveal the outcome of the daughter's effort. Conversely, RT/I's "l'aveva persuasa" (she had persuaded her) clearly states that the mother did ultimately join the league. Ambiguity (and character passivity, once again) is therefore lost in RT/I, while it is restored in both RT/D and /S. As for the "league," RT/I explicitates as ET/I did, rendering "to join a league" with "become member of an anti-alcohol league." Despite this case in which ambiguity is not restored, RT/I does reintroduce three important words that are missing in ET/I: "witness," which defines the social-psychological status of the daughter, "often," and "mother."

Similarly to what can be observed in ET/D and /S, ET/I shows several examples of explicitation and normalization, while RT/I's use of word-for-word translation strategies results in a text in which many instances of syntactical de-conventionalization and de-explicitation can be found. Nonetheless, explicitation is still present throughout RT/I. This may be due to the translator not having access, in the early 1970s, to annotated editions and criticism on the Uncle Charles Principle, which we know were used by the Dutch retranslators, for instance. As a result, RT/I often shows less subjective-emotional and more standardized single-voiced narratorial discourse, especially at the level of lexis. Whereas the translator's effort in ET/I seems to have been employed first and foremost in syntactical conventionalizations, RT/I does indeed dialogically re-accent ET/I by means of word-for-word renderings, although explicitations still occur. This word-for-word strategy has also allowed for the corrections of some mistranslations—a few examples are, from Excerpt 5, "macchina" (automobile) in ET/I; "carrozza" (carriage) in RT/I, or, from Excerpt 1, "imposte" (shutters) in ET/I; and becoming "tendina" (blind) in RT/I. In addition, some heteroglossia is preserved, for instance when "Earl Street" (Excerpt 5) is kept in English.

8.5. *Dubliners* in Spanish

There are a total of seven complete *Dubliners* translations into Spanish. The first translation, titled *Gente de Dublín*, by Ignacio Abelló and supervised by Félix Ros, was published in 1942 in Barcelona by Tartesos. Three years later, the first Latin American translation appeared in Chile, by Peruvian writer and politician Luis Alberto Sánchez, titled *Dublineses*. Since then, a number of retranslations has followed, but the most reedited translation (twenty-three reeditions) is the one by renowned Cuban author Guillermo Cabrera Infante titled *Dublineses* (1972). In the past thirty years, *Dubliners* has been retranslated four times: by Spanish author and journalist Eduardo Chamorro (1993), by Joseph Club (2001), by Marcos Mayer (2004), and by Fernando Velasco Garrido (2015). Also in that period a partial retranslation was published, of "The Dead," by María Isabel Butler de Foley (1994). For our analysis, we have selected Abelló's text as ET/S and Cabrera Infante's popular version as RT/S.

Excerpt 10

He lived his spiritual life without any communion with others. (ST 105)

En su vida spiritual se desenvolvía *sin tener en cuenta para nada* al prójimo. (ET/S 114; our italics)

Vivía su vida espiritual **sin comunión** con el prójimo. (RT/S 109; our bold face)

This is yet another example of the Uncle Charles Principle, taken from "A Painful Case." The text displays Mr. Duffy's repetitive daily routine from his own perspective. Accordingly, multivoicedness is visible in this passage, in which the third-person narrator's voice merges with the focalizing character by means of the idiom "without any communion with others." This expression reproduces, in the narrator's voice, a characteristic feature of Mr. Duffy's conservative Catholic discourse identity. RT/S has opted for "sin comunión con el prójimo," thus reproducing an equivalent effect of multivoicedness and a successful allusion to Catholicism by combining the word "comunión" with the evangelical term of "el prójimo" (your neighbor),[57] already present in ET/S. ET/S' rendering with "sin tener en cuenta para nada" (without taking into account at all), however, does not recreate Duffy's characteristic Catholic-conservative thinking. As a result, the reader can observe how ET/S has opted for explicitation, whereas RT/S manages to re-dialogize ET/S by reintroducing multivoicedness.

Excerpt 11

Her daughter had signed a contract for eight guineas and she would have to be paid. (ST 142)

Su hija había firmado un contrato *para los cuatro conciertos con un total de ocho guineas, y que haría que se las pagase*. (ET/S 154; our italics)

Su hija había firmado contrato por ocho guineas y **había que pagárselas**. (RT/S 146; our bold face)

This example is taken from "A Mother." Mrs. Kearny approaches Mr. Holohan because her daughter Kathleen has been hired to give concerts but has not been paid. Mr. Holohan then refers Mrs. Kearny to his secretary, Mr. Fitzpatrick. The sentence in this excerpt is a case of free indirect speech containing Mrs. Kearny's thoughts, namely that her daughter "would have to be paid," which highlights the character's inner sense of justice. ET/S, however, explicitates on several occasions, emphasizing something else, namely that Mrs. Kearny "would make them pay," thus turning her inner sense of justice into a rather vehement promise of imminent action. Similarly to what we saw earlier in the "Eveline" passages (Excerpts 2, 4, and 7), this modifies Mrs. Kearny's characterization in a way that is contrary to how Joyce highlights the inertia of Dublin's inhabitants. RT/S, on the contrary, stays close to ST word choice and word order, thus de-explicitating ET/S and reproducing Mrs. Kearny's inner voice in a more convincing way.

Excerpt 12

Lily, the caretaker's daughter, was literally run off her feet ... and she had to scamper along the bare hallway to let in another guest ... Though their life was modest they believed in eating well; the best of everything: diamond-bone sirloins, three-shilling tea and the best bottled stout. But

Lily seldom made a mistake in the orders so that she got on well with her three mistresses. They were fussy, that was all. But the only thing they would not stand was back answers. (ST 175–6).

Lily, la hija del conserje, <u>estaba que no sabía dónde tenía los pies</u> ... <u>y allá iba ella a grandes pasos</u> por el largo recibidor sin muebles, a dar paso a otro invitado ... Llevaban una vida modesta; <u>sin embargo</u>, creían en la buena mesa; lo mejor en todo: *solomillo del fino, de a tres chelines*, y el mejor *vino* embotellado<u>, y</u> como eran raras las veces que Lily cometía una equivocación en lo que la mandaban, se llevaba bien con sus tres dueñas. (ET/S 191–2; our italics and underlining)

Lily, la hija del encargado, <u>tenía los pies literalmente muertos</u> ... <u>y tenía que echar a correr</u> por el zaguán vacío para dejar entrar a otro ... **Aunque** llevaban una vida modesta, les gustaba comer bien; lo mejor de lo mejor: costillas de riñonada, **té** de a tres chelines y ***stout*** embotellado del bueno. **Pero** Lily nunca hacía un mandado mal, **por lo que** se llevaba muy bien con las señoritas. **Eran quisquillosas, eso es todo. Lo único que no soportaban era que les contestaran.** (RT/S 180–1; our underling and bold face)

Our final excerpt, from "The Dead, "is a classic example of the "Uncle Charles Principle," already mentioned by Kenner. According to other scholars as well,[58] "literally" is a characteristic feature of Lily's discourse, within the narrator's voice. Indeed, it is Lily who gets the difference between literal and figurative speech wrong (of course, she is figuratively run off her feet), while being merged with the third-person narrator's voice. One observes in this case how ET/S has conventionalized language ("she didn't know where her feet were"'), whereas RT/S opts for a strategy of re-dialogization by recovering the adverb "literally" and combining with a figurative expression containing "feet": "tenía los pies *literalmente* muertos" (she literally had dead feet). But this is about more than Lily making a silly mistake: her inner voice also connotes social class contrasts and power relationships. Her numerous tasks and hasty work rhythm as a servant are highlighted by the verb "she had to scamper." Here again, ET/S conventionalizes (and downplays) language, translating with "and there she went." RT/S, on the other hand, reproduces the way in which Lily's hard and fast work for her masters is highlighted in the narrator's choice of words: "tenía que echar a correr" (she had to run). In the second part of the excerpt, one can observe how the last two sentences have been omitted altogether in ET/S. Together with this, a series of misreadings have been corrected in RT/S—Abelló's ET refers to three-shilling sirloin instead of "tea" which is omitted, and to "wine" instead of "stout." But there also is an additional characteristic narratological feature in this second part of the excerpt, namely the use of conjunctions which, according to Michael Mayo,[59] are also characteristic features of a character's discourse and should therefore also be considered as parts of Kenner's "Uncle Charles Principle." Indeed, a comparison shows how, unlike ET/S, RT/S has managed to recreate all conjunctions except for the last "but," in order to adopt, in Spanish, Lily's colloquial voice as it appears in the ST narration.

For a final remark, we would like to go back to Excerpt 6, discussed above. This is the passage in which Gretta rather enigmatically admits to Gabriel, after several questions about her feelings for Michael Fury, that she "was great with him at that time" (ST 221). Terence Brown adds a note in which he explains that she "got along very well with him to the point where the relationship might well have become serious, though as yet without any great sexual connotation."[60] This ambiguity, which results from Gretta's reticence to explicitly express feelings that may well be unclear to her as well, increases the intensity of this critical scene: Gretta finally admits to having had a relationship with Michael Fury, yet the nature of that relationship remains unclear. In this case, a comparison of the two Spanish translations shows two different stories. In ET/S, Gretta explicitly admits that she was in love with Michael Fury: "lo estaba mucho entonces" (I was much [in love] at that time). Cabrera Infante, in RT/S, however, shows awareness of Gretta's ambiguity: "me sentía muy bien con él entonces" (I felt great with him at that time). Again, as we saw in all the excerpts discussed, ET/S has explicitated meaning, whereas RT/S recovers heteroglossia and ambiguity, thus recreating multivoicedness. The same occurs in RT/D as well, which reads "Ik was heel dik met hem indertijd" (I was very close with him at the time), using a colloquial expression that can refer to love, or deep friendship.

9. Conclusion: Retranslation as Re-dialogizing Re-accentuation

Our analyses show how heteroglossia and multivoicedness are indeed at odds with conventionalization and explicitation. However, these are not "universals of translation," as we have observed a substantial difference between ETs and RTs. For all languages examined, explicitation and conventionalization occur mostly in ETs, resulting in a loss of multivoicedness that alters character psychology and, due to the loss of ambiguity, the passive open-endedness of *Dubliners*' poetics. In RTs, however, explicitation and conventionalization occur far less and, as a result, multivoicedness is recreated more often. This is due to re-accentuation strategies to the second degree, by which retranslators de-explicitate what had been explicitated in ETs, and reintroduce heteroglossia where ETs had conventionalized. Interestingly, as we saw, this mainly occurs through word-for-word translation, which traditionally is not considered to be a creative translation strategy.[61] Another interesting discovery is that recreating multivoicedness benefits from de-explicitation as much as it does from de-conventionalization.

Nonetheless, multivoicedness is not always fully recreated in RTs. In the French context in particular, conventionalization occurs in RT and multivoicedness is only partially reproduced, as the centripetal forces of conventional literariness prove to be particularly strong. The German RT also reproduces some of the ST heteroglossia and conventionalizes less than ET, yet explicitates and, as a result, doesn't always preserve multivoicedness. However, RT/G is a five-dollar hardback (two-dollar e-book). We can therefore only imagine the translator's work rhythm to have been Tartarean. In some of the most recent and similarly low-priced Italian RTs, there is evidence of errors, carelessness, misinterpretations, and, indeed, many losses of multivoicedness. In comparison, the German retranslator did splendidly. What is at stake here is institutional (market) context, rather than whatever translation-immanent logic: in recent years, unfortunately, we see increasing numbers of translators who, like Lily, have to "scamper" while serving their masters. It is not them who are to be blamed.

With those caveats in mind, retranslations generally do recreate multivoicedness. This is not the case because RTs are more source-oriented, as the Retranslation Hypothesis suggests. Rather, the dichotomy of *either* source- *or* target-orientedness needs to be approached with much precaution. As retranslators re-accent *both* ETs *and* ST material, as we have shown, they respond dialogically to materials present in both source and target contexts. In that respect RTs are *both* source- *and* target-oriented. This is the very reason why retranslators achieve a more profound dialogical understanding—a re-accentuation to the second degree—of the ST material, in the TC. The work of their predecessors significantly contributes to that.

Although our analyses therefore confirm our hypothesis, we will not present re-dialogization as yet another "universal of translation" (or retranslation). First, what we claim here is that we believe our hypothesis to hold, with the caveats explained above, for this particular corpus. Much more work is needed, across a variety of STs and TCs before we can claim anything else. Second, the approach by which we selected a single ET and a single RT for each language may have resulted in a loss of gradation due to the bipolarity of such comparisons. Further scrutiny of all translations in different TCs is needed. In that respect, we believe that our Re-dialogization Hypothesis may have new heuristic value, in a field in which the Retranslation Hypothesis has run out of breath in recent years. In any case, it is not to be expected that each new translation will show the typical strategies of retranslation that we have commented on. In re-accentuation, context plays the key role. This is why the field of retranslation is to be seen, as Antoine Berman already argued in his seminal 1990 paper, as "a translation space" or "room" for potential improvement. This does not imply that every translation should always be an improvement as compared to the previous one. But what we have shown, for this particular corpus, is that a visible overall dynamic cuts across that re-accentuation "space" of subsequent translations. That improvement dynamic occurs over time, albeit in different degrees depending on contextual factors, as a result of re-accentuation to the second degree, and it can be described as a set of re-dialogizing translation strategies, such as de-explicitation and de-conventionalization. Such a diachronic "translation space" is traversed by the centripetal and centrifugal forces of language, and, in the case of translated narrative, by the two Stylistic Lines of the novel. What retranslations do, in this space for re-accentuation, is that they have the potential to undo the monologization of the classics in early translations, and to re-dialogize source text materials. Thanks to retranslation, the classics may reenter, in their target contexts, the Second Stylistic Line to which they belonged in the source context. That is, in a nutshell, the re-dialogizing power of retranslations' re-accentuation.

Notes

1. Mikhail M. Bakhtin, "Discourse in the Novel," in *The Dialogic Imagination: Four Essays*, ed. Michael Holquist, trans. Caryl Emerson and Michael Holquist (Austin: University of Texas Press, 1981), 259–422.
2. Simon Dentith, *Bakhtinian Thought. An Introductory Reader* (London: Routledge, 1995), 95–6; Gary Saul Morson and Caryl Emerson, *Mikhail Bakhtin: Creation of a Prosaics* (Stanford: Stanford University Press, 1990), 361–65; Slav Gratchev and Howard Mancing (eds.), *Don Quixote. The Re-accentuation of the World's Greatest Literary Hero* (Lewisburg: Bucknell University Press, 2017), 1–2.
3. Mikhail M. Bakhtin, *Art and Answerability: Early Philosophical Essays*, ed. Michael Holquist and Vadim Liapunov, trans. Vadim Liapunov (Austin: University of Texas Press, 1990).
4. Bakhtin, "Discourse in the Novel," 421.
5. Dentith, *Bakhtinian Thought*, 96.

6. Tzvetan Todorov, *Mikhail Bakhtin. The Dialogic Principle* (Minneapolis: Minnesota University Press, 1984), 56–9.
7. Bakhtin, "Discourse in the Novel," 293–95; Vyacheslav Ivanov, "Heteroglossia," *Journal of Linguistic Anthropology* 9, no. 1–2 (2000): 100–2; Caryl Emerson, "Editor's Preface," in Mikhail M. Bakhtin, *Problems of Dostoevsky's Poetics*, trans. Caryl Emerson (Minneapolis: Minnesota University Press, 1984), xxxiii.
8. Bakhtin, "Discourse in the Novel," 288.
9. The word *sobytie* has two meanings: it refers to the "event" of discourse, but it also means "together-being" (*so-bytie*), thus signaling that "within the arena of almost every utterance an intense interaction and struggle between one's own and another's word is being waged" (Bakhtin, "Discourse in the Novel," 354).
10. Bakhtin, "Discourse in the Novel," 263; Bakhtin, *Problems of Dostoevsky's Poetics*, 32–42, 181–204.
11. Bakhtin, "Discourse in the Novel," 354; Bakhtin, *Problems of Dostoevsky's Poetics*, 98, 285.
12. Bakhtin, *Problems of Dostoevsky's Poetics*, 185–99.
13. Mikhail M. Bakhtin, "The Problem of the Text in Linguistics, Philology and the Human Sciences," in *Speech Genres and Other Late Essays*, ed. Caryl Emerson and Michael Holquist, trans. Vern W. McGee (Austin: University of Texas Press, 1986), 119–20.
14. Andrew Robinson, "Bakhtin: Dialogism, Polyphony and Heteroglossia," *Ceasefire Magazine* (2011), ceasefiremagazine.co.uk/in-theory-bakhtin-1/, n.p.
15. Bakhtin, "Discourse in the Novel," 272; Ken Hirschkop, *Mikhail Bakhtin* (Oxford: Oxford University Press, 2000), 168.
16. Bakhtin, "Discourse in the Novel," 366–422; Gary Saul Morson and Caryl Emerson, *Mikhail Bakhtin: Creation of a Prosaics* (Stanford: Stanford University Press, 1990), 344–61.
17. Bakhtin, "Discourse in the Novel," 383.
18. Ibid.
19. Mikhail M. Bakhtin, "Epic and Novel," in *The Dialogic Imagination: Four Essays*, ed. Michael Holquist, trans. Caryl Emerson and Michael Holquist (Austin: University of Texas Press, 1981), 3–40.
20. Bakhtin, *Problems of Dostoevsky's Poetics*, 122–37, 156–77.
21. Bakhtin, "Epic and Novel," 19.
22. Gratchev and Mancing, *Don Quixote*.
23. Keith Easley, *Dickens and Bakhtin. Authoring and Dialogism in Dickens's Novels* (New York: Ams Press, 2014).
24. Ivanov, "Heteroglossia," 100.
25. For a useful overview of the literature on translation techniques and strategies, see Lucía Molina and Amparo Hurtado Albir, "Translation Techniques Revisited: A Dynamic and Functionalist Approach," *Meta* 47, no. 4 (2002): 498–512.

26. Pascale Casanova, *The World Republic of Letters* (Cambridge, MA: Harvard University Press, 2004), 135–36.
27. Lawrence Venuti, *The Translator's Invisibility. A History of Translation* (London: Routledge, 1995), 1–42.
28. Jan Willem Mathijssen, *The Breach and the Observance. Theatre Retranslation as a Strategy of Artistic Differentiation* (Utrecht: University of Utrecht, 2007), 61.
29. On the concepts of adequacy and acceptability, see Gideon Toury, *Descriptive Translation Studies—and Beyond*. Revised edition (Amsterdam: John Benjamins, 2012), 69–70.
30. Shoshana Blum-Kulka, "Shifts of Cohesion and Coherence in Translation," in *The Translation Studies Reader*, ed. Lawrence Venuti (London: Routledge, 2000), 298–313; Anna Mauranen and Pekka Kujamäki (eds.), *Translation Universals. Do They exist?* (Amsterdam: John Benjamins, 2004).
31. Anna Mauranen, "Universal Tendencies in Translation," in *Incorporating corpora. The Linguist and the Translator*, ed. Gunilla Anderman and Margaret Rogers (Clevedon: Multilingual matters, 2007), 32–48; Päivi Kuusi, "Features of Discourse Presentation in Translation: Literary and Narratological Insights into Translation Universals," *International Journal of literary Linguistics* 5, no. 3 (2016): 1–24.
32. Mauranen and Kujamäki, *Translation Universals*; Sara Laviosa, "Universals of Translation," in *Routledge Encyclopedia of Translation Studies*, ed. Mona Baker (London: Routledge, 2001), 288–91.
33. Yves Gambier, "La retraduction, retour et detour," *Meta* 39, no. 3 (1994): 413–17; Yves Gambier, "La retraduction: ambiguïtés et défis," in *Autour de la retraduction. Perspectives littéraires européennes*, ed. Enrico Monti and Peter Schnyder (Paris: Orizons, 2011), 49–66.
34. Antoine Berman, "La retraduction comme espace de la traduction," *Palimpsestes* 4 (1990): 1–7; Andrew Chesterman, "A Causal Model for Translation Studies," in *Intercultural Faultlines: Research Models in Translation Studies I: Textual and Cognitive Aspects*, ed. Maeve Olohan (Manchester: St. Jerome, 2000), 15–28; Kaisa Koskinen and Outi Paloposki, "Retranslation," in *Handbook of Translation Studies*, ed. Yves Gambier and Luc Van Doorslaer (Amsterdam: John Benjamins, 2010), 294–8.
35. Kris Peeters, "Traduction, retraduction, dialogisme," *Meta* 61, no. 3 (2016): 629–49; Kris Peeters and Guillermo Sanz Gallego, "Translators' Creativity in the Dutch and Spanish (Re)translations of "Oxen of the Sun": (Re)translation the Bakhtinian way," *European Joyce Studies* 30 (2020): 221–41.
36. Bakhtin, *Problems of Dostoevsky's Poetics*, 199.
37. Peeters and Sanz Gallego, "Translators' Creativity."
38. Uncle Charles is a character in *A Portrait of the Artist as a Young Man*. Hugh Kenner uses him in *Joyce's Voices* (Berkeley: University of California Press, 1978) to exemplify the "Uncle Charles Principle." Kenner argues that Joyce's

narrators, when speaking of a character, often use that character's idiom, thus revealing his or her inner voice and psychology, by means of what Leo Spitzer, Bakhtin's favorite philologist (Vyacheslav Ivanov, "Bakhtin's Theory of Language From The Standpoint of Modern Science," *Russian Journal of Communication* 1, no. 3 [2008]: 247), has described as "contagion of the narrator's speech by the character's conscience" (Leo Spitzer, "Sprachmischung als Stilmittel und als Ausdruck der Klangphantasie," *Germanisch-Romanisches Monatschrift* 11 [1923]: 201; our translation). In other words, Joyce's third-person narrators may seem detached, but actually it is quite the opposite.

39. Vanja Garic, "The Sense of the Unending in Joyce's *Dubliners*," *Folia Linguistica et Litteraria* 25 (2018): 87.
40. Ibid., 88.
41. James Joyce, *Dubliners*, Introduction and Notes by Terence Brown (London: Penguin Classics, 1993).
42. Geert Lernout and Wim Van Mierlo, *The Reception of James Joyce in Europe: Germany, Northern and East Central Europe, Volume 1* (London: Thoemmes Continuum, 2004), 414.
43. Ibid., 329–31.
44. Ibid., xx–xxiii.
45. Ibid., xxi–xxvii.
46. The word "Dublinezen" is not standard Dutch; it is a neologism inspired by existing words like "Chinezen" (Chinese) or "Albanezen" (Albanians).
47. All glosses in italics and between double quotation marks are ours.
48. "But I say to you that for every idle word men may speak, they will give account of it in the day of judgment." (*New King James* version, www.bible gateway.com).
49. The Dutch word used in RT/D for "idle" (ijdel) occurs in the 1637 *Statenbijbel* ("States Bible," which is comparable to the King James Bible in English) and the 1888 Jongbloed revision of it—which is the edition of Joyce's time—yet not in the most recent 2010 revision, which reads "nutteloos" (useless). RT/D therefore not only preserves the allusion, but also historicizes that allusion.
50. Interestingly, Frank's "peaked cap" was translated by both Du Pasquier and Tadié as a "casquette à visière," which alludes to the famous description of Charles Bovary's cap in the first chapter of Flaubert's *Madame Bovary*.
51. See *Oxford Dictionary of English*, www.oed.com.
52. Duden. *Das große Wörterbuch der Deutschen Sprache*, www.duden.de/woer terbuch.
53. Joyce, *Dubliners*, 316.
54. Marie-Dominique Garnier, "The Dubbing Theatre of *Dubliners*: Dubbing, Voiceovers and Post-synchronisation," in *Joyce's Dubliners. Lectures critiques/Critical Approaches*, ed. Claudine Reynaud (Tours: Presses universitaires François Rabelais, 2001), 44.

55. The libretto was translated into Italian in 1854, titled *La Zingara*, while ET/I and RT/I translate, respectively, *La ragazza di Boemia* and *La Zingarella*.
56. Anthony Pym, *Method in Translation History* (London: Routledge, 2014), 92–3.
57. As in *Matthew* 22: 39: "Amarás a tu prójimo como a ti mismo" (trans. Reina-Valera 1995), "You shall love your neighbour as yourself" (*New King James* version, www.biblegateway.com).
58. Margot Norris, "Stifled Back Answers: The Gender Politics of Art in Joyce's *The Dead*," *Modern Fiction Studies* 35 (1989): 479–80; Michael Mayo, "Beyond the Uncle Charles Principle," *James Joyce Quarterly* 56, no. 3–4 (2019): 245–66.
59. Mayo, "Beyond the Uncle Charles Principle."
60. Joyce, *Dubliners*, 316.
61. See Molina and Hurtado Albir, "Translation Techniques Revisited," 499, 506, 510.

Bibliography

Corpus of Translations

Dutch

(ET/D) *Dubliners*. Translated by Rein Bloem. Amsterdam: Polak and Van Gennep, 1969.
(RT/D) *Dublinezen*. Translated by Erik Bindervoet and Robbert-Jan Henkes. Amsterdam: Athenaeum-Polak and Van Gennep, 2016.

French

(ET/F) *Gens de Dublin*. Translated by Yva Fernandez, Jacques-Paul Reynaud and Hélène du Pasquier. Paris: Plon, 1969 [1926].
Dublinois. Translated by Jean-Noël Vuarnet. Paris: Aubier/Flammarion, 1974 [bilingual edition; partial translation containing *Counterparts* and *The Dead*]
Gens de Dublin. Translated by Jacques Aubert. Paris: Gallimard ("Du monde entier"), 1974. Republished in James Joyce, *Oeuvres I*, Paris: Gallimard ("Bibliothèque de la Pléiade"), 1982; Republished titled *Dublinois*, Paris: Gallimard ("Folio"), 1993.
(RT/F) *Gens de Dublin*. Translated by Benoît Tadié. Paris: Garnier Flammarion, 1993.
Dubliners/Gens de Dublin. Translated by Pierre Nordon. Paris: Librairie Générale Française ("Livre de Poche"), 1994 [bilingual edition; partial translation of seven stories].

Dubliners/Gens de Dublin. Translated by Lionel Dahan. Paris: Pocket, 2013 [bilingual edition; partial translation of *The Sisters, Eveline, The Boarding House* and *A Painful Case*].

German

Dublin. Novellen. Translated by Georg Goyert. Basel: Rhein-Verlag, 1928 [also *Dubliner*. Frankfurt am Main: Suhrkamp Verlag, 1967].
(ET/G) *Dubliner.* Translated by Dieter Zimmer. Frankfurt am Main: Suhrkamp Verlag, 1969 [until 1996] [also Wien: Buchgemeinschaft Donauland, 1981 and East-Berlin: Volk und Welt, 1983].
Dubliner. Translated by Harald Beck. Stuttgart: Reclam, 1994 [until 2012] [also Frankfurt am Main: Büchergilde Gutenberg, 1996].
Dubliner. Translated by Friedhelm Rathjens. Hamburg: Rowohlt Taschenbuch Verlag, 2003–16 [also Zürich: Manesse Verlag, 2019].
Dubliner. Translated by Harald Raykowsky. München: Deutscher Taschenbuch Verlag, 2012.
(RT/G) *Dubliner.* Translated by Jan Strümpel. Köln: Anaconda, 2014.

Italian

Gente di Dublino. Translated by Annie and Adriano Lami. Milano: Dall'Oglio, 1933 [until 1987].
(ET/I) *Gente di Dublino.* Translated by Franca Cancogni. Torino: Einaudi, 1949 [until 2012] [also Milano: Mondadori, until 1987].
Dublinesi [in later editions *Gente di Dublino*]. Translated by Margherita Ghirardi Minoja. Milano: Rizzoli, 1961 [until 2012].
Gente di Dublino. Translated by Maria Pia Balboni. Milano: Fratelli Fabbri [also *I dublinesi.* Milano: Bompiani, 1986 (until 1995)].
(RT/I) *Gente di Dublino.* Translated by Marina Emo Capodilista. Roma: Newton Compton, 1974 [until 2017] [also La Spezia: Club del libro, 1981].
Gente di Dublino. Translated by Marco Papi. Milano: Garzanti, 1976 [Revised by Emilio Tadini. Milano: Garzanti, 1989].
Gente di Dublino. Translated by Daniele Benati. Milano: Feltrinelli, 1987 [until 2008].
Gente di Dublino. Translated by Attilio Brilli. Milano: Mondadori, 1988.
Gente di Dublino. Translated by Massimo Marani. Roma: Gherardo Casini, 1988.
Gente di Dublino. Translated by Emilio Tadini. Milano: Garzanti, 1989 [Revision of the 1976 translation by Marco Papi.]
Gente di Dublino. Translated by Francesco Franconeri. Bussolengo: Demetra, 1993 [also Fidenza: Mattioli 1885, 2012].
Gente di Dublino. Translated by Gian Luca Guerneri. Rimini: Guaraldi, 1995.

I Dublinesi. Translated by Maurizio Bartocci. Milano: Bompiani, 2018.
Gente di Dublino. Translated by Stefano Bortolussi. Firenze: Giunti Editore/Demetra, 2018.

Spanish

(ET/S) *Gente de Dublín*. Translated by Ignacio Abelló. Barcelona: Tartesos, 1942.
Dublineses. Translated by Luis Alberto Sánchez. Santiago de Chile: Ercilla, 1945.
(RT/S) *Dublineses*. Translated by Guillermo Cabrera Infante. Barcelona: Lumen, 1972.
Dublineses. Translated by Eduardo Chamorro. Madrid: Cátedra, 1993.
Los muertos. Translated by María Isabel Butler de Foley. Madrid: Alianza Editorial, 1994 [partial translation containing *The Dead*].
Dublineses. Translated by Joseph Club. Madrid: Clásicos Universales, 2001.
Dublineses. Translated by Marcos Mayer. Buenos Aires: Losada, 2004.
Dublineses. Translated by Fernando Velasco Garrido. Madrid: Akal, 2015.

Criticism

Bakhtin, Mikhail M. "Discourse in the Novel." In *The Dialogic Imagination: Four Essays*. Edited by Michael Holquist. Translated by Caryl Emerson and Michael Holquist, 259–422. Austin: University of Texas Press, 1981.
Bakhtin, Mikhail M. "Epic and Novel." In *The Dialogic Imagination: Four Essays*. Edited by Michael Holquist. Translated by Caryl Emerson and Michael Holquist, 3–40. Austin: University of Texas Press, 1981.
Bakhtin, Mikhail M. "The Problem of Speech Genres." In *Speech Genres and Other Late Essays*. Edited by Caryl Emerson and Michael Holquist. Translated by Vern W. McGee, 60–102. Austin: University of Texas Press, 1986.
Bakhtin, Mikhail M. *Problems of Dostoevsky's Poetics*. Edited and translated by Caryl Emerson. Minneapolis: Minnesota University Press, 1984.
Bakhtin, Mikhail M. "The Problem of the Text in Linguistics, Philology and the Human Sciences." In *Speech Genres and Other Late Essays*. Edited by Caryl Emerson and Michael Holquist. Translated by Vern W. McGee, 103–31. Austin: University of Texas Press, 1986.
Bakhtin, Mikhail M. "The Problem of Content, Material and Form in Verbal Art." In *Art and Answerability*. Edited by Michael Holquist and Vadim Liapunov. Translated by Vadim Liapunov, 257–325. Austin: University of Texas Press, 1990.
Bakhtin, Mikhail M. *Art and Answerability: Early Philosophical Essays*. Edited by Michael Holquist and Vadim Liapunov. Translated by Vadim Liapunov. Austin: University of Texas Press, 1990.

Berman, Antoine. "La retraduction comme espace de la traduction." *Palimpsestes* 4 (1990): 1-7.

Blum-Kulka, Shoshana. "Shifts of Cohesion and Coherence in Translation." In *The Translation Studies Reader*. Edited by Lawrence Venuti, 298-313. London: Routledge, 2000.

Brisset, Annie. "Retraduire ou le corps changeant de la connaissance. Sur l'historicité de la Traduction." *Palimpsestes* 15 (2004): 39-67.

Casanova, Pascale. *The World Republic of Letters*. Cambridge, MA: Harvard University Press, 2004.

Chesterman, Andrew. "A Causal Model for Translation Studies." In *Intercultural Faultlines: Research Models in Translation Studies I: Textual and Cognitive Aspects*. Edited by Maeve Olohan, 15-28. Manchester: St. Jerome, 2000.

Dentith, Simon. *Bakhtinian Thought. An Introductory Reader*. London: Routledge, 1995.

Easley, Keith. *Dickens and Bakhtin. Authoring and Dialogism in Dickens's Novels*. New York: Ams Press, 2014.

Emerson, Caryl. "Editor's Preface." In *Problems of Dostoevsky's Poetics*. Edited by Caryl Emerson, xxix-xliii. Minneapolis: Minnesota University Press, 1984.

Gambier, Yves. "La retraduction: ambiguïtés et défis." In *Autour de la retraduction. Perspectives littéraires européennes*. Edited by Enrico Monti and Peter Schnyder, 49-66. Paris: Orizons, 2011.

Gambier, Yves. "La retraduction, retour et détour." *Meta* 39, no. 3 (1994): 413-17.

Garic, Vanja. "The Sense of the Unending in Joyce's *Dubliners*." *Folia Linguistica et Litteraria* 25 (2018): 87-104.

Garnier, Marie-Dominique. "The Dubbing Theatre of *Dubliners*: Dubbing, Voiceovers and Post-synchronisation." In *Joyce's Dubliners. Lectures Critiques/Critical Approaches*. Edited by Claudine Reynaud, 41-6. Tours: PU François Rabelais, 2001.

Gratchev, Slav, and Howard Mancing, eds. *Don Quixote. The Re-accentuation of the World's Greatest Literary Hero*. Lewisburg: Bucknell University Press, 2017.

Hirschkop, Ken. *Mikhail Bakhtin*. Oxford: Oxford University Press, 2000.

Ivanov, Vyacheslav. "Heteroglossia." *Journal of Linguistic Anthropology* 9, no. 1-2 (2000): 100-2.

Ivanov, Vyacheslav. "Bakhtin's Theory of Language from the Standpoint of Modern Science." *Russian Journal of Communication* 1, no. 3 (2008): 245-65.

Kenner, Hugh. *Joyce's Voices*. Berkeley: University of California Press, 1978.

Koskinen, Kaisa, and Outi Paloposki. "Retranslation." In *Handbook of Translation Studies*. Edited by Yves Gambier and Luc Van Doorslaer, 294-8. Amsterdam: John Benjamins, 2010.

Kuusi, Päivi. "Features of Discourse Presentation in Translation: Literary and Narratological Insights into Translation Universals." *International Journal of Literary Linguistics* 5, no. 3 (2016): 1-24.

Laviosa, Sara. "Universals of Translation." In *Routledge Encyclopedia of Translation Studies*. Edited by Mona Baker, 288–91. London: Routledge, 2001.

Lernout, Geert, and Wim van Mierlo. *The Reception of James Joyce in Europe: Germany, Northern and East Central Europe, Volume 1*. London: Thoemmes Continuum, 2004.

Mathijssen, Jan Willem. *The Breach and the Observance. Theatre Retranslation as a Strategy of Artistic Differentiation*. Unpublished PhD, University of Utrecht, 2007.

Mauranen, Anna. "Universal Tendencies in Translation." In *Incorporating Corpora. The Linguist and the Translator*. Edited by Gunilla Anderman and Margaret Rogers, 32–48. Clevedon: Multilingual matters, 2007.

Mauranen, Anna, and Pekka Kujamäki, eds. *Translation Universals. Do They Exist?* Amsterdam: John Benjamins, 2004.

Mayo, Michael. "Beyond the Uncle Charles Principle." *James Joyce Quarterly* 56, no. 3–4 (2019): 245–66.

Molina, Lucía, and Amparo Hurtado Albir. "Translation Techniques Revisited: A Dynamic and Functionalist Approach." *Meta* 47, no. 4 (2002): 498–512.

Morson, Gary Saul, and Caryl Emerson. *Mikhail Bakhtin: Creation of a Prosaics*. California: Stanford University Press, 1990.

Norris, Margot. "Stifled Back Answers: The Gender Politics of Art in Joyce's 'The Dead.'" *Modern Fiction Studies* 35 (1989): 479–80.

Peeters, Kris. "Traduction, retraduction, dialogisme." *Meta* 61, no. 3 (2016): 629–49.

Peeters, Kris, and Guillermo Sanz Gallego. "Translators' Creativity in the Dutch and Spanish (Re)translations of 'Oxen of the Sun': (Re)translation the Bakhtinian Way." *European Joyce Studies* 30 (2020): 221–41.

Pym, Anthony. *Method in Translation History*. London: Routledge, 2014.

Robinson, Andrew. "Bakhtin: Dialogism, Polyphony and Heteroglossia." *Ceasefire Magazine*, July 29, 2011, ceasefiremagazine.co.uk/in-theory-bakhtin-1/.

Spitzer, Leo. "Sprachmischung als Stilmittel und als Ausdruck der Klangphantasie." *Germanisch-Romanisches Monatsschrift* 11 (1923): 193–217.

Todorov, Tzvetan. *Mikhail Bakhtin. The Dialogic Principle*. Minneapolis: Minnesota University Press, 1984.

Toury, Gideon. *Descriptive Translation Studies—and Beyond. Revised Edition*. Amsterdam: John Benjamins, 2012.

Venuti, Lawrence. *The Translator's Invisibility. A History of Translation*. London: Routledge, 1995.

2

Bakhtin's Dialogism and Language Interpretation

Ida Day

In an increasingly globalized and interconnected world, language remains a barrier to human communication. Despite technological advancements in Google's language processing and automated translation tools, human emotions and understanding are the key to language interpretation. Electronic devices can help translate simple phrases or messages; however, they fail to convey interpersonal communication, which is not only a linguistic process, but also cultural and emotional. As Mikhail Bakhtin observed in *The Dialogic Imagination*, "a passive understanding of linguistic meaning is no understanding at all, it is only the abstract aspect of meaning."[1] For a "living dialogue" to be created, multiple voices come into contact: "understanding and response are dialectically merged and condition each other; one is impossible without the other."[2] To facilitate this understanding, the language interpreter needs to consider the entire context of the dialogue, including the cultural background and feelings of the speakers.

The Russian philosopher and literary critic Mikhail Bakhtin was one of the most influential scholars of the twentieth century, whose work has widened the horizons of various disciplines. Bakhtin discussed the extralinguistic qualities of language and the sociocultural background of communication in the 1930s—long before these perspectives began to influence the fields of translation, interpretation, and communication studies. This essay demonstrates how his principles of dialogism can be extended and applied to the field of language interpretation. I examine this process—specifically Spanish/English over-the-phone medical interpretation—and draw upon my own over-a-decade-long practical experience as an interpreter for CyraCom International, the leading provider of language interpretation and translation services to health care, business, and government in the United States.

In accordance with the dialogic principles of Bakhtinian theory, the linguistic aspect is just one element of communication, since any utterance is affected by other factors such as context, background, mood, and point of view. For the message to be transmitted accurately, the interpreter needs to be sensitive to the cultural context of the patient in order to provide not only a linguistic but also a cultural bridge between a provider and a patient who do not have a common worldview. Such dialogue involves "a multiplicity of social voices"—worldviews, perspectives, and ideologies—affecting one another, which Bakhtin calls *heteroglossia*.[3] The role of interpreter is to transfer the original meaning to a different language and culture through a process of re-accentuation of these *heteroglot* verbal exchanges. Apart from a linguistic conversion from one language to another, the interpreter helps overcome communication barriers resulting from class, educational, religious, and other social differences. My essay aims to demonstrate how this is done in practice.

CyraCom was founded in 1995 in response to the increasing immigration to the United States. Since then, the role of the health care interpreter has been constantly evolving due to a concern regarding the quality of services for cultural-linguistic groups, for whom English as a medium of communication posed a barrier. Two main tendencies have shaped the role of the CyraCom's interpreter: an unobtrusive linguistic "message conveyer" on one hand, and a cross-cultural facilitator of communication on the other. María-Paz Beltran Avery, in "The Role of the Health Care Interpreter," traces the evolution of this process, describing the early dichotomy identified as "the interpreter in a historically traditional neutral interpretation role perspective versus the interpreter with varied responsibilities in health care and in her community perspective."[4] According to the first model, the interpreter is neutral, unobtrusive and nonrelational, and his/her function is "message passing" from one language to the other. In contrast, the active interpreter is a cross-cultural facilitator of communication, and his/her role extends beyond the linguistic sphere, including a broader context: the interpreter's knowledge of the cultural background of the speaker is central to "the ability to understand the 'intended meaning' of the messages that are being conveyed and make the appropriate equivalent conversions."[5] Gradually, these two polar extremes of "neutral interpreter" and "mediating interpreter" started to find a common ground. This dialogue resulted in the emergence of new conceptualizations of the role, such as "the interpreter as conduit," who provides a linguistic and, at times, cultural bridge between a provider and a patient, but without offering his/her own explanations. This approach continues to inform practice in the field today, including CyraCom's protocols and procedures.

The interpreter as conduit, in certain aspects, coincides with the Bakhtinian model, as s/he maintains the flow of the conversation, in which "the intersects of both the cultures overlap and assimilate."[6] S/he transmits the message without interfering, adding, or elaborating; however, unlike the "neutral interpreter," the process requires more than literal conversions and is meant to enhance comprehension: "accurate message transmission has to be based on equivalencies of concepts and this requires knowledge of the cultural context and background of the patient as well as the medical culture."[7] In Bakhtinian terms, this is a process of re-accentuation, in which the interpreter plays an engaged and central role. On the other hand, the interpreter as conduit is not expected to perform an active social function in the clinical/cultural encounter, for instance, offering suggestions or clarifications in order to facilitate communication. Such actions do not pertain to the role of the interpreter as conduit because "the simple addition of a third party inevitably shifts the dynamics of power between patient and provider, acknowledges that it is only the interpreter who has full access to what is going on at any given point in time. This knowledge invests the interpreter with the power of information."[8] That is why the interpreter is expected to remain impartial and not to get involved in the conversation.

CyraCom's code of ethics also emphasizes the impartial role of the interpreter as conduit: "Always remain in the role of the conduit. Be as transparent as possible and avoid involving yourself in the conversation."[9] However, it is not realistic to remain completely neutral. No matter how impartial the interpreter is, the patient will form a connection with him/her, due to the fact that they share the same language. Even though the interpreter adopts the third-person form, "this is the interpreter speaking," and does not introduce himself/herself with his/her name, the patient feels a certain kinship and affinity because s/he is understood. For example, at the end of my recent interpretation session for the health insurance provider, the patient stated: "Gracias a usted por la información" (Thank you, sir, for the information), and then referred to the interpreter: "y gracias, mi amor, por tu ayuda. Que dios te bendiga" (and thank you, my love, for your help. God bless you). Not only was the tone directed to the interpreter more friendly than that directed to the insurance representative, but also the form "tú" versus "usted" was familiar and informal. According to the CyraCom protocol, translating the second part of this statement requires an indirect speech form, which does not convey the emotional aspect of the expression, and even sounds awkward: "the patient also said that she was grateful to the interpreter and blessed her." This message is not essential to maintain the natural flow of the conversation, since in this particular communicative interaction the provider (the CyraCom's client) is interested in message transmission and not in all the forms, nuances, and subtleties of language. Therefore, the most natural option is to communicate "thank you" to both parties, which also includes the interpreter's acknowledgment to the patient and to the provider, and vice versa. Inevitably, even though the interpreter maintains the role as conduit, the interpretation is not direct, and the relations formed during this conversation are not equal or impartial.

The concluding exchanges of thanks reflected the mood pervading that conversation. The patient's tone and choice of language communicated the attitudes she had developed toward both parties. From a Bakhtinian perspective, the interpreter's brief acknowledgment was sufficient to form a mutual relation with the patient: "being heard as such is already a dialogic relation."[10] According to Bakhtin, each utterance in a living discourse anticipates a response (verbal or nonverbal), and the interpreter's role is to assimilate that utterance into the context and to merge it with the response: "language is not a neutral medium that passes freely and easily into the private property of the speaker's intentions; it is populated—overpopulated—with the intentions of others."[11] The circumstances accompanying this conversation (the *heteroglossia* of intentions, expectations, and interests) led it in a certain direction, which was unique due to these circumstances, in this specific context.

This example demonstrates that language interpretation is a living dialogue and a creative process, which depends on variety of conditions and cannot be reduced to a direct verbal transmission of information between two parties. As Michael Holquist claimed in his introduction to *The Dialogic Imagination*, "the impossibility of being neutral is one of the founding assumptions of dialogism."[12] Particular relations unfold during the dialogue, and they are created by all the voices involved, including the interpreter's, who "has to build the relationship and sustain it to complete the task of translation."[13] That is why the CyraCom's commitment to maintaining the neutral role of the interpreter as "the voice of the speaker," who conveys "the exact message," "without adding, omitting, or substituting information," does not correspond to the Bakhtinian notion of a living dialogue.[14]

A Bakhtinian approach assumes that language interpretation prepares the ground for active understanding—one that "goes beyond the boundaries of the word's context" and enriches it with new elements.[15] The interpreter does not convert the original linguistic utterance, but creates a new one, often replacing the specific elements (names, concepts, references, etc.) by their cultural equivalents. An example of such re-accentuation is the use of the conventional words for letters while spelling the name of a street, medication, or last name. In one of my sessions, an English-speaking receptionist spelled a doctor's name, "Dimac," in the following way: "D like David, I, M like Mary, A, C like Charles." Even though the names—David, Mary, and Charles—have their equivalents in Spanish, people would commonly say: "D de dedo (finger), M de mamá (mom), C de casa (house)," and so that was my choice of interpretation. The message was rendered, but the original words were substituted with the culturally familiar elements in order to enhance understanding. As Bakhtin says, the word was assimilated "to be understood into its own conceptual system filled with specific objects and emotional expressions."[16] This type of re-accentuation, referred to as "domestication," is a strategy of conforming an interpretation to the culture of the target language. Domestication is used to communicate a good understanding and to minimize the strangeness of the foreign culture for the target audience.[17]

The strategy of domestication demonstrates that language interpretation is inseparable from the concept of culture. In the contemporary translation and interpretation field, Eugene Nida, considered an advocate of domestication, points out that translation cannot be successful as mainly linguistic-oriented process, and "biculturalism is even more important than bilingualism, since words only have meanings in terms of the cultures in which they function."[18] Bakhtin discussed and emphasized these connections already in the second half of the twentieth century, long before this perspective started to emerge as domestication in translation. His process of re-accentuation, through which the message becomes "better understood and better heard," have challenged the idea of literal and neutral translation, offering a reflection on the intimate link between linguistic, cultural, social, and emotional aspects of language.[19]

Another strategy of re-accentuation, opposed to domestication, is foreignization, which "deliberately breaks the target conventions by retaining something of the foreignness of the original."[20] The proponent of this strategy, Lawrence Venuti, discussed it in the context of the Anglo-American cultural values, which tend to dominate and domesticate other cultures. According to the author, foreignization in translation is desirable in order to preserve and "register the linguistic and cultural difference of the foreign text, sending the reader abroad."[21] A phenomenon of foreignization can also be present in other contexts, for example among Spanish language speakers living in the United States. Due to the presence of English, various words are adapted to Spanish as semantic extensions, where the speakers use a word with the meaning of its cognate rather than its standard meaning. Examples of such usages in a medical setting include "condición" incorrectly used for "sickness," "desorden" for "illness, impairment," "chequear, checar, or chequiar" for "examine," or "aplicación" for "application." Another common example is the Spanglish expression "Le llamo para atrás" (intended to mean "I'll call you back"), which David T. Gies described as a "hilarious and bizarre linguistic hybrid" that would mean to an orthodox Spaniard something like "I'll call up your backside."[22] In these examples, the foreignization is not a deliberate strategy to respect the cultural values; it is in fact closer to the function of domestication—to minimize the differences between the two cultures and facilitate understanding. There are no written rules banning the use of these words from professional interpretations. The interpreter should use his/her own criteria to analyze the situation, such as: "Who are the speakers/patients?," "Where are they from?," "Is this term easier for them to understand than a proper term?," "Do the medical providers use this terminology in their documents and forms in Spanish?," and so on. If a certain term (a loan word or a semantic extension) was already used by the patient during the interpretation session, the interpreter knows that this is a familiar term, and therefore responds accordingly—by using it. Thus, the Bakhtinian relation between response and understanding is the guiding principle for this communication—the interpreter's choice of words is a response to a given situation, and it "prepares the ground for active and engaged understanding."[23] As Gies observed, the examples of Spanglish "hardly seem conducive to intellectual exchange and open communication, yet we must continue to struggle for mutual understanding."[24]

As the above examples illustrate, in certain circumstances the process of re-accentuation is legitimate and even productive. The boundaries of re-accentuation are set by the interpreter's intention to maintain a smooth flow of communication and the integrity of the message. However, sometimes these boundaries are crossed, producing an altered or simplified version of the original message, which can affect the course and the outcome of discussion. The following scenario is a common example of the controversies that take place during the calls regarding the health insurance issues. A patient is trying to figure out the medical bills, which are not covered by the insurance, and in a raised voice expresses his frustration and annoyance: "Increíble esa vaina de verdad! Me joden otra vez!" According to the CyraCom code of ethics, the interpreter is obligated to remain in the role of the conduit, but not to literally translate profanity. Thus, the first option is to follow the protocol and say: "The client is upset and using profanity. How would you like me to proceed?," and the second option is to render the general meaning of the statement: "This is really unbelievable! Same thing again!" In the second case scenario, the interpretation downplays the patient's attitude/emotions and softens the intensity of his message. This can potentially be beneficial for the patient, because the insurance representative may be more inclined to help solve the problem instead of terminating or transferring the call. In re-accentuation of this kind, the general meaning is conveyed, but the emotional aspect is radically distorted.

The conversation described above involved colloquial language, which is culturally bound, and therefore not easy to translate. Colloquial and everyday Spanish expressions have a wide variety of meanings, depending on the country or region of origin. Some words are considered inappropriate or profane in some dialects while they are not in others. Some words can have a totally different meaning when used by certain groups of people. In Colombia, the word "vaina" (mentioned in previous example) is used in a number of different contexts. It refers to the English "stuff" or "thing," but also can describe problems or difficult situations. Here, the interpreter is presented with the task of finding an equivalent, by using re-accentuation. Another example, in Colombian Spanish, "aburrido," apart from its standard meaning "bored," can also mean "sad, upset, depressed." In one of my interpretation sessions for psychological therapy, the patient's mother described the condition of her daughter in the following words: "está muy aburrida, no quiere hacer nada" (she is very depressed/bored, does not want to do anything). The context is essential here to figure out the meaning of this message, and the interpreter needs to consider the diversity of languages included in this dialogue—*heteroglossia* of voices within both languages: medical, colloquial, and Colombian Spanish. Again, the meaning here evolves out of interactions among language, culture, and intentions of all the speakers.

A problematic issue in medical interpretations is the fact that the parties involved not only speak different languages (English and Spanish), but also different variations of dialects, accents, and jargons within one language (medical, English with a foreign accent, colloquial, regional, etc.). Bakhtin gives examples of this "social diversity of speech types" present in one language, such as social dialects, professional jargons, language of age groups, language of authorities, literary language, and so on.[25] He analyzes this phenomenon in the context of the novel, a genre which is characterized by "internal stratification of language" and a "variety of individual voices."[26] The language of the novel is dynamic—the social-linguistic *heteroglossia* dialogues with the "centripetal forces"—a unitary language "working toward concrete verbal and ideological unification and centralization."[27] Bakhtin describes this dialogic process using examples from literary works, but this interaction between the centralizing and decentralizing tendencies takes place in any context where language is involved. For instance, a dialogue between a medical provider and a patient is not governed by a common or singular language; rather, it represents a coexistence of social and professional differences. The interpreter serves as a mediator or a unitary force in this heteroglot environment—his/her translation of medical terminology needs to be accurate and direct, but at the same time understood by a patient who does not have a medical background.

Many medical terms are complex words composed of root words (base words that hold the basic meaning), prefixes (attachments added to the beginning of a root word), and suffixes (attachments added to the end of a root word). Common prefixes and suffixes that can be added to root words to build different, complex words are anti- (opposing or against), intra- (within or inside), hyper- (above, excessive, beyond), -logy (the study of), -itis (inflammation), -ectomy (surgical removal), and -oma (tumor). When the interpreter comes across a complex word in interpretation sessions, s/he can deconstruct it and figure out its meaning by its root, prefix, and suffix. For example, if the root word "cholecyst" means "pertaining to the gallbladder," then it is gathered that "cholecystitis" is inflammation of the gallbladder, and "cholecystectomy" is removal of the gallbladder. It is important for the interpreter to translate these words into everyday language because patients usually are not familiar with the specialized medical terminology derived from the Latin, and, unless the provider explains the condition or procedure, it is the role of the interpreter to make sure that the language used is understood by the patient. Therefore, in the above example, it would be productive and beneficial to translate "cholecystitis" as "inflamación de la vesícula" (inflammation of the gallbladder), instead of "colecistitis." According to Bakhtinian, this would be a legitimate re-accentuation, in which there is no "violation of the author's will"—the meaning is the same, although different words are used.[28] In the case of cholecystitis, the provider most likely would explain the condition to the patient; however, there are other common medical conditions that are usually used in their standard medical form, such as "hypertension," and patients are expected to understand them. During my sessions, I usually translate "hypertension" into common language—"alta presión" (high blood pressure), instead of "hipertensión," because from my experience, it is usually better understood, and does not require repetition or clarification.

Another example where the interpreter needs to use a "unitary language" to overcome cultural barriers to communication is during the assessment of patients' mental functional abilities, such as memory, attention, and orientation. It is a common practice for nurses to ask hospitalized patients questions regarding their name, location, date of birth, or current affairs in order to evaluate their mental condition. Some of these questions require a cultural clarification because the answers may be specific to the speaker's circumstances. For example, a question regarding the first day of the week in the calendar may be problematic, because, according to the international standards, Monday is the first day of the week, except in the United States and Canada, where it is considered the second day of the week. Another type of question that may cause miscommunication is the one regarding the current president, because patients will sometimes refer to the presidents of their countries of origin. Also, a common experience is to say "pesos" instead of "dollars" while discussing monetary issues. In this situation, the interpreter serves as a cross-cultural facilitator of communication—as a "force that unites and centralizes verbal-ideological thought ... defending an already formed language from the pressure of growing heteroglossia."[29] One of the techniques that helps the dialogue to flow without interruptions is using the cultural equivalents, for example, translating "pesos" into "dollars." However, the interpreter needs to be sensitive to the circumstances in which the dialogue takes place, since even if this incorrect usage of currency is very common, in some cases it may indicate the patient's mental confusion.

The above examples illustrate dialogues in which the interpreter uses different types of re-accentuation to facilitate communication and to make the messages relevant to the circumstances. However, there are also situations where the message needs to be delivered verbatim, without any replacements or omissions. Examples of such situations are disclosures for medical treatment and financial charges. Disclosure statements are official documents written in legal language, which is meant to communicate in a precise and accurate manner; however, this language is often hard to understand by the common people who do not have a legal background. According to Bakhtin, professional jargons "may be treated as objects, as typifications, as local color. For the outsiders, the intentions permeating these languages become *things*, limited in their meaning and expressions."[30] Also, the disclosures are documents written in formalized language, not designed for oral delivery, so there is an additional obstacle to communication when they are delivered by an insurance representative, translated from a script by an interpreter, and then agreed upon by a patient (neither of them being a lawyer). I have had multiple interpretation sessions in which it was clear that neither party understood what was being read. It is usually indicated by a monotonous tone of an insurance agent, pauses that do not make sense, and the inability to clarify the message when asked by a patient. In such sessions, the speaker is lacking intention, and thus there is no "responsive understanding"—"a fundamental force, one that participates in the formulation of discourse."[31] Bakhtin says that dialogue is formed when the speaker appropriates the word, "adapting it to his own semantic and expressive intention," and until that moment, the word exists "in other people's contexts, serving other people's intentions."[32] Many words resist and remain alien—"they cannot be assimilated into the context and fall out of it; it is as if they put themselves in quotation marks against the will of the speaker."[33] This is often the case when disclosures are introduced into the dialogue.

The delivery of disclosures is an example of a verbal interaction in which there is no mutual understanding and reciprocation. It is also an example of a communication in which the interpreter remains neutral, focusing only on the linguistic conversion from one language to another and avoiding re-accentuation. Such actions produce situations that do not fit the

Bakhtinian notion of a living dialogue. According to the author, "language is not a neutral medium," and it needs the speaker's intention to make a dialogue alive.[34]

To conclude, Bakhtin perceives language as "ideologically saturated, language as a world view, even as a concrete opinion, insuring a maximum of mutual understanding in all spheres of ideological life";[35] therefore, language interpretation is a process that involves not only a linguistic transposition of message, but also the entire meaning and context in which a conversation takes place. It builds a bridge between language and culture. Dialogue is a potentially unlimited meaning-making process, created by intention and responsive understanding: "The word wants to be heard, understood, responded to, and again to respond to the response, and so forth *ad infinitum*."[36] Interpretation is a creative and pluralistic process, and thus, the untranslatable linguistic elements require re-accentuation to facilitate the mutual understanding. Sensitive to this plurality of experience (*heteroglossia*), the interpreter participates in the dialogue in an active and open-minded way, constantly ready to re-accentuate the message and extend across the linguistic boundaries.

Notes

1. Mikhail M. Bakhtin, *The Dialogic Imagination: Four Essays*, ed. Michael Holquist, trans. Caryl Emerson and Michael Holquist (Austin: University of Texas, 1983), 281.
2. Ibid., 282.
3. Ibid., 263.
4. María-Paz Beltran Avery, "The Role of the Health Care Interpreter: An Evolving Dialogue," The National Council of Interpreting in Health Care. Working Paper Series (April 2018): 4. As a response to the increasing demand for health care interpreting, a conference was held in Seattle in 1994 which brought together health care providers, interpreters, and educators from the United States and Canada. The central theme discussed by the working group was the nature and scope of the role of the health care interpreter: "If the meaning rather than literal conversion was the goal, was the interpreter also expected to convey the emotional tone and affective content of the message?" (3).
5. Beltran Avery, "The Role of the Health Care Interpreter," 4.
6. Amith Kumar, *Bakhtin and Translation Studies: Theoretical Extensions and Connotations* (Cambridge Scholars Publishing: Newcastle, 2015), 17.
7. Beltran Avery, "The Role of the Health Care Interpreter," 6.
8. Ibid., 8.

9. "Quality Evaluation," E-mail to Ida Day. December 18, 2019, n.p.
10. Mikhail M. Bakhtin, *Speech Genres and Other Late Essays* (Austin: University of Texas, 1986), 127.
11. Bakhtin, *Dialogic Imagination*, 294.
12. Ibid., i.
13. Kumar, *Bakhtin and Translation Studies*, 17.
14. *Interpreter Bulletin: Impartiality Refresher*, no. 246, October 18, 2019, n.p.
15. Bakhtin, *Dialogic Imagination*, 281.
16. Ibid., 282.
17. For more information regarding the cultural impact of domestication in translation, see Wenfen Yang's "Brief Study on Domestication and Foreignization in Translation," *Journal of Language Teaching and Research* 1 (2010): 77–80.
18. Eugene Nida, *Language and Culture-Contexts in Translation* (Shanghai: Foreign Language Education Press, 2001), 82.
19. Bakhtin, *Dialogic Imagination*, 420.
20. Yang, "Brief Study on Domestication and Foreignization in Translation," 77. For foreignizing strategy, see Lawrence Venuti's *The Translator's Invisibility: A History of Translation* (London: Routledge, 1995).
21. Venuti, *The Translator's Invisibility*, 20.
22. David T.Gies, "Drop Your Trousers Here for Best Results: Linguistic Diversity in a Post-Google World," *MIFLC Review* (2015): 16.
23. Bakhtin, *e Dialogic Imagination*, 282.
24. Gies, "Drop Your Trousers Here for Best Results," 16. The author explains the phenomenon of mixing languages and the presence of Spanglish in the United States in the context of current globalization and multiculturalism: "some 50 million people in the United States alone speak Spanish, and many of these people speak Spanish exclusively, that is, they do not know English. There are more Spanish-speaking people in the US than in Spain" (15).
25. Bakhtin, *Dialogic Imagination*, 263.
26. Ibid., 264.
27. Ibid., 271.
28. Ibid., 420.
29. Ibid., 271.
30. Ibid., 289; emphasis in original.
31. Ibid., 281.
32. Ibid., 293.
33. Ibid., 294.
34. Ibid.
35. Ibid., 271.
36. Bakhtin, *Speech Genres*, 127.

Bibliography

Bakhtin, Mikhail M. *The Dialogic Imagination: Four Essays*. Edited by Michael Holquist. Translated by Caryl Emerson and Michael Holquist. Austin: University of Texas Press, 1983.

Bakhtin, Mikhail M. *Speech Genres and Other Late Essays*. Edited by Caryl Emerson and Michael Holquist. Translated by V. W. McGee. Austin: University of Texas Press, 1986.

Beltran Avery, Maria-Paz. "The Role of the Health Care Interpreter: An Evolving Dialogue." Working Paper Series, The National Council of Interpreting in Health Care. April 2001.

Gies, David T. "Drop Your Trousers Here for Best Results: Linguistic Diversity in a Post-Google World." *MIFLC Review* 17 (2015): 11.

Interpreter Bulletin: Impartiality Refresher, no. 246, October 18, 2019.

Kumar, Amith. *Bakhtin and Translation Studies: Theoretical Extensions and Connotations*. Newcastle: Cambridge Scholars Publishing, 2015.

Nida, Eugene. *Language and Culture-Contexts in Translation*. Shanghai: Foreign Language Education Press, 2001.

"Quality Evaluation." E-mail to Ida Day. December 18, 2019.

Venuti, Lawrence. *The Translator's Invisibility: A History of Translation*. London: Routledge, 1995.

Yang, Wenfen. "Brief Study on Domestication and Foreignization in Translation." *Journal of Language Teaching and Research* 1 (2010): 77–80.

3

Heteroglossia, Liminality, and Literary Translation

Bo Li

Recent scholarship has seen burgeoning interest in Bakhtinian theory's connection to translation studies. For instance, Amith Kumar[1] has explored the theoretical extensions and connotations of Bakhtin's philosophical writing in relation to translation studies in order to conclude that "a Bakhtinian approach will prove to be a major step towards achieving a new theoretical perspective for an understanding of the intricacies that make translation an extremely complicated endeavor."[2] Similarly, Bo Li, the first Chinese scholar to bring Bakhtinian studies and translation studies together,[3] deploys Bakhtin's terminology in order to illuminate some of the problems intrinsic to literary translation through interdisciplinary fertilization. Among Bakthin's major concepts, heteroglossia has been especially popular with scholars of literature, cultural studies, and translation studies.[4] Literary scenarios in many contexts challenge our stereotyped conceptualization of translation as the transference of one linguistic code into another. Diaspora writing in particular brings to the fore the issue of juxtaposition of linguistic varieties, dialect, idiolect, eye-dialect, diglossia, code-switching, code-mixing, creole, and so on. Heteroglossia in literary texts contributes to the construction of the work's liminality, while diaspora writing itself is the result of liminal writing. This chapter aims to investigate how the concepts of heteroglossia, liminality, and literary translation are interconnected with reference to the Chinese translation of *Tripmaster Monkey: His Fake Book* by the much-acclaimed Chinese American writer Maxine H. Kingston.

1. Heteroglossia and Liminality

In "From the Prehistory of Novelistic Discourse," Bakhtin notes that "heteroglossia within a language, that is, the problem of internal differentiation, the stratification characteristic of any national language,"[5] is the convergence in language or speech of "specific points of view on the world, forms for conceptualizing the world in words, specific world views, each characterized by its own objects, meanings and values."[6] In "Discourse in the Novel," Bakhtin elaborates on how authors can artistically incorporate social heteroglossia into novels, and he proposes four basic models that result from this process: hybrid construction, posited author or teller, language used by characters, and finally incorporated genres[7]—all amply illustrated with examples from literary works by Fielding, Smollet, Sterne, Dickens, and the like. Yet Bakhtin is reluctant to offer any precise definitions of the term heteroglossia itself, which has prompted scholars to interpret it in a variety of ways.[8] While Karine Zbinden sees it as "the fight between various 'dialects' or languages in a polylingual society,"[9] Graham Robert interprets heteroglossia as the "conflict between 'centripetal' and 'centrifugal,' 'official' and 'unofficial' discourses within the same national language."[10]

What other scholars tend to overlook is Bakhtin's insistence upon the difference between these linguistic varieties and the cultural and ideological connotations embedded in them. While most agree that Bakhtin's heteroglossia is marked by centripetal and centrifugal forces always working both together and against each other, it is a lot less clear if it is meant to apply to monolingual and polylingual societies in equal measure. Caryl Emerson offers a solution to this riddle by suggesting the blurring of the boundaries between a national language and a polylingual community when she points out that "the boundaries between national languages [should be viewed] as only one extreme on a continuum, at whose other end translation processes were required for one social group to understand another in the same city, for children to understand parents in the same family, for one day to understand the next."[11]

Such a move can carry powerful political messages. For example, by drawing upon a Taiwanese case-study (Wang Chen-ho's *Rose Rose I Love You* in English translation), Li suggests that the erasure/erosion of the heteroglossic feature in the source text, marked by political overtones, will subtly subvert the source-culture by downplaying the symbolic value of the original heteroglossia.[12] Li explored "the intricate relationship between subtitling and heteroglossia by observing the translation strategies adopted for the film *Made in Hong Kong*, which reveal "the anxiety and uncertainty of the Hong Kong people" in the form of heteroglossic construction of their dialogues and inner monologues.[13] With the case study on subtitle translation, Li tries to shed light on the "problematic relationship between heteroglossia and translation."[14]

In addition to such new appreciation of the interconnectedness of literary translation and heteroglossia, scholarly attention to the links between liminality and translation practices has revealed the need to explore their interdependence further. According to Victor Turner's rather broad definition, "liminal entities are neither here nor there; they are betwixt and between the positions assigned and arrayed by law, custom, conventions, and ceremonial," and betwixt and between means "in the midway position: neither one thing nor the other."[15] Foucault's discussion of "heterotopia" tries to provide a more grounded approach to the term by highlighting the functions of liminality, as do related theoretical constructs, such as Giorgio Agamben's "threshold," Jacques Derrida's "limitrophy," and Soja's "Thirdspace."[16] Liminality and heterotopology can thus be considered interrelated chronological and spatial formations, respectively.[17]

The cultural and anthropological perceptions of liminality resemble Mikhail Bakhtin's aesthetic concept of the chronotope, as defined in *The Dialogic Imagination* (1981). Literary chronotopes fuse temporal and spatial dimensions and correspond to basic linguistic and aesthetic structures, as do liminality and heterotopology, which structurally resemble the elementary linguistic operations of the selection from paradigms and combination of syntagmata.[18] Liminality tries to capture the permanent inescapability of transitions and the existential as well as cultural consequences of such destabilizations. In other words, liminality tries to explain change through the description of boundary crossings. The boundary is not necessarily just a line but can also be a space with a density and dynamics of its own, following its own rules. Such liminal zones can develop chronologically between a previous and a resulting state, systematically between one and another state, and spatially between here and there.[19]

To translate, therefore, it is not to cross a border, but to wander from one border to another. To complicate the issue even more, the creative writing by some Chinese American writers is marked by their reference to classical texts—"textualized remainders" in Dominick LaCapra's[20] term— through translation, which results in the heteroglossic construction of discourse. Their writing is defined as the product of liminal spaces that complicate translation further, particularly when the literary works are translated, or back-translated, into the Chinese context. Against this background, the remainder of this essay will study the Chinese translation of Maxine H. Kingston's *Tripmaster Monkey*, in order to explore the intricate relationship between heteroglossia, liminality, writing, translation, and back-translation in literary works by Chinese American writers in general.

2. Maxine Hong Kingston's *The Tripmaster Monkey*

Maxine H. Kingston is an acclaimed Chinese American writer who is famous for her first two novels *The Woman Warrior* and *China Men*—both of which have been translated into Chinese. Much research has been done on the reception of those works in China, and on their translations in the Chinese context. For instance, Lo Kwai-chung has endorsed the "'Chineseness' in the translation of Chinese American literature," citing Kingston's fictions in Taiwan and Chinese mainland as an example.[21] Lee Ken-Fang, another Chinese scholar, has metaphorically interpreted Kingston's works on the whole as a kind of translation in which the hybrid Chinese American cultural identity is highlighted.[22] Kingston's latest novel *Tripmaster Monkey* has also received a lot of critical attention over the past two decades.[23] It differs from *The Woman Warrior* and *China Men*, because the early two works are to some extent translations of the character's inner world, while the latest one is a depiction of the social, cultural, and linguistic reality for the Chinese American community living in the multicultural United States.

Some critics have argued that Kingston's works should be considered Chinese literature, for her stories are about Chinese characters abroad and their life struggles. While controversial from a Western standpoint, such a claim is embraced by interpreters from the Mainland and Taiwan Chinese community, who have tried—through translation—to reclaim and even rework Kingston's writing in order to highlight "Chineseness" and cultural affinity between Chinese Americans and the people of the Chinese mainland and Taiwan. Inevitably, Chinese American writings are placed consciously or unconsciously in a different, imaginary *third* realm, outside both the home/ancestral cultural space and the *diasporic*/host place.

Kingston's *The Tripmaster Monkey* is an interesting story about border-crossing and liminal writing. It demonstrates the importance of boundary-crossing, but also the potential and creativity associated with the purposeful rearticulation of boundaries pregnant with new worlds, visions, and perceptions.[24] Wittman Ah Sing is a young Chinese American hippie in San Francisco during the late 1960s. Named after America's quintessential poet, indomitably garrulous and free-spirited, Wittman is as American as James Dean. Yet he also bears a striking resemblance to Monkey, the trickster-saint of Chinese legend who helped bring the Buddhist scriptures from India. Driven by his dream of writing and staging an epic production of interwoven Chinese novels and folktales, Wittman's life becomes an extraordinary journey through an era as fantastic as his ambition.

When it comes to the translation of Kingston's *The Tripmaster Monkey*, we can observe strategies very similar to those examined by Lo Kwai-chung in his analysis of earlier translations of Kingston's work in Mainland Chinese and Taiwan.²⁵ For example, it is not difficult to spot deletions guided by ideological reasons. When discussing the book, *The Water Verge* (*Shui Hu Zhuan*), the source text reads as follows:

> Wittman was getting his inspiration from a book known as *The Book of Evil*; its title is something like *The Water Verge*. <u>It's Mao's favorite book—his field guide—the acts of 108 revolutionaries</u>. In preparation for warfare in marshes and rivers and rice paddies, the Pentagon was using this book too. ²⁶

The underlined sentence is deleted in the Chinese translation out of ideological considerations:

> 惠特曼的这些想法得益于一本被称为坏书的书。这本书的书名大约是《水浒》。在沼泽地、河流和稻田里备战时，五角大楼都是用这本书。²⁷

To a large extent, it is understandable for the translator(s) to delete parts of the original that might cause censorship problems and endanger the publication of the book. In addition to highlighting ideological manipulations of the source text, the remainder of this study will focus on the heteroglossic features in the original and how they are dealt with in the Chinese rendition. I will make specific use of two new terms: "intralingual heteroglossic construction" and "interlingual heteroglossic construction."

2.1. Intralingual Heteroglossic Construction

Fang defines Wittman's Chinese American theaters as a practice of liminal art and highlights the cross-cultural juxtaposition and the internal subversion:

> With his Chinese American theatre, Wittman proves that liminal art is a source empowerment. It can help to subvert racial stereotypes, freeing Chinese Americans from their enslavement. It can also generate new energy from old texts, stories and images, attributing to them new codes. Liminal art such as cross-cultural juxtaposition and signifying are important means of expression for ethnic trickster writers who tend to show their strength, power and creativity through the appropriation of the works of their masters or predecessors.²⁸

In dealing with another well-known classic Chinese work, namely *The Romance of the Three Kingdoms*, the translators chose to leave it out of the Chinese translation. In the English novel, Kingston uses this classical work as a "textualized remainder," a term coined by Dominick LaCapra to denote "myths, legends, histories, films, novels, poems, or plays" either quoted directly, alluded to, or retold by the author.[29]
The following quote comes from Kingston's novel:

"My dove brother. My hawk brother. These peach trees are at their fullest and reddest bloom. We vow friendship. Repeat after me. 'We three—Liu Pei, Gwan Goong, and Chang Fei—though not born to the same families, swear to be brothers. Though born under different signs, we shall seek the same death day'"…

"'Heaven and Earth, read our hearts,'" Chang Fei continued. "'If we turn aside from righteousness or forget kindliness, may Heaven and man take out vengeance on us.'"[30]

The Chinese translation has:

"我的鸽哥鹰弟,<u>红花满枝的桃树</u>,我们发誓做朋友。跟我说,'我们三个—刘备、关公和张飞<u>—虽不同姓,我们却发誓永远是兄弟。不能同日生,但求同日死。</u>'"
"<u>天地知我们的心</u>,"张飞继续说道,"<u>假如我们不伸张正义或不以慈悲为,愿受天地惩罚。</u>"[31]

The textual remainder creeps into the creative writing through translation and intertextual reference. How to render the intertextual elements in Kingston's works back into Chinese merits further investigation. In this specific case, we can witness the translator's incompetence in bringing out the heteroglossic construction which plays an important role in the source text. If we take a look at the Chinese original and its early and recognized English translations, we can immediately point out the problems in the current Chinese translation. Here is the original Chinese text:

飞曰:"吾庄后有一桃园,<u>花开正盛</u>;明日当于园中祭告天地,我三人结为兄弟,协力同心,然后可图大事。" 玄德、云长齐声应曰:"如此甚好。" 次日,于桃园中,备下乌牛白马祭礼等项,三人焚香再拜而说誓曰:"念刘备、关羽、张飞,虽然异姓,既结为兄弟,则同心协力,救困扶危;上报国家,下安黎庶,<u>不求同年同月同日生,只愿同年同月同日死。皇天后土,实鉴此心。背义忘恩,天人共戮</u>!"[32]

The Chinese translation of Kingston's work sounds ridiculous to most native Chinese readers. "天地知我们的心" (Heaven and Earth, read our hearts) sounds like a sentence from a sensational Taiwanese TV drama. In my view, the better way to deal with such intertextual elements is to restore the original, which would immediately serve two purposes. First, this back-translation would enable the proper identification of the referenced work by the target (and at the same time the original) reader. Whether you have read *The Romance of the Three Kingdoms* or not, the Chinese translation of Chang Fei's words sounds ludicrous to Chinese ears. Second, the juxtaposition of the part from the Chinese classic and the current young American's narration would contribute to the passage's heteroglossic construction, which would reveal a deep understanding of Chinese canon and culture and can serve to accomplish what Lo sees as a reaffirmation of the work's Chineseness. As Sun observes, "Chinese American literary texts transmigrate Chinese into English, often revealing Chineseness being retained or reproduced in parallel with the construction of and interaction with literary Americanness. The invisible source text(s) is/are embodied notably by a trove of cultural references to play a central role in the functionality of transcoding ethnicity … It is interesting to observe that some Chinese American literary texts are translated into Chinese, exhibiting a peculiar linguistic and cultural displacement."[33] This better explains the situation of the Chinese translation of Kingston's story into, or back to, Chinese. Kingston's work transmigrates, via translation, Chinese classical stories into English; however, when her work tries to enter into the Chinese context, the misunderstanding and mishandling of the Chinese remainders in the English text leads to linguistic and cultural displacement.

2.2. English, Mandarin, and Cantonese

Marvin Carlson offers a very enlightening review and explanation of the ambiguous relationship between language, dialect, and accent. According to the critic, world languages present themselves in an exponentially complicated way, depending on social, ideological, cultural, geographical, chronological, and spatial loci. Take Chinese and its varieties as an example. Carlson, in reference to David Crystal's *Dictionary of Linguistics and Phonetics*, calls attention to the difficulty of preserving the difference between language and dialects in certain cases:

> The distinction between "dialect" and "language" seems obvious: dialects are subdivisions of languages. What linguistics (and especially sociolinguistics) has done is to point to the complexity of the

relationship between these notions. It is usually said the people speak different languages when they do not understand each other. But many of the so-called dialects of Chinese (Mandarin, Cantonese, Pekinese) are mutually unintelligible in their spoken form. (They do, however, share the same written language, which is the main reason why one speaks of them as "dialects of Chinese.") And the opposite situation occurs: Swedes, Norwegians and Danes are generally able to understand each other, but their separate histories, cultures, literatures and political structures warrant their being referred to as different languages.[34]

Maxine Hong Kingston's *Tripmaster Monkey* is full of creative transliteration of Cantonese; however, in most cases in the translation, the translator(s) misunderstand or mistranslate them. Kingston does not follow the traditional way of Romanization. Li Juan points out that

> Cantonese uses a Romanization system called pingyam (literally "write sound") to indicate pronunciation of words. Unlike Mandarin, Cantonese does not have one single unified Romanization system and a word may be Romanized in multiple ways. In Romanizing Cantonese words in the novel, Kingston uses English spellings that approximate Cantonese pronunciation and are easier for the Anglo audience to pronounce.[35]

This explains to an extent why the translators cannot figure out what Kingston wants to say; their poor Cantonese prevents them from understanding properly the meaning of the source text. Here are a few examples from the novel and their translations into Chinese:

> When Ah Sing takes his newly wed wife Taña back to his mother's house, Rube, the mother, is playing Mah-jogg with her friends.
> "Wit man, over here," said Ruby.
> "Coming, Mother," said Wittman. He stood behind her to look at her winning hand.
> "Talk to See Nigh here," said the mother.
> "You enjoying the game, See Nigh?" he said to the lady whom he had never met before.
> "Oh, how well behaved," said the See Nigh, the Lady. "So dock-yee. And such good manners. Most boys with beards are bum-how. He doesn't have to call me See Nigh. You call me Auntie, Wit Man."[36]

The Chinese translation reads as follows:

"过来，惠特曼。"鲁比说。
"来了，妈妈。"惠特曼站到她身后看她的好手气。
"找西奈伊说句话。"妈妈说。
"你爱玩这牌，西奈伊？"他问一个他从来未见过面的太太。
"多懂事，"西奈伊说，"多有修养。许多长胡子的家伙是孬种。他不必叫我西奈伊。你叫我姨好了，惠特曼。"[37]

As we can see, the translators render See Nigh as "西奈伊" following the pronunciation. However, that is not a proper name, and unfortunately, the translators have missed the author's creative use of language in this case. The term "See Nigh" is a transliteration of the Cantonese word "师奶," a common way to address married and middle-aged women in Hong Kong and Canton. The term "bum-how" is a transliteration of the Cantonese expression "不好" (but ho), which Kingston creatively chooses to use because of its phonetic proximity to the Cantonese words. In English, the word "bum" means a beggar or one with lower ability, and this pun is unfortunately lost in translation.

In chapter 6, "A Song for Occupations," an old lady asks Wittman to serve as her interpreter when she applies for unemployment:

They referred me on the telephone. My mistake, I put "No" on Seven the same as usual. So the Government lady sent me to interrogation. I said, "Oh dear, I forgot. Now I remember, you refer. The answer is 'Yes.' There had been a Sai Yun voice on the phone." To call them Sai Yun instead of White Demon shows the classiness of the speaker, and also gives the Caucasian person class. "For punishment, they delayed my Unemployment for one week."[38]

The Chinese translation is as follows:

他们通过电话，为我指点。是我的错，我还是一如既往地回答"不。"于是政府女职员让我去受质询。我连忙说："噢，天啊，我忘了。现在我记起来，你在指点。回答应该是是的。"电话里曾传来赛云的声音。"称她赛云，而不是白骨精，表明了说话人的优雅，同时也给白人划了等级。" 作为惩罚，我的失业救济金被推迟一星期发放。[39]

Sai Yun has actually appeared earlier in the novel. When Wittman meets the See Nighs, his mother's Mah-jong friends, one of them refers to her

Mr. Right as "Sai Yun."⁴⁰ The term is an English transliteration of the Cantonese phrase "西人" (saai yan), literally a western guy. The translators assume that this is a proper name because it is capitalized. And they even go farther by translating "White Demon" into "白骨精" (white bone ghost). This term has nothing to do with *The Journey to the West*, in which the main character is called Lady White Bone (白骨精), and it can never be used to refer to a woman. Instead, it should be rendered as "bok gwai" (in Cantonese 白鬼, literally "white foreign devils"), which is much closer to the original.

The following is another interesting example of translation failure. Wittman goes back home with his newly wed wife, Taña, but their marriage is a secret to his mother. This is shrewdly managed by Kingston through code-mixing, the juxtaposition between English and Cantonese:

> "Hey, Taña," he called over to her table. "Meet my mother, Ruby Ah Sing. Ma, meet my pahng yow, Tan-ah." "Pahng yow" means "friend"; maybe Taña would think it meant "wife."⁴¹

Though Wittman is an ABC, American-born-Chinese and he is a typical banana man, he was raised in a traditional Chinese family. He knows the Chinese tradition of seeking parental consent for one's marriage, and understands that by choosing to ignore it he is committing a grave filial sin. As it happens, Wittman has just lost his job, and he does not want to drive his mother mad in front of her friends in this scene. On the other hand, he doesn't want to hurt his newly wed wife by introducing her as a friend to his mother. So, he applies code-mixing to avoid this embarrassment. However, the Chinese translation fails to accomplish the same goal:

> "嘿，唐娜，" 他喊她过来，"这是我妈，鲁比•阿新。妈这是我的朋友，唐啊。" "Pahng yow" 就是 "朋友，"也许唐娜认为是 "妻子" 的意思。⁴²

The translation is a faithful rendering, while the code-mixing part is very confusing to Chinese readers, because the phrase "Pahng yow" here seems weird and out of place. The juxtaposition of English words with the Chinese does not make any sense to Chinese readers. It is not in Chinese Pinyin, and it is not typical English spelling either. This can be solved by the following tentative version: "嘿，唐娜 他喊她过来 "这是我妈，鲁比•阿新。妈这是我的Pahng yow，唐啊。" "Pahng yow" 就是广东话的 "朋友，"也许唐娜认为是 "妻子" 的意思。(Back-translation: "Hey, Taña," he called over to her table. "Meet my mother, Ruby Ah Sing. Ma, meet my pahng yow, Tan-ah."

"Pahng yow" means "friend" in Cantonese; maybe Taña would think it meant "wife.")

It is likely that you may challenge this by saying that this is too strange and difficult for Chinese readers, for again it is neither in Chinese Pinyin nor a proper English spelling. But if the author dares to risk this with the English and Cantonese juxtaposition, why should the translator not try to follow suit? Moreover, the explanation right after the dialogue will explicitly reveal its true meaning. In this way, the strategy applied by Wittman can still work in the Chinese context.

3. Interlingually Heteroglossic Construction

Traditionally, translation is defined as the rendering of one language into another. However, in literary contexts, it is often more complicated than that. Leo Chan's enlightening article about linguistic multiplicity in literature discusses four major categories of bilingual literary texts, namely translating the two tongues, translating the translated, translating interlinguality, translating intralinguality.[43] Sara Ramos Pinto also provides concrete methodologies for handling linguistic varieties.[44] In the following parts, I will study the necessity and feasibility of applying heteroglossic construction in the target text with reference to the translation of Kingston's *Tripmaster Monkey*.

A work's linguistic identity can be better revealed through its use of code-switching or code-mixing, which usually refer to the coexistence of two native or national languages. The two terms are interchangeable in many contexts, but the latter (code-mixing) often refers to intrasentential code-switching only. In explaining different situations and motivations for code-switching, Gumperz identifies three subcategories of code-switching, namely, situational, conversational, and metaphorical, and discusses major factors accounting for code-switching in each category.[45] In situational code-switching, changes of language choice are caused by a change of interlocutor, setting, or topic; conversational code-switching, usually considered as code-switching proper by linguists, is motivated by many factors within the conversation itself and often takes place outside the speaker's consciousness; metaphorical code-switching, a subdivision of conversational code-switching according to Gumperz, is more planned than automatic because changes in language choice are for specific rhetorical purposes.[46] We can find cases of each category easily in *Tripmaster Monkey*.

For example, one day Wittman comes back home, and one of the aunts' pet dog jumps on him. Auntie Jadine applies code-switching from her Chinese to English:

> A dog jumped on him. "Down, Queenie. Behave," said Auntie Jadine, its owner. "Where you manners, Queenie?" Those who usually spoke Chinese talked to the yapperdog in English. "Down, Queenie. Come heah." They spoke English to him and to the dog. American animals.[47]

The code-switching here serves several important purposes. Kingston herself admits that Wittman Ah Sing, the protagonist of the novel, is modeled on one of her biggest critics Frank Chin, and here it is not difficult to discern that she directs her bitter sarcasm toward him. In addition, this scenario also immediately reminds us of the insulting notice in one of Shanghai's parks in the early twentieth century, "Dogs and Chinese are not allowed." The Chinese translation is as follows:

> 一条狗朝他扑去。"下来，昆妮！老实点儿，" 狗的主人贾丁阿姨说道："昆妮，怎么不规矩点儿？" 那些平日里讲汉语的人都用英语与这只哇啦哇啦的狗说起话来。"下来，昆妮。过来。" 她们用英语同他和狗说话。是美国动物。[48]

Though it is stated out by the sentence "那些平日里讲汉语的人都用英语与这只哇啦哇啦的狗说起话来" (Those who usually spoke Chinese talked to the yapperdog in English.), the foregrounding effect cannot be fully achieved without the heteroglossic construction. The code-switching applied by China Town Chinese residents should be better presented, possibly through the juxtaposition of the two language systems involved in this scenario. Here is a better solution to the problem of preserving the heteroglossic construction of the original:

> 一条狗朝他扑去。"Down, Queenie. Behave"（下来，昆妮！老实点儿）狗的主人贾丁阿姨说道："Where you manners, Queenie?"（昆妮，怎么不规矩点儿）那些平日里讲汉语的人都用英语与这只哇啦哇啦的狗说起话来。"Down, Queenie. Come heah."（下来，昆妮。过来。）她们用英语同他和狗说话。都是美国动物。

The strategy applied here is to highlight the visual effect with the English sentence embedded in the Chinese translation. The heteroglossic construction has a twofold function. On the one hand, it reiterates the fact that the Chinese aunties, See Nighs, can do code-switching when their interlocutors change. On the other, it gives the reader a taste of the pidgin English of early Chinese immigrants in the United States. Expressions such as "Where you manners" and "come heah" must be preserved instead of replaced by standardized language in order to highlight important features of the relevant cultural and historical context.

Pidgin English is used on many occasions in the novel. The slight differentiation among these cases is highlighted by Juan Li in her article, "Pidgin and Code-Switching: Linguistic Identity and Multicultural Consciousness in Maxine Hong Kingston's *Tripmaster Monkey*."[49] I pick two examples to illustrate my contention of heteroglossic construction in the source language. In chapter 2, "Linguists and Contenders," Wittman reads his poems to Nanci Li in his apartment:

> He wadded it up and threw it over his shoulder. He jumped on top of the trunk, scrunching and scattering the whole shit pile, then pounced on a page, and returned with it to the desk. "This is it! Here's one you'll like. That is, likee. Gurarantee. Ah. I mean, aiya. 'Wokking on da waywoad. Centing da dollahs buck home to why-foo and biby. No booty-full Ah-mei-li-can gal-low fo me. Aiya. Aiya.'" He wiped his eyes with the paper, crushed it, and pitched the wad at the window, which was shut.[50]

As in all liminal states, here too ambivalence and polysemy supersede clarity and definability.[51] The writing immediately challenges the readers' comprehension. The poem is very funny in that it simulates the accent of an early immigrant's English. Li contends that "Kingston also draws on stereotypical features of the past Chinese Pidgin English to combat negative stereotypes of Chinese American' languages."[52] The linguistic expressions used in this passage—"likee"/like, "centing"/sending, "booty-ful"/beautiful—are good examples of this kind of stereotypical features of the early Chinese Pidgin English. Unfortunately, they are all erased by the standardization strategy adopted by the translators:

> 说着，揉成一团，往背后一扔。接着又跳上箱子，把整堆狗屁诗稿撒了一地，后又扑向一张纸，拿着那页纸走回书桌。"就是这首。这首，你会喜欢的。就是说，<u>喜爱的</u>。肯定的。啊，我是说，哎呀。'<u>顺着大路往前走，把美元寄给家中的妻儿老小。美国美女没我的份</u>。哎呀。哎呀。'" 他拿那页纸揉揉眼睛后，又搓成团，从窗口扔出去，窗子是关着的。[53]

What can be done to solve this problem? Heteroglossic construction might be one way out, though it may make the renditions a little lengthy.

说着，揉成一团，往背后一扔。接着又跳上箱子，把整堆狗屁诗稿撒了一地，后又扑向一张纸，拿着那页纸走回书桌。"就是这首。这首，你会喜欢的。就是说，<u>喜爱的</u>。肯定的。啊，我是说，哎呀。'<u>Wokking on da waywoad. Centing da dollahs buck home to why-foo and biby. No booty-full Ah-mei-li-can gal-low fo me. Aiya. Aiya.</u>' （顺着大路往前走，把美元寄给家中的<u>妻儿老小。美国美女没我的份</u>。哎呀。哎呀。）"他拿那页纸揉揉眼睛后，又搓成团，从窗口扔出去，窗子是关着的。

Such strategy is not rare in creative writing. Take Khaled Hosseini's *The Kite Runner* as an example:

The laughing man broke into song, a slurring, off-key rendition of an old Afghan wedding song, delivered with a thick Russian accent:

Ahesta boro, Mah-e-man, ahesta boro.

Go slowly, my lovely moon, go slowly.[54]

Why does the author bother to put something intangible to most English readers there? This interlingual heteroglossic construction of discourse serves to highlight the unique identity of the text, and such linguistic features need to be preserved in translation whenever possible.

4. Conclusion

Jochen Achilles points out that "Liminality as a concept of both demarcation and mediation between different processual stages, spatial complexes, inner states, and multiple identities is of obvious importance in an age of global mobility, digital networking, interethnicity, transnationality, ecological reconsiderations of species boundaries as well as technological redefinitions of the human."[55] The liminal existence of characters like those populating Kingston's novels finds linguistic expression in heteroglossic structures that pose great challenges to translators of her work into other languages, Chinese included. The difficulties are twofold. First, it is essential that heteroglossic constructions in the source text are identified correctly. And second, it is necessary that they are adequately rendered into the target language, as this essay has argued. Preserving the original's heteroglossia of works such as *Tripmaster Monkey* is the only way to ensure that the multilayered ethnic identity of Chinese diaspora is conveyed fully into the receiving culture.

Acknowledgement

The work described in this paper was fully supported by the Research Seed Fund from Lingnan University of the Hong Kong Special Administrative Region, China (LU 102240).

Notes

1. P. V. Amith Kumar, *Bakhtin and Translation Studies: Theoretical Extensions and Connotations* (Newcastle upon Tyne: Cambridge Scholars Publishing, 2015).
2. Ibid., 9.
3. Bo Li, 翻译研究的对话性路径: 巴赫金思想与翻译研究 (The Dialogical Approach to Translation Studies: Bakhtinian Thoughts and Translation Studies) (Beijing: China Social Sciences Press, 2017). The English translations of Chinese components in this article are done by the author himself, unless otherwise specified.
4. Paul Bandia, "Postcolonialism, Literary Heteroglossia and Translation," in *Caribbean Interfaces*, ed. Lieven D'hulst et al. (New York: Rodopi, 2007), 203–21; Lavinia Merlini Barbaresi, "Text Linguistics and Literary Translation," in *Translation Studies: Perspectives on an Emerging Discipline*, ed. Alessandra Riccardi (Cambridge: Cambridge University Press, 2002), 120; Reine Meylaerts, "Literary Heteroglossia in Translation: When the Language of Translation Is the Locus of Ideological Struggle," in *Translation Studies at the Interface of Disciplines*, ed. João Ferreira Duarte, Alexandra Assis Rosa, and Teresa Seruya (Amsterdam: John Benjamins, 2006), 85; Elzbieta Tabakowska, "Linguistic Polyphony as a Problem in Translation," in *Translation, History and Culture*, ed. Susan Bassnett and André Lefevere (London: Pinter Publishers, 1990), 71–8;; Bo Li, "Heteroglossia, Dialects and Literary Translation: A Case Study of Wang Chen-ho's *Rose Rose I Love You* and Its English Translation," *Translation Quarterly* 55 (2010): 64–99; Bo Li, "Subtitling *Made in Hong Kong* and Missing Heteroglossia," in *Translation and Academic Journals*, ed. Sun Yifeng (New York: Palgrave Macmillan, 2015), 179–93.
5. Mikhail M. Bakhtin, *The Dialogic Imagination: Four Essays*, ed. Michael Holquist, trans. Caryl Emerson and Michael Holquist (Austin: University of Texas Press, 1981), 67.

6. Ibid., 291.
7. Ibid., 301–31.
8. Graham Roberts, "Glossary" to *The Bakhtin Reader: Selected Writings of Bakhtin*, Medvedev and Voloshinov, ed. Pam Morris (London: Edward Arnold, 1994), 248;; Karine Zbinden, "The Bakhtin Circle and Translation," *Yearbook of English Studies* 36, no. 1 (2006): 157–67.
9. Karine Zbinden, "Traducing Bakhtin and Missing Heteroglossia," *Dialogism: An International Journal of Bakhtin Studies*, no. 2 (1999): 41–59.
10. Roberts, "Glossary," 248.
11. Caryl Emerson, "Translating Bakhtin: Does His Theory of Discourse Contain a Theory of Translation?" *University of Ottawa Quarterly* 53, no. 1 (1983): 23–33.
12. Li, "Heteroglossia, Dialects and Literary Translation," 64–99.
13. Li, "Subtitling *Made in Hong Kong* and Missing Heteroglossia," 179.
14. Ibid., 182.
15. Victor Turner, *The Ritual Process: Structure and Anti-Structure* (New York: Aldine, 1969), 95.
16. Rainer Guldin, "From Threshold to Threshold: Translation as a Liminal Activity," *Journal of Translation Studies*, no. 1 (2020): 5–25.
17. Alfred Bendixen, "The Liminal Spaces of Nathaniel Hawthorne's Short-Story Cycles: Rites of Passage in History and Storytelling," in *Liminality and the Short Story: Boundary Crossings in American, Canadian, and British Writing*, ed. Jochen Achilles and Ina Bergmann (New York: Routledge, 2015), 7.
18. Bakhtin, *Dialogic Imagination*.
19. Roland Borgards, "Liminale Anthropologien: Skizze eines Forschungsfeldes," in *Liminale Anthropologien. Zwischenzeiten, Schwellenphänomene, Zwischenräume in Literatur und Philosophie*, ed. Jochen Achilles, Roland Borgards, and Brigitte Burrichter (Würzburg: Königshausen & Neumann, 2012), 9–13; Manuel Aguirre, Roberta Ann Quance, and Philip C. Sutton, *Margins and Thresholds: An Enquiry into the Concept of Liminality in Text Studies* (Madrid: Gateway Press, 2000), 9, 65; Bakhtin, *Dialogic Imagination*.
20. Dominick LaCapra, "Rethinking Intellectual History and Reading Texts," *History and Theory* 19, no. 3 (1980): 247.
21. Kwai-cheung Lo, "Reaffirming 'Chineseness' in the Translations of Asian American Literature: Maxine Hong Kingston's Fictions in Taiwan and Mainland China," *Translation Quarterly* 18 and 19 (2000): 74–98.
22. Ken-Fang Lee, "翻譯者是叛徒：解讀湯亭亭的《猴行者》" (Is a Translator a Traitor: A Reading of Maxine Hong Kingston's *Tripmaster Monkey*), 中外文學 *(Chung Wai Literary)* 29, no. 6 (2000): 91.
23. Jennie Wang, "*Tripmaster Monkey*: Kingston's Postmodern Representation of a New 'China Man,'" *MELUS* 20, no. 1 (1995): 101–14; A. Noelle Williams, "Parody and Pacifist Transformations in Maxine Hong Kingston's

Tripmaster Monkey: His Fake Book," *MELUS* 20, no. 1(March 1995): 83–100;;l;; Lee, "翻譯者是叛徒：解讀湯亭亭的《猴行者》," 77–99; Debra Shostak, "Maxine Hong Kingston's Fake Books," in *Memory, Narrative, and Identity: New Essays in Ethnic American Literatures*, ed. Amritjit Singh, Josephe T. Skerrett, Jr., and Robert E. Hogan (Boston: Northeastern University Press, 1994), 51–74; Lo, "Reaffirming 'Chineseness' in the Translations of Asian American Literature," 74–9; Hsiao-Hung Chang, "雜種猴子—解/構族裔本源與文化傳承" ("Hybrid Monkey—Deconstruction/Construction of Nationality and Cultural Inheritance"), in 性別越界：女性主義文學理論與批評 (*Gender Transgression: Feminist Literary Theory and Criticism*), Taipei: UNITAS Publishing,1995.

24. Hong Fang, *Liminal Art in Kingston's Writing* (Tianjin: Nankai University Press, 2007), 96.
25. Lo, "Reaffirming 'Chineseness' in the Translations of Asian American Literature," 74–98
26. .Maxine Hong Kingston, *Tripmaster Monkey: His Fake Book* (New York: Knopf, 1989), 170; underlining added.
27. Maxine Hong Kingston, 孫行者 (*Sun Xing Zhe*), trans. Zhao Wenshu and Zhao Fuzhu (Guilin: Lijiang Publishing, 1998), 185.
28. Fang, *Liminal Art in Kingston's Writing*, 105.
29. Shostak, "Maxine Hong Kingston's Fake Books."
30. Kingston, *Tripmaster Monkey*, 144.
31. Kingston, 孫行者(*Sun Xing Zhe*), 156; all underlining added
32. Guanzhong Luo, 三国演义:二十四卷嘉靖壬午本《三国演义》(Three Kingdoms: A Historical Novel) (Beijing: People's Publishing House, 2008), 4.
33. Yifeng Sun, "Translation and Back-Translation: Transcultural Reinventions in Some Chinese-American Literary Works," *Asia Pacific Translation and Intercultural Studies* 1, no. 2 (2014): 107.
34. Marvin Carlson, *Speaking in Tongues: Languages at Play in the Theatre* (Michigan: University of Michigan Press, 2006), 8.
35. Juan Li, "Pidgin and Code-Switching: Linguistic Identity and Multicultural Consciousness in Maxine Hong Kingston's *Tripmaster Monkey*," *Language and Literature* 13, no. 3 (2004): 286.
36. Kingston, *Tripmaster Monkey*, 181–2.
37. Kingston, 孫行者 (*Sun Xing Zhe*), 198.
38. Kingston, *Tripmaster Monkey*, 231.
39. Kingston, 孫行者 (*Sun Xing Zhe*), 255–6.
40. Kingston, *Tripmaster Monkey*, 182.
41. Ibid.
42. Kingston, 孫行者 (*Sun Xing Zhe*), 199.
43. Leo Tak-Hung Chan, "Translating Bilinguality: Theorizing Translation in the Post-Babelian Era," *Translator* 8, no. 1 (2002): 49–72.

44. Sara Ramos Pinto, "How Important Is the Way You Say It? A Discussion on the Translation of Linguistic Varieties," *Target* 21, no. 2 (2009): 289–307.
45. John J. Gumperz, *Discourse Strategies* (Cambridge, MA: Cambridge University Press, 1982).
46. Ibid., 60–1.
47. Kingston, *Tripmaster Monkey*, 179.
48. Kingston, 孫行者 (*Sun Xing Zhe*), 196.
49. Li, "Pidgin and Code-Switching," 269–87.
50. Kingston, *Tripmaster Monkey*, 32–3.
51. Bendixen, "The Liminal Spaces of Nathaniel Hawthorne's Short-Story Cycles," 8.
52. Li, "Pidgin and Code-Switching," 269.
53. Kingston, 孫行者 (*Sun Xing Zhe*), 35.
54. Khaled Hosseini, *The Kite Runner* (New York: Riverhead Books, 2003), 124.
55. Jochen Achilles, "Modes of Liminality in American Short Fiction: Condensations of Multiple Identities," in *Liminality and the Short Story: Boundary Crossings in American, Canadian, and British Writing*, ed. Jochen Achilles and Ina Bergmann (New York: Routledge, 2015), 35.

Bibliography

Achilles, Jochen. "Modes of Liminality in American Short Fiction: Condensations of Multiple Identities." In *Liminality and the Short Story: Boundary Crossings in American, Canadian, and British Writing*. Edited by Jochen Achilles and Ina Bergmann, 35–49. New York: Routledge, 2015.

Achilles, Jochen, and Ina Bergmann, eds. *Liminality and the Short Story: Boundary Crossings in American, Canadian, and British Writing*. New York: Routledge, 2015.

Aguirre, Manuel Roberta, Ann Quance, and Philip C. Sutton. *Margins and Thresholds: An Enquiry into the Concept of Liminality in Text Studies*. Madrid: Gateway Press, 2000.

Bakhtin, Mikhail M. *The Dialogic Imagination: Four Essays*. Edited by Michael Holquist. Translated by Caryl Emerson and Michael Holquist. Austin: University of Texas Press, 1981.

Bandia, Paul. "Postcolonialism, Literary Heteroglossia and Translation." In *Caribbean Interfaces*. Edited by Lieven D'hulst et al., 203–21. New York: Rodopi, 2007.

Barbaresi, Lavinia Merlini. "Text Linguistics and Literary Translation." In *Translation Studies: Perspectives on an Emerging Discipline*. Edited by Alessandra Riccardi, 120. Cambridge: Cambridge University Press, 2002.

Bendixen, Alfred. "The Liminal Spaces of Nathaniel Hawthorne's Short-Story Cycles: Rites of Passage in History and Storytelling." In *Liminality and the Short Story: Boundary Crossings in American, Canadian, and British Writing*. Edited by Jochen Achilles and Ina Bergmann, 134–44. New York: Routledge, 2015.

Borgards, Roland. "Liminale Anthropologien: Skizze eines Forschungsfeldes." In *Liminale Anthropologien. Zwischenzeiten, Schwellenphänomene, Zwischenräume in Literatur und Philosophie*. Edited by Jochen Achilles, Roland Borgards, and Brigitte Burrichter, 9–13. Würzburg: Königshausen and Neumann, 2012.

Carlson, Marvin. *Speaking in Tongues: Languages at Play in the Theatre*. Michigan: University of Michigan Press, 2006.

Chan, Tak-Hung Leo. "Translating Bilinguality: Theorizing Translation in the Post-Babelian Era." *Translator* 8, no. 1 (2002): 49–72.

Chang, Hsiao-Hung. "雜種猴子—解/構族裔本源與文化傳承" (Hybrid Monkey—Deconstruction/Construction of Nationality and Cultural Inheritance). In 性別越界：女性主義文學理論與批評 (Gender Transgression: Feminist Literary Theory and Criticism). Taipei: UNITAS Publishing, 1995.

Crystal, David. *A Dictionary of Linguistics and Phonetics*. New Jersey: John Wiley, 2011.

Emerson, Caryl. "Translating Bakhtin: Does His Theory of Discourse Contain a Theory of Translation?" *University of Ottawa Quarterly* 53, no. 1 (1983): 23–33.

Fang, Hong. *Liminal Art in Kingston's Writing*. Tianjin: Nankai University Press, 2007.

Guldin, Rainer. "From Threshold to Threshold: Translation as a Liminal Activity." *Journal of Translation Studies* 4, no. 1 (2020): 5–25.

Gumperz, John J. *Discourse Strategies*. New York: Cambridge University Press, 1982.

Hosseini, Khaled. *The Kite Runner*. New York: Riverhead Books, 2003.

Kingston, Maxine Hong. *Tripmaster Monkey: His Fake Book*. New York: Knopf, 1989.

Kingston, Maxine Hong. 孫行者 (*Sun Xing Zhe*). Translated by Zhao Wenshu and Zhao Fuzhu. Guilin: Lijiang Publishing, 1998.

Kumar, Amith P. V. *Bakhtin and Translation Studies: Theoretical Extensions and Connotations*. Newcastle upon Tyne: Cambridge Scholars Publishing, 2015.

LaCapra, Dominick. "Rethinking Intellectual History and Reading Texts." *History and Theory* 19, no. 3 (1980): 245–76.

Lee, Ken-Fang. "翻譯者是叛徒：解讀湯亭亭的《猴行者》" (Is a Translator a Traitor: A Reading of Maxine Hong Kingston's *Tripmaster Monkey*). 中外文學 (Chung Wai Literary) 29, no. 6 (2000): 77–99.

Li, Bo. "Heteroglossia, Dialects and Literary Translation: A Case Study of Wang Chen-ho's *Rose Rose I Love You* and Its English Translation." *Translation Quarterly* 55 (2010): 64–99.

Li, Bo. "Subtitling *Made in Hong Kong* and Missing Heteroglossia." In *Translation and Academic Journals*. Edited by Sun Yifeng, 179–93. New York: Palgrave Macmillan, 2015.

Li, Bo. 翻译研究的对话性路径: 巴赫金思想与翻译研究 (The Dialogical Approach to Translation Studies: Bakhtinian Thoughts and Translation Studies). Beijing: China Social Sciences Press, 2017.

Li, Juan. "Pidgin and Code-Switching: Linguistic Identity and Multicultural Consciousness in Maxine Hong Kingston's *Tripmaster Monkey*." *Language and Literature* 13, no. 3 (2004): 269–87.

Lo, Kuan-chung. *Romance of the Three Kingdoms*. Translated by C. H. Brewitt-Taylor. Rutland: Charles E. Tuttle, 1990.

Lo, Kwai-cheung. "Reaffirming 'Chineseness' in the Translations of Asian American Literature: Maxine Hong Kingston's Fictions in Taiwan and Mainland China." *Translation Quarterly* 18 and 19 (2000): 74–98.

Luo, Guanzhong. *Three Kingdoms: A Historical Novel*. Translated by Moss Roberts. Berkeley: University of California Press/Foreign Languages Press, 1991.

Luo, Guanzhong. 三国演义:二十四卷嘉靖壬午本《三国演义》(Three Kingdoms: A Historical Novel). Beijing: People's Publishing House, 2008.

Meylaerts, Reine. "Literary Heteroglossia in Translation: When the Language of Translation Is the Locus of Ideological Struggle." In *Translation Studies at the Interface of Disciplines*. Edited by João Ferreira Duarte, Alexandra Assis Rosa, and Teresa Seruya, 85. Amsterdam: John Benjamins, 2006.

Pan, Min-fang. "The Paradox of Racial Self-Hatred and Self-Love: On the Body Writing of *Tripmaster Monkey: His Fake Book*." *Jinan Journal (Philosophy and Social Science Edition)*, no. 6 (2015): 4.

Pinto, Sara Ramos. "How Important Is the Way You Say It? A Discussion on the Translation of Linguistic Varieties." *Target* 21, no. 2 (2009): 289–307.

Roberts, Graham. "Glossary" to *The Bakhtin Reader: Selected Writings of Bakhtin, Medvedev and Voloshinov*. Edited by Pam Morris, 251. London: Edward Arnold, 1994.

Shostak, Debra. "Maxine Hong Kingston's Fake Books." In *Memory, Narrative, and Identity: New Essays in Ethnic American Literatures*. Edited by Amritjit Singh, Josephe T. Skerrett, Jr., and Robert E. Hogan, 51–74. Boston: Northeastern University Press, 1994.

Sun, Yifeng. "Translation and Back-Translation: Transcultural Reinventions in Some Chinese-American Literary Works." *Asia Pacific Translation and Intercultural Studies* 1, no. 2 (2014): 107–21.

Tabakowska, Elzbieta. "Linguistic Polyphony as a Problem in Translation." In *Translation, History and Culture Susan*. Edited by Bassnett and André Lefevere, 71–8. London: Pinter Publishers, 1990.

Todorov, Tzvetan. *Mikhail Bakhtin: The Dialogical Principle*. Translated by Wlad Godzich. Minneapolis: University of Minnesota Press, 1984.

Turner, Victor. *The Ritual Process: Structure and Anti-Structure*. New York: Aldine, 1969.

Wang, Jennie. "*Tripmaster Monkey*: Kingston's Postmodern Representation of a New 'China Man.'" *MELUS* 20, no. 1 (1995): 101–14.

Williams, A. Noelle. "Parody and Pacifist Transformations in Maxine Hong Kingston's *Tripmaster Monkey: His Fake Book*." *MELUS* 20, no. 1 (March 1995): 83–100.

Zbinden, Karine. "The Bakhtin Circle and Translation." *Yearbook of English Studies* 36, no. 1 (2006): 157–67.

Zbinden, Karine. "Traducing Bakhtin and Missing Heteroglossia." *Dialogism: An International Journal of Bakhtin Studies*, no. 2 (1999): 41–59.

4

What Is an "Original"?: Creation, Translation, "Re-accentuation," and the Question of Primacy

Michael Eskin

1. "Accentuation" Equals "Re-Accentuation"

Since at least the late 1920s, the Bakhtin circle had been reflecting on the question of "accentuation" (*aktsentuatsiya*) in speech and language. From Voloshinov's *Marxism and the Philosophy of Language* (1929) to such texts by Bakhtin as *Discourse in the Novel* (1934–5), *From the Prehistory of Novelistic Discourse* (1940), and *Epic and the Novel* (1941), the dual problem of a language's "accentual system" and its specific "accentuation" in the oral and written speech of individuals, their utterances—be they simple or complex, quotidian or artistic, for instance—constitutes one of foci of the circle's inquiry into the workings of language and literature.[1] By "accentuation" the Bakhtin circle means a wide range of social, linguistic, and aesthetic phenomena, including "the congeries of objects accessible to social attention and axiologically accentuated by it at any given stage of a society's development"; "the living, concrete accentuation of the sense and meaning of speech"; "an author's irony, that is, his accentuation, his active assessment of his material"; any language's "inner form," that is, its "evaluative-accentual system"; and, finally, the "accentual units," that is, utterances, idiolects, idioms, professional and social languages animating the "word in the novel."[2] In other words, insofar as we always already exist in a world that we cannot help making sense of one way or another—in terms of both its material conditions, broadly understood, and its ideological superstructure, again broadly understood to include any and all human-made and "intended" objects and artifacts (from pottery to poetry)—we find ourselves confronted with "accentuation," with the world's being always already axiologically nuanced and shaded, assessed and evaluated. Thus, fact, to the extent it is such only for the hermeneutically engaged mind (to the best of our knowledge, nonhuman earthly species have, presumably, no concept of fact), is always already steeped in value: in the Bakhtinian universe, Hume's guillotine does not apply.³ And not only that: our world's ubiquitous "accentuation," its axiological texture, is ever in flux, ever elastic, being constantly stretched, creased, crumpled, and bunched up every which way amid the unfolding dialogue of human, necessarily sense-making and, hence, "accentuating," existence. Bakhtin calls this irreducible phenomenon "re-accentuation" (*pereaktsentuatsiya*).⁴

The interplay of "accentuation" and "re-accentuation" can be read as Bakhtin's creative appropriation and reinterpretation, that is, precisely, "re-accentuation" (through the prism of his particular interest in all matters linguistic and verbal-aesthetic), of Nietzsche's insight that "there is only perspectival seeing, only perspectival cognition."⁵ Everyone by definition willy-nilly imposes their own viewpoint on everything, which, in turn, cannot but itself always already be imposed and impinged upon by others' viewpoints (read: "accentuations"), which latter thus reveal themselves, essentially, as "re-accentuations" in turn: "accentuation" equals "re-accentuation."

2. An "Interminable Process"

How, now, we need to ask, does "re-accentuation" work? How ought we to conceive of the actual, concrete dynamic of "re-accentuation," which, as Bakhtin specifies, is an "interminable social-ideological process"?⁶ In other words, what exactly happens when "re-accentuation" happens?

According to Bakhtin, "re-accentuation" unfolds as "translation" (*perevod*)—as the "translation" of any given meaningful datum "from one accentual register into another—for instance from the comical into the tragic or vice versa" in the case of "literary images" in particular.⁷ Whereby "translation" is here to be taken not figuratively or in a broad cultural-conceptual sense so much as quite literally in terms of "carrying" or "ferrying over" or "trans-ferring"—something that is much more salient and palpable in the Russian *perevod* (lit.: over-, or across-guiding, or -leading) than in the Latinate "translation." Which also means that actual translation, as commonly understood, that is, translation from one language into another, can be said exemplarily to articulate and most overtly to embody "re-accentuation." The latter notwithstanding, however, any form of translation whatsoever—be it intra- and interlingual, intersemiotic, intra- and intercultural, interpersonal, or inter- and intramental—presents, in and of itself, an instance of "re-accentuation."⁸

The following passage from Dostoevsky's *Diary of a Writer for 1873* (from the chapter entitled "Small Pictures"), cited in full by Voloshinov (who, incidentally, borrows it from Yakubinsky), offers a prime example of intralingual, interpersonal, inter- and intramental "re-accentuation," which Voloshinov also dubs "expressive intonation":

> Dostoevsky relates the following incident in his diary: "Late one Sunday night, I happened to be walking next to a bunch of drunken artisans ... and it was there and then that I realized that all thoughts and feelings could be expressed by merely using a single noun—a particular noun of utmost simplicity ... This is what happened: First, one of the bunch utters this noun in a shrill, emphatic voice, as if to deny a point of general contention made earlier in the conversation. Then another picks up that very same noun in response to the first, but in a very different tone of voice, as though to categorically contradict him. A third one now gets angry at the first, abruptly joining the fray and tauntingly throwing that very same noun back at him. The second one in turn gets angry at the third for being rude to the first, and cuts him off by merely uttering that same time-honored noun for a certain body part, as though saying: 'What the hell do you think you're doing butting in like this?! Me and Filka were having a nice quiet chat and just like that you come along and start cussing him out!' Whereupon, out of the blue—and as though he had just stumbled upon the solution to the entire problem—a fourth chap who had remained silent until now ecstatically shouts that very same unprintable noun (especially in the company of ladies), just that one single word alone ... Finally, the oldest in the bunch, a surly character, who apparently didn't think his friend's enthusiasm appropriate, turns on him and repeats, in a gruff and expostulatory bass—yes, you guessed it—that very same noun, whose usage is forbidden in the company of ladies ... And so, without uttering a single additional word, they all repeated just this one, obviously beloved, little noun of theirs, understanding each other perfectly."[9]

Another, particularly poignant instance of intralingual, interpersonal, and intra- as well as intercultural "re-accentuation"—this time plucked from a context closer to home—occurs in contemporary British poet Simon Armitage's "recreation" of Thomas Hardy's 1912 poem "The Convergence of the Twain (*Lines on the Loss of the 'Titanic'*)" by way of commemorating the 9/11 attacks on New York City.[10] Armitage's 2002 poem "The Convergence of the Twain" not only borrows—thus culturally-historically "re-accentuating"—its predecessor's title, eleven-part structure, three-line stanzaic form, and overall plot (two unwitting protagonists fatally colliding with one another on their appointed date with destiny—"the smart ship" with "the Iceberg" [ll. 22–4] in Hardy's and "a passenger plane" with "an office block" [l. 21] in Armitage's poems, respectively), but it also gives the "convergence of the twain"-motif an idiosyncratic ideological twist or spin, that is, precisely, "re-accentuation": while Hardy's poem is, essentially, "about" human "vanity" (l. 2) and "vaingloriousness" (l. 15), that is, about the tragic flaw of hubris, which gets cut down to size, as it were, by the "Spinner of the Years" (l. 31), the "immanent Will that stirs and urges everything" (l. 18), Armitage's "re-make" can be said to be "about" the fatally unintended consequences of global financial greed and economic disparity—"One half-excoriated Apple Mac still quotes the Dow Jones" (l. 12) in the midst of a post-apocalyptic "architecture of air" (l. 1) where "nothing stands but free sky, unlimited and sheer" (l. 3). Incidentally, Armitage's unmistakable, if implicit, poetic-political commentary on 9/11, pithily and comically-grotesquely captured in the compound image of the "half-excoriated Apple Mac"—which not only onomastically fuses the literally pitted "Big Apple" with its digital-technological namesake and, arguably, prime emblem of US capitalism and global reach, but which doubly underscores the fatality of the US's perceived imperialism by articulating the "Apple Mac" with *its* other namesake (other than the "Big Apple," that is), namely, McDonald's' "Big Mac," that other, much maligned symbol of putative US world domination—can be said exemplarily to illustrate "re-accentuation" in terms of what Bakhtin specifies as the "translation from one accentual register into another—for instance from the comical into the tragic or vice versa."

3. The Work of Translation

Both examples of "re-accentuation"—Dostoevsky's musings about a certain "unprintable noun" and its varied use by a range of speakers, and Armitage's rewriting of Hardy—raise, each in its own way, the question of the "original," which is at the very heart of "re-accentuation" qua "*re*-accentuation," that is, "accentuation" in and through *re*-iteration or *re*-petition of one kind or another. Something must have always already preceded "re-accentuation" for it to be precisely that: "*re*-accentuation." More specifically, "re-accentuation" must have always already been preceded by "accentuation," which in turn, however, as I explained above, paradoxically always already equals "re-accentuation." In other words, from the vantage point of "re-accentuation," there is and can be no "original," no pristine, originating pre-text or viewpoint that would not have always already been caught up in the "interminable social-ideological process" of "re-accentuation." (This, of course, perfectly fits in with Bakhtin's conception of language as constitutively devoid of an original position, of an inherent pristineness or originality—every word and viewpoint always already being rife with layers upon layers of voices, viewpoints, intentions, cultural histories, "accentuations," and "re-accentuations."[11]) Thus, in Bakhtin's view, there can be no "unprintable word" that would not have always already been spoken or written—"re-accentuated"—by someone or other in one context or another. Similarly, there can be no truly or essentially "original" poem or text, more generally, according to Bakhtin—a poem or text, that is, which would not, one way or another, be a "re-accentuation" of another "re-accentuation" and so on. Which makes Armitage's repetition of Hardy's title doubly significant: as a reference to its putative pre-text, the original "The Convergence of the Twain," and, concomitantly, as the very denial of its pre-text's originality through its titular, "re-accentual" arrogation.

But what if, *per impossibile*, there indeed be an "original," after all? What if "re-accentuation" were truly supervenient upon "accentuation," which would not necessarily be "re-accentuation" in turn? What if ... what if ... What matters, it seems to me, is that no matter how hard we may try to obliterate the notion of the "original"—and for whatever reason—we still cannot help (*pace* Bakhtin, Derrida, and others) operating with it (if only when it comes to royalties due to the "original" author ...). This, anyway, is what I have experienced in one particularly notable example of "re-accentuation" that was also a particularly memorable instance of our veritable obsession with "originality," and to a discussion of which I would like to devote the remainder of this essay.

4. Original as Translation, Translation as Original

Several years ago, I was handed the manuscript of a nonscholarly work. The text constituted an attempt—as the author has explained in numerous interviews since the publication, in late 2007, of the book that would ultimately emerge from the manuscript—to live up to her own expectations as a professional philosopher, one of whose central tasks is to tackle such core problems of existence as death, love, pain, and survival. If she couldn't do that, she had frequently said, she would have failed as a philosopher.

Handing me a slim, spiral-bound copy of her German manuscript, entitled *November-Rose: Eine Rede über den Tod*, Kathrin Stengel asked me to read it, critique it, and tell her what I thought. I read this philosophical meditation on the death of the beloved and the lover's survival and did not know quite what to think, as the book exploded the interpretive frameworks for thinking through and dealing with mortality that I had been accustomed to from Plato and the Stoics onwards—so unique, so novel, so unexpected were its ruthless and unflinching honesty, its insights, perspectives, and approaches. I asked the author if she would allow me to translate the book into English and she consented.

It took me almost a year to get back to *November-Rose*—I must have intuited that the task of rendering this particular book in another language would require all of my attention and personal investment. Whatever projects I had going at the time would either have to have been finished or put on hold before I sat down to get to work on *November-Rose*.

In the winter of 2006, finally, I began translating. Already with the very first sentence, however, I realized that short though this extraordinary book of about ninety pages may be, translating it would be a particular challenge. Much later, the poet Durs Grünbein would poignantly articulate what about the book might have made translating it so idiosyncratically resistant, yet enticing and beckoning: "*November-Rose* ... is a treatise of such conceptual density," Grünbein would write,

> that it seems to reveal itself to the reader only gradually and in spurts. I have read it in one sitting, but that was a mistake. Now it is sitting on my desk, on certain days I open it and read a couple of pages—that's much better. The ideal reading pace for this book would probably be about three sentences per day—only in this manner can this amazing book of consolation (amazing in its philosophical purity) achieve its full impact. What I mean is the subtle sense of vertigo in reading it: the reader is drawn into reflections about the inevitable, as if it had already long happened. And, indeed, it has—and not only for the one whose voice we hear in this book, but for each of us, who listen closely.[12]

How to translate something that ought to be read at a pace of three sentences per day? At what pace? And how to unpack the density of something that only gradually, if at all, reveals itself to you, and then only in its condensed polysemy. Trivial questions to the seasoned translator of poetry and literature, to be sure—yet questions whose singular force is not diminished for all that, since any true encounter with the discursive cosmos of another human being demands an absolutely singular response, an absolutely singular "re-accentuation"; and singularity means the absence of the trivial.

The book begins with the following tripartite statement: "Der Tod ist ein Wendepunkt im Leben. Eine Kehre für den, der ihn stirbt. Ein Angelpunkt für den, der ihn erlebt."[13] The first proposition seems clear enough: "Death is a turning point in life." But immediately a question arises: how to read it—especially, in light of what follows? After all, while we live we don't know what death is, and when we are dead, we are no longer alive to witness and tell about it. So, what does it mean to say, "Death is a turning point *in life*"? In whose life? The deceased's or the survivor's? All-important questions for the translator, who has to intuit and decide on how to tackle the next proposition: "A turning for the one who dies, a pivotal point for the one who experiences it"—this being a more or less literal translation of the German "original." However, how exactly are we to understand the fine semantics? How can it be a "Kehre," a "turning" for the one who dies? Where do the dead go? And why is it a "turning" (a term that in itself already invokes and "re-accentuates" Heidegger's famous "Kehre," that is, the latter's own "re-accentuation" of his philosophical focus, which would henceforth no longer be concerned with humans so much as with Being as such[14])? And how can death be a "pivotal point for the one who experiences it"? The "one who experiences it" is the one who dies, and it would seem quite problematic to speak of a pivotal point in reference to the dead, as it perforce implies life, or does it? And what about the living? Can they really experience death? Of course not—only the *dying* of another, or their own dying, but surely not death?

The strange thing about all of these quandaries is that they emerge only once you begin translating, which means, precisely, emphatically "re-accentuating" the text. If you just read the text, it makes perfect sense, unless you really slow down and poke and prick every word, weigh it on the scales of analytical rigor, and allow yourself to spiral down a linguistic *mise-en-abîme*. In other words, the patchwork of verbal-conceptual bridges and causeways that make up a good portion of all of the texts that we read and that allow us to get from point A to point B as we flit across them tend to give way and, sometimes, to collapse if for some reason we stop midway and peer down into the abysses between the insights or thoughts they connect. And translation is an essential slowing down and a coming to a halt at the most unexpected moments and places on those suspended bridges within language and speech.

Let me give you another example of what I mean: "Der Tod ist ein Erdbeben, bei dem das Epizentrum nah, näher oder im aller Innersten der Identität liegt und in jedem Fall auf alle ihre Bereiche übergreift." Reading this statement in the original—again, it feels, sounds, and indeed is perfectly clear, transparent as can be: "Death is an earthquake whose epicenter lies close, closer to, if not at the very center of identity, and, in any case, affects all of its regions." However: how to understand this? Even if we go along with the statement's hyperbolic progression, we cannot, as we begin parsing it, but stop in our tracks at "in any case"—"auf jeden Fall"—which seems to imply an opposition between the two propositions contained in it. And whose "identity" is meant—the deceased's or the survivor's?

What I am trying to pinpoint here is not the author's putative lack of logical rigor—after all, *November-Rose* is not a work of analytical geometry—but the fact that discourse, the tangled skein of ever-flowing speech and thought, possesses the miraculous ability to create and make perfect sense—conceptually, intuitively—by dint of certain *mots justes*, even though, logically speaking, the construction may appear somewhat wobbly or jarring. And while we remain in discourse's natural habitat, as it were—its mother tongue, say—these ostensible fissures in logic remain virtually unnoticeable and undetectable within the varied force field—ethical, intuitive, psychological, emotional—of "native sense." As soon as we try to transplant the latter onto new soil, however, it seems to disperse, no longer held together by the gravitational pull of its native planet.

Now, this surely is the situation most translators find themselves in: they are presented with a finished, often already published, work and have to deal with it—with its inconsistencies, logical solecisms, and so on. Whatever doesn't seem to make sense in the original upon the translator's repeated "re-accentuating" prodding must be made to make sense one way or another in the target language, must pass muster before the target language's editorial eye. The original, though, will perforce remain the metric with few exceptions, obviously—afforded, for instance, by the translator's own literary standing, as in the case of Paul Celan's unfaithful Mandel'shtam translations, Don Paterson's versions of Rilke, or Nabokov's notoriously literal rendering of Pushkin's *Evgeny Onegin*.

Not so in the case of *November-Rose*, however: for the original that I received had neither been published nor was it complete in the strict sense, as I had been asked to read and critique it before it would be revised, edited, and finalized. Thus, both the author of the "original" and I found ourselves in an interesting situation: since quandaries such as the ones mentioned above would frequently emerge, what happened in the process of translation was that both translation and original would be revisited and, if need be, rewritten with every new provisionally final version of either translation or original. To offer only one example: in the final versions of both books—*November Rose: Eine Rede über den Tod* and *November Rose: A Speech on Death*—the second of the above-mentioned passages reads: "Der Tod eines geliebten Menschen ist ein Erdbeben, dessen Epizentrum im Allerinnersten unserer Identität liegt und auf alle ihre Bereiche übergreift."—"The death of a beloved person is an earthquake whose epicenter lies buried deep within the innermost recesses of our selves. It cannot but impact all regions of our identity."[15] In other words, not only did the translation in and of itself constitute the most palpable "re-accentuation" of the original, but the latter in turn revealed itself as a retroactive or reverse "re-accentuation" of its own translational "re-accentuation." The "original" had become as much of a reverse "translation" of its own translation as the latter was a "true" translation of the "original," while the translation had molted into a kind of new "original" in its own right.

5. Copyright "Re-Accentuated"

During the process of translation, the author of the "original" and I realized that something had happened to the very concept of the "original," the German version's chronological-substantive anteriority notwithstanding: which of the two final texts—both of which had come into being hand in hand, in parallel fashion, and in a process of constant mutual "re-accentuation"—were we to consider the final "original" when it came to submitting the book to the United States Copyright Office for copyright protection? The book, the author and I felt, had been written in two languages simultaneously, and as such, both versions, the "original" and the translation, were originals, that is, each version was an original in its own right. And that is how we decided to copyright the book, by way of two originals written by the same author under the same title in two different languages.

We contacted the Copyright Office and filed all of the required forms for copyright registration, including the manuscripts of the two books as originals. Months passed before we heard back from the Copyright Office. Instead of the expected copyright certificates, however, the materials were returned to us: we could not file two originals of the same book by the same author. We contacted the Copyright Office again to inquire what was wrong. We explained to the copyright officer assigned to our registration case that the author considered both versions originals and would like to copyright both as such and under her name. We were told that this was impossible, as one of the books had to have been written first. We explained to the officer that while this may certainly be the case in general, in this particular instance, although there had been an initial manuscript that had provided the matrix for the entire endeavor, the copyright versions were to be considered true originals, each in its in its own right, rather than original and translation, respectively, and that, in any case, both ought to be copyrighted in the original author's name.

To cut a long story short, there *was* one way of doing what we had in mind—albeit with a minor concession: both books *could* in principle be copyrighted as originals in the author's name; however, we would have to choose which of the two to bill as the original and which as the translation (the Copyright Office didn't care about that), and we would have to provide proof of transfer of rights to the effect that the translator relinquished their de facto and de jure rights to the translation—it being up to us which of the two versions to consider such—if either version was to be deemed the "original." The reason provided: there can only be *one* original.

What is remarkable about this incident is that it reveals the ostensible contingency of originality, discursive axiological precedence, and, thus, of the very distinction between "accentuation" and "re-accentuation," more generally. We were given the option to decide which of the two texts should count as the original and which as its "re-accentuation"; which of the two should be declared the native, primordially "accentuated" creation, and which the "re-accentuated," derivative artifice, so to speak. For someone like me, who has always been critical of the very concept of a single, "original" language, as tacitly bespoken, for instance, by the notion of the "mother tongue" and the concomitant assumption of our ingrained, fundamental ontological monolingualism—the idea, that is, that however many languages we speak, there is only one that we truly speak *as* our native, "original" language—this was an astonishing event. For didn't the copyright officer flout the very notion of linguistic precedence based on ontology in translating it into the realm pure pragmatics? Not only did the disjunction between "original" and translation, between "accentuation" and "re-accentuation," forfeit its ontological valence, but the very notion that certain speech acts ontologically-axiologically trump others seemed to implode.

Certainly ignorant of state-of-the-art literary and translation theory, or the flights of post-structuralism, the copyright officer intuitively came down on the side of deconstruction: for once a decision as to textual precedence would have been made, an "original" would have come into being, an "origin" established—as a matter of convention and agreement alone. Until such time, however, a moment of perfect undecidability and discursive freedom could be savored—a space in which speech could emerge simultaneously in several tongues without being branded by the mark of Babel. All of which can also be said to have epitomized and vindicated—in the most concrete terms—the accuracy and veracity of Bakhtin's view that "re-accentuation" is an "interminable social-ideological process," whose temporary termination can only be a matter of contingent pragmatic convention or necessity, that is, of the given contextual strictures of real-life utterances, whatever they may be—for which someone must, presumably, become answerable. Together, moreover, the two "originals," that is, mutual translations or "re-accentuations" of *November Rose*, vividly embodied and articulated what Bakhtin considers the irreducible "hetero-" and "poly-glossia" as well as "polyphony" of the "interminable socio-ideological process" of "re-accentuation."[16] Indeed, as an intrinsically and inherently dual or compound, internally "re-accentuated" utterance, *November Rose* can be said to constitute the very epitome of both the "polyphony" of "re-accentuation" and the "re-accentuation" of "polyphony."

Notes

1. Valentin. N. Voloshinov, *Marksizm i filosofiya yazyka* [1929] (Moscow: Labirint, 1993), 26–8, 144, 169; Mikhail M. Bakhtin, *Slovo v romane* (1934–5), in *Voprosy literatury i estetiki: issledovaniia raznykh let* (Moscow: Khudozhestvennaia literatura, 1975), 101, 103–4, 110, 219–21, 228–33; Bakhtin, *Epos i roman (O metodologii issledovaniya romana)* [1941], in *Literaturno-kriticheskie stat'i*, ed. Sergey G. Bocharov and Vadim V. Kozhinov (Moscow: Khudozhestvennaia literatura, 1986), 394; Bakhtin, *Iz predistorii romannogo slova* [1940], in *Literaturno-kriticheskie stat'i*, ed. Sergey G. Bocharov and Vadim V. Kozhinov (Moscow: Khudozhestvennaia literatura, 1986), 372, 383–4. Throughout this essay all translations are my own unless otherwise stated.
2. Voloshinov, *Marksizm i filosofiya yazyka*, 26, 144, 169; Bakhtin, *Iz predistorii romannogo slova*, 272, 383–4; Bakhtin, *Slovo v romane*, 219.
3. David Hume, *A Treatise on Human Nature*, 3 vols. [1739–40] (Oxford: Clarendon Press, 1888), vol. 3, I, 1, 469: "I am surpriz'd to find, that instead of the usual copulations of propositions, *is*, and *is not*, I meet with no proposition that is not connected with an *ought*, or an *ought not*. This change is imperceptible; but is, however, of the last consequence. For as this *ought*, or *ought not*, expresses some new relation or affirmation, 'tis necessary that it should be ... explain'd ... that reason should be given, for what seems altogether inconceivable, how this new relation could be a deduction from others, which are entirely different from it" (emphasis in original)
4. Bakhtin, *Slovo v romane*, 219–21, 228–32; Bakhtin, *Epos i roman (O metodologii issledovaniya romana)*, 394.
5. Friedrich Nietzsche, *Zur Genealogie der Moral: Eine Streitschrift* (Leipzig: Naumann, 1887), III, §12.
6. Bakhtin, *Slovo v romane*, 232.
7. Ibid.
8. On intra- and interlingual as well as intersemiotic translation, see Roman Jakobson, "On Linguistic Aspects of Translation," in *Language in Literature*, ed. Krystyna Pomorska and Stephen Rudy (Cambridge, MA: Belknap Press, 1987), 429; on interpersonal, intra- and intermental translation (which occurs, for instance, in everyday dialogue, any and all

acts of understanding, as well as more complex forms of scientific and spiritual-emotional communication), see ibid.; Bakhtin, *Estetika slovesnogo tvorchestva*, ed. Sergey G. Bocharov (Moscow: Iskusstvo, 1979), 7–180; Lev Petrovich Yakubinsky, "O dialogicheskoy rechi" [1923], in *Izbrannye raboty: Yazyk i ego funktsionirovanie*, ed. A. A. Leont'ev (Moscow: "Nauka," 1986), 17–82; Michael Eskin, *Ethics and Dialogue in the Works of Levinas, Bakhtin, Mandel'shtam, and Celan* (Oxford: Oxford University Press, 2000), 87–92.

9. Voloshinov, *Marksizm i filosofiya yazyka*, 114–15; Yakubinsky, "O dialogicheskoy rechi," 29.
10. Thomas Hardy, *The Collected Poems of Thomas Hardy*, ed. Michael Irwin (Ware, Hertfordshire: Wordsworth Editions, 2002), 288; Simon Armitage, "The Convergence of the Twain" (2002; https://simonarmitage.typepad.com/homepage/2005/11/convergence_of_.html). For reasons of spatial economy and copyright, I dispense with quoting either poem in full, contenting myself with the sense that my remarks concerning "re-accentuation," as it applies to Armitage's recourse to Hardy, will be sufficiently clear as is.
11. Bakhtin, *Slovo v romane*, 106. Even the unprecedented neologism or nonce word—ostensibly, the only exceptions to Bakhtin's rule—will have been constructed from materials (phonemes, morphemes, graphemes) that will have always already been used and articulated by others.
12. In a letter to the author dated November 13, 2007.
13. Kathrin Stengel, *November-Rose: Eine Rede über den Tod* (New York: Upper West Side Philosophers, 2007), 15; Kathrin Stengel, *November Rose. A Speech on Death*, trans. Michael Eskin (New York: Upper West Side Philosophers, 2007), 15.
14. Martin Heidegger, "Brief über den Humanismus" [1946], in *Wegmarken* (Frankfurt am Main: Klostermann, 1976), 328.
15. Stengel, *November-Rose*, 16; Stengel, *November Rose*, 16.
16. According to Bakhtin, the "interminable socio-ideological process" of "re-accentuation" cannot but unfold—across the spectrum of what he calls "primary" and "secondary speech genres" (from everyday speech to the most complex works of art, literature, and science)—in and through the interface of the "diversity of speech" ("raznorechie"), the "diversity of languages" ("raznoyazychie"), and the "diversity of voices" ("raznogolositsa"), which dynamic as a whole is tersely captured in Bakhtin's master concept of "polyphony." For Bakhtin's discussion of "speech genres," "polyphony," "raznorechie," "raznoyazychie," and "raznogolositsa," see *Problema rechevykh zhanrov* [1952–3], in *Literaturno-kriticheskie stat'i*, 428–72; Bakhtin, *Problemy poetiki/ tvorchestva Dostoevskogo* [1929–63], ed. Oleg V. Garun (Kiev: Next, 1994), 26, 31, 122, 184, 220, 226, 238–42; Bakhtin, *Slovo v romane*, 75–6, 78. For a discussion of "polyphony" as encapsulating the intertwinement

of "raznorechie," "raznoyazychie," and "raznogolositsa," see Eskin, *Ethics and Dialogue in the Works of Levinas, Bakhtin, Mandel'shtam, and Celan*, 102–3.

Bibliography

Armitage, Simon. "The Convergence of the Twain" (2002). https://simonarmitage.typepad.com/homepage/2005/11/convergence_of_.html. Accessed April 25, 2022.

Bakhtin, Mikhail M. *Epos i roman (O metodologii issledovaniya romana)* [1941]. In *Literaturno-kriticheskie stat'i*. Edited by Sergey G. Bocharov and Vadim V. Kozhinov, 392–428. Moscow: Khudozhestvennaia literatura, 1986.

Bakhtin, Mikhail M. *Estetika slovesnogo tvorchestva*. Edited by Sergey G. Bocharov. Moscow: Iskusstvo, 1979.

Bakhtin, Mikhail M. *Iz predistorii romannogo slova* [1940]. In *Literaturno-kriticheskie stat'i*. Edited by Sergey G. Bocharov and Vadim V. Kozhinov, 353–91. Moscow: Khudozhestvennaia literatura, 1986.

Bakhtin, Mikhail M. *Literaturno-kriticheskie stat'i*. Edited by Sergey G. Bocharov and Vadim V. Kozhinov. Moscow: Khudozhestvennaia literatura, 1986.

Bakhtin, Mikhail M. *Problema rechevykh zhanrov* [1952-3]. In *Literaturno-kriticheskie stat'i*. Edited by Sergey G. Bocharov and Vadim V. Kozhinov, 428–72. Moscow: Khudozhestvennaia literatura, 1986.

Bakhtin, Mikhail M. *Problemy poetiki/tvorchestva Dostoevskogo* [1929–63]. Edited by Oleg V. Garun. Kiev: Next, 1994.

Bakhtin, Mikhail M. *Slovo v romane* [1934–5]. In *Voprosy literatury i estetiki: issledovaniia raznykh let*, 72–233. Moscow: Khudozhestvennaia literatura, 1975.

Bakhtin, Mikhail M. *Voprosy literatury i estetiki: issledovaniia raznykh let*. Moscow: Khudozhestvennaia literatura, 1975.

Eskin, Michael. *Ethics and Dialogue in the Works of Levinas, Bakhtin, Mandel'shtam, and Celan*. Oxford: Oxford University Press, 2000.

Hardy, Thomas. *The Collected Poems of Thomas Hardy*. Edited by Michael Irwin. Ware, Hertfordshire: Wordsworth Editions, 2002.

Heidegger, Martin. "Brief über den Humanismus" [1946]. In *Wegmarken*, 313–64. Frankfurt am Main: Klostermann, 1976.

Hume, David. *A Treatise on Human Nature*, 3 vols. [1739–40]. Oxford: Clarendon Press, 1888.

Jakobson, Roman. "On Linguistic Aspects of Translation." In *Language in Literature*. Edited by Krystyna Pomorska and Stephen Rudy, 428–35. Cambridge, MA: Belknap Press, 1987.

Nietzsche, Friedrich. *Zur Genealogie der Moral: Eine Streitschrift*. Leipzig: Naumann, 1887.

Stengel, Kathrin. *November Rose: A Speech on Death*. Translated by Michael Eskin. New York: Upper West Side Philosophers, 2007.

Stengel, Kathrin. *November-Rose: Eine Rede über den Tod*. New York: Upper West Side Philosophers, 2007.

Voloshinov, Valentin. N. *Marksizm i filosofiya yazyka* [1929]. Moscow: Labirint, 1993.

Yakubinsky, Lev Petrovich. "O dialogicheskoy rechi" [1923]. In *Izbrannye raboty: Yazyk i ego funktsionirovanie*. Edited by A. A. Leont'ev, 17–82. Moscow: "Nauka," 1986.

5

A Study of Three Scarletts:
The Homeopathic Effect of Role Language

Yumi Tanaka

1. Role Languages in Translations of *Gone with the Wind*

In the latter half of the 2010s, Margaret Mitchell's *Gone with the Wind* (1936) was extraordinarily prominent in Japan. Following the 2009 expiration of Mitchell's copyright in Japan,[1] there was a renewed interest in her most famous novel, which led to the publication of two new and unabridged Japanese translations in 2015. The first was the work of Konomi Ara, a scholar of American culture and professor emeritus at Tokyo University of Foreign Studies. Her Japanese rendition of the original is both scholarly and informative. The other was from Yukiko Konosu, an experienced literary translator. It is a more ornate, but also very accessible translation of Mitchell's novel. In 2018, Mariko Hayashi, a well-known novelist and essayist, began serializing a first-person retelling of the original story, titled *I Am Scarlett* in *Qui La La*, a monthly literary magazine. Hayashi's Scarlett recounts the famous episodes from the original narrative in a straightforward, casual language. I will show how these three Japanese translations "re-accentuate" the conflict between Scarlett's instinctive nature and the disciplined self in the cultural tradition of the American South by analyzing the language used to characterize and describe Scarlett and her world and by considering what is added in each translation. According to Mikhail Bakhtin, "new images in literature are very often created through a re-accentuating of old images, by translating them from one accentual register to another."[2] Ara's, Konosu's, and Hayashi's linguistic choices and the exercise of translator's prerogative present different shades of Scarlett's emotions and morality as a Southern woman and reveal the influence of language on meaning.

My analysis of the re-accentuation of *Gone with the Wind* focuses on Scarlett's language as well as the language used by black characters in the three translations. Ara, Konosu, and Hayashi use a special "feminine" language for

Scarlett's speech. Ara and Konosu translate the speech of black characters into non-standard Japanese while Hayashi uses standard Japanese. Both Scarlett's feminine language and the nonstandard Japanese language of the black characters are fictional and stereotypical languages that are common in Japanese popular culture. Known as "role languages," they are defined by Satoshi Kinsui as "sets of spoken language features (e.g. vocabulary and grammar) and phonetic characteristics (e.g. intonation and accent patterns) associated with particular character types."[3] An important element of role language is its fictional nature; actual Japanese people do not use it even if it derives from actual languages and dialects. Almost nobody uses or hears role languages in real life, but the virtual role languages "instantly convey the image of the user to the recipient."[4] Another significant feature of a role language is the high frequency of its association with minor or marginalized characters, while protagonists almost always speak standard Japanese. It seems that "the knowledge of role languages ... allows prejudice and discrimination to naturally emerge."[5] Scarlett's particularly feminine language and the rural language of black characters in the translations "instantly conveys the image of the user to the recipient," namely, Japanese readers. As the Japanese versions of Scarlett and the black characters are represented by role languages, readers automatically connect them to specific archetypes—in this case an upper-class woman, and uneducated and marginalized people, respectively. It is important to question such a dependence on role languages when representing characters in translations since "prejudice and discrimination" can be and often is reproduced through those means.

 Gone with the Wind, the source text of the three contemporary texts is full of stereotypical representations of women and African Americans, and romanticizes the American antebellum South, which rested on a foundation of slavery and the repression of women's individuality. Especially after the emergence of the Black Lives Matter movement,[6] we cannot help but see in Mitchell's novel and its film version "the ongoing, painful patterns of racial injustice and disregard for Black lives" and acknowledge the need to approach the original as an opportunity "for examining expressions of White supremacy in popular culture."[7] How do the three translations communicate the racial and gender-related problems of representation to people who do not have enough knowledge about the historical context of the novel? Should a translator use role languages to suggest the racist undertones of the source text? Or should a translator avoid role languages in an effort to erase the problematic original representations of gender and racial difference and accentuate other elements that can be appealing to people in a totally different culture? I will show how each translation addresses these issues by investigating its relationship to role languages and its translator's intervention in Michell's text. This case study is a unique version of the "afterlife"[8] of *Gone with the Wind* in Japan—a linguistically, historically, and geographically different place from the American South.

2. The Re-accentuation of Black Characters in Japanese Translations of *Gone with the Wind*

Prior to the appearance of the three translations above, Yasuo Okubo, a famous and prolific translator, created the first unabridged Japanese translation of *Gone with the Wind* in 1938. In the same year, Seisaku Fukazawa published another translation of the first volume of Mitchell's novel. In 1939, Tomoji Abe and Kunio Fujiwara each offered an abridged translation of the novel to Japanese readers. Considering that Mitchell published the original work in 1936, this prompt reaction and deep interest in *Gone with Wind* is remarkable. After the World War II, Okubo's translation was revised by Michinosuke Takeuchi, whose very popular version provided many people with easier access to Mitchell's novel. This revised edition of Okubo as well as Takeuchi's translation dominated the market in Japan until 2015 when Ara's and Konosu's translations were published at almost the same time.

Linguists and anthropologists have problematized Okubo and Takeuchi's usage of rural language, a stereotypical and fictional language reserved for black characters in the translation. Okubo and Takeuchi chose a role language similar to the dialects used by people from the Tohoku region when they translated the speech of Mitchell's African American characters. The "pseudo-Tohoku dialect"[9] is a fictional language mainly based on real Tohoku dialects; a hodgepodge of uncertain dialects, it has been conventionally utilized in popular culture to indicate the origin and the social position of a specific type of character. In this case, the pseudo-Tohoku dialect suggests the lower social standing of the black characters. For comparison, the main white characters speak in standard Japanese in this version. Okubo and Takeuchi's translation, then, presents a clear example of the application of "regional speaker types"[10] of role language to black characters. Miyako Inoue points out that Mammy and other African American characters speak an "unspecified 'regional dialect,'"[11] which emphasizes their marginalized identity. Mie Hiramoto shows that "neither the slaves nor the poor whites use SJ [Standard Japanese]" and demonstrates "the ways in which their speech is modeled after, without actually accurately portraying, the stigmatized Japanese dialect TB [Tohoku-ben, the dialect of Tohoku region]."[12] The use of fictional language imprecisely associates Tohoku dialects with the language of marginalized and discriminated people, leading to the emergence of the idea of the inferiority of the Tohoku dialect in regard to standard Japanese.

Fictional nonstandard Japanese still functions as an indicator of the marginalized position of black characters in Ara's translation.[13] According to Shigeko Kumagai, the language of enslaved workers in Ara's version is a compound of multiple dialects not only from the Tohoku region but also from western Japan. Kumagai also points out Ara's frequent addition of double consonants and many instances of voiced consonants, which ensures that Japanese readers identify the language of black characters as nonstandard.[14] Ara, who has substantial scholarly knowledge about enslavement in the South and the historical and social position of black people through the centuries, depends on the effects of the stereotypical role language to show to Japanese readers Mitchell's representation of the enslaved by the use of eye dialect[15] and ungrammatical English. If, as Kumagai suggests, Ara's language choice for black characters is a hodgepodge of various dialects and artificial phonetic changes, its lack of grounding in reality, which is a counterpart to Mitchell's stereotypical and racist descriptions of black characters, accomplishes its goals without disrespecting dialects associated with a specific region, such as Tohoku dialects. Still, Ara's use of this language for black characters relies upon the hierarchy between standard Japanese and various existing dialects.

Konosu uses role language much less than Ara does, but she almost always assigns the language to Prissy. Hayashi, meanwhile, does not use role language associated with certain dialects or wrong grammar at all. Black characters speak in deferential and honorific language when addressing white people, which clearly suggests the former's social class position, whereas both black and white characters use standard Japanese, which makes the marginality of black characters less visible.

The language of Scarlett O'Hara is also affected by cultural norms. According to Nakamura, the words spoken by women in the West tend to be translated in "women's" or "feminine" language, making Okubo and Takeuchi's translation of Scarlett's parlance a typical example of this phenomenon.[16] Women's language is characterized mainly by particular first-person pronouns such as "atai," "watakushi," and "wachiki," and sentence-final particles such as "teyo," "asobase," and "wa." Some interjections, including "ara" and "mā," also indicate that the speaker identifies him or herself as a woman.[17] Furthermore, Inoue compares Mammy's "ungrammatical," "no gender-based," and "dialectical" speech style to Scarlett's and Melanie's "grammatical" and "feminine" one, showing that black characters are not allowed to use "'gendered'—and grammatically acceptable—speech," thus confirming the equivalence of middle-class (or, aristocratic) status and whiteness (and heterosexuality).[18] Nakamura's and Inoue's arguments are mainly based on their analyses of the sentence-final particles of Scarlett's language in the Okubo/Takeuchi translation. Women's language is divided into some subcategories, such as language linked with women from a good family, rich married women, prostitutes, and so on. Scarlett's language is classified as a language conventionally associated with women from a good family, which is marked especially by characteristic final particles, such as "kashira," "koto," and "te (teyo)."[19] Again, the most important and interesting point about role languages is that they are rarely used by actual people. Scarlett's feminine language and the African American characters' pseudo-Tohoku dialects are not real in the sense that they only exist in novels, movies, animations, and other popular media. In other words, the women's language of characters like Scarlett O'Hara is marked by fictionality and convention, which dominate Japanese popular culture. I will refer to this kind of role language as a "lady's language" in this argument.

What about the three contemporary Scarletts in Ara's, Konosu's, and Hayashi's translations? All three speak both in a lady's language and in nongendered and actual language, which can be used by real living women. Hayashi's Scarlett, for example, uses the kind of arrogant or assertive language one can hear from both Japanese men and women today. The balance between the "lady's language" and the nongendered contemporary languages varies. Nakamura's and Inoue's investigations interpret final particles to be an indicator of role language, including women's language and pseudo-Tohoku dialects, but other elements also play important roles in Scarlett's characterization as a unique Southern woman in each translation.

3. Three Different Approaches to Scarlett

When observing Scarlett's languages in the three translations from the perspective of role language, we find that her language is a hybrid of lady's language and a more casual and sometimes arrogant language, which portrays the struggle between Scarlett's vibrant and practical nature and her identity as a Southern belle.[20] Scarlett is not a typical Southern beauty. As Eve Kosofsky Sedgwick has pointed out, *Gone with the Wind* "has most resonantly thematized for successive generations of American women the constraints of the 'feminine' role, the obstacles to and the ravenous urgency of female ambition, the importance of the economic motive, the compulsiveness and destructiveness of romantic love, and ... the centrality and the total alienation of female sexuality."[21] Even though the novel's problematization of women's traditional gender roles has its limitations within white bourgeois feminism, "in the life of Scarlett O'Hara, it is expressly clear that to be born female is to be defined entirely in relation to the role of 'lady,' a role that does take its shape and meaning from a sexuality of which she is not the subject but the object."[22] Sedgwick continues that "for Scarlett, to survive as a woman does mean learning to see sexuality, male power domination, and her traditional gender role as all meaning the same dangerous thing. To ... learn to manipulate them from behind a screen as objects of pure signifiers, as men do, is the numbing but effective lesson of her life."[23] In *Between Men*, Sedgwick posits that to enable her economic survival Scarlett must always negotiate with her own sexuality, men's domination, and her expected role as a Southern lady. The differences in Scarlett's languages in the three Japanese translations reveal how they each render this negotiation.

Ara's, Konosu's, and Hayashi's unique renditions of the heroine's language demonstrate that their attitudes toward Scarlett's multifaceted struggle are different. A comparison of three examples from the three translations exemplifies the difference. In chapter 19, Rhett Butler reveals his intention to have Scarlett as his mistress rather than his wife. Upon hearing this offensive offer, Scarlett struggles between two split selves as a lower-class woman, which is associated with her Irish-ness, and a properly disciplined Southern lady. Scarlett analyzes her feelings internally before she actually responds to Butler's offer:

> "Dear," he said quietly, "I am complimenting your intelligence by asking you to be my mistress without having first seduced you."
>
> Mistress!
>
> Her mind shouted the word, shouted that she had been vilely insulted. But in that first startled moment she did not feel insulted. She only felt a furious surge of indignation that he should think her such a fool. He must think her a fool if he offered her a proposition like that, instead of the proposal of matrimony she had been expecting. Rage, punctured vanity, and disappointment threw her mind into turmoil and, before she even thought of the high moral grounds on which she should upbraid him, she blurted out the first words, which came to her lips. They were as follows:
>
> "Mistress! What would I get out of that except a passel of brats?" And then her jaw dropped in horror as she realized what she had said.[24]

The description of Scarlett's emotional response suggests that Scarlett's "rage" was more powerful than "the high moral grounds," which should have led her to "feel insulted" and to "upbraid" Butler. However, "rage punctured vanity and this appointment" forces Scarlett to mention "a passel of brats," a presumed effect of her sexual relationship with Butler, which reveals her sexuality and her expectation of a physical relationship. In addition, the choice of the informal word "passel" is an indication of Scarlett's descent to lower class, which is rooted in her Irish heritage. At the same time, Scarlett attempts to resist "male power dominance" as she realizes that Butler is simply trying to see if she is enough of a fool to accept the position of his mistress, an inappropriate role for a Southern lady. Thus, Scarlett finds herself in the middle of a struggle between her "sexuality, male power domination, and her traditional gender role."

The implied conflict between the enslaving upper class and the lower class emerges within the hybridity of a lady's language and a more casual language utilized in the three modern Japanese translations. Casual language refers to a language that is informal and used by real living people in everyday life, while lady's language is a role language, rarely used by people identifying themselves as women. In conveying Scarlett's criticism of Butler's arrogance and depravity in offering her the position of mistress, all three translators use the same sentence-final particle for Scarlett's words, which is associated with a lady's language: "Aijin desutte!" (You said mistress!) This sentence-final particle suggests that she was raised as a woman in a white, enslaving, high society and that her upbringing obliged her to find Butler's proposal morally repugnant. The three translations point to Scarlett's class consciousness and gender role with different balances between these language uses. Compare the translations of what Scarlett actually says and her response to her own totally inappropriate blunder as a Southern lady:

Ara's translation:

"<u>Aijin desutte</u>! [Mistress + sentence-final particle of lady's language] Aijin ni natte chibitachi wo zorozoro umutteiuno?" sou itta atode, kuchibasitta kotono nakamini kizuki, osoroshikunatte shitawo muita.²⁵

("You said mistress! Do you mean that I'll make a bunch of little brats with you?" After she said so, she realized what she said and it terrified her. She dropped her head.)

Konosu's translation:

"<u>Aijin desutte</u>! [Mistress + sentence-final particle of lady's language] Aijin nante, kodomo wo zorozoro unde oshimai jyanaino!" itte shimatte kara kizuite zotto shi, omowazu kuchi wo pokan to aketa.²⁶

("You said mistress! If I become your mistress, I'll just have a bunch of children, and that's it!" After she said so, she shuddered with what she has just said, and she gaped at it.)

Hayashi's translation:

"<u>Aijin, aijin desutte</u>! [Mistress, Mistress, sentence-final particle of lady's language] Aijin nante beddo no ue no kotoni hagende, gaki wo zorozoro umunoga shigoto jyanaino! Fuzakenna!" Watashi wa ittai naniwo itteruno. Konna kitanai kotobawo ikura kitanai otoko nidemo kuchini surunante.[27]

("Mistress, you said mistress! A mistress's job is just getting busy in bed and making a bunch of brats! Don't be silly!" What on earth am I saying? What I said was too filthy even for such a nasty man.)

Ara's translation of Scarlett's speech emphasizes her traditional gender role as a respectable Southern woman. After her fury breaks out in the first two words of the utterance, Scarlett's lady's language temporarily disappears. Her language is real, the kind that can be heard in the streets. Ara's choice of words for "brats" is "little tots," which does not connote badly behaved children and means just youth and physical smallness. Scarlett's choice of the word "brats" suggests that she does not have the requisite affection for children a proper Southern lady would have. In this context, children are important only as a potentially visible expression of her sexual relationship with Butler—a forbidden topic in the polite society of America's antebellum South. Scarlett is shocked and ashamed at what comes out of her mouth. Ara uses a translator's creative prerogative when she translates "her jaw dropped in horror" into a physical response of dropping her head, an indication of serious regret and shame. Ara's Scarlett regrets her words more deeply than Mitchell's Scarlett, who is surprised by her own words. Ara's translation evokes a more conservative Scarlett influenced by the rules of self-discipline she has learned from her mother and Mammy.

Another important aspect of Ara's translation involves the great effort she makes to reveal to the Japanese reader the historical and cultural context of *Gone with the Wind*. Ara's six-volume translation is full of notes about the cultural and historical background of the South, and each volume contains a long "translator's commentary." This translation attempts to encapsulate not only Mitchell's fictional drama but also a scholarly introduction to the culture, society, and history of the South. Within this context, Scarlett emerges as a representation of the typical Southern woman even if her character on occasion goes against the stereotype. Ara's translation tends to put more emphasis on Scarlett's ties with Southern tradition than her individuality. At the end of chapter 9, Mitchell describes Scarlett as "a delicately nurtured Southern belle with her Irish up."[28] Ara translates this expression by adding more to the original meaning and using an old-fashioned and idiomatic metaphor:

> Onbahigasa de sodaterareta [Brought up by a wet nurse and protected by a sunshade] nanbu bijyo ni airurandojin kishitsu ga hisondeiru.[29]

Ara's translation of "delicately nurtured" into "brought up by a wet nurse and protected by sunshade" (onbahigasa de sodaterareta) is appropriate since Mammy, who raised Scarlett, always made her protect her white skin. The idiomatic Japanese expression actually connotes overprotection. Konosu, for example, translates "a delicately nurtured Southern belle" simply into "a well-bred Southern beauty" (osodachi no yoi nanbu bijin).[30] Ara discusses Scarlett's "marked personality,"[31] which distinguishes Scarlett from the traditional gender role, but she provides additional information about the Southern tradition of both subjugating women and placing them on a pedestal, and suggests Scarlett was nurtured in that context. On the whole, Ara's translation foregrounds Scarlett as a Southern lady, and her individualized and passionate personality associated with Irish-ness is more controlled and balanced by the lady's language and the detailed information about Southern culture.

Compared to Ara's translation with its extensive background information, Konosu's (an independent translator with abundant experience of translating mainly contemporary literary works by the likes of Margaret Atwood, J. M. Coetzee, etc.) shows a more intuitive Scarlett, surrounded by the romantically aristocratic world of the South.[32] Konosu emphasizes the contrast between the sensuous language connected with Scarlett's emotions and the classical vocabulary associated with the higher society of the South and its cultivated literary tradition. Konosu's Scarlett first responds to Butler's offer in a lady's role language, but her following reaction is described with more casual and onomatopoeic expressions. Konosu uses two onomatopoeias: "zotto" (shuddered) for "in horror" and "pokan" (gaped) for "dropped." The two onomatopoeias are words phonetically mimicking Scarlett's feeling (horror) and physical condition (gaping), which do not produce any actual sounds but conventionally help most Japanese people imagine specific emotional and physical states. Yukio Mishima points out frequent use of onomatopoeia in children's literature and women's writing, and suggests that "women's writers' skillful onomatopoeia communicates to the reader a sensuous and concrete world unique to women."[33] Masahiro Ono criticizes Mishima's stereotypical understanding of onomatopoeias,[34] underscoring, instead, that onomatopoeias are "an indispensable thing when you express physical and mental senses."[35] When Mitchell uses lower-class language like "a passel of brats," Konosu deploys onomatopoeias to capture Scarlett's emotional confusion vividly and to suggest a childish and instinctive response to Butler's words. Ultimately Scarlett's emotional, naïve character is highlighted more than her effort to show Butler the disciplined morality she has learned from her mother and Mammy.

Another characteristic of Konosu's translation is her choice of bookish vocabulary even for ordinary words in Mitchell's writing:

> In her face were too sharply blended the delicate features of her mother, a Coast aristocrat of French descent, and the heavy ones of her florid Irish father. But it was an arresting face, pointed of chin, square of jaw. Her eyes were pale green without a touch of hazel, starred with bristly black lashes and slightly tilted at the ends.[36]

> Sono <u>kanbase</u> [a literary word for face] ni wa, furansukei no kaigankizoku dearu haha no sensaina mehanadachi to, airurandojin dearu akaragao no chichi no <u>zousaku</u> [a literary word for features] ga, azayakani majiriatte iru.

> Towaie, ago no sen wa kukkirito kakuhari, <u>otogai</u> [a literary word of chin] nikakete sutto togatta rinkaku, kanari mewohiku kawodachidearu. Hitomi wa chairomi no nai <u>asamidori</u> [light green, using a literary and non-standard Chinese character for green] de, sikkaritoshita kuroi matsugeni fuchidorare, kokoromochi tsuriagatteita.[37]

> (In her face, delicate features of her mother coming from the seashore aristocrat of French descent and different features of her Irish florid father are vividly blended. The line of her jaw is clearly angular, and the chin is pointed; the features are very distinguished. The pupils are light green without any brownish part, and lined by thick and black eyelashes, which slightly turn up at the ends.)

Konosu uses "kanbase," an archaic word for "face," and "zousaku," a formal word for "features." She also chose "otogai," a literary word for "chin." These classic words evoke an idealized and refined world. Konosu's semantic choices underscore her efforts to represent nostalgia for an elegant world that has already completely disappeared. Scarlett's energetic character is set against romantic but antiquated scenery. Also, the contrast between the delicate features of Scarlett's mother's French ancestry and the heavy features of her Irish blood is removed, and only the mention of her delicate features remains in the translation, excluding the racial element from this passage.

The narrative prologue to the film version of *Gone with the Wind* has been criticized for its complete romanticization of the lost antebellum South founded by "Knights and Ladies Fair" and "Master and Slave."[38] Similarly problematic, Konosu's translation, with its classical and refined tone, invites readers to an idealized Southern world, whose superficial beauty ignores the harsh reality of slavery and racism. In addition, as previously mentioned, Konosu reserves the role language for black slaves only for Prissy. The reduced use of lower-class language also contributes to building an idealized world of the South.

Finally, I will discuss Mariko Hayashi's *I Am Scarlett*, a version of *Gone with the Wind* told both in the voice of Scarlett and from her point of view. Hayashi started her career as a copy writer. In 1982, she published *After Buying a Happy Mood, Let's Go Home* (Run run wo katte ouchi ni kaerou), her first collection of essays on women's desire for a thinner and good-looking body, a nice boyfriend as a future husband, and money. She became a best-selling writer and was awarded the Naoki prize, a prestigious award for popular literature, before becoming an independent novelist and essayist. She retells the story of *Gone with the Wind* based on the translation by Mari Sekiguchi and Hiroko Doi, who are credited as translation collaborators.

In contrast to Ara's and Konosu's translations, Hayashi's omits notes or background about the American South in her first-person re-accentuation of *Gone with the Wind*. Hayashi's translation portrays Scarlett's emotion more directly, using much more straightforward and aggressive language. Hayashi's Scarlett speaks and thinks in a lady's language, but a considerable part of her monologue is not characterized by the specific first-person articles and sentence-final particles typical of this kind of verbal expression. When Butler offers her the position of his mistress, Scarlett repeats "mistress," an unacceptable and vulgar word, twice, which emphasizes her emotionally charged response, but in her version, the term has acquired the sentence-final particle associated with a lady's role language. This indication of Scarlett's lady-like qualities, however, vanishes soon. Scarlett then directly mentions the result of what she is going to do "on the bed" with Butler, if she is to accept the position of his mistress. Her choice of the vulgar word "gaki" (brats or imps) for children reminds us of Scarlett's general indifference to children, including her own, which sets her apart from the morality of Sothern ladies. Scarlett's verbal response to Butler's impolite offer ends with an angry outburst: "Don't be silly!" ("Fuzakennna!"); this term implies a surprising expression of un-ladylike assertiveness.

Hayashi also adds a detailed description to the original scene of Melanie's delivery. In this interpretation, Scarlett reveals herself to be much more emotional than she is in Mitchell's version, and she narrates her experiences without the customary lady's language. Hayashi has added many new details to the retelling of this episode. For example, Scarlett comments on noticing the baby's wet hair between Melanie's legs and describes exactly how she pulls the baby out, how limp it appears to be at first, and how she cuts the umbilical cord with scissors. Her hands remain partly stained with blood even after washing up. After the birth, Scarlett, who had previously been terrified of serving as a midwife out of necessity, releases the tension by weeping bitterly alone.

Hayashi's translation does not hesitate to reveal the fact that Scarlett is not a rebel against the traditional gender roles in the cultural context of the American South. Hayashi adds more details about Scarlett's feelings, which the original text does not describe, to show her obedience to male dominance when it serves her financially and when her vanity is gratified. In chapter 13, Scarlett, who is in mourning for Charles, is fascinated by a beautifully designed green bonnet, which Butler has brought for her from Paris. When Scarlett reaches for the bonnet, Mitchell writes "'Put it on,' said Rhett, smiling,"[39] and she goes to the mirror wearing it. In Mitchell's original, there is no information about what Scarlett is thinking in the moment. Hayashi, however, inserts some sentences to show what Scarlet feels when Rhett asks her to try on the bonnet: "Retto wa watashi ni meirei shitakeredo, kininaranai. Totemo itooshisouni watashi ni hohoenndeitakarada. Watashi mo mou toritsukurowanakatta."[40] ("'Put it on'. Rhett ordered me to do so, but I don't care because he looks at me with a deep affection and smiles at me. I did not fake mourning for Charles anymore.") Hayashi's Scarlett hears the arrogance in Butler's "order" to put the bonnet on, but she decides to ignore it since Butler's smile is clearly a sign of his love for her. Her confidence in Butler's love and the enticingly beautiful bonnet make her obey.

The characteristics of Hayashi's translation suggest that it attempts to recreate *Gone with the Wind* as Japanese chick literature (chick lit). Helen Fielding's *Bridget Jones's Diary* (1996) is usually regarded as the founding text of this particular genre. The novel is a modern-day retelling of Jane Austin's *Pride and Prejudice* in the form of a diary. According to Suzanne Ferris, in *Bridget Jones's Diary* novel and film versions, "the transformation exploits the distinctive and incommensurate qualities of literature and cinema to represent the psychological development of a female character searching for self-esteem and security."[41] In other words, *Bridget Jones's Diary* was born as a result of its focus on "the psychological development" of Elizabeth in *Pride and Prejudice*, who is "searching for self-esteem and security."[42] The first-person narrative, including the diary form, is appropriate for the portrayal of the protagonist's psychological development. The connection between *Gone with the Wind* and Hayashi's first-person translation is parallel to that between *Pride and Prejudice* and *Bridget Jones's Diary*. Hayashi's use of monologue and minimal deployment of a lady's language transforms *Gone with the Wind* into a record of Scarlett's psychological development as she struggles to survive in the American South following the Civil War by forming strategic romantic relationships with men. If chick lit is traditionally defined as featuring "single women in their twenties and thirties 'navigating their generation's challenges of balancing demanding careers with personal relationships,'"[43] it may appear problematic to include the story of Scarlett's marriages in this genre. Hayashi, however, recreates Scarlett as a brutally honest, strong modern woman by emphasizing the heroine's emotions, practical thinking, and mental strength. She uses her intelligence and her feminine wiles to survive amid war and upheaval. At the same time, this modern Japanese retelling of *Gone with the Wind* contains such typical of chick lit characteristics as emphases on the heroine's sexual desire and consumerism, which are usually regarded as proof of the shallowness of the genre. The pink and flowery design for the cover of Hayashi's translation immediately calls to mind other examples of chick lit, thus establishing yet another, visual connection to the genre. However, Hayashi's translation then can be seen as offering a new afterlife to Mitchell's *Gone with the Wind* as period chick lit through its re-accentuation of the heroine's emotions, resilience, and practicality in line with women's sensibilities today.

4. Conclusion

After Margaret Mitchell's copyright expired in Japan, *Gone with the Wind* acquired unique afterlives as translations. Ara's translation, with its abundant scholarly apparatus to help the reader better understand the American South, ironically depends on stereotypical role languages—a lady's language and pseudo-Tohoku dialects as indicators of marginalized characters— to locate Scarlett in the presented historical and cultural context. Konosu maintains the romantic and classical air of the novel, using a lady's language and a formalized, bookish descriptive discourse. Hayashi retells *Gone with the Wind* from Scarlett's perspective. Hayashi's Scarlett utilizes a lady's role language much less than Ara's and Konosu's versions. She narrates her story in the casual modern language of contemporary Japan, to which the readers are accustomed. Also, Hayashi does not hesitate to add more detailed descriptions of Scarlett's emotions and uses some tactics to add depth to

Scarlett and bring the original character much closer to the novel's twenty-first century Japanese readers.

How can we situate these three translations' deployment of role language in the context of the current Black Lives Matter movement and modern understandings of racial and gender equality? As we have seen, the use of pseudo-Tohoku dialect for black characters has been criticized, leading to the tendency to avoid role languages in many contemporary literary and film translations.[44] Ara's Japanese rendition of the original, however, heavily depends on it. This means that Japanese stereotypical role languages are assigned to Mitchell's stereotypical language for black characters. In a sense, this can be a justifiable way of indicating the historical, racial, and cultural problems of *Gone with the Wind* in the Japanese translation even as this approach depends on the hierarchical relationship between standard Japanese and regional dialects. Hayashi's general avoidance of role languages provides one possible solution to the presented problems, but it results in obscuring the racism and preserving the controversial idealization of the antebellum South in Mitchell's text. Hayashi's translation seems to neutralize Mitchell's original by keeping away from role languages, particularly for black characters, while still employing a lady's language for the white women's characters and by re-accentuating Scarlett's individuality and emotion; however, in this interpretation, Mammy, Prissy, and others continue to be represented as loyal servants rather than brutalized slaves. Hayashi's Scarlett and Konosu's Scarlett, too, are energetic heroines surviving in the difficult times after the Civil War, which can be appealing to today's Japanese readers, but it is no longer possible to naively enjoy the text ignoring the reality of the antebellum South even in Japan—a culturally, geographically, and historically very different place. Japanese role languages in modern translations evoke prejudices and discrimination, but their effect should be reconsidered as a device for translating problematic representations in the source text into the target language.

Notes

1. Mitchell's copyright expires in the United States in 2031. All of the three translators say that the publishers approached them to translate *Gone with the Wind* around 2009, considering the imminent expiration of the copyright in Japan. Konomi Ara, "Yakusha atogaki" (Translator's Afterword), in *Kaze to tomoni sarinu* (Gone with the Wind), vol. 6 (Tokyo: Iwanami shoten, 2015), 373; Yukiko Konosu, "Yakusha atogaki" (Translator's Afterword), in *Kaze to tomoni sarinu* (Gone with the Wind), vol. 5 (Tokyo: Shinchosha,

2015), 546; Mariko Hayashi, "Maegaki ni kaete: koi shite nanbo (In Place of Forward: What's Life without Falling Love?)," in *Watashi wa sukâ-retto* (I Am Scarlett), vol. 1 (Tokyo: Shogakukan, 2019), Kindle.
2. Mikhail M. Bakhtin, "Discourse in the Novel," in *The Dialogic Imagination: Four Essays*, ed. Michael Holquist, trans. Caryl Emerson and Michael Holquist (Austin: University of Texas Press, 1982), Kindle.
3. Satoshi Kinsui, *Virtual Japanese: Enigmas of Role Language* (Osaka: Osaka University Press, 2017), 125–6.
4. Ibid., 123.
5. Main characters speaking in regional dialects are on the rise, especially in TV dramas today. See Minako Okamuro, "Hogen to aidenthithi: dorama hihyo no tachiba kara" (Dialects and Identity from the Perspective of TV Drama Criticism), in *Terebi dorama to hougen no atarashii kankei: "ka-ne-shon" kara "yae no sakura," soshite "amachan"* (A New Relationship between TV Drama and Dialects: From *Carnation* thru *Yae's Sakura* to *Amachan*), ed. Satoshi Kinsui, Yukari Tanaka, and Minako Okamuro (Tokyo: Kasama shoin, 2014), part 1–3, Kindle. See also Yukari Tanaka, "Amachan ga hiraita atarashii tobira: 'hougen kosupure dorama' ga dekirumade (A New Door Amachan Opened: The Birth of Dialect-costume Drama)" (in ibid., part 1–2).
6. In 2013, Alicia Garza, Patrisse Cullors, and Opal Tometi started a black political movement called Black Lives Matter. Black Lives Matter began as a social media hashtag, #BlackLivesMatter, after the acquittal of George Zimmerman in the shooting of Trayvon Martin in 2012. The movement grew nationwide in 2014 after the deaths of Eric Garner in New York and Michael Brown in Missouri. Since then, it has become a worldwide movement, especially after the murder of George Floyd in Minneapolis, Minnesota. According to the Black Lives Matter website, they were "founded in 2013 in response to the acquittal of Trayvon Martin's murderer. Black Lives Matter Foundation, Inc. is a global organization in the US, UK, and Canada, whose mission is to eradicate white supremacy and build local power to intervene in violence inflicted on Black communities by the state and vigilantes. By combating and countering acts of violence, creating space for Black imagination and innovation, and centering Black joy, we are winning immediate improvements in our lives." See "About," Black Lives Matter Global Foundation, accessed October 21, 2021, https://blacklivesmatter.com/about/.
7. Jacqueline Stewart, "Why We Can't Turn Away from 'Gone with the Wind,'" CNN, June 25, 2020, https://edition.cnn.com/2020/06/12/opinions/gone-with-the-wind-illuminates-white-supremacy-stewart/index.html.
8. Walter Benjamin, "The Task of Translator," in *Illuminations*, trans. Harry Zohn, ed. and introduced by Hanna Arendt (New York: Schocken Books, 2007), 71.
9. Momoko Nakamura, *Honyaku ga tsukuru nihongo: hiroin wa "onna kotoba" wo hanashi tsuzukeru* (Japanese Language Made by Translation: The

Heroine Keeps Talking in "Women's Language") (Tokyo: Hakutakusha and Gendai shokan, 2013), 51–60.
10. Kinsui, *Virtual Japanese*, 133–4.
11. Miyako Inoue, "Speech without a Speaking Body: Japanese Women's Language in Translation," *Language and Communication* 23 (2003): 327, https://doi.org/10.1016/S0271-5309(03)00011-9.
12. Mie Hiramoto, "Slave Speak Pseudo-Toohoku-*ben*: The Representation of Minorities in the Japanese Translation of *Gone with the Wind*," *Journal of Sociolinguistics* 13, no. 2 (2009): 250.
13. Ara distinguishes Rene Picard's Creole language from other White main characters by emphasizing vowels without using the rural language. "Pretty lak w'en I first see you at ze bazaar. You remembaire?" (Margaret Mitchell, *Gone with the Wind* [London: Macmillan, 2015], 580)

> "Bazâru de oaishitatokito kawarâzu outsukushi. Oboete oidedesukâ. (You are unchaaangingly beautiful like when I see you at bazaaar. Are you remeeember me?)

(Ara, *Kaze to tomoni sarinu*, vol. 4, 267).
14. Shigeko Kumagai, "Shinyaku ga hikitsugu tohoku hougen no imeji: 'Kaze to tomonisarinu' nimiru kokujin no kotoba zukai wo cyushin-ni" (The Image of Tohoku Dialect Inherited in New Translations: Mainly on Black People's Diction in *Gone with the Wind*), *Kotoba* 36 (2015): 23–4.
15. George Phillip Krapp coined the term "eye dialect" to point out that "a dialect writer often spells a word like *front* as *frunt*, or *face* as *fase*, or *picture* as *pictsher*, not because he intends to indicate here a genuine difference of pronunciation, but the spelling is merely a friendly nudge to the reader, a knowing look which establishes a sympathetic sense of superiority between the author and reader as contrasted with the humble speaker of dialect." George Phillip Krapp, *The English Language in America*, vol. 1 (New York: Modern Language Association of America, 1925; New York: Frederick Ungar Publishing, 1966), 228.
16. Nakamura, *Honyaku ga tsukuru nihongo*, 14–24.
17. Kinsui Satoshi et al. eds., *Yakuwarigo sho jiten* (Handy Dictionary of Role Language) (Tokyo: Kenkyusha, 2014), ix.
18. Inoue, "Speech without a Speaking Body," 326–7.
19. Kinsui et al., *Yakuwarigo sho jiten*, viii–ix.
20. The representation of Scarlett in one of three musical versions of *Gone with the Wind* produced by Takarazuka Revue (a famed Japanese all-female theater troupe) exemplifies a particular interest in Scarlett as a woman who is awkwardly balancing a strong desire to pursue what she really wants and a modesty that is expected of women from the upper classes of the American South. The version, known as the "Butler Version," divides Scarlett into Scarlett and Scarlett II. Scarlett II, who seems to be in the other Scarlett's mind, expresses what she thinks and desires, and urges Scarlett to

follow her own instinct and practicality. At the end of story when Scarlett recognizes and accepts her love for Butler, the split personality known as Scarlett II is absorbed in Scarlett. Thus, Scarlett internalizes the struggle between her own desire and pressure to conform to class expectations in the Japanese context.

21. Eve Kosofsky Sedgwick, *Between Men: English Literature and Male Homosocial Desire* (New York: Columbia University Press, 1985), 8.
22. Ibid., 8.
23. Ibid.
24. Mitchell, *Gone with the Wind*, 328.
25. Margaret Mitchell, *Kaze to tomoni sarinu* (Gone with the Wind), trans. Konomi Ara (Tokyo: Iwanami shoten, 2015), vol. 3, 133, all underlining added by author.
26. Margaret Mitchell, *Kaze to tomoni sarinu* (Gone with the Wind), trans. Yukiko Konosu (Tokyo: Shinchosha, 2015), vol. 2, 291.
27. Mariko Hayashi, *I Am Scarlett* (Tokyo: Shogakukan, 2019), vol. 3, chapter 20, Kindle.
28. Mitchell, *Gone with the Wind*, 189.
29. Mitchell, *Gone with the Wind*, trans. Ara, vol. 2, 136.
30. Mitchell, *Gone with the Wind*, trans. Konosu, vol. 2, 432.
31. Mitchell, *Gone with the Wind*, trans. Ara, vol. 1, 313.
32. The number and length of Konosu's additional notes are more moderate than Ara's, and "the translator's afterword" is attached only to the last of the complete five volumes.
33. Yukio Mishima, *Bunsho tokuhon* (A Guide of Writing) (Tokyo: Chuokoronsha, 1973 [1953]), 177.
34. Mishima shows a negative attitude toward the use of onomatopoeia. In addition to his attribution of onomatopoeia to women and children's writing, he says it is "each nation's accumulation of infantile experience" (180) and points out "the lack of abstractness of onomatopoeia," which means "it only communicates something as it is to people's ears, and the primary function of language is lost, and a corrupted form of the language" (178).
35. Masahiro Ono, *Onomatope: giongo/gitaigo no sekai* (Onomatopoeia: The World of Imitative Words and Mimetic Words) (Tokyo: Kadokawa shoten, 2019), chapter 5, Kindle.
36. Mitchell, *Gone with the Wind*, 5.
37. Mitchell, *Gone with the Wind*, trans. Konosu, vol. 1, 8–9.
38. Victor Fleming, *Gone with the Wind* (Warner Home Video, 1999), DVD.
39. Mitchell, *Gone with the Wind*, 233.
40. Hayashi, *I Am Scarlett*, vol. 2, chapter 15.
41. Suzanne Ferriss, "Narrative and Cinematic Doubleness: *Pride and Prejudice* and *Bridget Jones's Diary*," in *Chick Lit: The New Women's Fiction* (New York: Routledge, 2006), 72.

42. Ferriss, "Narrative and Cinematic Doubleness," 72.
43. Suzanne Ferriss and Mallory Young, "Introduction," in *Chick Lit: The New Women's Fiction* (New York: Routledge, 2006), 3.
44. Kumagai, "Shinyaku ga hikitsugu tohoku hougen no imeji," 18–19; Nakamura, *Honyaku ga tsukuru nihongo*, 49.

Bibliography

Ara, Konomi. "Yakusha atogaki" (Translator's Afterword). In *Kaze to tomoni sarinu* (Gone with the Wind), 369–73. Volume 6. Tokyo: Iwanami shoten, 2015.

Bakhtin, Mikhail M. *The Dialogic Imagination: Four Essays*. Edited by Michael Holquist. Translated by Caryl Emerson and Michael Holquist. Austin: University of Texas Press, 1982. Kindle.

Benjamin, Walter. "The Task of Translator." In *Illuminations*. Translated by Harry Zohn. Edited and introduced by Hanna Arendt, 69–83. New York: Schocken, 2007.

Black Lives Matter Global Foundation. "About." https://blacklivesmatter.com/about/. Accessed October 21, 2021.

Ferriss, Suzanne. "Narrative and Cinematic Doubleness: *Pride and Prejudice* and *Bridget Jones's Diary*." In *Chick Lit: The New Women's Fiction*, 71–84. New York: Routledge, 2006.

Ferriss, Suzanne, and Mallory Young. "Introduction." In *Chick Lit: The New Women's Fiction*, 1–13. New York: Routledge, 2006.

Fleming, Victor. *Gone with the Wind*. Warner Home Video, 1999, DVD.

Hayashi, Mariko. "Maegaki ni kaete: koi shite nanbo" (In Place of Forward: What's Life without Falling Love?). In *Watashi wa sukâ-retto* (I Am Scarlett). Volume 1. Tokyo: Shogakukan, 2019. Kindle.

Hayashi, Mariko. *Watashi wa sukâ-retto* (I Am Scarlett). 4 vols. Tokyo: Shogakukan, 2019–21. Kindle.

Hiramoto, Mie. "Slave Speak Pseudo-Toohoku-*ben*: The Representation of Minorities in the Japanese Translation of *Gone with the Wind*." *Journal of Sociolinguistics* 13, no. 2 (2009): 249–63.

Inoue, Miyako. "Speech without a Speaking Body: Japanese Women's Language in Translation." *Language and Communication* 23 (2003): 315–30. https://doi.org/10.1016/S0271-5309(03)00011-9.

Kinsui, Satoshi. *Vācharu nihongo yakuwarigono no nazo* (Virtual Japanese and the Mystery of Role Language). Tokyo: Iwanami Shoten. 2003.

Kinsui, Satoshi. *Virtual Japanese: Enigmas of Role Language*. Osaka: Osaka University Press, 2017.

Kinsui, Satoshi et al., eds. *Yakuwarigo sho jiten* (Handy Dictionary of Role Language). Tokyo: Kenkyusha, 2014.

Konosu, Yukiko. "Yakusha atogaki" (Translator's Afterword). In *Kaze to tomoni sarinu* (Gone with the Wind), 514–48. Volume 5. Tokyo: Shinchosha, 2015.

Krapp, George Phillip. *The English Language in America*. 2 vols. New York: Modern Language Association of America, 1925 [1966].

Kumagai, Shigeko. "Shinyaku ga hikitsugu tohoku hougen no imeji: 'Kaze to tomoni sarinu' nimiru kokujin no kotoba zukai wo cyushin-ni" (The Image of Tohoku Dialect Inherited in New Translations: Mainly on Black People's Diction in *Gone with the Wind*). *Kotoba* 36 (2015): 18–33.

Mishima, Yukio. *Bunsho tokuhon* (A Guide of Writing). Tokyo: Chuokoronsha, 1973 [1953].

Mitchell, Margaret. *Gone with the Wind*. London: Macmillan, 2015 [1936].

Mitchell, Margaret. *Kaze to tomoni sarinu* (Gone with the Wind). Translated by Konomi Ara. Tokyo: Iwanami shoten, 2015.

Mitchell, Margaret. *Kaze to tomoni sarinu* (Gone with the Wind). Translated by Yasuo Okubo and Michinosuke Takeuchi. Tokyo: Gutenberg 21, 2016 [1936]. Kindle.

Mitchell, Margaret. *Kaze to tomoni sarinu* (Gone with the Wind). Translated by Yukiko Konosu. Tokyo: Shinchosha, 2015.

Nakamura, Momoko. *Honyaku ga tsukuru nihongo: hiroin wa "onna kotoba" wo hanashi tsuzukeru* (Japanese Language Made by Translation: The Heroine Keeps Talking in "Women's Language"). Tokyo: Hakutakusha and Gendai shokan, 2013.

Okamuro, Minako. "Hogen to aidenthithi: dorama hihyo no tachiba kara" (Dialects and Identity from the Perspective of TV Drama Criticism). In *Terebi dorama to hougen no atarashii kankei: "kâ-nê-shon" kara "yae no sakura," soshite "amachan"* (A New Relationship between TV Drama and Dialects: From *Carnation* through *Yae's Sakura* to *Amachan*). Edited by Satoshi Kinsui, Yukari Tanaka, and Minako Okamuro. Tokyo: Kasamashoin, 2014. Kindle.

Ono, Masahiro. *Onomatope: giongo/gitaigo no sekai* (Onomatopoeia: The World of Imitative Words and Mimetic Words). Tokyo: Kadokawa shoten, 2019.

Sedgwick, Eve Kosofsky. *Between Men: English Literature and Male Homosocial Desire*. New York: Columbia University Press, 1985.

Stewart, Jacqueline. "Why We Can't Turn Away from 'Gone with the Wind.'" CNN. June 25, 2020. https://edition.cnn.com/2020/06/12/opinions/gone-with-the-wind-illuminates-white-supremacy-stewart/index.html. Accessed October 21, 2021.

Tanaka, Yukari. "Amachan ga hiraita atarashii tobira: 'hougen kosupure dorama' ga dekirumade" (A New Door Amachan Opened: The Birth of Dialect-costume Drama). In *Terebi dorama to hougen no atarashii kankei: "kâ-nê-shon" kara "yae no sakura," soshite "amachan" e* (A New Relationship between TV Drama and Dialects: From *Carnation* through *Yae's Sakura* to *Amachan*). Edited by Satoshi Kinsui, Yukari Tanaka, and Minako Okamuro. Tokyo: Kasamashoin, 2014. Kindle.

6

The Master-Stylizer and the Creative Act: Mikhail Bakhtin on Translation

Margarita Marinova

On March 23, 1973, the ailing, fragile Mikhail Bakhtin settled down for his sixth, and final, recorded conversation with Viktor Duvakin, the politically disgraced former Moscow State University literature professor. The two men felt comfortable in each other's company and chatted freely about anything that either found interesting or important. As always, time seemed to pause its incessant march forward, and ghosts of very different worlds joined them in the book-filled room, where the quiet spinning of the reel-to-reel tape recorder mixed the human voices and the occasional meowing of the house pet into a marvelous auditory album for posterity.

Duvakin had lost his official job at the university in 1966 because of his open support of a former student, Andrei Sinyavsky, who had been persecuted by the Soviet government for publishing satirical novels abroad under the pen name of Abram Terz. Even though very disappointing, the dismissal proved to be a blessing in disguise as it allowed him to refocus all his passion and creative energy on a project he had pondered for a while: the creation of a phono-library of interviews with leading figures of early-twentieth-century Russian culture, whose voices were disappearing from the official annals of USSR's history. Duvakin recognized the enormous value of their memories, which, he felt, needed to be preserved as faithfully as possible, even if that meant waiting patiently for the right time when they could finally be shared with the rest of the world. As he was wont to tell his interviewees, their audience had probably not been born yet: Duvakin's labor of love was meant for the twenty-first century.[1] The effect of that statement on his interlocutors always seemed to border on the miraculous: free of any fear of censorship and political repercussions, they could express their ideas and share past recollections without self-conscious restraint.

Bakhtin didn't like writing about himself, but speaking about his past with a sympathetic listener who had no immediate plans for transcribing and publishing their conversations was another matter. At seventy-eight years old and just recently allowed to return to the capital after years of internal political exile, he welcomed the opportunity to share a life's worth of memories about his family's history, the turbulent years of his youth, the catastrophic aftermath of the Soviet Revolution, the devastation of two world wars, and the excitement of moving in the most influential literary and artistic circles of the times before he was forced to relocate to Kazakhstan. His reminiscences of meetings and friendships with Russian intellectuals constituted a veritable "who's who" of Russian culture from the first half of the twentieth century. So many voices came alive in the twelve hours of lively conversations which Duvakin recorded during the months of February and March of that cold winter. Buoyed by never-ending cups of strong hot tea, Bakhtin not only remembered specific interactions with now famous figures of his contemporary creative milieu, but often also tried to imitate their specific verbal peculiarities and embody their presence to the best of his abilities, mostly while reciting poems that he had heard them perform in person. This self-conscious impersonation amounted to a transposition of an other's linguistic existence into the material reality of a dialogic speech act, marked by the utmost respect and indeed, oftentimes, genuine love for the original. Bakhtin showed similar admiration for the many French and German authors whose works he could recite—in their original language—from memory. On occasion, he would volunteer opinions about their renderings into Russian, but he did that always in passing or as an afterthought. As a subject of conversation, literary translation just didn't seem to hold his attention for very long. When it did take center stage, albeit briefly, as it did in that last interview with Duvakin, it appeared rather cryptic and superficial, as though Bakhtin assumed others already knew what he meant and didn't need him to go into serious explanations of his ideas.

It is anyone's guess why that might have been the case, but a closer look at his writings from the 1930s and 1940s about literary history and the emergence and dissemination of the novel, coupled with the oral remarks he made to Duvakin some thirty years later, offer glimpses at possible answers, which I will discuss in the following pages. While Duvakin's questions about individual translators forced Bakhtin to share verbally his thoughts on such topics as the qualities of a good translation, or who is best qualified to render poetry into Russian, his answers were consistent with ideas he had already espoused in his earlier works about the nature of literary practices as such. Of particular interest to me here will be Bakhtin's essays, "Discourse in the Novel" (1934–5), "Forms of Time and Chronotope in the Novel" (1937–8), and especially "From the Prehistory of Novelistic Discourse" (1940),[2] where he advances the idea that language first becomes aware of itself through contact with other languages, and grants a special role in the birth of novelistic discourse to "translators-stylizers."³ In his later (1959-61) methodological and philosophical musings⁴ about the relationships between texts, individual utterances, and culture, he also brings up the importance and possibility of linguistic translation while underscoring yet again the uniqueness of any text seen as an individual utterance. Clearly, translation was a topic Bakhtin came back to again and again as he explored the larger implications of human discourse throughout his career. In fact, it was perhaps because he saw it as such an integral part of literary creation (and life in general) that he didn't feel the need to discuss it separately.

Specialists in translation studies who admire Bakhtin as a philosopher and literary critic have often lamented the lack of clear pronouncements on the value and practice of translation in his published writing. Of course, as several modern scholars⁵ of his work have pointed out, we can still deduce a lot about his ideas about translation from what he has left us. Caryl Emerson's early examination of this topic is perhaps still the best. In her 1983 essay, "Translating Bakhtin: Does His Theory of Discourse Contain a Theory of Translation?," she makes an excellent case for the need to reframe this question in order to capture better his notorious distrust of any formal theory that precludes internal contradictions and sets clear boundaries around itself. She then argues that his writing contains embedded guidance on how to think about translation as both practice and artistic outcome. There are several postulates that emerge from Bakhtin's reflections on this subject: First, Bakhtin views "boundaries between languages as only one extreme on a continuum, at whose other end translation processes [are] required for one social group to understand another in the same city, for children to understand parents in the same family, for one day to understand the next."⁶ As we all speak a language foreign to those around us, and routinely make use of different stylizations of our native tongue, we constantly engage in the practice of translation: "To understand another person at any given moment, then, is to come to terms with meaning on the boundary of one's own and another's language: to translate."⁷ Second, while it is true that there is no unity to his approach to translation, no theory in the traditional sense of the word, that is something we must celebrate rather than be frustrated by. Bakhtin's formal disregard for any traditional categories is a natural outgrowth of his "rigorous, almost clinical respect for the non-reducible individual and how he speaks."⁸ This irreducibility of the speech act suggests that it will always be impossible to find adequate equivalent expression for it in the language of an other, but, and here we arrive at the third main characteristic of his implicit approach to translation in general, "non-equivalence is never a matter of despair, it is the impulse to life; the interaction of two different, discreet systems is the only way a true *event* comes to pass."⁹

In his last dialogue with Duvakin, Bakhtin comes as close to articulating similar ideas clearly as he ever did in a brief conversational detour that involves his reminiscences about hearing Pasternak read his translation of *Faust*. "And how was the reading received?," Duvakin wants to know. Bakhtin's response suggests his full appreciation of the success of the endeavor: "As it should have been ... Everybody appreciated the quality of the translation."[10] He does not doubt Pasternak's ability to convey the original in Russian, and is not bothered that, as Duvakin suggests, "his translation doesn't much sound like Goethe."[11] Sadly, an interruption in the recording doesn't allow us to hear the continuation of Bakhtin's reply, "A little, yes. But all translations ..."[12] but when the voices of the two interlocutors come back, we hear him discuss Zhukovsky's translations of Byron's poetry in glowing terms.

We could extrapolate from this trailing, "But all translation," that Bakhtin thought that good translations as a rule do not sound much like the source text—nor should they, as they are expressions of a new dialogic *event* between participants whose particular talents would re-accentuate[13] the original differently in their own languages. Even if some might say that Zhukovsky's and Byron's "The Prisoner of Chillon" are two different works,[14] Bakhtin admits that he "prefer[s] that kind of translation[15] to the work of someone with no talent, a person who is not a poet himself. Zhukovsky was a poet. His translations were, after all... Even when he moved away from the original author, he didn't sink below him, but stayed on the same level, just a little bit to the side. There's nothing worse than when the translator lowers the level."[16] Having thus expressed his dislike for literal translations done by talentless amateurs,[17] Bakhtin shares his approval of a much freer creative engagement with the source text if undertaken by the right (talented) interpreter—someone like Pasternak: "Overall, I thought Pasternak's translation was very good,"[18] he concludes. Obviously, Bakhtin thought his compatriot, a gifted poet in his own right, to have successfully positioned himself alongside Goethe's writing, and avoided the traps of "lowering" and "trivializing"[19] the original text—the two worst outcomes of an uneven interlinguistic encounter. In addition, what is especially important in Pasternak's case is that he approaches poetic language in the same way as spoken language—by focusing on

> the element of freedom so characteristic of it ... Spoken language fears and shuns literary clichés—which is the main thing, the main thing ... There can't be any clichés, any literary, "correct," we might say learned elements in poetic language. Poetic language must be as unrestricted as possible—language set free, and in this case close to ordinary conversational speech. So, there you have it.[20]

The freedom and originality of spoken discourse that Bakhtin appreciates so greatly can apply to translation practices as well. If translation can be seen as a fruitful dialogic event between two equals, it does not have to conform to expectations of linguistic equivalence or the merging of distinctive viewpoints. As Pasternak and Zhukovsky position themselves next to Goethe and Byron, they retain their "outsidedness" (*vnenakhodimost*) in order to engage in the process of "understanding," which for Bakhtin means going beyond the "translation from the other's language into one's own language"[21] and is never complete. As Antonio Traficante puts it, "Bakhtin openly rejoices in the *vitality of non-equivalence*, and sees the existing polarity between languages as crucial to any act of translation, or for that matter, any kind of dialogue as well. Dialogue, then, is only possible when two sides do not understand each other completely."[22] While knowledge (or, as Bakhtin called it, "explanation"[23]) of the producing culture and source language is needed, it is not enough. The encounter between the original author and the translator releases some of the source text's multiple encoded potentialities, and this dialogic act of cocreation invites the reader to find new meanings in the resulting text in turn. Of course, every translator is first a reader of the original work, so his/her responsibilities are especially vital: the creation of the first inner link between disparate authentic experiences. This duty cannot be interpreted as simply theoretical or aestheticized, but must be viewed as material and pragmatic,[24] which is consistent with ideas Bakhtin developed both in his early and his mature philosophical writings about answerability in art. Our "relation with the world (which of course also includes texts) is, at bottom, a deeply personal and momentous act,"[25] which cannot be accomplished by any other person. Taking responsibility for one's actions as they are performed (and translation is one such act) is seen by Bakhtin as both liberating and self-defining.[26] Even if translation at first requires that the interpreter situate him/herself in the position of "the other," he/she must return to his/her original place in order to fulfill the task[27] of letting the voice of the other come alive as an independent entity. Pasternak and Goethe must remain separate and their voices must be allowed to retain their autonomy at all times. In order to grant such freedom to the other's language, the creating self (author or translator) resorts to a peculiar device: stylization.

The image of the two poets standing side by side (one to the side of the other, but on the same level as him) is an especially helpful visual introduction to how Bakhtin imagined the role of the translator in his ever-evolving ideas about literary language and history. In his 1940 essay, "From the Prehistory of Novelistic Discourse," he broaches the subject of linguistic interaction as key to the production of novelistic discourse in order to highlight the importance of translation as stylization:

> From start to finish, the creative literary consciousness of the Romans functioned against the background of the Greek language and Greek forms. From its very first steps, the Latin literary word viewed itself in the light of the Greek word, *through the eyes* of the Greek word; it was from the very beginning a word "with a sideways glance," a stylized word enclosing itself, as it were, in its own piously stylized quotation marks.[28]

In the process of such linguistic interanimation the "phonetic system of [one's] own language," or the "distinctive features of [one's] own morphology" and "abstract lexicon" do not matter as much as that "which makes language concrete and which makes its world view ultimately untranslatable, that is, precisely *the style of the language as a totality*."[29]

The side remark about the "untranslatability" of the original's worldview has led some scholars to assume that Bakhtin questions translatability as a matter of principle. This view is usually further supported by evidence from a later essay, "The Problem of the Text in Linguistics, Philology, and the Human Sciences: An Experiment in Philosophical Analysis," in which he suggests that as a system of signs language can certainly be rendered into another language, but that as a unique text ("as distinct from the language as a system of means"[30]) it can never be fully translated.[31] However, as already submitted above, a more careful consideration of the general philosophical postulates that underlie his thinking about any utterance as an unrepeatable dialogic event undermine the idea that translation between languages is any more suspect than translation between dialogic encounters within the same language. If all language is untranslatable yet communication still occurs (a fact that Bakhtin would be the first to acknowledge and celebrate), then, paradoxically, translation is very much not just possible but also necessary for a culture to survive and thrive.

Translation brings about the needed alienation between the creating consciousness and its own native language, which ensures the success of the creative act. As Bakhtin points out in "From the Prehistory of Novelistic Discourse," the distance between the native Roman and the imported Greek makes room for the emergence of laughter.[32] When all available linguistic material is perceived as equally foreign, it can lend itself to comedic use with equal ease. The distinction between indigenous and foreign languages collapses even further when we realize that Roman literature is marked not just by bi- but also *tri*lingualism, and therefore "three souls—three language-cultures—lived in the breast of all the initiators of Roman literary discourse, all the translator-stylizers who had come to Rome from Lower Italy, where the boundaries of three languages and cultures intersected with one another—Greek, Oscan and Roman."[33]

While Bakhtin does not provide many details about these translator-stylizers, it seems logical to assume that they are ultimately successful in their work if it brings about the replacement of "a single, unitary sealed-off Ptolemaic world of language" with an "open Galilean world of many languages, mutually animating each other."[34] The mutual animation of languages can take place only with the help of translation, and Bakhtin is even more clear in his positive assessment of its value to literary history when he announces, in "Discourse in the Novel," that *"European novel prose is born and shaped in the process of a free (that is, reformulating) translation of others' works."*[35] Here, once again, stylization is highlighted as the device that best enables the copresence of distinct voices in literature:

> Every authentic stylization, as we have already said, is an artistic representation of another's linguistic style, an artistic image of another's language. Two individualized linguistic consciousnesses must be present in it: the one that *represents* (that is, the linguistic consciousness of the stylizer) and the one that is *represented*, which is stylized. Stylization differs from style proper precisely by virtue of its requiring a specific linguistic consciousness (the contemporaneity of the stylizer and his audience), under whose influence a style becomes a stylization, against whose background it acquires new meaning and significance.[36]

The "specific linguistic consciousness," within which two styles of artistic representation coexist, anticipates[37] both the Roman "translator-stylizer" of "From the Prehistory of Novelistic Discourse" and the recreators of texts from "Forms of Time and Chronotope in the Novel," which suggests that Bakhtin's views on the role of the translator and translation in general in the development and dissemination of literature around the world remained consistent throughout the 1930s and 1940s. It makes sense to extrapolate, then, that for Bakhtin more modern translators as carriers of "contemporary language" would also be quite capable of "cast[ing] a special light over the stylized language" of other cultures and epochs, and creating "a *free* image of another's language, which expresses not only a stylized but also a stylizing language and art-intention."[38] Translation is always free and oriented outwards—to both the original style being stylized, and the contemporary background, which reactivates the original in order for it to acquire new meanings and significance. The real people involved in the cocreation of texts (author, listener, reader, translator-stylizer) may be located in different "time-spaces, sometimes separated from each other by centuries and by great spatial distances," but they "participate equally in the creation of the represented world in the text."[39] The boundary separating the represented world and the material—or, as Bakhtin calls it, "historical"[40] world reflected in art—is there, but it is porous and unreliable, which actually helps avoid "an oversimplified, dogmatic splitting of hairs."[41] The work, like any organism, "resists fusion with its environment, but if it's torn out of its environment it dies ... We might even speak of a special *creative* chronotope inside which this exchange between work and life occurs, and which constitutes the distinctive life of the work."[42] By implication, the effective translator must enter the *creative* chronotope and participate in the exchange of meanings in order to keep the source text alive. Even though Bakhtin does not commit to a coherent exploration of the listener-reader or translator-stylizer in any of the essays from this period (the 1930s and 1940s), he does acknowledge his/her role in *renewing* the work of art, while also positing a certain balance in the distribution of powers between the text and its receiver when he claims that "every literary work *faces outward away from itself*, toward the listener-reader, and to a certain extent thus anticipates possible reactions to itself."[43] Rather than seen as being completely helpless and limited by its inherent untranslatability, the text emerges as capable of holding its own in the dialogic encounter with contemporary and future interpreters.

Bakhtin returns to the question of whether source languages and dialects can interact productively with others in the late 1950s in his methodologically explorative essay "The Problem of the Text in Linguistics, Philology, and the Human Sciences: An Experiment in Philosophical Analysis."[44] His answer is a resounding "Yes." It is true that the price paid for such positivity is a "*departure beyond the boundaries of linguistics*"[45] and literal meaning, but the results are both worth it and appropriate. While "the word cannot be assigned to a single speaker," the author, too, has "his own inalienable right to the word, and the listener also has his rights, and those whose voices are heard in the word before the author comes upon it also have their rights (after all, there are no words that belong to no one)."[46] As the first reader-listener of any foreign work, the translator, too, has rights, which enable him/her to transplant the original text into the fertile soil (the creative chronotope) of the target culture and language. In Bakhtin's universe, we are all on equal footing with each other, as long as our interactions are truly dialogic and respectful of the utterance that is already and forever someone else's. This "internalized Babel,"[47] in Douglas Robinson's apt expression, may deny any "inherent cohesion of meaning,"[48] but it also turns linguistic unpredictability into the very origins of creativity. Bakhtin knew this earlier than most of us. He never meant to celebrate universal intelligibility because he recognized that it was impossible (and counterproductive as an idea) in a world of multiple languages forever intermingling and reanimating each other.[49] Contemporary theorists of translation like Adeiano Marchetti and Annette Lindegaard admire his groundbreaking appreciation of the dialogic nature of any intercultural creative encounter and embrace his suspicion of originality in any shape or form.[50] As Galin Tihanov has already argued, as a thinker Bakhtin "de-emphasizes originality and property,"[51] which are often seen as the very foundations of our understanding of literature and its translation. This makes sense, considering the way Bakhtin himself worked with novels in translation, and at times borrowed/translated, and synthesized other philosophers' ideas into his own writing without bothering to provide proper references. Ideas, just as utterances and texts in general, can never be anyone's private property. They travel between individual consciousnesses, languages, and cultures; they evolve as a result of entering many productive dialogues along the way; and they give birth to new perspectives and articulations without ever "falling prey to terminological fetishism."[52] As such, Bakhtin's work in its totality is both the product of and a continuous meditation on translation.

Of course, that is not to say that Bakhtin didn't differentiate between an original text and its later reiterations. The source text does retain control over its message to an extent if not for anything else then certainly because it already anticipates and thus can regulate certain responses. Goethe's *Faust* remains his German author's work even when it's retold in the voice of a talented Russian interpreter like Pasternak. The stylization of the language of the other doesn't replace it with a completely new one as much as it interacts with it freely. Anything else would amount to a monologic usurpation of power, which would stifle the creative impulse enlivening the wonderful singularity of each utterance by imposing clear division lines in meaning production.

Boundary crossing, then, is not only one of the main hallmarks of Bakhtin's approach to language and literature, but also to translation. If Pasternak's original or translated poetry was deemed good, let us recall, it was because it was "as unrestricted as possible—language set free, and in this case close to ordinary conversational speech." True to himself, Bakhtin had to blur any genre-defining lines to bring poetic discourse[53] as close to speech as possible in order to preserve the utterance's absolute openness to the outside world and the words of others. In his conversations with Duvakin, he often performed the act of blurring the divide between languages and genres when he smoothly transitioned between free speech and recitation, prosaic ruminations and poetic quotations, Russian and French, or German. The ever-changing linguistic expression of Bakhtin's subjectivity in this only surviving auditory encounter with the master thus provides the perfect example of his thought's overall resistance to any formalization to the end.

As the official translator into English of the tapes, I was both intimidated by such linguistic fluidity, and emboldened to approach it with the same freedom and acceptance of my role in the stylization of his voice one heard in Bakhtin's own treatment of his many remembered interlocutors. I strove to preserve the image of the spoken word captured by Duvakin's tape recorder while being fully cognizant of the fact that I inhabited a very different world with its own expectations and dialogic capabilities. It was a privilege to enter the conversation with two incredible men, position myself, however briefly, by their side in order to listen, transcribe, and translate their ever-changing thoughts so that others might join us later and the dialogue would continue to evolve. Reading the time- and place-specific utterances of Bakhtin and Duvakin fifty years after they took place is not the same as being in that Moscow apartment in 1973 or listening to the original tapes. But the English-speaking readers who would encounter their voices in translation do not have to feel handicapped. Rather than limited in their response to the text, they are free to take it in any direction they want and continue the conversation with the famous Russian thinker leaving behind any predetermined expectations or even scholarly goals. The many surprising insights and new understanding of meaningful interpersonal events which await the curious modern interlocutor are definitely worth the risk of getting disoriented or unsure of where you belong at times. They are what communication is all about. They are also what translation helps us to achieve, as Bakhtin fully recognized, and for that, alone, its value is beyond doubt.

Notes

1. For more on the history of Duvakin's project, see Slav Gratchev's Introduction to *Mikhail Bakhtin, The Duvakin Interviews, 1973*, ed. Slav Gratchev and Margarita Marinova, trans. Margarita Marinova (Lewisburg: Bucknell University Press, 2019), 1–2.
2. All three essays appear in Mikhail M. Bakhtin, *The Dialogic Imagination: Four Essays*, ed. Michael Holquist, trans. Caryl Emerson and Michael Holquist (Austin: University of Texas Press, 1981).
3. Karin Zbinden makes a similar point in her essay, "The Bakhtin Circle and Translation," *Yearbook of English Studies* 36, no. 1 (2006): 157–67. However, her conclusions about Bakhtin's evolving ideas about the possibility of proper translation are very different from mine. She argues that Bakhtin grows more skeptical about translatability with time, while I believe that his

ideas do not change much since his early assessments of the importance of translation practices to literary history.
4. Here I have in mind his essay "The Problem of the Text in Linguistics, Philology, and the Human Sciences: An Experiment in Philosophical Analysis," in *Speech Genres and Other Late Essays*, ed. Caryl Emerson and Michael Holquist, trans. Vern W. McGee (Austin: University of Texas Press, 1992), 103–31.
5. I am especially interested in the work of such contemporary theorists of translations studies as Amith Kumar, Milind Malshe, George Lang, Annette Lindegaard, Antonio Traficante, and others, whose writing about Bakhtin's relevance to translation I will have the opportunity to reference later in this essay.
6. Caryl Emerson, "Translating Bakhtin: Does His Theory of Discourse Contain a Theory of Translation?" *University of Ottawa Quarterly* 53, no. 1 (1983): 23.
7. Ibid., 24.
8. Ibid., 25.
9. Ibid, emphasis in original.
10. Gratchev and Marinova, *Mikhail Bakhtin*, 241.
11. Ibid.
12. Ibid., 242.
13. "Re-accentuation" is a term Bakhtin coined in his essay "Discourse in the Novel" (in *The Dialogic Imagination: Four Essays*, ed. Michael Holquist, trans. Caryl Emerson and Michael Holquist [Austin: University of Texas Press, 1981], 259–422) to talk about the many reiterations of Don Quixote's character in different cultures and times. By extension, we could define "re-accentuation" as any alteration of an original hero achieved by placing it in a different context, which can be seen as synonymous with translation when linguistic boundaries are crossed in the process.
14. Duvakin certainly makes that claim. See Gratchev and Marinova, *Mikhail Bakhtin*, 242.
15. "That kind of translation" amounts to a reworking of the source text synonymous with cocreation, for which a special individual talent is necessary. Here Bakhtin's opinion aligns with that of modern translation studies scholars like Bassnett and Lefevere who assert that "translation is, of course, a rewriting of the original text" (in *Translation, History, and Culture*, ed. Susan Bassnett and Andre Lefevere [London: Pinter Publishers, 1990], ix). The goal of that kind of translation, therefore, is the successful manipulation of the original text so that it appears new to the target language readers (ibid., 19).
16. Gratchev and Marinova, *Mikhail Bakhtin*, 242.
17. Bakhtin makes a similar comment about the inexcusable "crudeness" of literal translations, when undertaken by talentless authors in his first conversation with Duvakin as well. There he assesses—in passing—the work

of Mikhail Pokrovsky, a well-known classicist from the beginning of the twentieth century, and finds him unable to evaluate properly the quality of poetic translations. For instance, Pokrovsky thought that Valery Bryusov's and Vikenty Veresaev's translations of the classics were terrible, but Bakhtin vehemently disagreed as far as Bryusov's work was concerned. Bakhtin especially admired Bryusov's early translations of Baudelaire into Russian, and credited him with introducing the French symbolists to Russian audiences. See, Gratchev and Marinova, *Mikhail Bakhtin*, 43, 45–6.
18. Ibid., 242.
19. Ibid.
20. Ibid., 242–3.
21. Quoted in Caryl Emerson, "Perevodimost,'" *Slavic and East European Journal* 38, no. 1 (Spring 1994): 88, emphasis in original.
22. Antonio Traficante, "Translating the Other: Lawrence, Bakhtin, and Verga," *Etudes Lawrenciennes: The Poetics of Travel and Cultural Otherness* 36 (2007): 234.
23. Emerson, "Perevodimost,'" 88.
24. Pavel Ol'khov assesses Bakhtin's position on the importance of "answerability" in any human or artistic interaction similarly in "The Old New Bakhtin," *Russian Studies in Literature* 50, no. 4 (2014): 11–12.
25. Traficante, "Translating the Other," 235–36.
26. Ibid., 236.
27. Amith Kumar and Milind Malshe, "Translation and Bakhtin's 'Metalinguistics,'" *Perspectives: Studies in Translatology* 13, no. 2 (2005): 116, Kumar and Malshe continue to elaborate that "this dialogic act enables translators to preserve the difference between the self and the other. Translation attains a voice of its own that is neither an imitation of the source text nor a completely detached work. 'Active understanding' is what makes translation an 'answering word'" (116).
28. Mikhail M. Bakhtin, "From the Prehistory of Novelistic Discourse," in *The Dialogic Imagination: Four Essays,* ed. Michael Holquist, trans. Caryl Emerson and Michael Holquist (Austin: University of Texas Press, 1981), 61, emphasis in original.
29. Bakhtin, "From the Prehistory of Novelistic Discourse," 62, emphasis in original.
30. Bakhtin, "The Problem of the Text in Linguistics, Philology, and the Human Sciences," 261.
31. For more on this particular critical stance, see, for example, Karin Zbinden, "The Bakhtin Circle and Translation," *Yearbook of English Studies* 36, no. 1 (2006): 166–7. Léon Robel accepts the validity of such an interpretation of Bakhtin's early thoughts on the topic, but argues that Bakhtin espouses very different views in his later studies of the novel. While Karin Zbinden is right to call attention to Robel's error in dating the essays under consideration and therefore undermines his point that Bakhtin changes his ideas about

translation later, his suggestion that Bakhtin sees novels as translatable does stand when we consider Bakhtin's work on the genre in its totality.
32. Bakhtin, "From the Prehistory of Novelistic Discourse," 63.
33. Ibid.
34. Ibid., 65.
35. Bakhtin, "Discourse in the Novel," 378, emphasis in original.
36. Ibid., 362, emphases in original.
37. "Discourse in the Novel" predates "From the Prehistory of Novelistic Discourse" by about five years.
38. Bakhtin, "Discourse in the Novel," 362, emphasis added.
39. Bakhtin, "Forms of Time and Chronotope in the Novel," in *The Dialogic Imagination: Four Essays*, ed. Michael Holquist, trans. Caryl Emerson and Michael Holquist (Austin: University of Texas Press, 1981), 253.
40. Ibid.
41. As Bakhtin puts it, "there is a sharp and categorical boundary line between the actual world as source of representation and the world represented in the work ... But it is also impermissible to take this categorical boundary line as something absolute and impermeable (which leads to an oversimplified, dogmatic splitting of hairs)," ("Forms of Time and Chronotope in the Novel," 253).
42. Bakhtin, "Forms of Time and Chronotope in the Novel," 254, emphasis in original.
43. Ibid., 257, emphasis in original.
44. Although written during the period of 1959–61, these notes were not published in Russian until 1976.
45. Bakhtin, "The Problem of the Text in Linguistics, Philology, and the Human Sciences," 119, emphasis in original.
46. Ibid., 121–2.
47. Douglas Robinson, *The Translator's Turn* (Baltimore: Johns Hopkins University Press, 1991), 106.
48. George Lang, "La Belle Altérité: Towards a Dialogical Paradigm in Translation Theory?" *Canadian Review of Comparative Literature* (March/June 1992): 250.
49. Annette Lindegaard agrees that we have learned a lot from Bakhtin when she writes in "Translations: Originals in Dialogue," *Perspectives, Studies in Translatology* 4, no. 2 (1996) that "today we no longer believe in a universal intelligibility amid the plurality of languages... Thus, modern concepts of translation are primarily concerned with the *untranslatability of languages* rather than with *equivalence*" (157).
50. As Adeiano Marchetti argues in "Traduzione e inesauribilita del 'dire,'" *Anno II- Fasciocoli* 1–2 (1992), "The original, individual text, in which one author speaks, is an illusion" (159).

51. Galin Tihanov, "Ferrying a Thinker Across Time and Language: Bakhtin, Translation, World Literature," *Modern Languages Open* (2018), https://www.modernlanguagesopen.org/articles/10.3828/mlo.v0i0.230/
52. Ibid.
53. For more on Bakhtin's ideas about the nature of poetic discourse, see Margarita Marinova, "The Art and Answerability of Bakhtin's Poetics," in *Mikhail Bakhtin's Heritage in Literature, Arts, and Psychology: Art and Answerability*, ed. Slav Gratchev and Howard Mancing (Lanham, MD: Lexington Books, 2018), 41–62.

Bibliography

Bakhtin, Mikhail M. *The Dialogic Imagination: Four Essays*. Edited by Michael Holquist. Translated by Caryl Emerson and Michael Holquist. Austin: University of Texas Press, 1981.

Bakhtin, Mikhail M. "The Problem of the Text in Linguistics, Philology, and the Human Sciences: An Experiment in Philosophical Analysis." In *Speech Genres and Other Late Essays*. Edited by Caryl Emerson and Michael Holquist. Translated by Vern W. McGee, 103–31. Austin: University of Texas Press, 1992.

Bassnett, Susan, and Andre Lefevere, eds. *Translation, History, and Culture*. London: Pinter Publishers, 1990.

Emerson, Caryl. "Perevodimost'." *Slavic and East European Journal* 38, no. 1 (Spring 1994): 84–9.

Emerson, Caryl. "Translating Bakhtin: Does His Theory of Discourse Contain a Theory of Translation?" *University of Ottawa Quarterly* 53, no. 1 (1983): 23–33.

Gratchev, Slav, and Margarita Marinova, eds. *Mikhail Bakhtin, The Duvakin Interviews, 1973*. Translated by Margarita Marinova. Lewisburg: Bucknell University Press, 2019.

Kumar P. V., Amith. "Translation as 'Reported' Verbalization: An Extension of the Theoretical Postulates of 'the Bakhtin Circle.'" *International Journal of Comparative Literature & Translation Studies* 3, no. 1 (January 2015): 16–23.

Kumar P. V., Amith, and Milind Malshe. "Translation and Bakhtin's "Metalinguistics." *Perspectives: Studies in Translatology* 13, no. 2 (2005): 115–22.

Lang, George. "La Belle Altérité: Towards a Dialogical Paradigm in Translation Theory?" *Canadian Review of Comparative Literature* (March/June 1992): 237–51.

Lindegaard, Annette. "Translations: Originals in Dialogue." *Perspectives, Studies in Translatology* 4, no. 2 (1996): 153–62.

Marinova, Margarita. "The Art and Answerability of Bakhtin's Poetics." In *Mikhail Bakhtin's Heritage in Literature, Arts, and Psychology: Art and*

Answerability. Edited by Slav Gratchev and Howard Mancing, 41–62. Lanham, MD: Lexington Books, 2018.

Ol'khov, Pavel. "The Old New Bakhtin." *Russian Studies in Literature* 50, no. 4 (2014): 9–15.

Paz, Octavio. "Translation: Literature and Letters." Translated by Irene del Corral. In *Theories of Translation*. Edited by John Biguenet and Rainer Schulte, 152–63. Chicago: University of Chicago Press, 1992.

Robel, Léon. "Bakhtine et la traduction." In *Melanges offerts a Jean Peytard*. Edited by Jacques Bourquin and Daniel Jacobi, 641–4. Paris: Belles Lettres, 1993.

Robinson, Douglas, *The Translator's Turn*, Baltimore: Johns Hopkins University Press, 1991.

Tihanov, Galin. "Ferrying a Thinker Across Time and Language: Bakhtin, Translation, World Literature." *Modern Languages Open* (2018). https://www.modernlanguagesopen.org/articles/10.3828/mlo.v0i0.230/. Accessed December 2, 2020.

Traficante, Antonio. "Translating the Other: Lawrence, Bakhtin, and Verga." *Etudes Lawrenciennes: The Poetics of Travel and Cultural Otherness* 36 (2007): 219–53.

Zbinden, Karine. "The Bakhtin Circle and Translation." *Yearbook of English Studies* 36, no. 1 (2006): 157–67.

7

Eduardo Mendoza, Lost and Found in Translation

Melissa Garr

In a 2002 speech at the Universitat Pompeu Fabra in Barcelona titled "Translation and Its Discontents," famed Spanish author Eduardo Mendoza discussed the difficulty of translating humor into other languages, using an example from his 1990 novel *No Word from Gurb*. The novel, originally published in serial form in the *El País* newspaper, features an alien protagonist whose partner, Gurb, goes missing. When Gurb decides to take on human form to study human behavior, Mendoza has him transform into Spanish singer Marta Sánchez. Translators from various nations approached him wondering if they could use an equivalent because in France, Denmark, and Germany, no one knows Marta Sánchez. When he asked who the equivalent would be in those countries, the translators suggested Madonna. Mendoza said no, because "Madonna wouldn't be funny to the Danish, the way that Marta Sánchez is to us."[1]

Eduardo Mendoza is certainly an authority when it comes to translating: he worked as a simultaneous interpreter for the United Nations in the 1970s, and has published literary translations of such English-language works as E. M. Forster's *Howard's End* and Shakespeare's plays *Antony and Cleopatra* and *A Midsummer Night's Dream*. He is far better known for his original literary work, however. Since the publication of his first novel, *The Truth About the Savolta Case*, in 1975, Eduardo Mendoza has been one of Spain's most bestselling authors. His works have been nationally and internationally recognized, and he has won several of Spain's most prestigious literary prizes, including the Premio Cervantes in 2017, and the Premio Planeta in 2010 for *An Englishman in Madrid*, which also won the European Book Prize. His 1986 novel *The City of Marvels* has won at least four national and international awards and was made into a graphic novel in 2020. In addition to his novels, Mendoza has also written plays, nonfiction, travel guides, and books for children. Five of the Mendoza novels that have been rendered into English were translated by the award-winning Nick Caistor, who has received the

Valle-Inclán prize for translation twice for his exceptional literary translation work. It is notable, however, that compared to the translations of Mendoza's work into other languages, relatively little of his work has been translated into English. Moreover, English translations of his more explicitly humorous novels, such as *The Mystery of the Enchanted Crypt* (1979) and *No Word from Gurb* (1990), lag significantly behind the publication of the original works compared to English translations of his other works. Nearly thirty years separate the publication of the original Spanish text of *The Mystery of the Enchanted Crypt* and its English translation; seventeen years elapsed before *No Word from Gurb* had an English version. In contrast, Bernard Molloy's translation of *The City of Marvels* came out a scant two years after the novel's initial publication, *The Year of the Flood* and *An Englishman in Madrid* were both translated into English within four years, while *A Light Comedy* had an English language translation within seven. This is possibly because literary translation can result in the creation of beautiful, more nuanced texts, or conversely, may cause a peculiar "flattening" effect whereby much of the texture of the original text is lost. This "flattening" can be defined in Bakhtinian terms as a "fusion of authorial intentions with the image ... under changed conditions for perceiving an image, the curve may become less sharp and may even be stretched out into a straight line."[2] The task is rendered more difficult in the case of parodic novels and polyphonic novels, particularly if the author of the original work is a translator himself.

Because of his own literary translations and interpretation work, Mendoza is highly sensitive to what may be lost in translation; in his speech at the Universitat Pompeu Fabra, Mendoza asserted that a translation "can only worsen the original text, because if it improved it, it would betray it."[3] He further noted that the translators of a work are rarely recognized for it, and if they are it is "to make objections and point out its defects" unless it is nearly a recreation of the original work.[4] Maarten Steenmeijer advocates for celebrating the artistry of the translator, whom he describes as "a two-faced writer whose motherland is the phantasmal zone where the style of the author and the style of the translator come together and are interwoven."[5] Because of this interweaving, Mendoza posited the need for a pact between the reader and the translator, whereby the translator may assume that a reader has sufficient intelligence to understand that the work is not identical to its original, but the reader will also assume that the translator is working as honorably as possible, considering the difficulties that a particular text presents. Translating novels such as *No Word from Gurb* and *The Mystery of the Enchanted Crypt* is complicated not only because they are removed from their English-language readers by nation, language, culture, and, importantly, by the significant amounts of time between their publication, but also by the humor. These two novels also are parodies of literary genres—detective fiction and science fiction—and both include heteroglossia in the ways in which multiple languages intersect and interact dialogically in the original Spanish text, and double-voicedness in the parodic re-accentuation of genres and the carnivalesque representations of tropes and characters. Caistor's challenge as translator of these two novels in particular is to avoid the reader perceiving a text that is distant from them "against a background that is completely foreign to it," because then "it may be subject to a re-accentuation that radically distorts it."[6] This is especially true with these two novels, because double-voiced discourses, upon being perceived, can "very easily lose their second voice and fuse with single-voiced direct speech. Thus, a parodic quality ... may under certain circumstances be easily and quickly lost to perception, or be significantly weakened."[7] Caistor avoids this flattening effect by approaching the translations as re-accentuations, maintaining the double voicedness and heteroglossia of the original but in a re-accented way: through the grotesque body, juxtaposition of erudition and vulgarity, and the manipulation (or not) of cultural reference. He therefore is able to preserve humor in the text for English readers and avoid what Bakhtin calls a "crude violation of the author's will."[8] Following the explicit philosophy of the original text's author (made perhaps more challenging given that the author is himself a literary translator), Caistor keeps at the forefront of his translation the humor of his target-language audience, rather than rigid adherence to linguistic codes and systems.

The humor in both of these novels relies heavily on what Bakhtin refers to as "the grotesque body," which is a body "in the act of becoming":

> It is never finished, never completed; it is continually built, created, and builds and creates another body ... This is why the essential role belongs to those parts of the grotesque body in which it outgrows its own self, transgressing its own body, in which it conceives a new, second body: the bowels and the phallus.[9]

Acts that are performed at the boundaries between the body and the world, particularly involving parts of the body that protrude (Bakhtin lists eating, drinking, defecation, perspiration, sneezing, copulation, and pregnancy among these acts) represent the renewal and constant recreation of the body and its unfinalizability. In this category, I would argue, we should also include the breasts, as they protrude beyond the normal confines of a woman's body in times of fertility and menstruation, and they excrete milk, the production of which is quite literally fundamental to the renewal and creation of another body. The "grotesque" understanding of these parts of the body, and the acts associated with them, represents the carnivalizing spirit that upends hierarchies and celebrates the low, the vulgar, and the degraded in order to transform fear through laughter, for it "degrades and relieves at the same time, transforming fear into laughter."[10] The grotesque, as Tiffany Gagliardi Trotman points out, does not exist to disgust or repel, but rather indicates "an attempt to reflect true life by portraying characters realistically."[11]

In *The Mystery of the Enchanted Crypt*, this type of transformation is linked to the move from the oppressive, authoritarian Franco regime into the Movida of the 1980s. *The Mystery of the Enchanted Crypt* leverages the grotesque body to shoot down institutions of Francoist Spain including censorship, the police, the medical establishment, and religion by making them ridiculous and bringing them down to the level of the protagonist, an unnamed informant who is released by the police from a criminal mental institution to gather information about the disappearance of a young girl from a religious boarding school. Both Mendoza's and Caistor's texts, for example, render the protagonist's body odor as a fetid stench that should alienate him from others, particularly in enclosed, indoor spaces, but which does not impede him from engaging with a taxi driver who, when the protagonist pretends to be a member of the secret police, reveals that he, also, is in the secret police. The secret policeman engages in natural, professional chitchat in a taxi with a man who has, among other things, played a soccer match at high noon, fallen into a garbage dump, urinated on himself, spent a day in a train car full of rotten fish, and spilled rancid wine all over himself, as if the protagonist were a normal policeman and nothing were odd about him. Interactions and depictions of the grotesque body in both Mendoza's and Caistor's texts are similarly humorous because they are universal to the human experience; as Bakhtin notes, "in all languages there is a great number of expressions related to the genital organs, the anus and buttocks, the belly, the mouth and nose."[12] In these cases, the re-accentuation in *The Mystery of the Enchanted Crypt* comes not from the use of relatively inequivalent terms in a linguistic sense, because the terms used are very similar, but rather the cultural understanding of the effects of the grotesque body on the target culture reading them. The translator serves as a facilitator for dialogic understanding between the author of the source text, Mendoza, and the readers of the target culture: they are "brought to a dialogic interaction in which meaning arises out of shared understanding."[13] The understanding, here, is the laughter that debases and renews, brings down the institutions of authority that had repressed the characters in the novel, and allows us to see them as flawed and, ultimately, human.

Similarly, in *No Word from Gurb*, the grotesque body carries much of the humor in the novel, in this case thanks to the incorporeal (and also unnamed) alien protagonist. One example is when the protagonist has waited by the side of a road, in human form, for five hours hoping that his colleague Gurb will pass by. He takes a moment to reflect on his difficulty remembering to breathe in and out, and how when he forgot to do that for the space of five minutes, his eyes popped out and went rolling away, and he had to retrieve them from traffic and put them back in.[14] While Bakhtin observed that there were many expressions in multiple languages that involved genitals, arms, buttocks, the belly, mouth and nose, he also noted that "there are few expressions for the other parts of the body: arms and legs, face and eyes."[15] This is because these parts of the body are not generally rendered grotesque in order to carnivalize, to create renewing laughter. In *No Word from Gurb*, however, these body parts are rendered grotesque by the *alienness* of the subject. The unfamiliar eyes transgress the boundaries of the body and become new bodies in a (dangerous) world, requiring the alien to put himself at risk of being hit by cars in order to make himself whole again. The danger to the alien is purely hypothetical, as he has already been hit by several cars, and his primary concern is not to be conspicuous. The re-accentuated motivation—from fear of death to fear of being noticed—makes this scenario laughable, and the otherness of the protagonist and his observations about humanity cause human readers to laugh at themselves. In this way, the alien protagonist functions as a translator of the self, as "translation requires 'outsideness'—putting the self in the place of the other without losing oneself in the process."[16] It is difficult to read the episode about respiration without suddenly becoming aware of one's own breathing, literally re-accentuating one's normal, unconscious rhythm of breath. On top of the re-accentuation via translation of the self to the other, Caistor's translation additionally re-accentuates the transgression of the body in the way he describes the eyes separating from it. Mendoza writes that the eyes "le han salido disparados de las órbitas"—this Spanish phrase gives the image of eyes shooting, as from a gun, out of their sockets.[17] Caistor, on the other hand, renders this as "my eyes came out on stalks,"[18] which initially seems to maintain the connection to the body, until the next sentence in which the protagonist must retrieve them from the middle of the street. By transforming the nature of this transgression of the body, the dialogic encounter between the alien body and the environment it inhabits "opens both self and other up to the new and implies a notion of translation not as a relation of equivalence or sameness, but as an incessant movement of reciprocal transformation."[19] Caistor's translation heightens the unexpectedness of the protagonist's response, provoking laughter not just from the grotesque body, but also from the inversion of social and mortal fear relating to that body.

A danger in translation, however, especially with respect to a universalizing human experience such as the grotesque body, is that if one becomes "engulfed in the foreign text without referring to it in [one's] own language ... when there is too much harmony between the two, meaning disappears."[20] Bakhtin frames this as a merging of the source text and the target text; I have defined it here as a flattening effect. In order to overcome that, the translator keeps the other firmly in mind when choosing how to communicate it to the target culture's audience of readers. In *No Word from Gurb,* the alien's otherness from humanity keeps the flattening of the text at bay. In Caistor's translation of *The Mystery of the Enchanted Crypt,* this is evidenced primarily in two ways: descriptions of women's bodies and descriptions of bodily elimination. Early in the novel, the protagonist explains to us how he is showing restraint in not assaulting the nurse who has brought him a Pepsi-Cola by fondling what he describes as her "peras abultadas y jugosas que se rebelaban contra el níveo almidón de su uniforme,"[21] which literally translates as "swollen, juicy pears that rebelled against the snowy starch of her uniform." Caistor opts to use a fruit more commonly compared to breasts in English: "soft, juicy pair of melons straining against the starched white front of her uniform."[22] It is notable that these two descriptions indicate a significant difference in the size of the woman's breasts, as well as the attitude assumed by the breasts under the constraint of the uniform. In the English text, the breasts are straining outward, implying that they are being held back and contained successfully. In the Spanish text, the breasts are described as rebelling, implying a desire for freedom and autonomy (consistent with the myth of bra burning in the 1960s and 1970s, which is mentioned in chapter 9 when the protagonist depicts his suspect Mercedes's breasts in a similar way). The breasts as part of the grotesque body assume, in the 1970s Spanish text, an attitude of transgression against repression and imminent freedom for the female body (although still objectified by the male gaze) that had been forcefully reined in by the Sección Femenina during the Franco dictatorship. The breasts in Caistor's English text need no such deliberate thrust for freedom for female readers in the English-speaking world of 2008, and they represent a shift in beauty standards for women across the time and space between the two texts. In addition to carrying the humor associated with the grotesque body, the breasts in Caistor's translation can be considered a dialogic event in that they represent "the open-ended and never-ending dialogue between the translators' consciousness and the source and target cultures."[23] They also metonymically represent the progress achieved by women in the intervening twenty-nine years, and how much women continue to be subject to the patriarchy.

Another example of re-accentuation via the grotesque body in *The Mystery of the Enchanted Crypt* is the ways in which Caistor translates passages relating to bodily elimination or emissions. The Spanish text frequently uses explicit language and expletives to describe bodily functions related to the phallus and the anus. The general style of the text in Spanish, however, borrows its ornate and erudite (even Baroque) syntax from the picaresque novels of Spain's Golden Age, creating a jarring juxtaposition between "high" and "low" linguistic registers and situations that can be quite shocking, and funny. In the novel's first scene, the narrator describes chairs that are no longer in his psychiatrist Dr. Sugrañes's office because another patient "se hizo caca"[24] on one of them. Literally translated, the patient pooped himself on the chair. Caistor opts for the more euphemistic translation, "forgot himself on one of them,"[25] which additionally highlights how the diversity of the target-language culture can affect the reader's experience of the text—as a native speaker of American English myself, some of Caistor's euphemisms as a speaker of British English in this regard are quite foreign-sounding to my ear, or, as in this case, ambiguous. Another example of this is in a diatribe in chapter 13 from a bystander about pornographic magazines such as the one the narrator has just been perusing. In Caistor's translation, the bystander comments that "each time I read one of those magazines it drives me nuts."[26] The original Spanish text is much more explicit: the man says "me la pelo," which literally means "I jerk off." The English translation ends there, but in the original Spanish text, the bystander continues to speak, saying, "No me importa propagarlo a los cuatro vientos; todos estamos hechos de la misma pasta, ¿qué le parece?"[27] The phrase "propagarlo a los cuatro vientos" (spreading it to the four winds) is double-voiced in Spanish; it refers to the fact that the man has no compunction about telling anyone who will listen about his masturbatory proclivities regarding the magazines, and it also implies that he does not mind spreading his masturbatory emissions to the four winds, meaning do it anywhere he likes. It is perhaps to avoid losing the double-voicedness of this phrase relating to the grotesque body that Caistor opted to omit it entirely, as it would not necessarily add anything to the meaning for his target-language audience. It also wouldn't make sense following the euphemism "it drives me nuts," as that does not explicitly refer to masturbation.

Caistor does not always euphemize the original language referring to bodily emissions and the grotesque body, however. In some cases, he becomes even more explicit or uses expletives that are not present in the original Spanish text of *The Mystery of the Enchanted Crypt*. In chapter 16, as part of a plan to distract the dogs that patrol the boarding school, the narrator picks up what the Spanish text calls "excremento de perro"[28] (dog's excrement), and Caistor boldly calls "dog-shit."[29] Also, in chapter 8, prior to the narrator breaking into a wealthy family's home to interrogate the daughter, a group of maids suddenly disperse like startled pigeons who will, in Mendoza's words, defecate on you,[30] while Caistor opts for the phrase "crap on you."[31] When in chapter 5, two policemen are "searching" (or rather, destroying) the narrator's sister's house, the narrator remarks that they don't know what they're getting into. In the Spanish text, one of the policeman responds, "¿Y eso?" (What's that?).[32] Caistor, on the other hand, has him say, "What the fuck?"[33] And as a final example, when the narrator is interrogating Mercedes about whether her friend was sexually involved with a much older man as a young girl, the narrator asks her, "¿Se la …?"[34] The ellipses here omit the verb, which could be any verb that refers to a sexual act done by him to her. Caistor makes the verb more explicit in his translation into English, but *also* censors the expletive: "He **** her?"[35] Despite the fact that the verb "fuck" has been used both in its metaphorical and literal meanings several times elsewhere in the translation, he chooses to omit it here, which oddly renders the word *more* vulgar than when he actually comes out and says it. The softer, more euphemistic general tone of the English translation makes the use of explicit language in Caistor's re-accentuation much more jarring and crude by comparison. In this way, without imitating the Baroque style and syntax (which would be difficult to render in English), Caistor has translated the shock of grotesque and vulgar language, particularly relating to the grotesque body, being juxtaposed with erudite style, in a different way that resonates more linguistically and culturally with English-language readers in the twenty-first century. Mendoza would undoubtedly salute him for managing this; Mendoza himself described the work of translation as work "that is done as a duet between the author of a text and its translator, and its translator and the receiver of this text, that is neither universal nor atemporal."[36] In other words, the translation is dependent upon the time, space, and culture of the target audience, not just its language; this is what makes it necessarily a re-accentuation. This is also why, as Mendoza points out, "any classic text must be translated by every generation"[37]—while the original texts never seem to have an expiration date, translations need to be redone over and over as the time and culture that produced them no longer speaks to the time and culture that wants to read the work in translation.

Another way in which Mendoza's humorous texts are re-accentuated in Nick Caistor's translations is in the way they transform the texts' original heteroglossia. By this, of course, we refer to "another's speech in another's language, serving to express authorial intentions but in a refracted way."[38] Mendoza's texts are often set in, and created in, the heteroglot environment of Barcelona, home to two native languages, and in which circulate hundreds of other languages through immigration, tourism, and travel. Although Barcelona is fiercely proud of its multilinguistic heritage, the constant push and pull of language hegemony, explicitly imposed from Franco's government on Cataluña during the dictatorship, makes the city a setting that is constantly in linguistic tension, ripe for the spirit of parody to amplify ambiguities and stress points. Bakhtin notes that parody flourishes under these conditions because "only polyglossia fully frees consciousness from the tyranny of its own language and its own myth of language."[39] Mendoza himself is fully aware of the mechanism of heteroglossia; he notes that, as an author, he benefits from his experience as an interpreter and translator because the knowledge of language conferred by this experience helps the writer "understand that each language has many languages."[40] The linguistic richness of Barcelona is not only found in the dialogic interplay among Catalan, Spanish, and the many other languages that move through and make their homes there, but also in the sociocultural languages operating dialogically *within* each of them. The translation of such a text, then, presents particular linguistic challenges beyond just the level of the humor of the text (which, in the case of *The Mystery of the Enchanted Crypt* and *No Word from Gurb*, is also often linguistic). Take the case of character names in *The Mystery of the Enchanted Crypt*, for example. Characters bear such colorful names as "Cagomelo Purga" (the first name refers to someone shitting themselves, and the last name means "laxative"), Vicenzo Hermafrodito Halfmann, and Plutonio Sobobo Cuadrado (whose middle name is reflective of both the verb "to fondle" and a slang term for "stupid"). Caistor mostly[41] opts to keep these character names the same in the English translation. While the semantic play and double-entendre are largely lost on the target-language audience, leaving them in Spanish serves a different purpose: it encourages the reader to maintain a sense of *place* at the forefront of their mind. Barcelona is an integral part of the story, not just its backdrop, and the English-language reader who comes across these unfamiliar (even in Spanish) names does not forget that the text is not taking place just anywhere, but rather, in the Barcelona of the late 1970s. In this way Caistor maintains a dialogic understanding between the readers of the target language text and their source language author; this understanding "makes the other's words mine without completely obliterating their foreignness, their origin outside myself. There can be no response if this outsideness is forgotten."[42] The awareness of this outsideness creates a space for re-accentuation that might otherwise be lost. It is successful here because, as Bakhtin asserts, the re-accentuation of languages in the novel is conditioned by "a change in the background animating dialogue, that is, changes in the composition of heteroglossia."[43]

It is not merely the characters' names that highlight the heteroglossia of the texts and provide for re-accentuation through it; *The Mystery of the Enchanted Crypt* includes other languages and dialects throughout the characters' speech. The text includes, for example, several Latinisms such as "in fraganti," "ecce homo," and "mutatis mutandis," which Caistor preserves as they serve a similar function in the English text: to highlight the unexpectedly erudite narrative style of the uneducated, insane narrator. It may perhaps be more marked in English, as the English text cannot grammatically render the overelaborate baroque syntax in which these phrases appear in the Spanish text. Another example is when the protagonist meets a prospective client for his sister, Candida, who is a prostitute. He deduces from the man's blue eyes and blond hair that he must be a Swedish sailor, and decides to attempt to speak to him in English. The original Spanish text renders the protagonist's words in English: "'*Me*,' [I said, drawing on my English, somewhat rusty from disuse], "*Candida: sisters. Candida, me sister, big fart. No, no big fart: big fuck. Strong. Not expensive.*"[44] It is notable that the use of English within the Spanish text harkens back to the grotesque body. The humor relies on Spanish speakers understanding the difference in English between "fart" and "fuck" and that the designation "sisters" does not grammatically refer to mixed-gender sibling groups in either English or Spanish. The humor is additionally marked given the response by the "Swedish" man, who tells the protagonist in perfect Spanish to shut his trap; the protagonist even believes he detects a slight accent from the neighboring region of Aragón. Caistor, in his translation, omits the Spanish dialogue marker referring to the protagonist's rusty English, opting instead for the protagonist "tak[ing] advantage of the opportunity fate had cast me to show off my English."[45] The tone in which the protagonist's English utterance is rendered is the opposite of the original in Caistor's translation: instead of the protagonist apologizing for the poor state of his English, he expresses pride in it before butchering it and using offensive language. Instead of the humor relying on the audience understanding the meaning of the English words, it now relies on the disconnect between the protagonist's self-assessment of his English language proficiency and his demonstrated proficiency when he speaks. Likewise, in *Sin Noticias de Gurb*, the alien laments that human languages are laborious and childish because they cannot even understand a simple sentence such as "109328745108y34-19«poe8vhqa9enf087qjnrf-09aqsd nfñ9q8w3r4v21dfkf=q3wy oiqwe=q3u 1o9=853491926rn 1nfp24851ir093 48413k8449f385j9t830t82 = 34 ut t2egu34851mfkfg-231lfgklwhgq0i2ui347 56=13ir2487-23 49r20i45u62-4852ut-34582-9238v43 597 46 82 = 3t98458 9672394ut945467 = 2-3tugywoit = 238tej 93 46 7523 fiwuy6-23f3yt-238984rohg- 2343ijn87b8b7ytgyt65 4376687by79."[46] These scenes, as parodic discourse, require that two languages, the language being parodied and the language of parody, cross one another; the parodying language, "against whose background the parody is constructed and perceived, does not ... enter as such into the parody itself, but is invisibly present in it."[47] This is what Caistor must, and does, recreate and maintain in the English translation, and the shifted accentuation of the parody translates the humorous effect to the audience of the other language.

Although Caistor generally leaves characters' names in the original Spanish in both novels, there are other names, mostly cultural references, which he often translates or modifies according to the rule of thumb proposed by Mendoza himself: that it provokes the same humor in an English-speaking audience as the reference would for the Spanish-speaking audience. In the case of *The Mystery of the Enchanted Crypt*, this often means that references to famous people, songs, or other pop culture are changed in the English version, either because the English-speaking audience wouldn't get the joke or because it might cause confusion. For example, the narrator's sister was told (erroneously) in her youth that she looked like Juanita Reina, a Spanish singer and actress from the 1940s and 1950s. Caistor uses instead the image of Judy Garland, and instead of the narrator's sister being deemed too ugly to sing "María de las Mercedes" (a copla of the type sung by Juanita Reina) on the radio, she was forbidden to sing "Somewhere over the Rainbow."[48] Cándida's client is described as looking like the child of Boris Karloff and Mae West in the English translation, rather than Kubala (a heavy-browed soccer player) and la Bella Dorita[49] (a famous Spanish cabaret performer frequently compared with Mae West) in the original Spanish. On another occasion, a picture of a man in red is described as looking like the Hulk instead of famous Spanish tenor Luis Mariano,[50] and the protagonist is compared to Frankenstein's monster instead of fictional pirate Sandokan.[51] Nor do these changes refer only to people; when the protagonist is in the crypt at the end of the novel, a black man appears and cites "the classical author" as saying "I've had a long time to consider it!"[52] In the Spanish text, the classical author in question is Tirso de Molina, whose character Don Juan uses the phrase "cuán largo me lo fiáis" (appearing in Mendoza's text[53]) to express disdain for the idea that he will have a reckoning for his sins any time soon. In Mendoza's Spanish text, the quote is accompanied by a salacious glance by Mercedes toward the black man's genitals, creating a context in which the adjective "largo," or "long" (which in Tirso de Molina's text refers to the time Don Juan may have left) is implied to refer to how long the other characters believe his penis might be, although he wants to be a poet instead of a sex object. The deep cultural reference of this quote, coupled with the sexual comment made by Mercedes, creates the double-voiced parody of the scene in Spanish. In the

English version, Mercedes's comment that his true talent would be wasted if he only wrote poetry, and her glance toward his genitals, shifts the humorous emphasis to her own statement of desire rather than to his response, as his rejoinder in English doesn't justify by his deep knowledge his desire to be a poet or skewer her for racially stereotyping him. These changes reflect not only linguistic realities of creating an "answering word" that will "meet the anticipation of target readers,"[54] but also takes into account the amount of *time* that has passed between the novel's original publication and the release of Caistor's translation. Even if Caistor had left these cultural references the same in the English text and allowed readers to just Google them, they still would not carry the weight of the humor that they carry if he finds the humorous equivalent that would anticipate the response of an English-speaking reader in the twenty-first century.

Caistor takes a different approach in *No Word from Gurb*, however. The majority of the cultural references remain the same in both the Spanish and English texts. This is because a translation can sometimes "fail to render the dynamic double-voicedness in the source text"; in those cases, leaving the words in the source language instead of translating them can "infuse one more voice to the already existing multiple voices … and thus contribute to the dialogic appeal" of the translation.[55] In *No Word from Gurb*, unlike in *The Mystery of the Enchanted Crypt*, the humor of the reference is often clear because of the *context* in which the reference is employed, rather than knowledge of the reference itself. For example, on Day 10, the alien protagonist appears in Barcelona in the form of the Count-Duke of Olivares with a primary objective of "not attracting attention."[56] Appearing as a notable noble personage would hardly serve that goal, even if a reader were not aware of him being a sixteenth- to seventeenth-century noble personage, complete with Baroque wardrobe. Similarly, after being injured, the protagonist changes himself into Tutmosis II, because, he reasons, then he'll already have bandages on;[57] on another occasion he transforms himself into Mahatma Gandhi so as to have more appropriate clothing to deal with the heat[58]; when he has to appear in front of a judge, the narrator turns himself and another prisoner from his cell into famous Spanish authors and philosophers José Ortega y Gasset and Miguel de Unamuno.[59] In the last instance, the judge is confused and decides to let them go because he "wants a quiet life" and doesn't want to deal with all of this. In both cases, the humor comes from the context rather than intimate knowledge of the historical figures or the way Spanish people would have related to them. The humor is able to be preserved in this way in *No Word from Gurb* more than in *The Mystery of the Enchanted Crypt* because the otherness that preserves the "outsideness" of the subject, rather than one's fusion with it and therefore flattening of the double-voicedness, comes from the fact that the protagonist and narrator is as alien to a Spanish-speaking audience as to an English one. His attempts to approximate and imitate human behavior and interactions are universally ridiculous. The protagonist becomes as much as reflection of us as the text is a reflection of the world that produced it; Bakhtin points out that when a text "becomes the object of our cognition, we can speak about the reflection of a reflection" as a "subjective reflection of the objective world."[60] In this text, *we* are the object of cognition for the protagonist, as well as the text for us, creating a reflection of a reflection of a reflection. The translation doesn't need to carry the weight of the double-voicedness linguistically; it is largely preserved in the premise of the novel itself. The translation into English serves more to re-accentuate the angle from which that alien observes human life.

In his speech at the Universitat Pompeu Fabra, Eduardo Mendoza asserted that "there exists no translation that does not carry with it a re-elaboration of the text, for the simple reason that a literary work is not a mere accumulation of words meant to inform," but something that has what is called in Spanish "voluntad de estilo."[61] This Spanish phrase (which is difficult to translate) refers to the conscious, deliberate decisions on the part of the translator to style the work in a certain way. Mendoza's words echo Bakhtin's idea of re-accentuation, or "translating from one accentual register to another."[62] Thus, it is clear that by even undertaking to translate these underrated comic novels into English at all, Nick Caistor has dedicated himself to re-accentuating them. In addition to the self-evident challenges of transforming the language so that a target-language reader can still access the essence of the original text, he must also bridge cultural gaps between the source language culture and the target language culture, as well as the many cultures that speak the target language; he must also make the translation accessible to English language audiences seventeen to twenty-nine years removed from the novels' original publication. One problem inherent in translation is that it is subject to the processes of transformation known as canonization and re-accentuation. These two processes mirror competing forces described by Bakhtin in "Discourse in the Novel:" centripetal force, pushing toward linguistic centralization and unification, the idea of a "correct language" that imposes heavy limits on heteroglossia; and centrifugal force, which is stratifying, dynamic, linguistically lively, and splits languages up, accentuating the nuances and differences between them.[63] I would argue that canonization is a centripetal force, whereas re-accentuation is a centrifugal force. When texts become canonized, they become reified. Many of Mendoza's texts are becoming canonized, particularly *The City of Marvels*; it is the novel of Barcelona and its plucky picaresque character is now the quintessence of the postmodern pícaro, which works against the novel's irreverent, heteroglot, parodic qualities. Then there are these misfit novels, *The Mystery of the Enchanted Crypt* and *No Word from Gurb,* generally overlooked by the big literary awards because their purpose is just to be funny, even though they are also much more than that. Both novels are already re-accentuations—of detective fiction and science fiction, respectively— and both feature first-person narrators who are also misfits, who, instead of seeking to build a coherent narrative that makes sense to everyone, destabilize their own narration to the extent that the novels even laugh at themselves. It is perhaps no wonder that translations of these novels in particular came out so much later; other, equally unrepentantly comedic novels in the series begun by *The Mystery of the Enchanted Crypt* have still never been translated. Nick Caistor leaned into the multiple intentions of the text, including the "refracted intention of the author,"[64] and, consistent with Bakhtin's definition of double-voicedness, created a text that is dialogically interrelated to its source text, and internally dialogized in itself. He identified the essences of the text in its juxtaposition of erudition and vulgarity in its style, its call to popular culture, and its carnivalesque celebration of the grotesque body, and he re-accentuated these elements in such a way that the heteroglossia and double-voicedness are still available to English language readers. The texts for English readers are perhaps not celebrating post-dictatorship freedom or exploring ontological and political uncertainty of the post-Franco period, but they certainly reflect the globalized, multicultural world of the twenty-first century and the decentralization of authority that characterizes the information age in which the translations were born.[65]

Notes

1. Eduardo Mendoza, "La traducción y sus descontentos," *Inaugural Lessons* (Barcelona: Universitat Pompeu Fabra, 2002), https://www.upf.edu/en/web/traduccio/llicons-inaugurals#collapse--69354058117.
2. Mikhail M. Bakhtin, "Discourse in the Novel," *The Dialogic Imagination: Four Essays,* ed. Michael Holquist, trans. Caryl Emerson and Michael Holquist (Austin: University of Texas Press, 1981), 419–20.
3. Mendoza, "La traducción y sus descontentos." My translation.
4. Ibid. My translation.
5. Maarten Steenmeijer, "Sobre la traducción literaria y la identidad del traductor," *Pasavento: Revista de estudios hispánicos* 4, no. 2 (Summer 2016): 281–92.
6. Bakhtin, "Discourse in the Novel," 420.
7. Ibid., 419.
8. Ibid., 420.

9. Mikhail M. Bakhtin, *Rabelais and His World*, trans. Hélène Iswolsky (Bloomington: Indiana University Press, 1984), 317.
10. Ibid., 335.
11. Tiffany Gagliardi Trotman, *Eduardo Mendoza's Crime Novels: The Function of Carnivalesque Discourse in Post-Franco Spain, 1979–2001* (Lewiston: Edwin Mellen Press, 2009).
12. Bakhtin, *Rabelais and His World*, 319.
13. Kumar P. V. Amith and Milind Malshe, "Translation and Bakhtin's 'Metaliguistics,'" *Perspectives* 13, no. 2 (2005), doi: 10.1080/09076760508668980, 120.
14. Eduardo Mendoza, *Sin noticias de Gurb* (Barcelona: Seix Barral, 2001), Kindle.
15. Bakhtin, *Rabelais and His World*, 319.
16. Amith and Malshe, "Translation and Bakhtin's 'Metaliguistics,'" 116.
17. Mendoza, *Sin noticias de Gurb*.
18. Eduardo Mendoza, *No Word from Gurb* (London: Telegram, 2013), 11.
19. Esther Peeren, "The Subject as Translator: Mikhail Bakhtin and Jean Laplanche," *Doletiana: revista de traduccio Litteratura/Arts* 1 (2007): 3.
20. Ibid., 4.
21. Eduardo Mendoza, *El misterio de la cripta embrujada* (Barcelona: Seix Barral, 1979), 23.
22. Eduardo Mendoza, *The Mystery of the Enchanted Crypt* (London: Telegram, 2008), 17
23. Amith and Malshe, "Translation and Bakhtin's 'Metaliguistics,'" 116.
24. Mendoza, *El misterio de la cripta embrujada*, 17.
25. Mendoza, *Mystery of the Enchanted Crypt*, 11.
26. Ibid., 137.
27. Mendoza, *El misterio de la cripta embrujada*, 147. My translation: "I don't mind spreading it to the four winds; we're all made of the same stuff, what do you think?"
28. Ibid., 172.
29. Mendoza, *Mystery of the Enchanted Crypt*, 161.
30. Mendoza, *El misterio de la cripta embrujada*, 88.
31. Mendoza, *Mystery of the Enchanted Crypt*, 79.
32. Mendoza, *El misterio de la cripta embrujada*, 63.
33. Mendoza, *Mystery of the Enchanted Crypt*, 55.
34. Mendoza, *El misterio de la cripta embrujada*, 116. This could be translated into English as "Did he…?"
35. Mendoza, *Mystery of the Enchanted Crypt*, 107.
36. Mendoza, "La traducción y sus descontentos." My translation.
37. Ibid. My translation.
38. Bakhtin, "Discourse in the Novel," 324.
39. Mikhail M. Bakhtin, "From the Prehistory of Novelistic Discourse," *The Dialogic Imagination: Four Essays*, ed. Michael Holquist, trans. Caryl

Emerson and Michael Holquist (Austin: University of Texas Press, 1981), 61.
40. Lourdes de Rioja, "Eduardo Mendoza, sobre interpretación," *YouTube*, uploaded by Lourdes de Rioja, January 26, 2013, www.youtube.com/watch?v=Xv7K7L0RGaA&feature=emb_logo.
41. The one character name he does translate is the name the protagonist's mother wanted to give him at his baptism: "Gonewiththewind." As this corresponds to the official translation of the name of the movie as it appears in Spanish in the text, it is notable only for being the only name of an active character in the story to be rendered into English, and was perhaps done because it could be done with little loss of humor or meaning.
42. Peeren, "The Subject as Translator," 4.
43. Bakhtin, "Discourse in the Novel," 420.
44. Mendoza, *El misterio de la cripta embrujada*, 44. The text in italics is originally in English; the non-italicized text is my translation of the Spanish phrase.
45. Mendoza, *Mystery of the Enchanted Crypt*, 36.
46. Mendoza, *No Word from Gurb*, 30–1; it means "Give me 9 kilos of turnips," undoubtedly a very useful sentence.
47. Bakhtin, "From the Prehistory of Novelistic Discourse," 75.
48. Mendoza, *Mystery of the Enchanted Crypt*, 32; Mendoza, *El misterio de la cripta embrujada*, 40.
49. Mendoza, *Mystery of the Enchanted Crypt*, 35; Mendoza, *El misterio de la cripta embrujada*, 43.
50. Mendoza, *Mystery of the Enchanted Crypt*, 73; Mendoza, *El misterio de la cripta embrujada*, 82.
51. Mendoza, *Mystery of the Enchanted Crypt*, 77; Mendoza, *El misterio de la cripta embrujada*, 86.
52. Mendoza, *Mystery of the Enchanted Crypt*, 174.
53. Mendoza, *El misterio de la cripta embrujada*, 186.
54. Amith and Malshe, "Translation and Bakhtin's 'Metaliguistics,'" 115.
55. Ibid., 120.
56. Mendoza, *No Word from Gurb*, 8.
57. Ibid., 129.
58. Ibid., 77.
59. Ibid., 19–20.
60. Mikhail M. Bakhtin, "The Problem of the Text," *Speech Genres and Other Late Essays*, ed. Caryl Emerson and Michael Holquist, trans. Vern W. McGee (Austin: University of Texas Press, 1986), 113.
61. Mendoza, "La traducción y sus descontentos."
62. Bakhtin, "From the Prehistory of Novelistic Discourse," 421.
63. Ibid., 270–2.
64. Ibid., 324.

65. The reader may be holding onto a very important question regarding the example Mendoza gave in his speech about who to choose as the humorous equivalent for Marta Sánchez in the translation of *No Word from Gurb*. Nick Caistor had the benefit of the author's thoughts on the subject, and decided to make the text his own: he went with Madonna.

Bibliography

Bakhtin, Mikhail M. "Discourse in the Novel." *The Dialogic Imagination: Four Essays*. Edited by Michael Holquist. Translated by Caryl Emerson and Michael Holquist, 259–422. Austin: University of Texas Press, 1981.

Bakhtin, Mikhail M. "From the Prehistory of Novelistic Discourse." *The Dialogic Imagination: Four Essays*. Edited by Michael Holquist. Translated by Caryl Emerson and Michael Holquist, 41–83. Austin: University of Texas Press, 1981.

Bakhtin, Mikhail M. "The Problem of the Text." *Speech Genres and Other Late Essays*. Edited by Caryl Emerson and Michael Holquist. Translated by Vern W. McGee, 103–31. Austin: University of Texas Press, 1986.

Bakhtin, Mikhail M. *Rabelais and His World*. Translated by Hélène Iswolsky. Bloomington: Indiana University Press, 1984.

Bakhtin, Mikhail M. "Response to a Question from the *Novy Mir* Editorial Staff." *Speech Genres and Other Late Essays*. Edited by Caryl Emerson and Michael Holquist. Translated by Vern W. McGee, 1–9. Austin: University of Texas Press, 1986.

De Rioja, Lourdes. "Eduardo Mendoza, sobre interpretación." YouTube video, uploaded by Lourdes de Rioja, January 26, 2013. www.youtube.com/watch?v=Xv7K7L0RGaA&feature=emb_logo.

Gagliardi Trotman, Tiffany. *Eduardo Mendoza's Crime Novels: The Function of Carnivalesque Discourse in Post-Franco Spain, 1979–2001*. Lewiston: Edwin Mellen Press, 2009.

Kumar P. V., Amith, and Milind Malshe. "Translation and Bakhtin's 'Metalinguistics.'" *Perspectives* 13, no. 2 (2005): 115–22. Accessed August 27, 2020. doi: 10.1080/09076760508668980.

Mendoza, Eduardo. *El misterio de la cripta embrujada*. Barcelona: Seix Barral, 1979.

Mendoza, Eduardo. "La traducción y sus decontentos." In *Inaugural Lessons*. Barcelona: Universitat Pompeu Fabra, 2002. https://www.upf.edu/en/web/traduccio/llicons-inaugurals#collapse--69354058117.

Mendoza, Eduardo. *The Mystery of the Enchanted Crypt*. Translated by Nick Caistor. London: Telegram, 2008.

Mendoza, Eduardo. *No Word from Gurb*. London: Telegram, 2013.

Mendoza, Eduardo. *Sin noticias de Gurb*. Barcelona: Seix Barral, 2001. Kindle.

Peeren, Esther. "The Subject as Translator: Mikhail Bakhtin and Jean Laplanche." *Doletiana: revista de traduccio Litteratura/Arts* 1 (2007): 1–12.

Steenmeijer, Maarten. "Sobre la traducción literaria y la identidad del traductor." *Pasavento: Revista de estudios hispánicos* 4, no. 2 (Summer 2016): 281–92.

8

Dialogue Disrupted

Victor Fet

1. Introduction

It is widely accepted today that "translation is a double writing, a rewriting of the foreign text according to domestic cultural values."[1] Translation is a Bakhtinian dialogue between the frozen past and the changing present, a time-transcending light beam connecting pixels of our civilization. It exists only as long as this dialogue continues—as long as one can recognize, and take seriously, a relevant signal coming from the past. The intensity and success of this dialogue depends on cultural receptivity and the needs of those on the receiving end.

Many classical European texts have been translated to my native Russian over the last century and under very different circumstances, as Russia and its language underwent rapid, dramatic changes. Among these, *The Hunting of the Snark* (1876) by Lewis Carroll appears today—quite unexpectedly—to be among the most frequently translated English poems.[2] In this, it rivals Edgar Poe's *The Raven* (twenty-two major translations listed in the Russian Wikipedia) and Shakespeare's Sonnet 66. However, an examination of the nearly forty Russian translations of *The Hunting of the Snark* published since 1991 reveals a disturbing trend that I will discuss here.

2. Lewis Carroll in Russia

There are over twenty translations of the *Alice* books in Russia. Nina Demurova's classical translations of the two *Alice* books (first version published in 1967) brought Lewis Carroll to my generation during the Soviet period; both used a clear, traditional language with little slang. Demurova (1930—2021), who passed away recently in Moscow, was also the most prominent Russian scholar of Carroll's oeuvre for many decades. As part of her interviews with fellow connoisseurs of Carroll's work, she often liked to ask them what they attributed Carroll's popularity in Russia to. Perhaps the best answer came from the poet Olga Sedakova (b. 1949), who in 1978 provided translations of parody poems for Demurova's *Alice in Wonderland*: "My guess is that it is because of that ethereal irrationality, I would say, that dance of meanings which somewhat relieves the perception of the absurd that surrounds us. The absurd in everyday Russia is heavy and desperate, it seems to swallow one like a swamp; but here, one finds hidden play. One can play freely with the absurd environment! This is what, I feel, consoles and pleases our domestic reader."[3] Yuri Vashchenko (b. 1941), one of the best illustrators of Carrollian translations in Russia, agreed: "What in Europe and England is a subject of nonsense, in Russia more often than not is a subject of reality … In Russia, we have very definite relationships with nonsense: sometimes it becomes so real it is not nonsense anymore. It's a murky rocking back and forth, just like Humpty-Dumpty, like rocking in a chair: a little bit this way, and you are sitting in a dense, legitimate reality, nothing unusual; but a little bit that way, and it is a lunatic's raving, you break your neck, and there is no rocking anymore."[4] Another great illustrator Oleg Lipchenko (b. 1953) explained the attraction further: "Carroll and his Alice were among the little that was available for us from the 'free world,' the world of free thought. *Alice* is not dissident literature, but maybe it is a different order of dissent … The entire trip is improvised; all encounters are unexpected and not defined by previous events. It is that NON-following of fairy-tale rules, its standard structures, which is the most appealing, the most delightful. It is a feeling of freedom—as in a dream."[5]

All of Demurova's interviewees agreed: Carroll indeed wrote about our life, about our, Soviet absurd, about the totalitarian neglect of truth and logic. We in the USSR took our cues from his dry humor, gentle paradoxes, and existential despair. As the literary scholar and translator Evgeny Vitkovskii summed it up, "We were told we lived in *Wonderland*, while in reality we lived *Behind the Looking-Glass*."[6]

Of course, those comments largely refer *not* to the original English texts of Lewis Carroll, but rather the translations of his *Alice* books read by Russian readers in the 1960–70s. The times have changed, and we see a different trend in the 1990–2000s, reflected, since 1991, in Russian translations of *The Hunting of the Snark*.

3. The Original Poem and Its Many Translations

Lewis Carroll's third (after the *Alice* books of 1865 and 1871) highest achievement, *The Hunting of the Snark* (1876), resembles a Victorian parody of heroic ballads. It has a clear surrealist streak, akin to the light parody Carroll used already in his early "Anglo-Saxon parodies" and the famous "Jabberwocky." Carroll, a life-long Oxonian, was well acquainted with the tradition of "macaronic" scholastic parody that Bakhtin discussed in detail in "From the Prehistory of Novelistic Discourse"[7]—although the carnivalesque nature of traditional parody was consciously Bawdlerized by Carroll for his children audience. This genre is reflected in both *Alice* books in their parodies of nursery rhymes, the didactic verse by Isaac Watts, and the like.

Light, often raucous, parody English verses (such as limericks) were favored by many Soviet translators since the 1920s. Often, however, they created very remote equivalents, as they followed rigid templates such as the typical AABBA rhyming scheme of a limerick, but ended up replacing most of the original content. This playful, deceptively easy approach required much more of skill from the translator than was often available.

Unlike *Alice* (the first Russian translation of the first book was published in 1879), it took hundred years for Bellman and his crew to reach the Russian shores. The very first full published *Snarks* appeared only in 1991 in two separate translations by Grigory Kruzhkov and Mikhail Pukhov. My 2016 research on the bibliographic history of this poem's publication in Russia revealed the existence of eighty-five translations (sixty-seven full and eighteen partial), by forty-two translators, dating from 1958 to 2015.[8] The list includes thirty-six different full versions by thirty-three translators, and all discovered full reprintings.

While this attention is remarkable, and even cult-like, most of the translations suffer from a severe detachment from the original text. Within the last twenty-five post-Soviet years, when, finally, much more freedom was allowed in print in Russia, many translators used this opportunity to develop peculiar, runaway versions of Carroll's texts. Lewis Carroll became an excuse for an unbridled slang and rudeness due to his "eccentric foreign aura," as Valerii Anan'in put it. Many translators clearly just wanted to invent their own nonsense by painting over the canvas provided by the famous Victorian. Often, this debased Lewis Carroll's original text, or the Russian language, or both.

Is an "adequate translation" of such a poem as the *Snark* even possible? Only some of the many attempts can be characterized as decent. What criteria for "being close to the original" (minimal re-accentuation) can be deployed, and how could they be combined with inevitable replacements (domestication)? It is easier to determine what *should not be done*. As a minimum, in my opinion, a translator clearly should not use vocabulary and expressions that the author could, but did not use.

While no one can completely and faithfully render all of Carroll's images and expressions in Russian, many translators followed the text diligently and made an honest effort to recast it in a meaningful, polite Russian. Interestingly, no one has yet attempted to approximate this Victorian poem into the literary Russian of the 1870s, which had its parallel tradition of nonsense poetry in the oeuvre of "Koz′ma Prutkov," a fictional character created by Alexei K. Tolstoy and his friends, starting from the 1850s.

Many versions modernize the original Victorian poetry intentionally—and often excessively. A few translators attempted to follow the important Russian absurdist tradition of the Oberiu (the acronym for the Group of Real Art) of 1920s–30s, which was close to Surrealism and Dadaism (especially Daniil Kharms). Some translators tend to invent new words and names. Others change the tone of the text so much that it becomes a parody, a mockery that cannot be called an honest, or faithful, translation.

4. Name Choices

The tone and attitude of a translator are often easily discerned from their choice of vocabulary. One can get an immediate feeling of a Snark translator's attitude looking at how the names of the crew are translated. Demurova[9] compared four Russian translations (by Kruzhkov, Kliuev, Lipkin, and Iakhnin), discussing the various "degrees of freedom" within which the translators work. "Bellman," for example, is difficult to translate. Sometimes this name is retained in the Russian version, which is admissible as it looks like a proper surname, and it is quite common in modern Russian to use English words such as *Barmen* or *Biznesmen*). "Bellman" has often been rendered as "Botsman" (boatswain), which is probably the only available maritime term. (We should note, though, that Carroll himself could have used "Boatswain" if he chose to, but did not.)

When Evgenii Kliuev playfully morphs "Botsman" into an invented "*Bomtsman*" (*bom* is a bell sound), his translation parts ways with Carroll, who used no neologisms for crew names; moreover, the word is hardly pronounceable. Mikhail Matveev's "*Bill Sklianki*" (strike [the ship's] bell), an admissible word pun, draws on a great Russian tradition of translating English nonsense poetry. However, it makes the tone of the poem more playful—akin to the poetry of the *Alice* books, or nursery rhymes translated by the famous Russian poets Samuil Marshak and Kornei Chukovsky—than it actually is. Other transformations of the Bellman are more random: he becomes a "*Brandmeister*" (a chief fireman) in the prose retelling by Aleksandr Floria, or "*Barabanshchik*" (a drummer) in my own 1981 version.

The name "*Blagozvon*" (*blago*—"good," *zvon*—"toll"), invented by Mikhail Pukhov, and adopted also by Andrei Moskotel′nikov, remains one of the best choices. It suits a Tennyson-like Bellman as depicted by Henry Holiday, as it evokes "*blagovest*" (church bell toll). It is an admissible choice, although a church bell is clearly different from Bellman's handbell (or a ship's bell, "*rynda*"). Mikhail Vainshtein's "*Zvonar*" is, in fact, a church bellman. Unfortunately, "*Blagozvon*" also evokes a similarly built Russian noun, which is a mild expletive indicating a person (usually a public official) talking nonsense. At the same time, "*Balabon*" (from *balabonit*′ —"to jibber-jabber") of Grigorii Kruzhkov's most well-known translation, is, in my opinion, a poorer choice since it intentionally adds rudeness and lightness that is absent in Carroll's text. Other versions embrace this rudeness as well by choosing names such as "*Balabol*" (same as above), or "*Balamut*" (troublemaker); some use an intentionally rude slang, and still call this a translation of Lewis Carroll. I doubt that Charles Dodgson would approve of any profanities so nonchalantly introduced by these "translators."

5. Carrollian Markers

One simple marker for evaluating a translation of *The Hunting of the Snark* is the attempt to retain the names of the four languages (Hebrew, Dutch, German, and Greek) that Baker, one of the main characters of the story, uses when he forgets that the crew speaks only English. Carroll's choice in this case is far from random as two of these languages have a classical religious connection and two others, philosophical. While it is not easy to work all four into a translation, several attempts have been made to accomplish that. Even a lengthy Russian word for Hebrew, "*drevneevreiskii*," can be easily utilized in a verse, or replaced by the more modern "*ivrit*." One can see some translators trying to reproduce at least some of Carroll's language assignments faithfully while others veer far away from the original language(s), and even invent some. This kind of "heteroglossia" does not represent well Carroll's artistic choices and can serve us only as a starting point for evaluating translations and especially a translator's attitude toward their work.

6. Neologisms

Another easily recognizable characteristic of Lewis Carroll's language is the so-called "portmanteau" neologism (a new word formed by combining parts of existing words). Its usage abounds in Russian Carrollian translations.

While Carroll probably did not invent the portmanteau, he used it extensively and even commented on it in his known preface to the *Snark*. Indeed, the word "Snark" itself could be seen as a simple portmanteau, and Lewis Carroll himself told Beatrice Hatch that "snark" is a portmanteau word (snail + shark). Other combinations are also possible, such as "snake + shark" and the like. Interestingly, it has also been suggested that some of Carroll's linguistic experimentation might have been the result of his 1867 trip to Russia and his fascination with the Cyrillic alphabet.[10] Portmanteau words, which Carroll himself discussed in his preface to *The Hunting of the Snark* ("Richard + William = Rilchiam"), link the poem to the second *Alice* book, specifically to "Jabberwocky" and to Humpty Dumpty's "linguistic" commentary on this ballad (a complex and shrewd academic parody).

7. Examples

Below, I have provided a brief overview of the main characteristics and examples from eight representative translations of *The Hunting of the Snark*, all published in Russia between 1991 and 2015. The texts were chosen according to their diversity of tone (from moderate to very offensive), presence of neologisms (sometimes "Anglicized" ones, a Russian tradition of nonsense translation that has no equivalents in Carroll's original), and the intended target audience (presumably, some are more directed at children due to the absence of adult slang and the publisher's specialization).

(a) *Grigorii Kruzhkov*.[11] Kruzhkov's was the first full published translation, and the only one widely reprinted. Thorough and inventive, it also introduced an arguable tradition of treating the poem lightly, freely deviating from Carroll's original. Jarring slang is used sparingly: for example, *bo-bo* (a boo-boo), *dokhliak* (wimp). Here, Bellman's remark "His form is ungainly—his intellect small" was translated as "neither a mind of a Socrates, nor a face of a Paris." This is not what Carroll wrote, although he could easily have written it, had he wanted to have done so. Baker's important Hebrew language becomes, somewhat randomly, Turkish. Bellman is "*Balabon*"; Bandersnatch is "*Krovopir*" (from *krov'*—"blood" and *vampir*—"vampire").

(b) *Evgenii Kliuev*.[12] Kliuev did not try to stay close to Carroll, and his text is often hard to read. Not only is there slang, but "absurdized" words are often carefully "Anglicized" by using a double "l" or double "s" (not used in Russian), as in "*bollvan*," from "*bolvan*" (idiot), "*bolbess*," from "*balbes*" (blockhead)—or just scrambled. The invented names are

Dialogue Disrupted 153

extremely, overly playful, and not relevant to anything in Carroll's names or their construction: Bellman is *"Bomtsman"*; Baker is *"Bandid,"* from *Bandit* (a bandit), Anglicized with a "did"; Bandersnatch is *"Burnostai,"* from *burnyi* (stormy) + *stai* "[of] herds" + *"gornostai"* (ermine); Boojum is just *Bez*, from *"bes"* (a devil), and *"bez"* (without); and Jubjub is *"Chërdt,"* from *"chërt,"* (a devil, but with a Germanic ending).

(c) Leonid Iakhnin.[13] This exaggerated, freewheeling version is possibly directed at children, since it does not have much slang. It uses funny, childish made-up names like *"Billy-Bell"* for Bellman, *"Buka-Biaka"* (bogey-nasty) for Butcher, *"Biskvit"* (biscuit) for Baker, and *"Zhutkonos,"* from *"zhutkii"* (dreadful) + *"utkonos"* (duckbill, platypus), for "Jub-jub." A big problem with this translation is that it has a lot of randomly added, invented lines, which cannot be found in Carroll. For example, instead of referencing hyenas and bears, stanza 12 of "Fit the First" reads: "They say that he [Baker] called Snark a marmot, offending the poor thing mortally; Snark wrote a letter to the Parliament about that, and sent it in an envelope with a courier." Baker's languages are Finnish, Arabic, and Welsh. In addition, he "was understood by both monk and fellah." Or, "Snark is a Snark, it is not a hare in the bush, or a stupid Guinea fowl." The Pig in Barrister's Dream becomes a *"Svinaia Otbivnaia"* (pork chop). In the end, not only Baker but the entire crew disappears.

(d) Vladimir Gandel'sman.[14] This is an inventive but jarring text, straying very far away from Carroll. While it is one of the rare instances where the name *"Bellman"* is retained, in this version all monsters are heavily recast: "Boojum" is *"Zlodiuka,"* an invented childish portmanteau word from *"zlodei"* (evil-doer) and *"gadiuka"* (viper) while "Jubjub" is *"F'iuzhas,"* from *"uzhas"* (dread). The translation is sprinkled with intentionally rude, modern slang: *"pudrit' mozgi"* (to jive), *"patly"* (a rude word for "hair"), *"shmotki"* (rags) for Baker's things; even Yiddish-based *"tsimes"* ("tzimmes," a sweet carrot stew) to characterize Snark's taste. In this translation, Baker speaks "120 languages plus Swahili."

(e) Yurii Fel'dman.[15] The tone here is supposed to be playful and strange. There are "Snarkoman," "Snarkotic," and "Snarkenstein;" dozens of invented words, Jabberwockystyle. "Bellman" is *"Balaban,"* a meaningless word; "Barrister" is *"Balabol"* (jibber-jabber[er]), "Butcher" is *"Bedokur"* (troublemaker), and "Bandersnatch" is *"Barabashka"* (poltergeist). This is a free retelling in a heavy modern slang, light years removed from Lewis Carroll. Clearly, it is not a "Treasure of Classical Poetry" as marketed.

(f) Sergei Shorgin.[16] Shorgin changed B-names into S-names, "Bellman" is a "Speaker," while "Beaver" has turned into a *Surok* (marmot). Both are rodents, and it probably would not matter (in some Alice translations, even the iconic Dormouse becomes a sleepy Marmot; see my "Russian Translations of Lewis Carroll's *Alice* Books"[17]), but the translator mentions Groundhog Day, thus mixing epochs and continents. Other heavy intentional domestication and modernization includes *"Cheburashka"* (a popular Soviet animated cartoon character, which first appeared in a 1966 story by Eduard Uspensky); quotes from Pushkin; "Jubjub" as *"Solovei-Razboinik"* (a medieval Russian folklore character); and "Bandersnatch" as *"Bandiugad,"* a portmanteau from slang *"bandiugan"* (gangster) + *"gad"* (monster). The Baker, who has become *"Stiuard"* (steward) is for some unexplained reason overly Jewish (his languages are not only Hebrew, which is true to the original, but also Yiddish, and even Ladino!). There is jarring slang full of profanity: *"Stervets"* (rascal), *"kretin"* (cretin), *"olukh"* (blockhead), and shaky versification.

(g) Valerii Anan´ in.[18] This text is accompanied by a detailed translator's commentary. It is an exercise in author's own (definitely not Carroll's) version of an ebullient nonsense, inventive in words and irreverent in style, but full of heavy slang. Detailed, overdone comments of the same mocking kind are supplied. "Bellman" is *"Bomboltain,"* a made-up anglicized word (from *bom*, a bell sound, and *boltat´* "to chatter"), "Butcher" is *"Buzodërl"* (an anglicized *Buzotër*, "troublemaker"), "Baker" is *"Bufetcher,"* an anglicized *"Bufetchik"* (steward). This is a good example of *"stëb,"* a novel Russian term for an aggressive, often sadistic, mockery, which is amusing mostly to the author.

(h) Dmitrii Ermolovich.[19] Here, "Snark" is *"Ugad"*—a portmanteau construct that is not easily decoded. According to the translator himself, it is supposed to be a hybrid of a (hardly visible) *"ugor´"* (an eel) and *"gadiuka"* (a viper), as well as *"naugad"* (at random). It also can be decoded as *"U, gad"* (you monster) and an invented noun derived from *"ugadyvat´"* (to guess). "Boojum" is *"Obum,"* from *naobum* (haphazard); note that *"naugad"* and *"naobum"* are near synonyms. Butcher is a cumbersome five-syllable *"Boinevladelets"* (slaughterhouse owner). Slang is limited. The last stanza states that Baker actually got into Snark's "lair" (*berloga*).

8. Conclusions

The quality of the Russian versions varies dramatically. In addition to poetic skill, the quality of the translation is primarily a matter of taste and tact—which, unfortunately, are often lacking in the constant attempts to translate

The Hunting of the Snark. Alas, many translators apparently think that Bellman, being the ship's captain, should *talk like a sailor* and enhance his speech with profanities. In the original poem, however, Bellman is a wise and solemn leader in the sea of the unknown, and his bell tolls incessantly measuring the passing of life.[20]

Most of the Russian translators treated the *Snark* as light verse, akin to *Alice* parodies—remaining completely unaware that this was one of Carroll's darkest, death-related, deeply philosophical works. As a result, they did not even attempt to convey this depth—in a way, mimicking the Victorian reaction, since for most of Carroll's contemporaries the poem appeared to be a light entertaining piece, similar to William Schwenck Gilbert's *Bab Ballads*.[21]

Many of the modern translators of Carroll into Russian clearly are *not interested* in the original, and as they replace the author with their own fantasies, this type of domesticated translation (intended possibly as the macaronic mockery discussed by Bakhtin in "From the Prehistory of Novelistic Discourse"[22]) does not work. Most translations fail to address the essence of Carroll's iconic poem—in Nina Demurova's words,[23] the "apotheosis of Carroll's nonsense, which ... combines this author's lightness and 'irresponsibility' with depth and loftiness of his thought and diction."

A more detailed lexical-semantic study is warranted, but in my initial opinion, the cultural interaction between the Victorian English and post-Soviet Russian is rapidly decaying and fading in contemporary translations. The Bakhtinian dialogue is disrupted; the re-accentuation process is damaged; and an attempt at a translation becomes a disappointing travesty.

Acknowledgements

I am grateful to Sergei Camyshan, Michael Everson, Emma Fet, Galina Fet, Iakov Fet, Vladimir Fet, Doug Howick, Clare Imholtz, August A. Imholtz, Jr., Vladimir Krasavchikov, Sergei Krupodër, Sergei Kurii, Olga Liudvig, Irina Mishina, Andrei Moskotel′nikov, Sergei Shevchenko, Sergei Simonov, Iurii Sokolov, Vladimir Uspenskii, Mikhail Vainshtein, Ivan Vorob′ëv, and Marina Zagidullina for their help and support. I am especially thankful to my good friend, an indefatigable Snarkology veteran Byron W. Sewell, for the many fascinating hours he spent with me over my Carrollian manuscripts. Above all, I am honored to acknowledge all the mentorship and encouragement that were kindly given to me by Nina Demurova, who brought Lewis Carroll to my generation in Russia. I thank Slav Gratchev for inviting me to contribute to this volume, and Margarita Marinova for her expert editing help.

Notes

1. Lawrence Venuti, *Translator's Invisibility: A History of Translation* (New York: Routledge, 1995), 312.
2. Victor Fet, "An Annotated Bibliography of Russian Translations of *The Hunting of the Snark*," in L´iuis Kérroll, *Okhota na Snarka: v Vos'mi Napastiakh* (Lewis Carroll, The Hunting of the Snark: In Eight Troubles), trans. Victor Fet (Portlaoise: Evertype, 2016), 119–65.
3. Olga Sedakova, "Eta vozdushnaiia irratsional´nost´… etot tanets smyslov kak-to oblegchaet vospriiatie okruzhaiushchego nas absurda …" (That Ethereal Irrationality, … That Dance of Meanings Somewhat Relieves the Perception of the Absurd that Surrounds Us), in *Kartinki i razgovory: Besedy o L´iuise Kérrolle* (Pictures and Conversations: Talks about Lewis Carroll), ed. Nina M. Demurova (Sankt-Peterburg: Vita Nova, 2008), 155. All translations, unless otherwise noted, are mine.
4. Yurii Vashchenko, "Eta kniga kazalas´ mne zamechatel´nym prostranstvom dlia igry s real´nost´iu …" (This Book Seemed to Me as a Wonderful Space to Play with Reality), in *Kartinki i razgovory: Besedy o L´iuise Kérrolle* (Pictures and Conversations: Talks about Lewis Carroll), ed. Nina M. Demurova (Sankt-Peterburg: Vita Nova, 2008), 41–2.
5. Oleg Lipchenko, "Kerroll—sokrovennyi chelovek …" (Carroll Is an Enigmatic Man), in *Kartinki i razgovory: Besedy o L´iuise Kérrolle* (Pictures and Conversations: Talks about Lewis Carroll), ed. Nina M. Demurova (Sankt-Peterburg: Vita Nova, 2008), 202.
6. Victor Fet, "Beheading First: On Nabokov's Translation of Lewis Carroll," *Nabokovian* 63 (2009): 62–3.
7. Mikhail M. Bakhtin, "From the Prehistory of Novelistic Discourse," in *The Dialogic Imagination: Four Essays*, ed. Michael Holmquist, trans. Caryl Emerson and Michael Holmquist (Austin: University of Texas Press, 1981), 74–6.
8. Fet, "An Annotated Bibliography of Russian Translations of *The Hunting of the Snark*," 119.
9. Nina M. Demurova, "O stepeniakh svobody. Perevod imën v poeme L´iuisa Kérrolla 'Okhota na Snarka'" (On Degrees of Freedom. Translation of the Names in the Poem by Lewis Carroll *The Hunting of the Snark*), in *Almanakah perevodchika* (Translator's Almanac) (Moskva: Rossiiskii gosudarstvennyi gumanitarnyi universitet, 2001), 37.
10. Victor Fet and Michael Everson, "Is *SNARK* part of a *Cyrillic Doublet*?" *Knight Letter* 99 (2018): 16–17.
11. L´iuis Kérroll, *Okhota na Snarka: Agoniia v vos´mi vopliakh* (Lewis Carroll, The Hunting of the Snark: An Agony in Eight Screams), trans. Grigorii Mikhailovich Kruzhkov, illustr. Leonid Aleksandrovich Tishkov (Riga: Rukitis, 1991) (in Russian).

12. L′iuis Kérroll, "Okhota na Smarka: Agoniia v vos′mi pristupakh" (Lewis Carroll, The Hunting of the Smark [sic]: An Agony in Eight Fits), trans. Evgenii Vasil′evich Kliuev, in Edvard Lir and L′iuis Kérroll, *Tselyi tom chepukhi. Angliiskii klassicheskii absurd XIX veka* (Edward Lear and Lewis Carroll. The Whole Volume of Nonsense. English Classical Absurd of XIX Century), ed. Evgenii V. Kliuev (Moskva: Ob″edinenie "Vsesoiuznyi molodëzhnyi knizhnyi tsentr," 1992), 76–119.
13. L′iuis Kérroll, "Okhota na Snarka: Perepolokh v vos′mi okhakh" (Lewis Carroll, The Hunting of the Snark: A Commotion in Eight Ouches), trans. Leonid L′vovich Iakhnin, in L′iuis Kérroll, *Alisa v Strane Chudes; Alisa v Zazerkal′e; Okhota na Snarka; Pis′ma k detiam* (Lewis Carroll, Alice's Adventures in Wonderland; Through the Looking-Glass, and What Alice Found There; The Hunting of the Snark; Letters to Children), trans. and retold by Leonid Iakhnin and Iulii Danilov (Moskva: Eksmo, 1999), 316–54.
14. L′iuis Kérroll, *Okhota na Snarka: Bred v vos′mi paroksizmakh, ili Svershenie v vos′mi pesniakh* (Lewis Carroll, The Hunting of the Snark: A Delirium in Eight Paroxysms, or a Deed in Eight Songs), trans. Vladimir [Arkad′evich] Gandel′sman (Volga, 2000), 4: 131–7.
15. L′iuis Kérroll, "Okhota na Snarka: Trali-vali v vos′mi fintakh" (Lewis Carroll, The Hunting of the Snark: Blah-blah in Eight Feints), trans. Evgenii Davydovich Feld′man, in L′iuis Kérroll, *Shedevry klassicheskoi poezii dlia iunykh chitatelei* (Lewis Carroll, Treasures of Classical Poetry for Young Readers), ed. Evgenii Vitkovskii (Moscow: Eksmo, 2003).
16. L′iuis Kérroll, "Okhota na Snarka: Gonenie v vos′mi voiakh" (Lewis Carroll, The Hunting of the Snark: A Chase in Eight Howls), trans. Sergei Iakovlevich Shorgin, in L′iuis Kérroll, *Okhota na Snarka* (Lewis Carroll, The Hunting of the Snark) (Sankt-Peterburg: Azbuka-klassika, 2007), 97–124.
17. Victor Fet, "Russian Translations of Lewis Carroll's *Alice* Books: A Bakhtinian Re-accentuation," in *Mikhail Bakhtin's Heritage in Literature, Arts, and Psychology*, ed. Slav N. Gratchev and Howard Mancing (Lanham, MD: Lexington Books, 2018), 64.
18. L′iuis Kérroll, *Okhota na Snarka, ili Snarkova travlia: Predsmerdie v vos′mi ambzatsakh, ili Tragonia v vos′mi vzrydakh* (Lewis Carroll, The Hunting of the Snark, or Snark Chase), trans. Valerii Zosimovich Anan′in (Petrozavodsk, 2011).
19. L′iuis Kérroll, "Okhota na Ugada: Terzaniia v vos′mi sodroganiiakh" (Lewis Carroll, The Hunting of the Ugad: The Excruciations in Eight Shudders), trans. Dmitrii Ivanovich Ermolovich in L′iuis Kérroll, *Okhota na Ugada i drugie strannye istorii* (Lewis Carroll, The Hunting of the Ugad and Other Strange Stories), trans. Dmitrii Ivanovich Ermolovich (Moskva: Auditoria, 2015), 21–83.
20. Edward Giuliano, *Lewis Carroll: The World of His Alices* (Brighton: Edward Everett Root, 2019), 125.
21. Giuliano, *Lewis Carroll: The World of His* Alices, 131.

22. Bakhtin, "From the Prehistory of Novelistic Discourse," 74.
23. Demurova, "O stepeniakh svobody," 37.

Bibliography

Bakhtin, Mikhail M. "From the Prehistory of Novelistic Discourse." In *The Dialogic Imagination: Four Essays*. Edited by Michael Holmquist. Translated by Caryl Emerson and Michael Holmquist, 41–83. Austin: University of Texas Press, 1981.

[Carroll, Lewis] Kérroll, L′iuis. "Okhota na Smarka: Agoniia v vos′mi pristupakh" (The Hunting of the Smark [sic]: An Agony in Eight Fits). Translated by Evgenii Vasil′evich Kliuev. In Edvard Lir and L′iuis Kérroll. *Tselyi tom chepukhi. Angliiskii klassicheskii absurd XIX veka* (Edward Lear and Lewis Carroll. The Whole Volume of Nonsense. English Classical Absurd of XIX Century). Edited by Evgenii V. Kliuev, 76–119. Moskva: Ob″edinenie "Vsesoiuznyi molodëzhnyi knizhnyi tsentr," 1992 (in Russian).

[Carroll, Lewis] Kérroll, L′iuis. *Okhota na Snarka: Bred v vos′mi paroksizmakh, ili Svershenie v vos′mi pesniakh* (The Hunting of the Snark: A Delirium in Eight Paroxysms, or a Deed in Eight Songs). Translated by Vladmir Arkad′evich Gandel′sman, 4: 131–37. Volga: Saratov, 2000 (in Russian).

[Carroll, Lewis] Kérroll, L′iuis. "Okhota na Snarka: Gonenie v vos′mi voiakh" (The Hunting of the Snark: A Chase in Eight Howls). Translated by Sergei Iakovlevich Shorgin. In L′iuis Kerroll. *Okhota na Snarka* (Lewis Carroll, The Hunting of the Snark), 97–124. Sankt-Peterburg: Azbuka-klassika, 2007 (in Russian; an anthology of four translations, by Kruzhkov, Gandel′sman, Shorgin, and Lifshits.)

[Carroll, Lewis] Kérroll, L′iuis. "Okhota na Snarka: Trali-vali v vos′mi fintakh" (The Hunting of the Snark: Blah-blah in Eight Feints). Translated by Evgenii Davydovich Fel′dman. In L′iuis Kerroll. *Shedevry klassicheskoi poezii dlia iunykh chitatelei* (Lewis Carroll. Treasures of Classical Poetry for Young Readers), compiled by Evgenii Vitkovskii. Moskva: Eksmo, 2003 (in Russian).

[Carroll, Lewis] Kérroll, L′iuis. "Okhota na Ugada: Terzaniia v vos′mi sodroganiiakh" [The Hunting of the Ugad: The Excruciations in Eight Shudders]. Translated by Dmitrii Ivanovich Ermolovich. In L′iuis Kérroll. *Okhota na Ugada i drugie strannye istorii* (Lewis Carroll. The Hunting of the Ugad and Other Strange Stories). Translated by Dmitrii Ivanovich Ermolovich, 21–83. Moscow: Auditoria, 2015 (in Russian).

[Carroll, Lewis] Kérroll, L′iuis. *Okhota na Snarka, ili Snarkova travlia: Predsmerdie v vos′mi ambzatsakh, ili Tragonia v vos′mi vzrydakh* (The Hunting of the Snark, or Snark Chase). Translated by Valerii Zosimovich Anan′in. Petrozavodsk, 2011 (in Russian).

[Carroll, Lewis] Kérroll, L′iuis. *Okhota na Snarka: Agoniia v vos′mi vopliakh* (The Hunting of the Snark: An Agony in Eight Screams). Translated by Grigorii Mikhailovich Kruzhkov. Illustrations by Leonid Aleksandrovich Tishkov. Riga: Rukitis, 1991 (in Russian).

[Carroll, Lewis] Kérroll, L′iuis. "Okhota na Snarka: Perepolokh v vos′mi okhakh" (The Hunting of the Snark: A Commotion in Eight Ouches). Translated by Leonid L′vovich Iakhnin. In L′iuis Kérroll. *Alisa v Strane Chudes; Alisa v Zazerkal′e; Okhota na Snarka; Pis′ma k detiam* (Lewis Carroll. Alice's Adventures in Wonderland; Through the Looking-Glass, and What Alice Found There; The Hunting of the Snark; Letters to Children). Translated and Retold by Leonid Iakhnin and Iulii Danilov, 316–54. Moskva: Eksmo, 1999. Title on cover: *Prikliucheniia Alisy* (Alice's Adventures) (in Russian).

Demurova, Nina M. "O stepeniakh svobody. Perevod imën v poeme L′iuisa Kérrolla "Okhota na Snarka" (On Degrees of Freedom. Translation of the Names in the Poem by Lewis Carroll *The Hunting of the Snark*). In *Almanakah perevodchika* (Translator's Almanac), 29–49. Moscow: Rossiiskii gosudarstvennyi gumanitarnyi universitet, 2001 (in Russian).

Fet, Victor. "An Annotated Bibliography of Russian Translations of *The Hunting of the Snark*." In L′iuis Kerroll. *Okhota na Snarka: v Vos′mi Napastiakh* (Lewis Carroll. The Hunting of the Snark: in Eight Troubles). Translated by Victor Fet, 119–65. Portlaoise: Evertype, 2016.

Fet, Victor. "Beheading First: On Nabokov's Translation of Lewis Carroll." *Nabokovian* 63 (2009): 62–3

Fet, Victor. "Russian Translations of Lewis Carroll's *Alice* books: A Bakhtinian re-accentuation." In *Mikhail Bakhtin's Heritage in Literature, Arts, and Psychology*. Edited by Slav N. Gratchev and Howard Mancing, 63–84. Lanham, MD: Lexington Books, 2018.

Fet, Victor, and Michael Everson. "Is *SNARK* Part of a *Cyrillic Doublet*?" *Knight Letter* 99 (2018): 16–17.

Giuliano, Edward. *Lewis Carroll: The World of his Alices*. Brighton: Edward Everett Root, 2019.

Lipchenko, Oleg. "Kerroll—sokrovennyi chelovek…" (Carroll Is an Enigmatic Man). In *Kartinki i razgovory: Besedy o L′iuise Kerrolle* (Pictures and Conversations: Talks about Lewis Carroll). Edited by Nina M. Demurova, 101–204. Sankt-Peterburg: Vita Nova, 2008 (in Russian).

Sedakova, Olga. "Eta vozdushnaiia irratsional′nost′ … etot tanets smyslov kak-to oblegchaet vospriiatie okruzhaiushchego nas absurda …." (That Ethereal Irrationality, … That Dance of Meanings Somewhat Relieves the Perception of the Absurd That Surrounds Us). In *Kartinki i razgovory: Besedy o L′iuise Kerrolle* (Pictures and Conversations: Talks about Lewis Carroll). Edited by Nina M. Demurova, 149–56. Sankt-Peterburg: Vita Nova, 2008 (in Russian).

Vashchenko, Yurii. "Eta kniga kazalas' mne zamechatel'nym prostranstvom dlia igry sreal'nost'iu" (This Book Seemed to Me as a Wonderful Space to Play with Reality). In *Kartinki i razgovory: Besedy o L'iuise Kerrolle* [Pictures and Conversations: Talks about Lewis Carroll]. Edited by Nina M. Demurova, 36–62. Sankt-Peterburg: Vita Nova, 2008 (in Russian).

Venuti, Lawrence. *Translator's Invisibility: A History of Translation.* New York: Routledge, 1995.

9

Accentuation and Re-accentuation in Language, Literature, and Translation

Susan Petrilli and Augusto Ponzio

1. Intonation and Tone in Accentuation

In "Rilettura di Sylvie" (Rereading Sylvie) (1999), the afterword to his translation of *Sylvie* by Gérard de Nerval (1999 [1853]),[1] Umberto Eco begins by saying that every text should be able to construct its own "Model Reader" (*Lettore Modello*), to say to whomever reads it: this is how you should read me.[2] This is true for the translator too, given that translation is a particular way of reading—"to read translating" (*leggere traducendo*), to be precise.[3]

Every text has its own specific accentuation, and insofar as it is a written text, it calls on the reader to understand the right intonation by reading it and listening to it. Considering that reading is *translation* (an *intralingual translation*[4]), if the reader is also the translator of the text (*translates it* in the sense of *interlingual translation*), the text requires its "same other" (*stesso altro*) (the translated text, similar and different at the same time) to maintain the right *re-accentuation*.[5]

As in spoken language, written texts too, and literary texts in particular, create forms of *listening* that are not only specific to musical language. Speaking of "intonation," "accentuation," and "re-accentuation" do not only refer to the auditory sense.[6] Listening to an utterance, to a text, like listening to a piece of music, cannot be reduced to sound; it is not directed toward "meaning" but to "sense." Here *sense* involves different senses; it implies forms of *synaesthesia*, *giving color to sound*, not only as the expression of the exceptional "alchemy" of the poet, as in Rimbaud,[7] but also as the essential modality of the artistic text for the sake of listening and responsive understanding. And this draws literary writing, not only music, closer to expressive modalities like painting and the figurative arts in general.[8]

Eco begins his afterword "Rilettura di Sylvie" describing "the atmosphere in Sylvie" (*l'atmosfera di Sylvie*) in terms of color (*colorazione*): it is "bluish and purple" (*bluastra e purpurea*), deriving not from the words themselves but "between one word and another" (*tra una parola e un'altra*), and adds: "like a morning mist in Chantilly" (*come la nebbia di un mattino a Chantilly*), an expression taken from Proust's "Gérard de Nerval"[9] (in Proust, *Contre Sainte-Beuve*[10]).

2. Interpreting and Translating

Not in words but "between one word and another": with Eco's expression we are led to reflect on the relationship between the original text and the translated text, with particular attention to literary texts.[11]

In a letter to Gide dated May 19, 1916, Conrad[12] noted that

> Par exemple: si j'écrivais, disons que dans les circostances racontées, un certain "Mr. X had taken his own life," la traduction la plus fidèle serait par l'idiome français: "Monsieur X s'était donné la mort." Il est vrai qu'on pourrait dire: "s'était ôté la vie," mais c'est toujours l'idiome le plus simple, le plus énergique qui est préférable. Quant à la traduction littérale: "Monsieur avait pris sa propre vie," elle me parait impossible.
>
> (For example: if I wrote, let's say in the narrated circumstances, a certain "Mr. X had taken his own life," the most faithful translation in French idiom would be: "Monsieur X s'était donné la mort." True that one could also say: "s'était ôté la vie," but the simplest, the most energetic idiom is always preferable. As to the literal translation: "Monsieur avait pris sa propre vie," sounds impossible to me.)

Gide translated "*à sa façon*" (in his own manner), as he claimed, in order to preserve the sense rather than the letter, the literal meaning of the word. In "Lettre sur la traduction" (1930), Gide states that we must translate sentences (we prefer the term "*utterances*"), not words, expressing the thoughts and emotions therein as if they had been written in the target language: "Ce qui ne se peut que ... par d'incessants détours et souvent en s'éloignant beaucoup de la simple littéralité" (Something that can only be done ... through incessant detours and often moving a long way from a mere literal translation).[13] As Karl notes,[14] the translation of Gide's *Typhon* aims to keep the global sense and sentiment of the work rather than its literal meaning.

Apart from what frequently results in a lack of clarity in the opposition between sense and literal meaning, between "faithfulness to sense" and "faithfulness to the letter," what is particularly interesting, considering the relationship between *Typhoon* by Conrad and *Typhon* by Gide—between "le plus beau roman de Conrad" (Conrad's best novel) and "La plus belle traduction de Gide" (Gide's best translation), as the back cover of the Gallimard edition states—is precisely *the relation between accentuation in the original and re-accentuation in the translation.*

The transfer of discourse from one language to another, from English to French in the text by Gide, leads to what can be described as a *linguistic lightening* through the use of omission and condensation, and, simultaneously and somewhat paradoxically, to the *enrichment* of the English text.[15] There are certain parts that offer several equivalents of one syntagm, for example adjectives, to clarify, reinforce, and give value to the original expression; there are those in which more words are added in order to better describe an event, or new details to make the narrative more interesting. Re-accentuation in Gide's translation occurs on the level of syntax, too, as a type of reformulation, changes in punctuation, the joining of two sentences into one or the break of one sentence into two. Whatever might be said about the arbitrary nature of such "license," we must admit that this re-accentuation through reorganization of the discourse generally allows for a better rendering of the original accentuation.

As Valerio Magrelli[16] notes, Gide's translation sometimes manifests not only a change of tone, of accentuation, but also of sense. That is to be expected, considering that both inter- and intralingual translation often turn reported speech into a form of indirect discourse; *translated text, then, becomes indirect discourse masked as direct discourse.*[17] As Valentin Voloshinov has already posited in relation to indirect discourse, this generally leads reporting discourse to dominate over reported discourse. But it also implies *responsibility*, that, with reference to Bakhtin's work from 1919 to the mid-1920s, can be defined as "moral responsibility"—a concept that goes beyond mere "technical responsibility."[18]

3. Translation: "Saying Almost the Same Thing" or "Indirect Discourse Masked as Direct Discourse"?

Eco entitled his book on translation *Dire quasi la stessa cosa* (Saying Almost the Same Thing), where "almost" is indicative of the relationship between the original text and the translation. As mentioned above, Voloshinov, in the third part of *Marksizm i filosofija jazyka* (Marxism and Philosophy of Language)[19] suggests that the passage from direct to indirect discourse entails reformulation due to its "analytical tendency"—indirect discourse describes, explains, and somehow re-accentuates direct discourse. In much the same way, in interlingual translation, the accentuations in the original discourse, when reported into another language, must undergo reformulation. This means that, in some cases, in order to render the "color" of the original, it will be necessary to introduce other words,[20] for example, adjectives or adverbs.

At this point we must ask: is there *a same thing*, expressed in the original text, that the translated text must in turn say, that is, express "almost" the same thing, as Eco suggests. Eco is aware that the expression "saying almost the same thing" used to describe translation is not adequate, for it reifies simultaneously that which the text speaks of, the text itself and the language used. Reflecting on the term "almost," he adds in a footnote that[21] *Lo stesso altro* (The Same Other), the title introduced by Susan Petrilli for a collective volume on translation,[22] captures the meaning of transposing one text into another more effectively[23] as it expresses better the relationship that is established, in what Derrida[24] would call "relevant" translation, between the original and the translated text. The two texts look similar, but in what ways?[25]

This similarity is complex and not at all obvious. Charles S. Peirce would describe it as an "iconic" resemblance, likeness. What we are dealing with here is not a simple reproduction, but a relationship characterized by reciprocal alterity: we might speak of a *dialogic* relation. The paradox of translation resides in the fact that the text *must stay the same while becoming other*. This emerges in the way in which the same text in translation must be reorganized to express, see, project, evaluate, imagine, and plan in another language. *The same other*: the translated text is both identical and different. Presenting translation in this way, rather than as "saying almost the same thing," concurs with De Abreu Chulata,[26] whose subtitle to the book *Il traduttore*, reveals how *the deconstruction of an identity*, that of the translator, challenges the "myth" of the purely technical function of translating and of the role of the translator as a simple transmitter or spokesperson of language.

After agreeing with us that translation is indirect discourse masked as direct discourse, and observing that as a consequence the implicit metalinguistic formula that precedes every translated text is "such and such Author in his own language expressed the following" (L'Autore tale ha detto nella sua lingua quello che segue), Eco goes on to add that "this metalinguistic announcement implies the *deontology of the translator*".[27]

4. The "Mist-Effect" (*Effetto-Nebbia*) in Rendering Literary Chronotopes

For Umberto Eco, "the mist-effect"[28] is the recurrent sensation he feels each time he rereads *Sylvie*. The sentence that opens the work as the protagonist leaves the theater in the evening uses a verb in the imperfect tense ("Je sortais d'un théâtre": an action that is taking place but that is also iterative, having taken place many times before). In his essay about this text, "Rilettura di Sylvie," Eco considers the important role this indicative imperfect construction—this "imperfect tense," an "imperfect time,"—plays in *Sylvie* in dissolving the boundaries of time.[29] In the second part of "Note sulla traduzione" (Notes on Translation), Eco revisits this opening but does not concern himself with the chosen verb form further, principally because in Italian translations from French the imperfect tense presents no problem to the translator. Still, the topic continued to interest him greatly especially given the fact that, beyond the ten Italian translations written before his, Eco also consulted four English versions of *Sylvie* in order to "examine a language that has no imperfect tense" (fare il confronto con una lingua che non ha l'imperfetto).[30] Eco also discussed the use of the imperfect tense at the beginning of *Sylvie* in his *Norton Lectures* (1992–3), at Harvard University,[31] where he had to deal[32] with the English language by necessity.

In a language like English, where there is no imperfect tense, the translator needs to find a way of rendering this double duration (an unfinished action that is repeated in time) with other words: "Je sortais d'un théâtre où tous le soirs je paraissais aux avant-scènes en grande tenue de soupirant" ("Uscivo da un teatro, dove ogni sera mi esibivo al palco di proscenio in gran tenuta di primo amoroso," Eco's translation) (I would leave the theater, where I appeared every evening in the proscenium boxes in the grand attire of a suitor). The "sortais" at the beginning of *Sylvie*, Eco notes, is a duration form while "paraissais" expresses both duration and repetition.

In English, the iterative aspect of the French "paraissais" can be re-accentuated by making do with the textual indication of time "every evening." This is, however, no small difference, Eco notes, because the narrative enchantment of *Sylvie* resides in the careful, indeed calculated alternation of the imperfect tense and the simple past tense. Moreover, the use of the imperfect tense bestows an oneiric tone on the narrative. Nerval's "Model Reader," to whom he directs the right accentuation and the right tone, was not, as Eco affirms, an English speaker, English being too precise a language to render Nerval's narrative style.

Another difficulty inherent in the passage from French to English concerns Eco's decision to call the first-person narrator "Je-rard" in order to distinguish him from the voice of the author Gérard. In the "Norton Lectures," this play on words has no correspondent in English, and Eco is forced to find another form for Je-rard: "We will call him the Narrator" (Lo chiameremo il Narratore).

How does *Sylvie* conclude? With a "J'oubliais de dire" ("Dimenticavo di dire") (I forgot to mention).[33] The speaker is the narrator who initiated the story with "Je sortais d'un théâtre," Je-rard. What has Je-rard forgotten to mention? He says it by reporting the direct speech of Sylvie: "Pauvre Adrienne! Elle est morte au convent de Saint-S***, vers 1832" ("Povera Adrienne! È morta nel convent di Saint-S***, verso il 1832") (Poor Adrienne! She died in the convent of Saint-S***, around 1832).[34] In *Sylvie*, as in other literary works,[35] the narration begins with a cut, a wound that death has inflicted in real time.[36]

In addition to time, places too are never precisely defined so that Sylvie's story involves "shifts" in time and space. Using one of Bakhtin's favorite terms, we might say that the *chronotope* here, found in the relation between fabula and siuzhet, is rather unique and particularly significant. This gives the narrative its peculiar accentuation that the interlingual translator not only has to take into account, but has to render in the target language, making it heard through *re-accentuation* in the *other*, different language.

5. The Chronotope of a New Life

The last chapter, chapter 14, "Dernier feuillet," ends with a vague indication of the year in which Adrienne died. And based on what we gather from this last chapter, the story that is recounted begins there. The final date is not "un rintocco funebre che chiude la storia" (a death knell that ends the story),[37] but instead signals a new start, the beginning of a search for lost time. Literary writing reveals the possibility of a *new life* here as well, and once again, as in other cases of literary writing, the narrative begins from the rupture that death has produced in an attempt to search for lost time. Here, too, the awareness that "all has ended" does not block the narration but, on the contrary, provokes it, motivates it, directs it, and gives tone, motive, and rhythm to it.

The realization that separation (through death) is forever introduces the other time of literary writing, which is also another space. From this other time and this other space, the relationship reality-madness is turned upside-down and, with Maurice Blanchot, we can speak of reality as "the madness of the day."[38] The dialectic between rationality and irrationality, logic and dreaming, realism and pure fantasy is not resolved in Nerval with the victory of one over the other, but with a form of unstable (dramatic) accord between the two.[39]

Similarly to Pushkin's poem "Razluka," analyzed by Bakhtin in his fragment from the first chapter of *Autor i geroi v estetičeskoj dejatel'nosti*

Accentuation and Re-accentuation   167

(Author and Hero in Aesthetic Activity), published postumously by Bocharov,[40] in *Sylvie*, too, the context of the narrative is that of knowledge of the beloved's death, for the time of writing is part of that time in which the extreme separation has already occurred. In Pushkin's poem, as in *Sylvie*, the intonation, accentuation, and orientation of the narrator's voice is imbued with the awareness of her death. This contributes to confusing voices and events, merging events in the present with memories, blurring temporal and spatial distances. The result, as Bakhtin shows in the context of "Razluka," is the creation of a dialogic dimension in the narrative.

In literary writing then, the intonation, accentuation, and re-accentuation of the *dramatis personae* giving voice to the text come together and encounter each other: the author-creator (as distinct from the author-man and identifiable through the style and form of the text) meets with the hero and the addressee ("the model reader"). Each has his own time, point of view, values, his own chronotope, his own real and imagined relations. The translator must take all of this into account, continually calculating the effect that transposition from one language to another has on the dialogue between them as it is woven into the text.

6. Original Accentuation and Re-accentuation in Translation

6.1. The Space of the Word: "Le cimetière marin" by Paul Valéry

In this section, we aim to show the role of re-accentuation in translations into Italian and Spanish of Valéry's poem "Le cimetière marin." This of course requires citations from the original verses as much as the translated. Not to be excluded is the possibility that poetic rendition and translative re-accentuation may shine through in the original, superseding it in poetic creativity. Valéry's poem starts with the following stanza:

[I]
Ce toit tranquille, où marchent des colombes,
Entre les pins palpite, entre les tombes;
Midi le juste y compose de feux
La mer, la mer, toujours recommencée!
Ô récompense après une pensée
Qu'un long regard sur le calme des dieux![41]

Here the sea is presented as a roof, something that encloses, protects, something solid, still and stable, but with the movement of doves above, from whose symbolic meaning it receives a sense of peace. This sea is calm yet at the same time palpitating, alive. It is set between the cypress trees and the graves, the final resting place of the dead. It is both a destination and a point of departure, forever new. Its dynamic tranquility guides the gaze toward the lure of the horizon, where it loses itself.

The Spanish translation by Jorge Guillén, *Le cimetière marin*, runs as follows:[42]

> Ese techo, tranquillo de palomas,
> Palpita entro los pinos y la tumbas,
> El Melodía justo en él enciende
> El Mar, el mar sin cesar empezando ...
> Recompensa después de un pensamiento:
> Mirar por fin la calma de los dioses.

And here is the Italian translation of the same stanza by A. Ponzio:[43]

> Quel tetto quieto, sparso di colombe,
> Fra i pini palpita, e pur fra le tombe;
> In fuoco il giusto Meriggio combina
> Il mare, il mare, sempre rinnovato!
> Quale compenso a un pensier passato
> Un lungo sguardo alla calma divina.

By the time the poem moves into its eleventh section, the sea has undergone important transformations.

> [XI]
> Chienne splendide, écarte l'idolâtre!
> Quand solitaire au sourire de pâtre,
> Je pais longtemps, moutons mystérieux,
> Le blanc troupeau de mes tranquilles tombes,
> Éloignes-en les prudentes colombes,
> Les songes vains, les anges curieux!

The sea is now a faithful dog that—shining and bright—protects the graves. Its task is to keep the white flocks of quiet graves from idolaters, the prudent pacifiers of conscience, "les prudentes colombes," the curious and all those who disrupt the peace of this special place with their hypocrisy. "Éloignes-en":

Spanish translation by J. Guillén:[44]

¡Al idolatra aparta, perra esplendida"
Cuando, sonrisa de pastor, yo solo
Apaciento, carneros misteriosos,
Blanco rebaño de tranquillas tumbas,
Aléjame las prudentes palomas,
Los sueños vanos, los curiosos ángel.

Italian translation by A. Ponzio:[45]

Chi idoli vuol scaccia, cane splendente!
Se io solitario, pastor sorridente,
Vado pascendo, agnelli misteriosi,
Il bianco gregge di mie quiete tombe,
Tieni lontane le prudenti colombe,
I sogni vani, gli angeli curiosi.

[XXI]
Zenon! Cruel Zénon! Zénon d'Elée!
M'as-tu percé de cette flèche ailée
Qui vibre, vole, et qui ne vole pas!
Le son m'enfante et la flèche me tue!
Ah! Le soleil ... Quelle ombre de tortue
Pour l'âme, Achille immobile à grands pas!

In stanza XIII, the immobility of the sun at noon, "Midi là-haut, Midi sans mouvement," is juxtaposed with movement, the changing life below: "Je suis en toi le secret changement." Now, instead, there is a recognition that in life, all changes, all transformations are in vain. This confirms the paradox of Zeno, the cruel Zeno who reveals the illusion of movement with the syllogism of the arrow in flight that never reaches its target because it must pass through an infinite number of half-way stages on its journey. Similarly, the swift-footed Achilles will never overtake the extraordinarily slow tortoise, and thus will never recover the advantage initially allowed it. The self exhausts itself, running, fighting against time, but always stays the same—there is nothing new under the sun. The self is immobile, like the defeated Achilles; instead, the sun, while seeming to stand still, moves forward like Zeno's tortoise.

Spanish translation by J. Guillén:⁴⁶

¡Zenón, cruel Zenón, Zenón de Elea!
Me has traspasado con la flecha alada
Que vibra y vuela, pero nuca vuela.
Me crea el son y la flecha me mata.
¡Oh sol, oh sol! ¡Que sombra de tortuga
Para el alma: si en marcha Aquiles, quieto!

Italian translation by A. Ponzio:⁴⁷

Zenon! Crudele! Zenone eleata!
M'hai tu trafitto con la freccia alata,
Che vibra, vola, eppur in vol non è!
Mi dà il suon vita che la freccia fuga,
Ah! Questo sole ... Ombra di tartaruga
per l'io, l'immoto Achille lesto piè.

6.2. The Paradox of Achilles and the Tortoise

Significantly, Jorge L. Borges dedicates two of his writings to the paradox of the tortoise in the collection *Discusión* following "Las versiones homéricas," in which he offers reflections on the translation of the Homeric poems "La perpetua carrera de Aquiles y la tortuga" and "Avatares de la Tortuga."⁴⁸ Borges tags as "avatares de la tortuga" all discourses that reproduce Zeno's paradox. The discourse of translation is a case in point.

Doesn't the swift-footed Achilles, who chases after the slow but unreachable tortoise, somehow resemble a valid translation, or what Derrida calls "rélevante" translation, which strives to overtake the original whose sole advantage, like the tortoise, is that it began first?

Translation does not *represent* the original text, but *portrays* it, *depicts* it;⁴⁹ it is a *re-velation* of the original text, not its *unveiling*; translation belongs to the sphere of the *icon*, not the *idol*.⁵⁰ It implies a process of deferral from *said* to *saying*, from *sayable* to *unsayable*. We could suggest then, after Eco's "Dire quasi la stessa cosa,"⁵¹ that fidelity in translation does not mean that there exists one unique definitive translation, *the* translation. Instead, it means that translation is always possible, ever again—in other words a translation is always perfectible, thanks to renewed dialogue, renewed re-accentuation.

The translated text stands in relation to the original as both itself, the same, and as an other. Their resemblance is—as we have said—of the iconic order, in Peirce's sense when he establishes a difference, in the sign, in terms of prevailing iconicity, indexicality, or symbolicity.⁵² The two texts, the original and the translation, exist in a reciprocal relationship of alterity. And in literary texts such alterity appears in both cases as absolute alterity. As Bakhtin in particular has shown, this occurs to the extent that as literary texts they do not belong to representational discourse genres, that is, to discourse genres representing the direct, objective word. Instead, literary texts reside in figurative discourse genres, the genres of depiction, where the indirect word is portrayed, depicted according to different degrees of extralocalization.[53]

The translated text is always *the same other*. Not even Menard's *Quijote* is identical to Cervantes's *Quijote*, even though, paradoxically, it is "translated into the same language," as Borges explains in the story in *Ficciones*.[54] To prove the difference, Borges quotes a passage from *Quijote* (part I, chapter IX) with its corresponding "translation" by Menard: it is immediately obvious that Menard's style is affectedly archaic while Cervantes's *Quijote* is written quite simply in the Spanish of his time.[55]

Because the original is itself an icon semiotically understood,[56] as is a translation, it too an icon, the translation may surpass the original in terms of depiction, as Borges demonstrates in the example of "Le cimetière marin" by Valéry translated by Néstor Ibarra, comparing "La pérdida del rumor de la ribera" with "Le changement des rives en rumeur." Maintaining otherwise, based on the prejudice that the verse from Valéry is "original," implies confusing Valéry the author-man, first in the temporal sense, with Valéry the author-creator, who, in terms of depiction, according to Borges,[57] comes second, given that his verse looks like a pale imitation of the Castilian text. This is possible because between the two texts, both icons, the author's and the translator's, of which the latter may well supersede the former in iconicity, depicting better what it aims to depict.

Another case in which the text that comes later claims to come before the original, indeed claims that it is the original, paradoxically subverting the logic and the order of discourse, is Antonin Artaud's[58] translation of Lewis Carroll. Artaud questions the order of discourse, interrogates it, challenging not only the pre-written (pre-scribed) text, but also the language in which it is translated.[59] In *L'arve et l'aume*, just as Alice looks through the looking-glass, Artaud reads *through* Carroll's text in his translation of the Humpty Dumpty chapter in *Alice Through the Looking-Glass*, scrutinizing it in a cruel anti-grammatical exercise against Carroll himself and against the French language. What is at stake, what Artaud plays with in his translation, as in his *Theatre of Cruelty*, is "existence" and "flesh," body and life.

Carroll's puns, his playing on words, do not supersede a playful enactment of the exchange relation between signified and signifier, which he caricatures. But his language games do not succeed in denouncing the hypocrisy, on whose repression such relations are based; his word play does not affect or undermine social structures, production cycles, or the ideological assumptions that language, the order of discourse, serve.

In the Alice books[60] the wonders of word play are reduced to language games played out on the surface level.[61] Here it is interesting to note that originally *Alice's Adventures in Wonderland* was significantly titled *Alice's Adventures Underground*, which from a semiotic perspective evokes the realm of semantic meaning that goes under such banners as "implicit meaning," "hidden meaning," "stratified meanings," enthymemes, and assumptions, which direct human behavior as it occurs "above ground," accentuated by these signifying undercurrents. In Wonderland, we witness anomalies and deviations from familiar semiosis that lead to questioning the very nature and proper functioning of language.

But, as Artaud points out, Carroll's word play, his language games, the linguistic acuteness, the cunning, the psychical trickeries performed in Wonderland are all bloodless. Carroll caricatures language and the equal exchange relation between signified and signifier, but without actually denouncing the hypocrisies that such exchange is based upon, or destroying existing social structures and ideological assumptions. Carroll peeps through the looking glass but keeps away from the shadows behind it. This is why Artaud requested that the published version of his work, *L'arve et l'aume*, be prefaced by a statement of paradox: Carroll's work is to be seen as the bad imitation of his own translation.

6.3. *Antigone*, "Pious Sacrilege": Pasolini Translates *Antigone*

Pasolini's translation of *Antigone* by Sophocles goes back to 1960.[62] Unfinished, it ends after the scene in which Creon hears of Polynices's burial. In the context of literary re-accentuation in translation, what is especially interesting in Pasolini's rather "faithful" translation[63] of Sophocles's play are his lexical choices, particularly adjectives involving the two female protagonists Antigone and Ismene. Here we present a few fragments of this work along with the Italian translation by Cantarella from 2007 (RC).[64] Compare the following. In the dialogue between the two sisters, Ismene and Antigone, the latter declares her will to disobey Creonte's order not to bury their brother's body, Polynices. This will lead to her being condemned to death:

(l. 1) Antigone: "*O koinon autadelphon Ismenes kara*," [a term of endearment referring to their common origins and destiny] "*Ismenes kara*."

Tr. RC: "Ismene, sorella nel sangue comune" (Ismene, sister of our common blood).

Pasolini: Dolce capo fraterno, mia Ismene (Sweet fraternal head, my Ismene).

(l. 38) Antigone, "*eit'eugenes pephykas.*"

Tr. RC: "di nobile razza" (of noble race).

Pasolini: *degna dei padri* (worthy of your fathers).

(l. 39) "*o talaiphron*" [spoken by Ismene]

Tr. RC: "o infelice" (O unhappy wretch).

Pasolini: Io, povera sciagurata che sono! (Poor wretch that I am).

(l. 47) "*o sketlia*" [Ismene expresses concern and commiseration for her sister]

Tr. RC: "Sventurata" (unlucky).

Pasolini: O infelice (O unhappy wretch).

(l. 48) Antigone: "*all'ouden autho thon emon <m>'eirgein meta.*"

Tr. RC: "Ma egli non ha alcun diritto di impedirmelo" (But he has no right to stop me).

Pasolini introduces the adjective "lontana" (distant, Antigone uses the word to refer to herself): "Non ha il diritto di tenermi lontana da lui" (He has no right to keep me distant from him) (from her brother Polynices who was denied the right of burial by Creon).

Ismene, begging her sister to reflect carefully before acting, in light of the recent tragedies, at a certain point says:

(l. 58) "*nyn d'au mona de no leleimmena.*"

Tr. RC: "Ora siamo rimaste noi due sole" (Now it is just the two of us alone).

Pasolini connects this line with the following two lines (ll. 59–60) and translates:

"Pensa ora come miseramente anche noi / moriremo, sole, senza nessuno, se andremo contro il volere del Re" (Think how miserably we too / will die, alone, with nobody, if we go against the King's wishes).

Beyond the invitation to reflect upon the obvious fact of their being left alone, his translation includes a warning that going against the wishes of the king will lead to their deaths, and that they will die alone, by themselves: "moriranno sole, senza nessuno" (we will die alone, with nobody).

Ismene's resignation follows, summarized in the reflection that they are born women "nate donne," thus unable to fight against men (ll. 60–8):

Tr. RC: "siamo nate donne, sì da non poter lottare contro gli uomini; sottoposte a chi è più forte, dobbiamo obbedire ... : non ha alcun senso fare cose troppo grandi" (we are born women, unable to fight against men; subjugated to the strongest, we must obey ... : there is no sense in doing things that are bigger than us).

Pasolini: Ah, ricordo, infine, che siamo nate donne, / che contro gli uomini non possiamo lottare: / dobbiamo chinare la testa e soffrire / anche angosce peggiori di questa. / Io per me, pregherò le anime dei morti / perché mi perdonino: non posso non obbedire a chi tiene il potere. / I gesti disperati sono vani (Ah, remember, in the end, we are born women, / who against men cannot fight: / we must bow our heads and suffer / hardships even far worse than this. / For myself, I will pray to the dead souls / that they pardon me: I can do nothing but obey those who are in power. / All desperate acts are in vain).

(ll. 71–4) Antigone: "*keinon d'ego / thapso. kalon moi touto poiouse(i) thanein / phile met'autou keisomai, pliloy phllou / hosia panourgesas' epei.*"

Tr. RC: "io lo seppellirò, e per me sarà bello fare questo, e morire. Amata giacerò insieme a lui che io amo, avendo commesso un santo crimine" (I will bury him, and it will be good ["good" translates the Italian "bello" here, "beautiful"] to do this, and to die. Beloved I will lay with him whom I love, having committed a holy crime).

Pasolini: io lo seppellirò, nostro fratello, / e mi sarà dolce per questo morire. / Starò sotterra con lui legata d'amore / piamente sacrilega. (I will bury him, our brother, / and I will die sweetly for this. / I will lie underground with him tied by love / in pious sacrilege).

(ll. 86–7) Antigone: "*Oimoi, katauda· pollon echthion ese(i) / sigos' ean me pasi keryxe(i)s tade*" [This is Antigone's reply to Ismene's advice to say nothing of her disobedience, as indeed she does.]

Tr. RC: "Ahimè, gridalo forte, sarai molto più odiosa se, tacendo, non la proclamerai a tutti." (Ah, I will shout it out loud, it will be more odious if, by keeping silent, I do not proclaim it to all.)

Pasolini: "Ah dillo, invece, fallo sapere! Mi sarai / più odiosa tacendo che gridandolo a tutti." (Ah, say it then, let them all know! It will be/ more odious keeping quiet than shouting out the truth to all.)

(ll. 87–99) Ismene: "*thermen epi psychroisi kardian echeis.*" Antigone: "*all'oid'areskous' ois malisth'hadein me chre.*" ... Ismene: "*áll'ei dokei soi, stiche· touto d'ìsth,' hoti / anous men erche(i), toís phílois d'orthos phile."*

Tr. RC: Ismene: "Hai un cuore ardente per cose che raggelano." Antigone: "Ma so di riuscire gradita a chi soprattutto devo piacere." ... Ismene: "Certo, tu sei davvero dissennata, ma giustamente cara ai tuoi cari" (You have a heart that burns for things that freeze. Antigone: But I know that I am welcomed above all by those whom I must please ... Ismene: No doubt, you are truly foolish, but rightly dear to your loved ones).

Pasolini: Ismene: "Hai un cuore che arde di cose che gelano ..." Antigone: "So di essere approvata da chi se lo merita" ... Ismene: "Fa' come vuoi: ma sappi che chi t'ama, / benché folle, continuerà ad amarti" (You have a heart that burns for things that freeze ... Antigone: I know I am accepted by those who deserve it ... Ismene: "Do as you wish: but know that those who love you, / even though you are mad, will continue to love you).

The adjective "dolce" (sweet) that was used previously in Antigone's words ("Dolce capo fraterno, mia Ismene" / Sweet fraternal head, my Ismene), and again later, after having made the decision to bury her brother ("e mi sarà dolce per questo morire" / and I will die sweetly for this), is used by Pasolini to translate the first words of the Chorus describing the sunrise.

The superlative form, referring to the new dawn following Antigone's night-time burial of her brother, Antigone's act of "pious sacrilege," functions as a tie between her words and those of the Chorus. With *"più dolce,"* "the sweetest" Pasolini translates *"kalliston ... phaos"* as "la luce più bella" (the most beautiful light).

(l. 100) *"aktis aleliou, to kal- / liston eptapylo(i) phanen / Theba(i) ton proteron phaos / ephanthes pot."*

Tr. RC: "Raggio di sole, / luce bellissima fra quante ne apparvero / a Tebe dalle sette porte [si distingue così la Tebe di Boezia dalla Tebe egiziana, dalle cento porte], / sei apparso alfine" (Ray of sunlight, / beautiful light of all that appeared / to seven-gated Thebes [distinguishing Thebes in Boeotia from Egyptian Thebes, the city of one hundred gates], / you finally appeared).

Pasolini: Barlume del giorno, il più / dolce che sia mai apparso / sulle porte di Tebe! (Light of the day, the sweetest / light that ever appeared / on the gates of Thebes!).

The quotes above offer a concrete example of the determining importance of re-accentuation in translation. To accentuate in one way rather than another makes a difference, involves perceptions and interpretations that vary, whether a question of different[65] translations within the same historical-natural language or of translations across different languages, involving the need to find the right words and turns of phrase able to render the original accentuation. Pasolini's Italian translation offers a rendition of the ancient Greek original, which by far exceeds in poetic sense the second Italian translation reported here. Of course, to appreciate the difference requires that we compare texts, in our case referring to the Italian translation by Pasolini, and by contrast, to evidence the difference, particularly significant when considering the problem of accentuation and re-accentuation, to another official Italian translation, generally well regarded, but far less effective than Pasolini's: hence the necessary presence of ancient Greek and Italian.

7. Literary Writing and Translation in the Linguistics of the Utterance

The moment has come to ask the question why we should consider *the characterization of the text*—the "problem of the text," referencing the title of Bakhtin's essay from 1959–61 ("Problema teksta v lingvistike"[66]—*referring specifically to the literary text and its translations*). As Bakhtin underlines in "The Problem of Speech Genres" ("Problema rechevych zhanrov"),[67] the dialogic complexity of speech can be best identified in the *depiction of the word that characterizes literary genres*.[68] This is of particular interest when we view the utterance as the object of analysis, the living cell of dialogic exchange, rather than the sentence or proposition, the dead cell of the *langue*.[69] Literary writing allows us to capture from verbal language that which the direct word is not able to communicate, even though it's there as a part of the objective word. Literary genres are actually better able to reflect on intonation, sense, responsive understanding, all essential prerogatives of the live word.

The writer of literature, who is different from the speaker or the "scrivener" (the letter writer, journalist, literary critic, expert in a particular field, etc.), "uses language from the outside," he does not speak directly, in his own name, he does not *represent*, but *depicts*, *portrays* in his writing. In the literary work "the primary author clothes himself in *silence*," as Bakhtin puts it in "From Notes Made in 1970–71" ("Iz zapisej 1970–71 godov"),[70] and this silence can assume various forms of expression, from parody to irony, allegory, the various forms of "reduced laughter," and the like. This notion dominates much of Bakhtin's work through the 1970s, and it is also reflected in "Methodology for the Human Sciences" ("K metodologij gumarnitarnykh nauk").[71]

The translator, like the writer, uses language from the outside; he says nothing in his own name. They are joined, translator and writer, by the very fact that they do not use language directly and by the fact that they do not speak in their own name. Both have to express the word of the other, the word as a living utterance, with its intonation, accentuation, sense, and specific intentionality. Thus, from the point of view of the writer and the translator, and even more so for the *writer-translator*—considering their condition of *extralocalization* with respect to language, and to their "own" language—the word is perceived in all its *alterity*, as a word that is always semi-other, internally dialogized.[72] The literary text and the translated text, both "complex texts" that *portray* the words of the other, are then those that we must consider when we want to know how "simple" texts and utterances work in ordinary discourse, in everyday representation, with their expedients (in the first place accentuations and re-accentuations), in order to achieve their primary goal: listening. *Linguistica generale, scrittura letteraria e traduzione* (general linguistics, literary writing and translation)[73] are thus inseparable in any reflection on the word.[74]

8. Synaesthesia in Literary Writing and Anesthesia in Ordinary Life

À *propos* accentuation and re-accentuation in the literary text, we started out this essay by discussing the organization of sense in listening and responsive understanding in terms of *synaesthesia*. Going back to Conrad's *Typhoon*,[75] which we considered in relation to Gide's translation, we can now make the observation that the work concludes with the description of a form of *anaesthesia* that dominates ordinary life. In the drawing room of her beautiful house, Captain MacWhirr's wife "reclined in a push-bottomed and gilt hammock-chair near a tiled fireplace," and "glanced wearily here and there in the many pages" of the letters her husband had sent her regularly, and which she found "so prosy, so completely uninteresting." Mrs. MacWhirr "stifled a yawn—perhaps out of self-respect—for she was alone."

Mrs. MacWhirr skips negligently from one page of her husband's letters to the next, and it turns out that the first words she glimpses, with her superficial gaze, are "see you and the children again": "It did not occur to her to turn back overleaf to look. She would have found it recorded there that between 4 and 6 A.M. on December 25th Captain MacWhirr did actually think that his ship could not possibly live another hour in such a sea, and that he would never see his wife and children again."

Thus, we learn that the events recounted on the previous pages regarding the danger to Captain MacWhirr's ship and crew when struck by the typhoon had occurred on Christmas Day. Captain MacWhirr's wife then goes out shopping with her daughter. She knows "there is a sale at Linom's." Along the way she engages in "a swift little babble of greetings and exclamations both together" with another lady who, like her, is intent on shopping. From behind the shop windows we glimpse the movement of people busy buying gifts for Christmas. As Magrelli observes,[76] Conrad was especially critical of the bourgeois convention of giving and receiving gifts as occasioned and preestablished traditions on fixed festivities.

If we consider the context in which we wrote the present text—Christmas 2020 and New Year's 2021—we cannot help but notice the similarities with the holiday scene described in *Typhoon*. People continue behaving in the same way, regardless of the threat to life presented by the pandemic, which has already translated into a tremendous loss of lives around the world.[77] Indifference, ignorance, lack of responsibility to others: we might describe this as *anaesthesia*; a condition of unreflexive, superficial feeling, a consequence of the *hyperaesthesia* characteristic of global communication today.[78]

Bakhtin underlines the responsibility of literary writing, indeed the capacity for unlimited responsibility/answerability characteristic of literature in the face of everyday speech genres, its capacity for *aesthesia*, which the work of translation has the capacity to amplify. Such expressive enhancement inevitably involves the work of accentuation and re-accentuation, thereby evidencing the enormous moral or, better yet, ethical responsibilities involved in the work of the translator. Clearly in a global world moving toward its very own destruction, a voice like Mikhail Bakhtin's, so insistent on the moral responsibilities of the author (the self; the writer, or translator) and the hero (the other), demands that we listen. In our example from Conrad's *Typhoon*, parodying, ironizing, and critiquing (all forms of suspending the order of discourse and of listening) the ordinary behavior of the everyday person, the writer conveys the widespread lack of a sense of responsibility, in this particular case during the Christmas festivities. Gide the translator succeeds in doing exactly the same thing in his own text, thus transferring the specific accentuation of Conrad's writings to the context of dominant behaviors and ideologies.

Notes

1. Eco's translation is published as a parallel text edition by Einaudi in the series "Scrittori traducono scrittori" (Writers Translate Writers), 1999. Eco reflects on his experience as a translator in his introduction to *Dire quasi la stessa cosa* (Milan: Bompiani, 2003). He refers not only to *Sylvie* but also to his translation of *Exercices de style* by R. Queneau (Turin: Einaudi, 1983). In *Sei Passeggiate nei boschi narrativi* (Milan: Bompiani, 1994), Eco returns to *Sylvie*: "L'ho letto a vent'anni, e da allora non ho mai cessato di rileggerlo … Ogni volta che riprendo in mano *Sylvie*, pur riconoscendo a fondo la sua anatomia, e forse proprio per questo, me ne innamoro come se lo leggessi per la prima volta" (I read it at the age of twenty, and from then on have never stopped rereading it … Each time I pick up *Sylvie*, and though I am profoundly familiar with its anatomy, and perhaps just because of this, I end up falling in love with it as if I were reading it for the first time) (in Umberto Eco, *Sei passeggiate nei boschi narrativi*, 14–15; all English translations in this essay are ours, unless otherwise stated).
2. Gerard de Nerval, *Sylvie*, Italian trans. and ed. Umberto Eco (Turin: Einaudi, 1999), 97.
3. "Leggendo traducendo" (Reading Translating) is the title of the second part of Augusto Ponzio's *La coda dell'occhio* (Rome: Aracne, 2016). The first part is entitled "Leggendo" (Reading) and contains Italian translations of poems by Donne, La Fontaine, Pushkin, Heine, Baudelaire Mallarmé, Verlaine, Valery, Apollinaire, Borges, as well as Ορνιθες (*Uccelli* [*Birds*]) by Aristophenes. The title of the book as a whole, *La coda dell'occhio* (The Corner of the Eye), recalls the words of Edgar Allan Poe's character Dupin who explains that observing an object directly always alters the way we see it, while the best vision is reached "out of the corner of the eye."
4. See Roman Jakobson, "On Linguistic Aspects of Translation," in *On Translation*, ed. R. A. Brower (Cambridge, MA: Harvard University Press, 1959), 232–9.
5. *Intonacija* and *akcentuacija* are terms used frequently by Mikhail Bakhtin and Valentin Voloshinov. Referring to Dostoevsky, Bakhtin uses the expression *pluriaccentuation*.
6. In *Cours de linguistique générale*, Ferdinand de Saussure connotes *signifiant* with respect to *signifié* as an "acoustic image."
7. See Arthur Rimbaud, *Une Saison en enfer* (Paris: Compton Auberge Veerte, 1993 [1873]). Italian trans. and ed. G.-A. Bertozzi. Parallel edition (Milan: Newton, 1995).
8. See Susan Petrilli, ed., *L'immagine nella parola, nella musica e nella pittura*. Serie Athanor, XXVIII, 21 (Milan: Mimesis, 2018); Susan Petrilli "Vision of the Other: Word and Image in Mikhail Bakhtin," *International Journal of Semiotics and Visual Rhetoric* II, no. 1 (2018): 120–36; also, Augusto Ponzio, *L'Écoute de l'autre* (Paris: L'Harmattan, 2009).

9. Nerval, *Sylvie*, 99.
10. Marcel Proust, *Contre Sainte-Beuve* (Paris: Gallimard, 1954).
11. See Susan Petrilli and Augusto Ponzio, *Views in Literary Semiotics* (Ottawa: Legas, 2003) and Susan Petrilli and Augusto Ponzio, *La raffigurazione letteraria* (Milan: Mimesis, 2006).
12. In Frederick R. Karl, "Conrad and Gide. A Relationship and a Correspondence," *Comparative Literature* 29, no. 2 (1977): 269, cited in Valerio Magrelli, "Gide traduttore di Conrad," in Joseph Conrad, *Typhoon*. French trans. André Gide, Italian trans. U. Mursia, ed. Valerio Magrelli (Turin: Einaudi, 1993 [1902]), 345–75.
13. In Magrelli, "Gide traduttore di Conrad," 361.
14. Karl, "Conrad and Gide," 361.
15. See Magrelli, "Gide traduttore di Conrad," 367.
16. Ibid., 370.
17. See Susan Petrilli, ed., *Lo stesso altro*, Serie Athanor XIII, 4 (Rome: Meltemi, 2001).
18. Augusto Ponzio, *Michail Bachtin* (Bari: Dedalo, 1980); Augusto Ponzio *La rivoluzione bachtiniana* (Bari: Levante, 1997); Augusto Ponzio *Tra semiotica e letteratura* (Milan: Bompiani, 2015); Susan Petrilli, *Altrove e altrimenti* (Milan: Mimesis, 2012).
19. In Bachtin e il suo Circolo, *Opere 1919–1930*. Parallel edition Russian/ Italian, ed. A. Ponzio (Milan: Bompiani, 2014), 1750–61.
20. Augusto Ponzio, *Rencontre de paroles* (Paris: Baudry, 2010); Augusto Ponzio, *In altre parole* (Milan: Mimesis, 2012).
21. Eco, *Dire quasi la stessa cosa*, 10.
22. Petrilli, *Lo stesso altro*, is the title of the third collective volume of a trilogy dedicated to translation theory and practice edited by Susan Petrilli. The trilogy is hosted in the Serie Athanor. *Semiotica, filosofia, Letteraturea, Arte*, founded by Augusto Ponzio in 1990. See note 23 for more details.
23. The volumes forming the *Athanor* trilogy include: *La traduzione* (Serie Athanor X, 2. Rome: Meltemi, 2019); *Tra segni* (Serie Athanor XII, 3. Rome: Meltemi, 2000); and *Lo stesso altro* (Serie Athanor XIII, 4. Rome: Meltemi, 2001). The English essays from this trilogy were later published as a separate collected volume, also edited by Susan Petrilli, *Translation Translation* (Amersterdam: Rodopi, 2003).
24. Jacques Derrida, "Qu'est-ce que c'est une traduction 'relevante,'" 1998. Italian trans. J. Ponzio, in Susan Petrilli, ed., *Tra segni* (Rome: Meltemi, 2000), 25–45.
25. Susan Petrilli and Augusto Ponzio, "Iconicity, Otherness and Translation." *Chinese Semiotic Studies* 7, no. 1 (2012): 11–26; Susan Petrilli and Augusto Ponzio, "Propriedades iconicas da traducao," in *Tradução, Transposição e Adaptação*, ed. Daniella Aguiar and João Queiroz (São Carlos: Pedro & João, 2016), 135–98.

26. Katia De Abreu Chulata, *Il traduttore. Mito e (de) costruzione di una identità*, preface by A. Ponzio (Milan: LED, 2015).
27. Eco, *Dire quasi la stessa cosa*, 20; emphasis added.
28. Nerval, *Sylvie*, 99–100.
29. Ibid., 126.
30. Ibid., 94.
31. Eco, *Sei passeggiate nei boschi narrativi*, 15–16.
32. Nerval, *Sylvie*, 2–3.
33. Ibid., 88–9.
34. Ibid., 89.
35. Our immediate references here are to Dante Alighieri, *Vita Nova* (1294–5); Pushkin, "Razluka," 1830, analyzed by Bakhtin in "*Autor i geroi v esteticheskoj dejatel'nosti*," Italian trans. A. Ponzio, in Bakhtin e il suo Circolo, 169–215; R. Barthes, *Journal de deuil*, ed. Nathalie Léger (Paris: Seuil, 1977); R. Barthes, *Vita nova*, in *Oeuvres complètes, V, Livres, Textes, Entretiens 1977–1980* (Paris: Seuil, 1979); R. Barthes, *La chambre claire* (Paris: Seuil, 1980); R. Barthes, *La préparation du roman*, I et II, ed. N Léger (Paris: Seuil, 2003).
36. Susan Petrilli, "Tempo di scrittura, tempo di vita nuova." In *Tempo, corpo, scrittura*, ed. S. Petrilli et al. (Lecce: Pensa MultiMedia, 2012), 85–112.
37. Nerval, *Sylvie*, 138.
38. Maurice Blanchot, *La follie du jour* (Paris: Fata Morgana, 1973).
39. Vito Carofiglio, *Nerval e Baudelaire. Discorsi segreti* (Bari: Edizioni dal Sud, 1987), 170.
40. In Mikhail M. Bakhtin, *Autor i geroy* (S. Petersburg: Ažibuca, 2000) and in Italian translation in Bachtin e il suo Circolo, *Opere 1919–1930*.
41. Paul Valery, *Le cimitière marin*, ed. G. Sansone (Turin: Einaudi, 1995), 2.
42. Ibid., 3.
43. Paul Valéry, "Il cimitero marino," Italian translation in Ponzio, *La coda dell'occhio*, 329.
44. In Valéry, *Le cimitière marin*, 9.
45. In Ponzio, *La coda dell'occhio*, 331.
46. In Valéry, *Le cimitière marin*, 16.
47. In Ponzio, *La coda dell'occhio*, 333.
48. Jorge Luis Borges, "La perpetua carrera de Aquiles y la Tortuga," in *Discusión* (Buenos Aires: Manuel Gleizer, 1932), 151–61, and in Jorge Luis Borges, *Obras Completas*, ed. J. E. Clemente (Buenos Aires: Emecé, 1957), 113–20; "Avatares de la tortuga." *Sur* 63, no. 11 (1939): 18–23, in Borges, *Obras Completas*, 129–36.
49. When a question of depiction, *izobrazhenie*, the objective, direct word, the word of power, the transcribed, inscribed, recited, repeated, sanctioned word, the word of representation becomes the objectified, indirect word, writing that announces that repetition of the identical is impossible, that the other cannot be reduced to the same. This is the word of literary

writing, the depicted word extralocalized to varying degrees. See Pavel N. Medvedev, *Formalnyj metod v literatuovedenii* (1928), Mikhail M. Bakhtin, *Problemy tvorchestva Dostoevskogo* (1929), and Valentin N. Voloshinov, *Marksizm i filosofija jazyka* (1929/1930), in Bachtin e il suo Circolo, ed. A. Ponzio (Milan: Bompiani, 2014), respectively, 702–15, 1103–9, 1863–9.
50. Luciano Ponzio, *Visioni del testo* (Lecce: Pensa MultiMedia, 2016).
51. Eco, *Dire quasi la stessa cosa*, 364.
52. See Susan Petrilli, "Iconicity in Translation," *American Journal of Semiotics* 24, no. 4 (2008): 237–302; Susan Petrilli, "Translation, Iconicity, and Dialogism," in *Signergy*, ed. C. Jac Conardie et al. (Amsterdam: Benjamins, 2010), 367–86; Petrilli and Ponzio, "Iconicity, Otherness and Translation" ; Petrilli and Ponzio, "Propriedades iconicas da traducao, 135–98.
53. *Vnenakhodimost (exotopy, or extralocalization)* plays in important role in Bakhtin's conception of the aesthetic vision, present throughout all his writings. See, for example, his essay redacted between 1920 and 1924, *Toward a Philosophy of the Act* (Austin: University of Texas Press, 1993), 66–7, and for the Russian original with parallel Italian translation, see Michail Bachtin e il suo Circolo, *Opere 1919–1930*, 150–4.
54. In Borges, *Obras Completas*.
55. Jorge LuisBorges, "Pierre Menard, autor del Quijote," *Sur* 56, no. 5 (1939): 7–16. In Borges, *Obras Completas*, 45–57.
56. According to Peirce, the "icon" is one of three types of sign in a triad where the other two signs are the "index" and "symbol." In the icon, the relation between sign and the object It refers to is characterized by similarity, which does not imply dependency (see Charles Perice, *Collected Papers*, ed. C. Hartshorne, P. Weiss, and A. W. Burks. 8 Vols. (Cambridge, MA: Harvard University Press, 1931–58).
57. Jorge Luis Borges, "Paul Valéry: El cementerio marino," preface by J. L. Borges, trans. Néstor Ibarra (Buenos Aires: Les Editions, Schillinger, 1932).
58. Antonin Artaud, *L'arve et l'aume* (Paris: L'arbalète, 1985).
59. Susan Petrilli, "La traduzione crudele di Artaud contro Artaud," in Susan Petrilli and Augusto Ponzio, *Fuori campo. I segni del corpo tra rappresentazione ed eccedenza* (Milan: Mimesis, 1999), 273–8.
60. Lewis Carroll, *The Annotated Alice. Alice's Adventures in Wonderland and Through the Looking Glass*, ed. Martin Gardiner (Harmondsworth: Penguin, 1978).
61. See Gilles Deleuze, *Critique et clinique* (Paris: Minuit, 1993), Italian translation titled *Critica e clinica* (Milan: Cortina, 1996), 37–8; also, Susan Petrilli and Augusto Ponzio, "Exchange in Alice World," in *Semiotics and Linguistics in Alice's Worlds*, ed. R. Fordyce et al. (Berlin: De Gruter, 1994), 74–8.
62. *Antigone*, in Pier Paolo Pasolini, *Teatro* (Milan: Mondadori, 2001), 1013–24.

63. Augusto Ponzio, "Il femminile in Pasolini traduttore dell'*Antigone* e dell'*Orestiade*, in Ponzio, *In altre parole*, 41–8.
64. In Sofocle, *Le tragedie*, Italian trans. Raffaele Cantarella et al. (Milan: Mondadori, 2007). [All italics added by us to the text, transliterated from the ancient Greek original, to distinguish it from its Italian translations.]
65. Slav Grachev and Howard Mancing, eds., *Don Quixote: The Re-accentuation of the World's Greatest Literary Hero* (Lewisburg: Bucknell University Press, 2017).
66. In Mikhail M. Bakhtin, *Estetica slovesnogo tvorchestva* (Moscow: Iskusstovo, 1979).
67. In Mikhail M. Bakhtin, *Speech Genres and Other Late Essays*, ed. C. Emerson and M. Holquist (Austin: University of Texas Press, 1986), 60–102.
68. Ibid., 109–12.
69. Augusto Ponzio, *Linguistica generale, scrittura letteraria e traduzione* (Perugia: Guerra, 2018), preface titled "La parola e l'ascolto" (The Word and Listening).
70. In Bakhtin, *Speech Genres and Other Late Essays*, 149.
71. Ibid., 159–72.
72. See Susan Petrilli, "Listening, Otherness and Translation" and "Philosophy of Language as the Art of Listening," in S. Petrilli, *Signs, Language and Listening* (New York: Legas, 2019), 139–56 and 157–98; also Susan Petrilli, "Translation as Listening to the Other," *Acta Translatologica Helsingiensia*. INTER 2 (2013): 116–45; and Susan Petrilli and Augusto Ponzio, "Translation as Listening and Encounter," *Traduction, Terminologie, Rédaction* XIX (2006): 191–224, and Susan Petrilli and Augusto Ponzio, "In Name of the Other. Translation as Listening and Encounter," in *Challenges to Living Together*, ed. S. Petrilli (Milan: Mimesis, 2017), 197–231.
73. This is the title of a book by Augusto Ponzio (Perugia: Guerra, 2018), of which the first edition appeared with the same publishers in 2004.
74. See Susan Petrilli, "Lifelong Listening to M. Bakhtin's Word in the Context of His 'Circle,'" *Philology* 3 (2017): 361–95.
75. Conrad, *Typhoon*.
76. Magrelli, "Gide traduttore di Conrad," 336.
77. See Pierre DallaVigna, *I luoghi del coronavirus* (Milan: Mimesis, 2020).
78. See Susan Petrilli and Augusto Ponzio, *Il sentire della comunicazione globale* (Roma: Meltemi, 2000); Susan Petrilli and Augusto Ponzio, *Semioetica* (Rome: Meltemi, 2003); and Susan Petrilli and Augusto Ponzio, *Semiotics Unbounded* (Toronto: Toronto University Press, 2005); see also Susan Petrilli, *Sign Studies and Semioethics. Communication* (Berlin: De Gruyter Mouton, 2014); Susan Petrilli, "Sensibility in the Era of Global Communication," *Social Semiotics* 18, no. 4 (2008): 503–28; and Susan Petrilli, ed., *Semioetica e comunicazione globale*,

Serie Athanor XXIV, 17 (Milan: Mimesis, 2014); see also A. Ponzio, *Da dove verso dove. La parola altra nella comunicazione globale* (Perugia: Guerra, 2009).

Bibliography

Artaud, Antonin. *L'arve et l'aume*. Paris: L'arbalète, 1985.

Bachtin e il suo Circolo. *Opere 1919–1930*. Parallel edition Russian/Italian. Edited by A. Ponzio. Parallel Russian/Italian text edition (Translated into Italian with L. Ponzio). Contains: by Bachtin, "Iskusstvo i otvetstvennost'" (Arte e responsabilità); "K filosofi postupka" (Per una filosofia dell'atto responsabile); "Sovremenny vitalizm" ("Il vitalismo contemporaneo"), firmato da Kanaev; *Avtor i geroi v esteticheskoj dejatel'nosti* (L'autore e l'eroe nella attività estetica. Frammento del I capitolo); *Problemy tvorchestva Dostoevskogo* (Problemi dell'opera di Dostoevskij); by Medvedev, *Formalnyj metod v literatuovedenii* (Il metodo formale nella scienza della letteratura); by Voloshinov, "Slovo v zhizni i slovo v poezii (La parola nella vita e nella poesia); *Frejdizm* (Freudismo); *Marksizm i filosofija jazyka* (Marxismo e filosofia del linguaggio); the three essays of "Stilistika chudozhestvennoj rechi" ("Stilistica del discorso artistico"; "O Granicach poetiki i linguistiki [Sui confini tra poetica e linguistica]). Milan: Bompiani, 2014.

Bakhtin, Mikhail M. *Autor i geroy*. S. Petersburg: Ažibuca, 2000.

Bakhtin, Mikhail M. *Estetica slovesnogo tvorchestva*. Moscow: Iskusstvo, 1979. Translated into Italian as *L'autore e l'eroe*. Edited by C. Strada Janovič. Turin: Einaudim, 1988.

Bakhtin, Mikhail M. *Speech Genres and Other Late Essays*. Edited by C. Emerson and M. Holquist. Austin: University of Texas Press, 1986.

Barthes, Roland. *Journal de Deuil*. Edited by Nathalie Léger. Paris: Seuil, 1977.

Barthes, Roland. *La chambre Claire*. Paris: Seuil, 1980.

Barthes, Roland. *La préparation du roman*. Vols. I and II. Edited by N Léger. Paris; Seuil, 2003. Translated into Italian by J. Ponzio and E. Galiani as *La preparazione del romanzo*. Milan: Mimesis, 2010.

Barthes, Roland. *Vita nova*. In R. Barthes. *Oeuvres complètes, V, Livres, Textes, Entretiens 1977–1980*. Paris: Seuil, 2002.

Blanchot, Maurice. *La follie du jour*. Paris: Fata Morgana, 1973.

Borges, Jorge Luis. "Avatares de la tortuga" *Sur* 63, no. 11 (1939): 18–23.

Borges, Jorge Luis. *Discusión*. Buenos Aires: Manuel Gleizer, 1932.

Borges, Jorge Luis. *Ficciones*. Buenos Aires: Sur, 1944.

Borges, Jorge Luis. "La perpetua carrera de Aquiles y la Tortuga." In *Obras Completas*. Edited by J .E. Clemente, 113–20. Buenos Aires: Emecé, 1957.

Borges, Jorge Luis. "Las versiones homéricas." In *Obras Completas*. Edited by J.E. Clemente, 105–12. Buenos Aires: Emecé, 1957.
Borges, Jorge Luis. *Obras Completas*. Edited by J.E. Clemente. Buenos Aires: Emecé, 1957. [New edition 1958.]
Borges, Jorge Luis. "Paul Valéry: El cementerio marino." Preface by Jorge Luis Borges. Translated by Néstor Ibarra. Buenos Aires: Les Editions, Schillinger, 1932.
Borges, Jorge Luis. "Pierre Menard, autor del Quijote" *Sur* 56, no. 5 (1939): 7–16.
Borges, Jorge Luis. *Tutte le opere*. Vols. I and II. Edited by D. Porzio. Milan: Mondadori, 1984–5.
Carofiglio, Vito. *Nerval e Baudelaire. Discorsi segreti*. Bari: Edizioni dal Sud, 1987.
Carroll, Lewis. *The Annotated Alice. Alice's Adventures in Wonderland* and *Through the Looking Glass*. Edited by Martin Gardiner. Harmondsworth: Penguin, 1978.
Carroll, Lewis. *Humpty Dumpty*. Translated into French by Antonin Artaud, *L'Arve e l'aume*. Translated into Italian by G. Almansi and G. Pozzo. Edited by C. Pasi, Turin: Einaudi, 1993.
Conrad, Joseph. *Typhoon*. Translated into French by André Gide. Translated into Italian by U. Mursia. Edited by Valerio Magrelli. Turin: Einaudi, 1993. https://www.gutenberg.org/files/1142/1142-h/1142-h.htm.
Dalla Vigna, Pierre. *I luoghi del coronavirus*. Milan: Mimesis, 2020.
De Abreu Chulata, Katia. *Il traduttore. Mito e (de) costruzione di una identità*. Preface by A. Ponzio, Milano: LED, 2015.
Deleuze, Gilles. *Critique et clinique*, Paris: Minuit, 1993. Translated into Italian by A. Panaro as *Critica e clinica*. Milan: Cortina, 1996.
Derrida Jacques. "Qu'est-ce que c'est une traduction 'relevante,'" 1998. Translated into Italian by J. Ponzio. In *Tra segni*, Serie Athanor XII, 3. Edited by S. Petrilli, 25–45. Rome: Meltemi, 2000.
Eco, Umberto. *Dire quasi la stessa cosa*. Milano: Bompiani, 2003.
Eco, Umberto. *Experiences in Translation*. Toronto: Toronto University Press, 2001.
Eco, Umberto. *Sei passeggiate nei boschi narrativi*. Milan: Bompiani, 1994.
Gide, André. "Lettre sur les traductions." In W. Shakespeare. *Hamlet: Premier acte*. Translated into French by A. Gide. Paris: Editions de la tortue, 1930.
Grachev, Slav N., and Howard Mancing, eds. *Don Quixote: The Re-accentuation of the World's Greatest Literary Hero*. Lewisburg, MD: Bucknell University Press, 2017.
Jakobson, Roman. "On Linguistic Aspects of Translation." In *On Translation*. Edited by R. A. Brower, 232–9. Cambridge, MA: Harvard University Press, 1959.
Karl, Frederick R. "Conrad and Gide. A Relationship and a Correspondence" *Comparative Literature* 29, no. 2 (1977): 148–71.

Magrelli, Valerio. "Gide traduttore di Conrad." In Joseph Conrad, *Typhoon*, 345–75. Turin: Einaudi, 1993 [1902].

Monod, Sylvère. "Note sur la traduction de *Typhoon* par Andreé Gide." In Joseph Conrad, *Œuvres*. Volume 2. Paris: Gallimard, 1985.

Nerval, Gérard de. *Sylvie*. Parallel French/Italian text edition. Translated into Italian by Umberto Eco, 97–165. Turin: Einaudi, 1999 [1853].

Pasolini, Pier Paolo. *Teatro*. Milan: Mondadori, 2001.

Peirce, Charles S. *Collected Papers*. Edited by C. Hartshorne, P. Weiss, and A. W. Burks. 8 vols. Cambridge, MA: Harvard University Press, 1931–58.

Petrilli, Susan. *Altrove e altrimenti*. Milan: Mimesis, 2012.

Petrilli, Susan. "Iconicity in Translation." *American Journal of Semiotics* 24, no. 4 (2008): 237–302.

Petrilli, Susan. "La traduzione crudele di Artaud contro Artaud." In *Il sentire della comunicazione globale*. Edited by A. Ponzio and S. Petrilli, 273–8. Rome: Meltemi, 2000.

Petrilli, Susan, ed. *La traduzione*, Serie Athanor X, 2. Rome: Meltemi, 1999.

Petrilli, Susan. "Lifelong Listening to M. Bakhtin's Word in the Context of His 'Circle.'" *Philology* 3 (2017): 361–95.

Petrilli, Susan, ed. *L'immagine nella parola, nella musica e nella pittura*. Serie Athanor, XXVIII, 21. Milan: Mimesis, 2018.

Petrilli, Susan, ed. *Lo stesso altro*, Serie Athanor XIII, 4. Rome: Meltemi, 2001.

Petrilli, Susan. ed. *Semioetica e comunicazione globale*. Serie Athanor XXIV, 17. Milan: Mimesis, 2014.

Petrilli, Susan. "Sensibility in the Era of Global Communication. *Social Semiotics* 18, no. 4 (2008); 503–28.

Petrilli, Susan. *Signs, Language and Listening*. New York: Legas, 2019.

Petrilli, Susan. *Studies and Semioethics. Communication, Translation and Values*. Berlin: De Gruyter Mouton, 2014.

Petrilli, Susan. "Tempo di scrittura, tempo di vita nuova." In *Tempo, corpo, scrittura*. Edited by S. Petrilli et al., 85–112. Lecce: Pensa MultiMedia, 2012.

Petrilli, Susan. "Translation, Iconicity, and Dialogism." In *Signergy*. Edited by C. Jac Conardie et al., 367–86. Amsterdam: Benjamins, 2010.

Petrilli, Susan, ed. *Translation Translation*. Amsterdam: Rodopi.

Petrilli, Susan, ed. *Tra segni*, Serie Athanor XII, 3. Rome: Meltemi, 2000.

Petrilli, Susan. "Translation as Listening to the Other." *Acta Translatologica Helsingiensia*. INTER 2 (2013): 116–45.

Petrilli, Susan. "Vision of the Other: Word and Image in Mikhail Bakhtin." *International Journal of Semiotics and Visual Rhetoric* 2, no. 1 (2018): 120–36.

Petrilli, Susan, and Ponzio, Augusto. "Exchange in Alice World." In *Semiotics and Linguistics in Alice's Worlds*. Edited by R. Fordyce et al., 74–8. Berlin: De Gruyter, 1994.

Petrilli, Susan, and Ponzio, Augusto. *Fuori campo. I segni del corpo tra rappresentazione ed eccedenza*. Milan: Mimesis, 1999.

Petrilli, Susan, and Ponzio, Augusto. "Iconicity, Otherness and Translation." *Chinese Semiotic Studies* 7, no. 1 (2012): 11–26.
Petrilli, Susan, and Ponzio, Augusto. *Il sentire della comunicazione globale*. Milan: Mimesis, 2000.
Petrilli, Susan, and Ponzio, Augusto. "In Name of the Other. Translation as Listening and Encounter," 197–231. In *Challenges to Living Together*. Edited by S. Petrilli, 197–231. Milan: Mimesis, 2017.
Petrilli, Susan, and Ponzio, Augusto. *La raffigurazione letteraria*. Milan: Mimesis, 2006.
Petrilli, Susan, and Ponzio, Augusto. "Propriedades iconicas da traducao." In *Tradução, Transposição e Adaptação*. Edited by Daniella Aguiar and João Queiroz, 135–98. São Carlos: Pedro & João, 2016.
Petrilli, Susan, and Ponzio, Augusto. *Semioetica*. Rome: Meltemi, 2003.
Petrilli, Susan, and Ponzio, Augusto. *Semiotics Unbounded*. Toronto: Toronto University Press, 2005.
Petrilli, Susan, and Ponzio, Augusto. "Translation as Listening and Encounter." *Traduction, Terminologie, Rédaction* 19 (2006): 191–224.
Petrilli, Susan, and Ponzio, Augusto. *Views in Literary Semiotics*. Ottawa: Legas, 2003.
Poe, Edgard Allan. *Lettera rubata*. Edited by J. L. Borges. Milan: Franco Maria Ricci, 1979.
Ponzio, Augusto. "Il tempo e lo spazio nella scrittura letteraria." In *Tempo, corpo, scrittura*. Edited by S. Petrilli et al., 113–149. Lecce: Pensa MultiMedia, 2012.
Ponzio, Augusto. *Da dove verso dove. La parola altra nella comunicazione globale*. Perugia: Guerra, 2009.
Ponzio, Augusto. *In altre parole*, Milan: Mimesis, 2012.
Ponzio, Augusto. *L'Écoute de l'autre*. Paris: L'Harmattan, 2009.
Ponzio, Augusto. *La coda dell'occhio*. Rome: Aracne, 2016.
Ponzio, Augusto. *La rivoluzione bachtiniana*. Bari: Levante, 1997.
Ponzio, Augusto. *Linguistica generale, scrittura letteraria e traduzione*. Perugia: Guerra, 2018.
Ponzio, Augusto. *Rencontre de paroles*. Paris: Baudry, 2010.
Ponzio, Augusto. "Il femminile in Pasolini traduttore dell'*Antigone* e dell'*Orestiade*." in Susan Petrilli, *Altrove e altrimenti*, 41–48. Milan: Mimesis, 2012.
Ponzio, Augusto. *Michail Bachtin*. Bari: Dedalo, 1980.
Ponzio, Augusto. *Tra semiotica e letteratura*. Milan: Bompiani, 2015.
Ponzio, Luciano. *Visioni del testo*. Lecce: Pensa MultiMedia, 2016.
Proust, Marcel. *Contre Sainte-Beuve*. Paris: Gallimard, 1954.
Queneau, Raymond. *Exercices de style—Esercizi di stile*. Translated into Italian by U. Eco. Turin: Einaudi, 1983.
Rimbaud, Arthur. *Une Saison en enfer*. Paris: Compton Auberge Veerte, 1993. Translated into Italian and edited by G.-A. Bertozzi. Parallel edition. Milan: Newton, 1995 [1873].

Saussure, Ferdinand de. *Cours de linguistique générale*. Edited by C. Bally and A. Secheaye. Paris: Payot, 1916.

Sofocle. *Le tragedie*. Translated into Italian by Raffaele Cantarella et al. Milan: Mondadori, 2007.

Valery, Paul. *Le cimitière marin*. Edited by G. Sansone. Torino: Einaudi, 1995.

10

Sifting through Dialogic Ashes: Translating Complex Meanings in Muñoz Molina's *Beatus Ille*

Steven Mills

Mikhail M. Bakhtin's concept of re-accentuation explores the author's voice within the social contexts of polyphonic and dialogic novels in which characters function as independent agents in their story world much as we do in our real world. Furthermore, the authorial voice is itself another shade that nuances their story world, often recasting the real world it represents with new hues in the process. In this light, Spanish author Antonio Muñoz Molina recreates, and in so doing re-accentuates, the contemporary Spanish society in his first novel, *Beatus Ille* (1986), which debuted during the first decade of the transition to democracy after the Franco dictatorship (1939–75). The novel explores the people's sentiments and social contexts during the regime as well as the effects of intentionally forgetting the difficult memories of oppression as the Spanish society emerges from the dictatorship. What we find through the authorial voice in this novel about memory is a re-accentuation of Spain's transition: the Spaniards want to forget their oppression as they move on to democracy, but Muñoz Molina recasts that Spanish society into one that recovers the past and finds hope in the future.

However, his society is recast again in 2008 when Edith Grossman publishes an English translation of *Beatus Ille*, which she titled *A Manuscript of Ashes*. While the story is the same, the new title refocuses the entire message of the book away from hope and toward the lost memories of previous generations. In essence, Grossman re-accentuates what Muñoz Molina had already re-accentuated. In so doing, she recreates the sentiment of loss that Muñoz Molina's novel had attempted to resolve in his work, thus adding her voice to that of Muñoz Molina's and his characters. Her focus on the feelings experienced by the Spanish people under Franco inspires a dialogic connection between the original *Beatus Ille*'s effect on Spaniards of the transition during the 1980s and the English readers of the twenty-first century, in the process helping them understand life under dictatorship better.

The novel tells the story of Minaya, who as a college student in 1969 relocates to his family's hometown Mágina to escape the regime's violence in Madrid. Claiming to be writing a dissertation on Jacinto Solana, a deceased subversive poet and a childhood friend of his uncle Manuel, Minaya moves in with his uncle, now one of the region's wealthy and influential landowners. As Minaya researches Solana, to maintain pretenses, he uncovers romance, political agendas, jealousy, betrayals, and social unrest among Manuel's and Solana's family and friends. Gradually, Minaya's interest in the case becomes genuine as he stumbles upon Solana's forgotten manuscripts, his love affair with Manuel's bride Mariana, and the identity of Mariana's murderer. Minaya discovers these secrets as he interviews various people who share their memories with him, but the novel's structure is complicated by the mysterious first-person omniscient narrator who shares his own perspectives along the way and who resides just outside the plot as the lover of Inés, a young woman who works as a servant in Manuel's house, and who has also become romantically involved with Minaya. Inés spies on Minaya and the house's inhabitants and reports back to this narrator, who turns out to be Solana himself (he has been hiding all those years following his presumed assassination by the regime in 1947). When Solana and Minaya meet in 1969, Solana informs the younger man that he has recently written the manuscripts Minaya had found as a sort of a game, while the originals were all burned just before he feigned his death. Throughout the novel, the plot and the investigation revolve around these recuperated memories, the enigmatic manuscripts, and Solana's domineering presence in the past and present.

1. *Beatus Ille*: The Title

The key element of this study is the title of the book: it is fundamental to the original story's message, and the new title of the book's translation orchestrates a crucial change in meaning in English. Muñoz Molina's re-accentuation of Spanish society during the transition stems from the title, and Grossman's new title re-accentuates Muñoz Molina's message. Titles are always important, as they often try to guide readers toward a particular interpretation of the narrated events. In this case, they are even more significant, as they can arguably be seen as the first enigma, in a series of many, to be noted and deciphered as the readers engage with the text's meanings.

Muñoz Molina's title *Beatus Ille* comes from a classical trope and a Spanish Golden Age poet who employed that trope. The Latin phrase, associated with

Horace's oeuvre, means *"blessed the one,"* or *"blessed is he,"* and can be found in many of the poems by the well-known Spanish Golden Age poet Fray Luis de León. De León used the expression to laud those who can escape the hassle of the city and dwell in the serene peace and freedom of the countryside. This phrase's history highlights Jacinto Solana's and Minaya's efforts in the novel to escape the city and the regime's oppression centered there, and find refuge in rural Mágina. Of the two characters, it is Minaya who truly deserves to be called "blessed" as he finds love and success in the countryside, while Solana fails to escape the regime or find peace and freedom in Mágina. Nevertheless, the key point upon which the novel is built is hope, and the reader is meant to receive this message as he/she navigates the narrative in Minaya's steps. Hope is what Solana has lost, what Minaya holds onto, and what Spain of the 1980s needs. In short, Muñoz Molina declares: blessed is he (*beatus ille*) who finds hope and peace through this novel.

2. *Beatus Ille*: Minaya

As already noted, Minaya is the blessed one referenced in the novel's title. While he seeks refuge from the regime and its oppression in Mágina in 1969, he is also much younger than Solana and his uncle Manuel, which means that, unlike them, he can hope to outlive Franco. Solana, Manuel, and their generation of friends accept they will never be free of the regime: "Don't have any illusions, Manuel, ... you and I will never see the Third Republic. We're condemned to Franco in the same way we're condemned to grow old and die."[1] Minaya's readers in the real world, on the other hand, know that if he can survive six more years, he will see the death of Franco in 1975, and he will find the peace and freedom that Solana never achieved.

Through Minaya, Muñoz Molina redraws the perspective of 1986 Spain so that the mysteries of the past give way to Minaya's future, which Muñoz Molina's reader is living. This process begins in Manuel's house, where Minaya is staying, because it is a microcosm of Spain and its political and ideological situation in the 1960s. Elvira, the conservative matriarch, akin to Franco, holds together the family fortune and business—and thereby its power and influence—while Manuel, the liberal son who originally wanted to escape to France with his bride and abandon the family traditions and pressures, now faces his depressing life wherein both his best friend and bride have died. The parallels to the oppressive Franco regime during this period are clear. However, the dictator, like Elvira, is aging, and his death would open a new era for Spain. In this way, the family, the friends, and the house represent

Minaya's Spain: a country of destroyed pasts, painful memories, constant fear, and heavy oppression.

Through Manuel's house, then, combined with Minaya's search for peace and freedom, Muñoz Molina re-accentuates Spain: he takes the memories and events of the past, of Solana and Manuel, of Spaniards under Franco, and then recasts them. The effect is that the harshness of the past can turn into a paradise in the present; as Solana at one point contemplates, "what a strange logic of memory and pain conspires silently to transform the prison of another time into paradise."[2] Muñoz Molina's reimagining of Spain's identity reflects Bakhtin's idea that every author re-accentuates their own society through the work's polyphonic voices. In this process, particularly in *Beatus Ille*, the characters, their memories, their words, and their perspectives recreate, and consequently dialogue with, the readers' own histories. Fictional voices reflect real voices as the past converses with the present, liberal with conservative, hope with despair. Through those dialogic voices, Muñoz Molina "builds a superstructure ... made up of his own intentions and accents, which then becomes dialogically linked with them. The author encases his own thought in the image of another's language."[3] Molina's Spain is a country of hope shifting away from dictatorship to democracy, which is reflected in Minaya's story as it changes its focus from the memories of Solana and his friends, who are dead or dying, to Minaya and his generation.

By recognizing its problematic past and actively facing its future, Spain becomes the "blessed one." Like the main characters in the novel, it, too, must recover and process its painful memories in order to write the real history of Franco's regime. As Minaya unearths truths previously lost or hidden, we see the process that real Spaniards must undergo to find their own past. Thus, Miguel Martinón argues that *Beatus Ille* "es más bien [una novela sobre] la recuperación de la historia contemporánea de España negada por el franquismo" (is [a novel about] the recovery of the contemporary history of Spain rejected by Francoism).[4] Essentially, through Solana and Minaya, Molina is attacking the falsifications of the old regime and allowing the new generation the opportunity to discover the truth and move onward because of it.

However, there were those who accepted the doctored histories or who supported Franco and wanted the new Spain to stay true to his ideals even after his death. Their fidelity threatened the needed political and social unity during the political shift to democracy. This troubled transition from the old generation to the new, from past to present, and from dictatorship to democracy among the Spanish people is evident in the novel through Inés's transition from being Solana's lover to becoming Minaya's. Throughout the novel she and Minaya have an affair, but she also maintains a sexual relationship with the narrator Solana, with whom she had been involved long before Minaya arrives in Mágina. Playing both sides, Inés refuses to let go of the past (her relationship with Solana) and journey into her future with Minaya. Solana, as narrator, explains that Minaya and the future he represents are unwanted, "like a guest who has not yet accepted the obligation to leave," and that she, like Spain, clings to her past, to the regime, to what she has known: "Inés had already excluded [Minaya] from her tenderness and from the world and embraced me ... as if she were defending me, as if when she turned her back on Minaya and the future, she had expelled them from us."[5] He is old, she is young, this relationship has no hope of continuing, and yet she refuses to move onward as do many Spaniards who choose to hold onto Franco despite (or perhaps because of) their troublesome past and ignore the future. Solana recognizes the goodness, the blessedness the young generation faces, because for him Inés is genuine, as "she was the only thing that never had contained even the slightest hunger for lies or guilt."[6] Still her purity does not prevent her from making the wrong choice by refusing to move forward with Minaya at first.

The threat Spaniards face, then, is that if they cannot recover their memories and move on together, they would no longer be "blessed," as it happened for Solana and Manuel. Minaya and Inés have the hope of peace and freedom, but they can only be *beatus* if they move forward, leave the oppressive city, and enter the idyllic countryside of democratic liberty. In the novel, Solana plans to commit suicide, which will be the end of his and, symbolically, Spain's past, the end of the Franco era, and mark the beginning of a new relationship and a new future for Minaya and Inés, who would finally understand that, as Solana states, "she could not undo my purpose and that when she left she would fulfill the final, delicate, necessary tribute to our mutual loyalty."[7] Only by moving forward, without Solana and the dictatorship era he represents, can they overwrite the past. It is fitting that while Solana curses Minaya for being able to escape, he also envies him because Minaya will realize that his idyllic future with Inés is not a dream, that "she is not another illusion constructed by his desire and despair," but a reality. As such, Solana also blesses him with the final two words of the novel, "*beatus ille*."[8] He may despise the hope and joy they can have together, but he also knows that they are blessed for it, as are the new generation of Spaniards.

Another important element of this hope for democratic Spain is reflected in the transferal of the entire estate, of the house that is Spain, from Manuel to Minaya. As wealthy landowners, Manuel's family controls the land and business, and yields a great deal of influence in the rural region. Before he dies, Manuel names Minaya as his heir thus bequeathing to his nephew the power he used to have. Similarly, Solana sends his writings along with Inés to Minaya so that Minaya becomes Solana's artistic heir; as the aging writer explains, "now you're the owner of the book and I'm your character, Minaya. I've obeyed you too."[9] Thus, Minaya is tasked with carrying on both for Solana, in writing and in love, and for Manuel and the family estate, because he is the future landowner. Martinón comments that "Manuel y Solana ven in Minaya la posibilidad de salvar sus vidas de un fracaso y un olvido totales, a través del rescate y glorificación de aquella época ya distante (prebélica)" (Manuel and Solana see in Minaya the possibility of saving their lives from a total failure and oblivion, through the rescue and glorification of that distant (prewar) period).[10] As Minaya uncovers the true story of the past and then moves into the future, he "personifica la recuperación de la memoria histórica"[11] (personifies the recovery of historic memory) to process what the regime has altered or what the people have forgotten, and then he moves on. At the end of their journey, he and Inés take the estate's deed and Solana's manuscripts, and, as Solana narrates, "closed the door and didn't turn around to look at me because I had forbidden it"; instead, they look "at the red lights and the tracks and the cars stopped at the end of the station and of the night."[12] These train tracks symbolize the beginning of their journey together into the future and the end of the past generation. Like the Spaniards of the transition, Minaya emerges from his encounter with the past ready to take responsibility for the family's (or Spain's) future.

3. *Beatus Ille*: Blessed the Reader

Minaya is "*beatus*" because Muñoz Molina's re-accentuation and symbolic treatment of Minaya's relationship with Inés and his inheritance of the estate reflects the author's visions for the Spanish society's future. But Molina does not stop there. The title *Beatus Ille* also extends to the reader and makes them co-heirs in Minaya's blessedness through a metafictional connection with the main character. In this way the author ultimately re-accentuates his own society in which the new, democratic voices, along with the recovery of memories from the regime, make the real reader of the novel the blessed one, the *beatus ille*. Spanish readers at the book's publication are able to find peace, not through distancing themselves from the city, as the fictional heroes try to accomplish, but through distancing themselves from the past as they have adopted the new democratic perspective of the future. For Muñoz Molina, *beatus ille* refers to is his blessed reader.

Through the title *Beatus Ille*, the novel mixes Minaya's and the reader's contexts in such a way that the reader and the fictional character join the same social, diegetic, and thematic space. They begin to share a world.

The title is the key here because the novel *Beatus Ille* shares the same title as Solana's incomplete manuscript, "Beatus Ill," which is referenced more than twenty times throughout the work. Given that the title orients the reader's interpretation of the text, one possible conclusion is that the novel *Beatus Ille* is about Solana's manuscript. While this is a logical assumption, the connections run much deeper because the manuscript itself appears to be the book *Beatus Ille* that we, the real readers, hold in our hand, as if the fictional text has emerged into the real world. For example, at one point Minaya describes the narrative and stylistic structure of the manuscript in the following manner: "at times Solana wrote in the first person and at other times he used the third, as if he wanted to hide the voice that was telling and guessing everything and in this way give the narration the tone of an impassive history."[13] This description applies to the novel itself, and our book seems to be the same that Minaya holds as they blend into one. "Who is the author of the book I am reading," the reader cannot help but wonder, "Molina, or Solana?"

This confusion of voices leads to a peculiar layering of the past onto the present. If, as Bakhtin suggests, a text becomes "a subjective reflection of the objective world, ... an expression of consciousness, something that reflects,"[14] then Muñoz Molina's re-accentuation of 1969 Spain can also be a re-accentuation of his own 1986 Spain. The two worlds blend into one, "as if the plot of a book had suddenly occurred to me,"[15] says Solana, and thus the manuscript/novel relationship becomes virtual and real, and mirrors their world, according to Julio Prieto: "el juego de espejos en virtud del cual el texto se reproduce a sí mismo dentro del texto" happens precisely because *Beatus Ille* is "el título no sólo de la novela escrita por Muñoz Molina sino, también, de la novela concebida pero nunca escrita por el narrador de ésta (Jacinto Solana)" ("The game of mirrors through which the text reproduces itself through the text" happens precisely because *Beatus Ille* is "the title of not only the novel written by Muñoz Molina but, also, of the novel conceived but never written by its narrator (Jacinto Solana)").[16] Either could be the author of our text, so we also must accept that essentially both Solana and Molina seem to say: blessed are they who read this novel, because, like Minaya, as they face the horrors of the past, they also find hope in the prospects for a better future. The title makes this metafictional relationship possible, which enables Muñoz Molina to forge a re-accentuation of the Spain of his time for his reader of 1986.

Yet, because Muñoz Molina has linked his novel's fictional society with his contemporary and transitioning Spanish society, what does it say about modern Spain? First, Minaya, well-placed to take over for Manuel and Elvira, reflects the young Spanish leaders who assume leadership of the country. After Franco dies in 1975, for example, the country begins a political transition to a democracy that ultimately takes hold after the landslide election of Felipe González and his socialist party PSOE in 1982. This election marks the emergence of the country's political and social liberal thought that had been suppressed under Franco. John Hooper explains that many expected the new government to facilitate necessary change: the voters were "convinced that [the PSOE] were going to change everything. Just by being who they were—young men and women unencumbered by the intellectual baggage and ballast of the totalitarian past—they would be able to bring about a revolution in Spanish society when they applied to the nation's affairs attitudes regarded as normal in the rest of democratic Europe."[17] The new government officials, as Hooper describes them, resemble Minaya who is also young and unencumbered by the dealings of Manuel, Solana, and their friends. In one clear example, Felipe González, in his acceptance speech, urges his fellow Spaniards to prepare for change: "Desde este mismo instante, quiero hacer un llamamiento … a todos los sectores de la vida nacional para que se sientan integrados y presten su apoyo participativo en la tarea común de consolidar definitivamente la democracia en España … La colaboración de cada español, dentro de su ámbito, es imprescindible para lograr el objetivo de sacar a España adelante" (From this very instant, I want to extend a call … to all sectors of national life so they feel integrated and lend their participatory support in the common task of definitively consolidating Spain's democracy … The collaboration of every Spaniard, within his or her own sphere, is essential to achieve the objective of moving Spain forward).[18] Like Minaya, Spain can collapse under the weight of the past as they try and reinvent their future if they are unable to move forward effectively. Indeed, as Omar Encarnación explains, contemporary scholars recognized this threat early on and "warned about the return of the old habits that for centuries have nourished the well-known myth of the two Spains: a country tragically divided into two halves that can never find a way to get along."[19] However, unlike Minaya who chooses to process the past, many real Spaniards feared that delving too deep into the horrors of Franco's regime might compromise their future. As a result, Spain mounted an unofficial yet "concentrated effort to repress the memory of selective events from the past in order to envision possible futures."[20] Consequently, the Spaniards in the 1980s—*Beatus Ille*'s original audience—found themselves in an awkward position: they craved to "be part of the future," while at the same time being "keen to escape from the past"[21] as they searched for a new national identity.

In short, then, Muñoz Molina's re-accentuation introduces into 1986 Spain the hope for the blessings of the country's new identity and freedom under democracy. While in the first decade post Franco the political situation is volatile—with a new constitution (1978), the first free elections (1981), an attempted military coup (1981), a second, decisive election and political shift away from the results of the first election (1982), and political violence "quite characteristic of the era,"[22]—Muñoz Molina creates a Spain in his novel that can overcome all these challenges. Much like Minaya and Inés, who are able to overcome their troubled past and are ready to board the train to their future, the people of modern Spain too have much to look forward to. As a result, Molina's re-accentuated Spain in *Beatus Ille* "begins to sound in a different way, or is bathed in a different light, or is perceived against a different dialogizing background."[23] This new sound, new perspective, allows for Spain to emerge as a much better version of itself: "for the word is, after all, not a dead material object in the hands of an artist equipped with it; it is a *living* word and ... under changed conditions this meaning may emit bright new rays, burning away the reifying crust that had grown up around it."[24] Muñoz Molina's readers can declare, as Solana does, that "it's in your imagination where we were born again, much better than we actually were, more loyal, better looking, free of cowardice and truth."[25] The Spaniards who read this book in the 1980s can become, like Minaya, the blessed ones also. They have the potential to overcome their problematic present and establish their own democracy, to finish the transition and become truly free. But they also must recognize their reality for what it actually is.

4. *Beatus Ille*: Lost in Translation

I have demonstrated that Muñoz Molina refocuses his reader from the past to the potential of the future in *Beatus Ille*, and that he does this through the complex yet subtle play between the title and the roles performed by his characters. Unfortunately, in Edith Grossman's translation this nuanced interplay crumbles as soon as she changes the title from *Beatus Ille* to *A Manuscript of Ashes*. The possibility of a blurred real/fictional line through which the reader is actually reading Solana's manuscript breaks down because the two texts no longer share a title, and now the new English title can no longer imply that the reader may be the *beatus ille*. Instead, Grossman's title undermines Muñoz Molina's nuanced hope and replaces it with a darker, more fleeting meaning in the novel.

By changing the title from *Beatus Ille* to *Manuscript of Ashes*, Grossman submerges the novel into shadow and decay rather than hope. Her title *Manuscript of Ashes* still references Solana's manuscript, but whereas Muñoz Molina promises blessings to the one that can find hope in the future, Grossman's title conjures up loss and destruction. Her *Manuscript of Ashes* directly alludes to the writings that Solana burns as the fascists are arriving to kill him, a symbolic destruction of his past, his future, his identity, and this burning is a prelude to him feigning death and existing only as a memory until Minaya discovers him in 1969. He relates to Minaya the powerful fury that overcame him after he burned his papers: "I ground my foot into the ashes with the same fury I would have used to grind my foot into the pieces of a broken mirror that kept reflecting me. There was, of course, no blue notebook, no manuscripts I had forgotten in Manuel's house ... There was nothing but the ashes of blank pages."[26] Once turned to dust, the references to Solana's writings, even the manuscript and blue notebook that Minaya finds can never be anything other than ashes, pulverous remnants of what once was but is no longer. The English title, then, lacks the optimism behind the phrase "blessed is he," and replaces it with the image of ashes, which emphasizes the destruction of the past rather than an anticipated future.

With this new title, the book is not about the preserved manuscript, as the Spanish title implies, nor is it about the characters that escape the city and its oppression, but it is about the destructive past. To begin with, we must recognize there are two manuscripts: the first, which Solana burns, and the second, which he leaves for Minaya to find. For example, while Solana claims he never writes his book, in actuality he does but after Minaya arrives. He emerges from his self-imposed artistic and social exile and creates a manuscript to draw Minaya into their complicated past: "I invented the game," explains Solana to "build him the labyrinth he wants" through a second manuscript.[27] While both novels' titles reference Solana's manuscript, each refers to a different one: the Spanish *Beatus Ille* refers to the version Solana writes for Minaya, while the English title refers to the original manuscript he burns. *A Manuscript of Ashes*, then, dwells on what was written earlier and then destroyed before the regime could discover it, which emphasizes both the fear in which Solana and other liberals lived and the end that they expected under Franco: death. Thus the title places a heavy weight over the entire novel because it begins the book with the image of destruction and the ephemeral nature of writing, art, and life. To put it differently, Grossman's choice reverses Muñoz Molina's message embedded in *Beatus Ille*, and replaces hope with hopelessness.

Consequently, Grossman's title re-accentuates Muñoz Molina's already re-accentuated message and turns it toward darkness. The burnt manuscript referenced in *Manuscript of Ashes* implies the destruction of Solana's, and his friends', memories; they, as his past, have burned to powder. Such ashes not only lose all resemblance the original, but they will shortly succumb to the elements and blow away to oblivion. And, like Solana and Manuel's past chronicled in Solana's text, the postwar memory becomes fleeting and lost like Solana's memories of "years and bodies and blame not recovered from its own ashes."[28] The English-speaking reader watches Minaya face the past as does the Spanish-speaking reader, but in English as the record crumbles, the effect is exactly the opposite of the Spanish title: there is no merging of fiction and reality, and there is no hope. There is only the ephemeral and temporary memory of postwar Spain. What once was—like the manuscript—will be gone, and there remains nothing to carry Minaya into the future.

This substantial shift in meaning between the two novels is not a criticism of Grossman's choice as translator, nor is it necessarily a detriment to the English novel, principally, on both accounts, because the readership of both texts is substantially different, and so the accents, the messages, and the dialogic content between novel and reader must also be different. For example, Grossman's English-speaking public of 2008, twenty years removed from Muñoz Molina's immediate audience, would most likely lack the experiences of those of the Spanish transition of the 1980s. Furthermore, if Grossman would have maintained the phrase *Beatus Ille* as the title, it would not mean to her public what it means to Muñoz Molina's. Grossman's readers cannot be expected to have solid knowledge of Franco's regime, Spain's new democracy, or its Golden Age, so Fray Luis de Leon's reliance on *beatus ille* would also certainly elude Grossman's audience.

Such contextual diversity behind utterances themselves drives Bakhtinian re-accentuation because the contextual (e.g., cultural, linguistic, historical) differences between the two publics subtly change the meanings of words and messages. Bakhtin, for example, argues that while words may be identical in two different contexts, and may be directly translated (i.e., the English title could still be *Beatus Ille*), the meaning most certainly is not. He differentiates between language and speech communication (or utterance), the first being words and the second being meaning. While words can be identical, or even translated, for our purposes, identically, the meaning can never be perfectly recreated because contexts inexorably and incessantly change. Words, therefore, can be repeated, but utterances cannot:

> Two or more sentences can be absolutely identical..., but as an utterance (or part of an utterance) no one sentence, even if it has only one word, can ever be repeated: it is always a new utterance (even if it is a quotation) ... A sentence can be repeated within the bounds of one and the same utterance..., but each repetition makes it a new part of the utterance, for its position and function in the entire utterance have changed.[29]

Consequently, the original Latin title would be an utterance in a new language for a new reader. In this light, the phrase *Beatus Ille* cannot produce for Grossman's reader the nuances that it has for Muñoz Molina's reader, and its message of hope for a new democratic Spain would be lost on the English reader anyway.

Furthermore, any attempt to recreate Muñoz Molina's original re-accentuation would not only be lost on the English-reading public, it could be considered neglectful because the author must connect to the reader, and Grossman's reader is inevitably different than Molina's. We can, then, claim that a translator must consider changes that can draw the reader into the text according to their own context, and even create a comparable connection to that which the original text had with its public. Bakhtin recognizes this need, because "when a work is distant from us and when we begin to perceive it against a background completely foreign to it, ... [it] may be subjected to a re-accentuation that radically distorts it," which would make it inaccessible to the new audience.[30] Grossman, then, must do more than merely translate words; she must re-accentuate the work to help bridge the gap between *Beatus Ille* as Muñoz Molina writes it and her public's socially, historically, geographically, politically, and linguistically different context.

In this sense, Grossman writes the text anew and shows that the translator becomes a second author, and as such she re-accentuates the world, and the novel, yet again. Authors create dialogic voices (cultures, characters, themes) in their novels, and translators must do the same to carry the original over into the new culture and contexts. The writer's text dialogues with its receiving audience and culture, and the translator must prepare that text for a new receiving culture. Petrilli elaborates on Bakhtin's dialogism and explains that "the voice is always oriented towards another voice ... One's own utterance alludes always and in spite of itself, whether it knows it or not, to the utterance of others."[31] Muñoz Molina orients his novel toward his society, and he communicates utterances that include emotions, memories, and hopes to his audience. But if Grossman were only to translate words, this could undermine such utterances for her own audience, which is far removed from the Spain of the transition. Instead, Grossman recreates the text for her new audience with new voices, and she, therefore, becomes as much a writer of *Manuscript of Ashes* as Muñoz Molina is. For example, Grossman argues that translators do not replace or undermine the original author, but throughout the process of rewriting the author's own story "the work becomes the translator's (while simultaneously and mysteriously somehow remaining the work of the original author) as we transmute it into a second language."[32] Because she has authorial powers over *Manuscript of Ashes* as Muñoz Molina does over *Beatus Ille*, it follows that her work dialogues with her audience, but she also dialogues with Muñoz Molina's text and context at a different level than he had originally intended, and the resulting re-accentuation becomes more complex and distanced from his original text. In *Manuscript of Ashes*, there is a new set of voices, the translator and the translator's reader, with new contexts, new perspectives, and new challenges.

Still, as she translates the text from Spanish to English, Grossman considers the complexities of Muñoz Molina's text and context, and as a translator, she attempts to convey the nuances and intricacies of the original author to her own reader. She comments that translators "endeavor to hear the first version of the work as profoundly and completely as possible, struggling to discover the linguistic charge, the structural rhythms, the subtle implications, the complexities of meaning and suggestion in vocabulary and phrasing, and the ambient, cultural inferences and conclusions these tonalities allow us to extrapolate."[33] Similar to her comments on listening to the author, Suan Petrilli argues that "the task of translation ... transposition of sense and signifying materiality, of the very musicality and rhythm of language, calls for a *listening* attitude towards the text, towards the other in translation."[34]

Grossman recognizes that writers such as Molina re-accentuate their societies through a variety of literary techniques, and she must be aware of them to make them available to the new audience. Her readers in English would not be Spaniards who experienced the period of transition to democracy; they may have never lived under a dictator, and would have no historical or literary connection to the phrase "*beatus ille*." Therefore, her challenge with the novel *Beatus Ille* would be to introduce once more her own authorial voice and re-accentuate the text to not only translate the language for a new reader, but also translate the culture and the novel's impact in order to provide a similar experience for her public and their different context and worldview. She argues, for example, that translators must take the author's complex voice and then "repeat what we have heard, though in another language, a language with its own literary tradition, its own cultural accretions, its own lexicon and syntax, its own historical experience, all of which must be treated with as much respect, esteem, and appreciation as we bring to the language of the original writer."[35] Effective translation must account for both the original and the target reader and must include, as Lawrence Venuti explains, "varying cultural assumptions and interpretive choices, in specific social situations, in different historical periods. Meaning is a plural and contingent relation, not an unchanging unified essence, and therefore a translation cannot be judged according to mathematics-based concepts of semantic equivalence or one-to-one correspondence."[36] The objective is to give the original text meaning in the new culture, syntax, and historical context while preserving the impact the original had for Molina's reader in 1986, "hoping that readers of the second language ... will perceive the text, emotionally and artistically, in a manner that parallels and corresponds to the esthetic experience of its first reader."³⁷ The product becomes a new text meant for a new culture, for it must resonate with them as the original did for its own audience. Venuti explains, "Whatever difference the translation conveys is now imprinted by the receiving culture, assimilated to its positions of intelligibility, its canons and taboos, its codes and ideologies."³⁸ The translation, then, is another re-accentuation beyond what the author creates. Grossman must recognize Molina's dialogic elements of the transition, dissect their impact on his reader, and rewrite the novel in English in such a way that the story and its impact carries through.

Here we must ask: what does the new title accomplish since we know what it does not, and how does it affect this new reader? While Grossman's *Manuscript of Ashes* erases the original meaning of the Spanish title, a new message dialogues with the receiving culture's context, and refocuses her public on Spain's emotionally charged, disappearing past. Instead of pointing to the future, Grossman's title effectively brings the past to life for a reader who can thus connect better with Solana. Grossman's title thus highlights for the translation's reader what was lost rather than what may be gained in the future for Spain.

5. *Beatus Ille*: Grossman's Re-accentuation

While Grossman cannot recreate the original text's context, history, and experiences for her audience because it is too complex, she can connect her reader with important parts of the original text's world through a dialogue with the original's context. For example, Petrilli argues that "the relation between texts in translation does not merely involve one text reproducing another, nor pouring the same content from one linguistic container into another. Instead, to translate means to relate differences, to create a dialogue among differences, among singularities."³⁹ Even though the English readers are not likely to have first-hand knowledge of Franco's Spain, they can still relate to the sense of loss and frustration Molina's original audience would have experienced.

Grossman's title emphasizes the erasure of personal and national memory—and, with it, the loss of identity—that plague both Minaya and Spain as a whole. This is a major theme in the novel, expressed openly by both Solana and Minaya on separate occasions. For example, at one point Solana tries to recapture his feelings in the past: "that was how I looked at everything then: it all fled, devoured by the magnet of time while I, motionless, advanced toward the empty future where ... I didn't exist."⁴⁰ Similarly, Minaya felt has if he were a "forsaker of memory"[41] as he thought about leaving forever "to a part of his life that very soon would no longer belong to him, inaccessible to returning and to memory, because remembering and going back ... are exercises as useless as demanding explanations from a mirror of the face that an hour or a day or thirty years ago had looked into it."[42] Later on, Minaya feels that he does not belong among his family, his family's history, and their friends, that "the city and the house had never accepted him as one of their own, because even before he left, the furniture, the cool odor of the wood and the sheets, the mirror ... were denying him like suddenly disloyal accomplices and hurrying to erase every proof or trace of the time he had spent among them."[43] His identity is linked to this place, but his memory is unreliable, and his loss of personal connection leaves him unanchored as he moves on with his life.

This is where Molina's and Grossman's interpretations diverge drastically, as their different titles suggest. *Beatus Ille* emphasizes the blessedness of Minaya: in the end he is still his uncle's hope; he inherits the estate; he gets the girl; he uncovers the truth of the past; he moves onward despite his unstable past. While these same events happen in the English novel, the title *Manuscript of Ashes* underscores the darker imagery that permeates the novel. Minaya, his past, his identity, his life, resembles the ashes and are forever doomed to be as incomplete as a manuscript. This dark re-accentuation of the hero works well in Grossman's translation because it can connect the new audience to important aspects of the original's message. As Petrilli has pointed out, translating often must

> enhance the signifying otherness of the texts involved in renewal processes in the shift across languages, whereby the same text is rendered altogether other, reorganized in another language. The translated text is always *the same other*. The paradox of translation is that the text *must remain the same while becoming other* simply because it is reproduced and at once recreated in a different language.[44]

Ultimately, Grossman's readers are able to see the Other, and the book becomes a window into the Other's world. By altering the original enigma of the title, she may have refocused the entire message of the novel, but she has also succeeded in connecting her reader to Molina's first audience, thus illustrating Bakhtin's claim that bridging cross-contextual gaps unites people because "the mutual understanding of centuries and millennia, of peoples, nations, and cultures, provides a complex unity of all humanity, all human cultures (a complex unity of human culture), and a complex unity of human literature."[45]

Notes

1. Antonio Muñoz Molina, *A Manuscript of Ashes*, trans. Edith Grossman (New York: Harcourt, 2008), 84.
2. Ibid., 60.
3. Mikhail M. Bakhtin, *The Dialogic Imagination: Four Essays*, ed. Michael Holquist, trans. Caryl Emerson and Michael Holquist (Austin: University of Texas Press, 1981), 409.
4. Miguel Martinón, "Género y narrador en *Beatus Ille*, de Antonio Muñoz Molina," *Revista de Filología de la Unviersidad de la Laguna*, no. 14 (1995): 95–6.
5. Molina, *Manuscript of Ashes*, 303.
6. Ibid.
7. Ibid., 304.
8. Ibid., 305.
9. Ibid., 300.
10. Martinón, "Género y narrador," 94.
11. Ibid.
12. Molina, *Manuscript of Ashes*, 1–2.
13. Ibid., 94.
14. Mikhail M. Bakhtin, "The Problem of the Text in Linguistics, Philology, and the Human Sciences: An Experiment in Philosophical Analysis," *Speech Genres and Other Late Essays*, trans. Vern W. McGee, ed. Caryl Emerson and Michael Holquist (Austin: University of Texas Press, 1986), 113.
15. Molina, *Manuscript of Ashes*, 299.
16. Julio Prieto, "'Playing the Sedulous Ape': Antonio Muñoz Molina y los espejos de la (meta)ficción en *Beatus Ille*," *Revista de Estudios Hispánicos* 36 (2002): 431–2.
17. John Hooper, *The New Spaniards* (New York: Penguin, 2006), 46.
18. FelipeGonzález, "Felipe González celebra la victoria del PSOE en las elecciones de 1982," *RTVE* (October 29, 1982): n.p.
19. Omar Encarnación, *Democracy without Justice in Spain: The Politics of Forgetting* (Philadelphia: University of Pennsylvania Press, 2014), 4–5.
20. Ibid., 20.
21. Hooper, *New Spaniards*, 2.
22. Encaranción, *Democracy without Justice*, 19.
23. Bakhtin, *Dialogic Imagination*, 420.
24. Ibid., 419, emphasis in original.
25. Molina, *Manuscript of Ashes*, 302.
26. Ibid., 298.
27. Ibid., 299.
28. Ibid., 131.
29. Bakhtin, "Problem of the Text in Linguistics," 108–9.
30. Bakhtin, *Dialogic Imagination*, 420.

31. Susan Petrilli, *Signs, Language and Listening: Semioethic Perspectives* (Mineola, NY: Legas, 2019), 139.
32. Edith Grossman, *Why Translation Matters* (New Haven, CT: Yale University Press, 2010), 8.
33. Ibid., 9.
34. Petrilli, *Signs, Language and Listening*, 149, emphasis in original.
35. Grossman, *Why Translation Matters*, 10.
36. Lawrence Venuti, *The Translator's Invisibility: A History of Translation* (New York: Routledge, 2008), 13.
37. Grossman, *Why Translation Matters* 7.
38. Venuti, *Translator's Invisibility*, 14.
39. Petrilli, *Signs, Language and Listening*, 150.
40. Molina, *Manuscript of Ashes*, 201.
41. Ibid., 260.
42. Ibid., 278–9.
43. Ibid., 257.
44. Petrilli, *Signs, Language and Listening*, 149, emphasis in original.
45. Mikhail M. Bakhtin, "Toward a Methodology for the Human Sciences," in *Speech Genres and Other Late Essays*, trans. Vern W. McGee, ed. Caryl Emerson and Michael Holquist (Austin: University of Texas Press, 1986), 167.

Bibliography

Bakhtin, Mikhail M. *The Dialogic Imagination: Four Essays*. Edited by Michael Holquist. Translated by Caryl Emerson and Michael Holquist, Austin: University of Texas Press, 1981.

Bakhtin, Mikhail M. "The Problem of the Text in Linguistics, Philology, and the Human Sciences: An Experiment in Philosophical Analysis." In *Speech Genres and Other Late Essays*, 103–31. Translated by Vern W. McGee. Edited by Caryl Emerson and Michael Holquist. Austin: University of Texas Press, 1986.

Bakhtin, Mikhail M. "Toward a Methodology for the Human Sciences." In *Speech Genres and Other Late Essays*, 159–72. Translated by Vern W. McGee. Edited by Caryl Emerson and Michael Holquist. Austin: University of Texas Press, 1986.

Encarnación, Omar G. *Democracy without Justice in Spain: The Politics of Forgetting*. Philadelphia: University of Pennsylvania Press, 2014.

González, Felipe. "Felipe González celebra la victoria del PSOE en las elecciones de 1982." *RTVE*. October 29, 1982. www.rtve.es/alacarta/videos/fue-noticia-en-el-archivo-de-rtve/felipe-gonzalez-celebra-victoria-del-psoe-elecciones-1982/2430160/. Accessed September 3, 2020.

Grossman, Edith. *Why Translation Matters*. New Haven, CT: Yale University Press, 2010.

Hooper, John. *The New Spaniards*. 2nd edition. New York: Penguin, 2006.

Martinón, Miguel. "Género y narrador en *Beatus Ille*, de Antonio Muñoz Molina." *Revista de Filología de la Unviersidad de la Laguna* 14 (1995): 87–108.

Muñoz Molina, Antonio. *Beatus Ille*. Mexico D.F.: Fondo de Cultura Económica, 2007.

Muñoz Molina, Antonio. *A Manuscript of Ashes*. Translated by Edith Grossman. New York: Harcourt, 2008.

Petrilli, Susan. *Signs, Language and Listening: Semioethic Perspectives*. Mineola, NY: Legas, 2019.

Prieto, Julio. "'Playing the Sedulous Ape': Antonio Muñoz Molina y los espejos de la (meta)ficción en *Beatus Ille*." *Revista de Estudios Hispánicos* 36 (2002): 425–56.

Venuti, Lawrence. *The Translator's Invisibility: A History of Translation*. 2nd edition. New York: Routledge, 2008.

11

The Many Faces of Alice in Carnival: From Intersemiotic to Intervisual Translation

Riitta Oittinen

She generally gave herself very good advice (though she very seldom followed it), and sometimes she scolded herself so severely as to bring tears into her eyes; and once she remembered trying to box her own ears for having cheated herself in a game of croquet she was playing against herself, for this curious child was very fond of pretending to be two people.[1]

1. Introduction

The goal of this chapter is to address the special issues concerning intersemiotic and intervisual translation, and Mikhail Bakhtin's views about carnival, heteroglossia, and dialogue as they relate to those two types of translation. I will base my discussion on an investigation of Lewis Carroll's first story in words, *Alice's Adventures under Ground* from 1864,[2] and compare his original illustrations with my own visual interpretations of the material in order to illuminate the carnivalistic changes in the used images and their influence on characterization in the story.

Roman Jakobson was among the first theorists of translation to explore the special features of visual translation. According to him, there are three kinds of translation: intralingual translation or rewording; interlingual translation or translation proper; and intersemiotic translation, such as translating words into images, or transmutating, such as illustrating.[3] Yet, similar factors are included in all of the three: there is always someone who is interpreting words and images, rewriting or redrawing them and aiming them at someone else. In this essay, I look at translation of images into images as intervisual translation.

In carnivalized storytelling, new ways of communication always bring about new ways of speaking and expressing ideas. They denote the skill to

Figure 11.1 "... for this curious child was very fond of pretending to be two people." (Source: Oittinen 2017–20).

go overboard and leave the tracks of the everyday life.[4] Carnival also allows the language of science and the arts (including translation) to express new ideas with new words. As Simon Dentith puts it, carnivalized writing "has taken the carnival spirit into itself and thus reproduces, within its own structures and by its own practice, the characteristic inversions, parodies and discrownings[5] of carnival proper."[6] In Figure 13.2, "dialogics" denotes interaction, where the "I" and the "you" meet and new meanings arise; "heteroglossia" refers to the set of conditions, time, place, and culture, where everything happens; and, finally, "carnival" is at the very core of dialogics, where (mock) crownings and decrownings take place and the crown keeps on moving from a pauper/child/clown to a queen/adult/authority and the other way around, and the fear of authority is conquered by human laughter.

At the heart of any form of translation, then, there is a never-ending process of dialogue and carnivalization, which includes writers, illustrators, translators, and readers, and the whole society where texts are born and reborn and read silently or aloud.[7]

The carnivalistic culture of laughter, which originated in Antiquity and kept on flourishing during the Middle Ages and the Renaissance, is a

Figure 11.2 Dialogics, heteroglossia, and carnival. (Source: Oittinen 2020).

combination of the grotesque and the philosophical, opposing anything self-important or clearly defined, and relying instead on language that is open-ended, unofficial, and anti-authoritarian. The carnival is full of satire, rituals, comic verbal twists, and rude expression[8]—"it liberates from the fear ... of the sacred, of prohibitions, of the past, of power."[9] In *Rabelais and His World* (1984), Bakhtin defines the carnivalistic world of laughter, where anything high is lowered and anything fearsome is made less dangerous. Through carnival, it is possible to defeat the fear of authority by means of laughter. Bakhtin's carnivalistic world is a paradoxical site of birth and death, where one becomes free of any dogmatic constraints—in Bakhtin's own words, benevolent "laughter, food, and drink defeat death."[10] Carnival is also full of constant metamorphoses and unexpected opposites, and even the devil is a funny fellow and the hell a comical place.[11]

Bakhtin speaks about dialogue[12] and dialogism in most of his texts. Yet there is one essay that is especially important to me: "Discourse in the Novel."[13] Michael Holquist, the editor of the essay, defines dialogism in the following way: "Dialogism is the characteristic epistemological mode of a world dominated by heteroglossia. Everything means, is understood, as a part of a greater whole—there is a constant interaction between meanings, all of which have the potential of conditioning others."[14] In this text, Bakhtin also discusses dialogism and words being born in some dialogue or situation where some other word, image, conversation, language, and culture are "dialogized," which implies that a word is never as such but always relativized. From this follows that dialogue is internally persuasive, not authoritarian or absolute, and that dialogue may also be external, such as between two persons or two cultures. A human being may also converse internally with her/his present and former selves.[15] In this sense, dialogue may be seen as a carnivalistic meeting-place for different authors, illustrators, readers, contexts, the past, the present, and the future.

As Bakhtin puts it so well, utterances are no monologues, but "*every utterance is by definition dialogic.*"[16] In fact, if we change any small detail, such as a word or an image, the whole situation of understanding will undergo a metamorphosis. As Bakhtin points out, at any time or place, all utterances are heteroglot and "there will be a set of conditions—social, historical, meteorological, physiological—that will ensure that a word uttered in that place and at that time will have a meaning different than it would have under any other conditions."[17] According to the picturebook artist Uri Shulevitz, it is even "the task" of the illustrations "to tell a story different from the story told by the author ... The pictures in a successful picturebook are more than a repetition of what is said in words."[18] Louise M. Rosenblatt raises a similar point: "A specific reader and a specific text at a specific time and place: change any of these, and there occurs a different circuit, a different event—a different poem."[19] This is what happens in illustrating and reillustrating stories: there occurs a different poem.

In the situations of understanding, the worlds of all the writers, illustrators, readers, presenters, and listeners are intertwined and the process of understanding goes on. Even though the reader is reading a book, alone by her/himself, s/he hears the voices emerging from the text, which are alive and meaningful. Of course, a text is also material, and it has a place in the material world—it is also read in the course of time. One way or the other, a reader always reaches toward another human voice: the reader has a renewing role in the life of a text.[20] This kind of reading, too, is carnivalized and carnivalizing and aimed at future readers. In other words, we are all in a constant dialogue with languages, the one of our own and the other of someone else.

All processes of interpretation, such as translation and illustration, may also be depicted as ephemeral answers given for the problems raised in the source text. Bakhtin often discusses the problematics of responding to the language of an other: "every word is directed toward an answer and cannot escape the profound influence of the answering word that it anticipates."[21] Similarly, translation or illustration may be understood as an answer, or several answers, to not only the original text but also to new texts and new readers. Yet not even the illustrators' and translators' answers, verbal and visual, are final but temporary and embodied in different translations, in new words and images. In a similar manner, a work written is never the same as the work retold, and an illustrated story is never the same as the story reillustrated.[22] Every word is heteroglot and requires the excess of vision of another word.[23]

I am looking at carnival and dialogue from at least two angles: the carnival and dialogue of all human understanding and the concrete situations of understanding texts. For example, in translation—such as intervisual translation—the original text and its creators have no authority over dialogic understanding, but every interpretation is in some way different, carnivalized and questioning the authority of the original text. Everything is heteroglot and constantly changing: no text, no original, no translation, remain the same. Thus translation signifies a never-ending chain reaction starting already before the author of the original has written one word. Metaphorically, in the carnival of verbal and visual translation, the one with the higher status may first be holding the crown of interpretation. Yet after crowning always comes decrowning and the crown of understanding is in a constant movement from one head to another. This implies ongoing metamorphoses involving the writers, illustrators, readers, translators, and so forth. "Crowning/decrowning is a dualistic ambivalent ritual."[24] This also certainly applies to translation as well: whatever we translate, verbally or visually, the audience, language, and culture will take up a different stance and a different tack.

2. Alice and Carroll

One of the most celebrated authors of nonsense literature is Lewis Carroll (1832–1898). His vast creative output includes books, puzzles, poems, and other stories.[25] Yet, he is most famous for his first two works about Alice: *Alice's Adventures in Wonderland* (1865) and *Through the Looking-Glass and What Alice Found There*[26] (1871). Alice's character first appeared in a manuscript called *Alice's Adventures under Ground. A Christmas Gift to a Dear Child in Memory of a Summer Day* (1965)[27]. The evolution of the story is summarized by Warren Weaver in the following way:

> There were to be four developments, over the succeeding period of three years and four months, before the book we all know—*Alice's Adventures in Wonderland*—was available to the general public. There was first written an unillustrated manuscript copy of a preliminary short version with the title *Alice's Adventures under Ground*; there was next produced by hand an illustrated copy of the same preliminary version; there was printed but not released for sale the true first, 1865, edition of the familiar longer version; and finally there was released to the trade the second, 1866, edition.[28]

While there have been many possible interpretations of the book—critics have seen it as a dream, a Freudian presexual fantasy, a version of the Holy Scriptures (especially Genesis), and a critique of the Victorian era[29]—first and foremost the story of Alice's adventures should be viewed as a satire of social institutions and existing power structures.

In the following section, I deal with the different visual representations of the story by Carroll and myself from the angle of satire depicted by Bakhtin as a carnivalized genre, a happy decrowning.[30] In other words, Carroll's first story of Alice is about carnivalizing the fear: the fear of authorities, of what is bigger, noisier, or nastier. The tale also depicts reason as a weapon against such a fear. The story of Alice takes place on two levels: the frame tale of the real world with Alice and her sister sitting on a river bank, reading a book with "no pictures or conversations,"[31] and the parallel, deeper level of storytelling, where Alice ends up after diving into the rabbit hole.

In the first published story about Alice from 1864[32], the seven-year-old protagonist wanders in a strange underground land, where everything is upside down.[33] During her adventures, Alice meets strange or outright crazy characters often behaving in atrocious ways, such as the Cheshire-Cat,[34] the Gryphon, the Mock Turtle, Father William, the Caterpillar, the Queen of Hearts, and many more. During the conversations with these creatures, Alice tries to keep her head and temper, but often flies into a rage at the impossible characters and situations.

In the following analysis of several images, I will take a look at scenes that both Carroll and I have illustrated—with a couple of exceptions, such as the verbally carnivalized Cheshire-Cat, which is a good example of Carroll's comic, rude and utterly nonsensical creations. My own visual interpretation of the character was inspired by Carroll's verbal descriptions in the very first printed version illustrated by John Tenniel. The Cheshire-Cat appears in the story in order to ridicule various human virtues and vices. In my own visualization,[35] the character has taken the look shown in Figure 11.3.

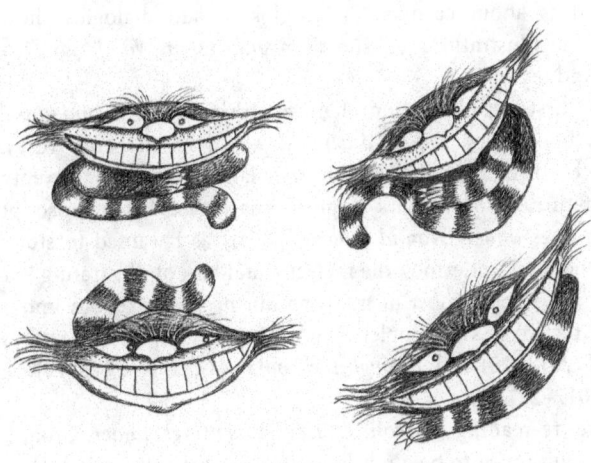

Figure 11.3 Cheshirecats. (Source: Oittinen 2017–20).

What makes Carroll so interesting, especially from the perspective of an illustrator, is his way of satirizing rulers, authorities, and institutions, such as school, church, and family life (babies and old people especially); yet his satire is seldom reflected in his original images. In other words, while Carroll's verbal text stresses the carnivalesque qualities of the narrated events, his original illustrations seem surprisingly serious and in sharp contrast with Tenniel's much better known images. While Tenniel's visual representations of the characters are funny, clever, and recognizably Victorian in their appearance, Carroll's seem to escape the confines of history and create a completely different universe. My illustration may also be seen as a response to this original interpretation of the girl and the metamorphoses she undergoes in the story.

3. Alice and I

I met Alice for the first time in the 1980s, when I was working on my very first university thesis. Since then, I have returned to this interesting protagonist in a number of articles, essays, book chapters, and books on Alice and her character in translation. I have also seen many different illustrations of the stories. In fact, I am not at all sure which of the Alices has influenced me most. Nevertheless, I am taking this new journey with Alice to be able to find the answer to a very important question: How do Bakhtin's ideas about carnival, heteroglossia, and dialogics show themselves in the illustrations of *Alice's Adventures in Wonderland* by Lewis Carroll and myself?

I created my first full illustration of *Alice's Adventures in Wonderland* in 1997 in my book titled *Liisa, Liisa ja Alice* (Liisa, Liisa and Alice), which introduced three Finnish-language translations of Alice.[36] Twenty years later, I returned to Carroll's original images for his manuscript of *Alice's Adventures under Ground* (1965a [1864]) as I wanted to study them carefully before I undertook the monumental task of illustrating her adventures myself. I spent most of my time during the next four and a half years drawing two sets of completely new images for *Alice's Adventures in Wonderland* (2017–20) and *Through the Looking-Glass and What Alice Found There* (2017–21).

Reading and re-reading Carroll's *Alice's Adventures under Ground* during this period proved to be a revelation for me. Carroll's visual Alice is a serious-looking, thoughtful girl, who is mostly still and either stands or sits concentrating on what she sees or hears. In other words, Carroll's visual depiction of Alice is very different from his verbal descriptions of the girl. In the narrative, when Alice meets new characters, she is usually polite and positive at first. While being tender-hearted most of the time, she also has a strong character that often shows when she gets angry due to experiencing unfairness or insults to her abilities to think and draw conclusions. Her rationality is stressed through various means. For instance, she is able to look at situations from different angles, which helps her to survive all her trying adventures. Alice also talks to herself as she strives to solve various problems she finds herself in. On the occasions when she fails to do so, she offers herself advice of the following kind: "The first thing I've got to do ... is to grow to my right size again."[37] At times, as she endeavors to sort out situations, she may fail in her effort and get angry. On those occasions, it seems that Alice is able to transform herself into an adult and scold herself appropriately: "You ought to be ashamed of yourself ... a great girl like you ... to go on crying in this way! Stop this moment, I tell you!"[38] All of these peculiarities of her character and behavior are not easy to capture visually.

As mentioned above, I first illustrated the story of *Alice's Adventures in Wonderland* in 1997.[39] Yet, when a later research project demanded that I take another look at Carroll's first story of Alice, *Alice's Adventures under Ground* (1864), I felt the urge to dive into the story once more and create new images, which would be able to reflect better the satirical elements and general carnivalesque atmosphere of the original verbal narrative. In my intervisualization, I paid special attention to Alice's thoughts and to the physical changes she undergoes not only as a result of indulging in food and drink, but also as a consequence of strong emotion. What interested me were the parallel worlds the girl experienced, and the carnivalization practices which accompanied her metamorphoses. In the following section, I will explore the differences in the dialogic situations the protagonist finds herself in, and her reactions to them.

4. Alice in Analysis

Alice's Adventures in Wonderland is a satire where social authorities and the fear of one's superiors are defeated by carnival. Through carnivalistic laughter, the lower, the smaller, the weaker are allowed to conquer their fear and reclaim power for themselves.

I will start my analysis upside down, so to speak, with Alice's very last image in the manuscript, which (Figure 11.4) reveals how Alice really looks after her final transformation at the end of her adventures. In Carroll's interpretation, the girl's face appears to be serious and inquisitive, even of her own little sister. So the boat wound slowly along, beneath the bright summer-day, with its merry crew and its music of voices and laughter, till it passed round one of the many turnings of the stream, and she saw it no more.

Then she thought, (in a dream within the dream, as it were,) how this same little Alice would, in the after-time, be herself a grown woman: and how she would keep, through her riper years, the simple and loving heart of her childhood: and how she would gather around her other little children, and make their eyes bright and eager with many a wonderful tale, perhaps even with these very adventures of the little Alice of long-ago: and how she would feel with all their simple sorrows, and find a pleasure in all their simple joys, remembering her own child-life, and the happy summer-days.

Figure 11.4 Alice's eyes. (Source: Carroll 1865).

Figure 11.5 Doublefold Alice. (Source: Oittinen 2017–20).

secretive. Her eyes are enthralling, in full control of the situation, looking directly into the eyes of the viewer. It seems clear to me that Carroll wanted to show how strong and fearless the young protagonist had become as a result of her mental and physical journey.

Compare that with my own image (Figure 11.5) of the dual Alice, which aims to highlight her multiple personalities. She, too, takes a look at the reader, but it is a side glance. She is totally at ease: a grinning, happy, chatty girl, who exists in many different forms. She escapes the confines of singularity in order to revel in her many-sided, carnivalesque existence. While Carroll's Alice is holding the reader's gaze, my Alice does not care about the external observer and remains focused on having a good time with her friends.

Let us now turn to the very beginning, to the early pages of the original story, where Alice—illustrated by Carroll (Figure 11.6)—is listening to

Figure 11.6 "… once or twice she had peeped into the book her sister was reading, but it had no pictures or conversations …" (Source: Carroll 1865).

her sister reading a book. In my own visualization of the opening scene, I chose to depict the girl right after the moment when she has entered the parallel world and fallen asleep (Figure 11.7). In the scene by Carroll, Alice looks like an obedient quiet little girl. As depicted by Carroll verbally, Alice finds the book boring, and it is hard to tell what, exactly, she is dreaming about.

In my image, Alice has already fallen asleep and drifted to a parallel world, the carnivalized Wonderland. The trusting girl is sleeping peacefully and has no idea about the strange, dangerous landscape surrounding her. Here Alice and the world around her are full of unexpected opposites: the carnival laughter is ambivalent, "gay, triumphant and at the same time, mocking, deriding."[40] The girl has no fear, despite the grinning toothy faces in the background that could be interpreted as a possible cause for concern. Alice's innocence protects her from any danger as all she needs to do to be safe is to retreat into her own mind. Carroll has chosen to depict the every-day situation before

Figure 11.7 "… for the hot day made her feel very sleepy and stupid …" (Source: Oittinen 2017–20).

moving into the wonderland; I have taken a step further and started my illustration of her story by depicting Alice already in Wonderland. In general, whereas Carroll prefers to stay away from the bizarre and the ridiculous in his visualization of the events, I choose to highlight the odd peculiarities of this other world.

In another illustrated scene in Figure 11.8, Alice is swimming with strange creatures in the pool of tears that she had cried herself when she was very big. Carroll's Alice (Figure 11.8) looks as if she wants to get out of the water as quickly as possible. All the creatures are following her.

In my intervisual translation (Figure 11.9), Alice is in the same pool, this time wondering where she is and trying to start a dialogue with the creatures—without any success. Even though some of the unconventional beasts look frightening, again the irritated Alice is more confused than afraid, asking, as a proper school-girl: Have you not learnt any manners? We can see a similar awkwardness in the following scenes with Alice and the Mouse, first in the same pool of tears, then on dry land. In Carroll's image (Figure 11.10) they have momentarily paused their swimming to look—with solemnity—into each other's eyes.

Figure 11.8 The pool of tears 1. (Source: Carroll 1865).

Figure 11.9 The pool of tears 2. (Source: Oittinen 2017–20).

My image (Figure 11.11) depicts Alice and the Mouse already out of the water. The characters are under a fairy tree surrounded by blueberries and pine cones.⁴¹ This scene is built on the contrast between the angry Mouse and the happy Alice against the background of a fantastic landscape. Here as an

Figure 11.10 The Mouse and Alice in the pool of tears. (Source: Carroll 1865).

Figure 11.11 The Mouse and Alice under the tree. (Source: Oittinen 2017–20).

illustrator I am playing with the terror of the original text in order to defeat "the fear by laughing at it; through carnival, the awesome, terrifying original becomes a 'comic monster.'"[42]

In this serene landscape, Alice feels safe and keeps happily chatting about cats and dogs, which makes her seem self-assured and the Mouse scared and beside itself. While her interlocutor desperately tries to change the subject, Alice is too happy to pay any attention to the Mouse's anger. In the end, the Mouse resorts to acting like a bully by showing its teeth in a desperate attempt to reassert power over Alice. Yet she is not intimidated and does not seem concerned about the Mouse's actions at all. At a closer look, it becomes clear that the huge Mouse, with its wide-open mouth, is carnivalized (and thus neutralized) by Alice's laughter. In the end, the Mouse surrenders and leaves Alice alone.

Throughout the story, every time Alice eats or drinks either she or her environment changes dramatically. In the image (Figure 11.12) by Carroll, Alice has once again eaten something and shrunk into an immovable, menacing, sulking head. Without any scenery around, Alice's head is huge and her body non-existent. The girl looks imposing and scary, more disgusted with her transformation than afraid of what it might mean.

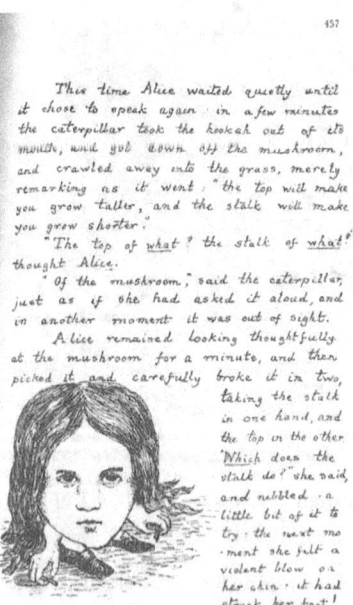

Figure 11.12 "… the next moment she felt a blow on her chin: it had struck her foot!" (Source: Carroll 1865).

Figure 11.13 "The first thing I've got to do," said Alice to herself, as she wandered about in the wood," is to grow to my right size again; …". (Source: Oittinen 2017–20).

In my representation (Figure 11.13) of a similar metamorphosis, the gigantic size of the bird next to Alice reveals how small she is at this point: as tiny as to find support in the stem of a flower. The bird seems angry but Alice looks straight in its eyes, her mouth open (she is talking to the bird) and almost smiling. Any potential fear the character might be expected to experience under the circumstances is neutralized by the carnivalized nature of her interlocutor, who has lost the ability to inspire terror. The brave child that she is, Alice tries to solve difficult situations by civil discussion and laughter.

As the story progresses, Alice tries to follow adult instructions to the best of her abilities. This is especially noteworthy in the scenes where the Caterpillar lectures Alice on which piece of a mushroom to eat (or not) if she wants to change her size. The Caterpillar is rude, oblivious, obsolete, odd, and probably—if we are to judge by the hookah—under the influence of some drug. It speaks in impossible terms and makes Alice feel intimidated. In the image (Figure 11.14), Carroll's confused Alice tries to begin a sensible discussion with the creature. At first, she listens

Figure 11.14 "'Who are you?' said the Caterpillar." (Source: Carroll 1865).

to the Caterpillar with an attentive ear and tries to behave properly. Although she is initially full of respect for him, she gradually begins to lose her temper.

In my image (Figure 11.15), too, Alice resembles an obedient child, hands crossed and solemnly listening to the Caterpillar, but my depiction of the latter takes on different dimensions and meaning. My Caterpillar, with its terrifyingly big teeth and eyes, is presented with exaggerated physicality to the point of crossing over into the ridiculous, in the process also carnivalizing and neutralizing its symbolic authority over the situation. The mushroom is taller than Alice and the fearsome looks of the Caterpillar make her remember everything wrong. In many scenes of the story, Alice tries, and usually fails, to recall poems she has learnt at school. This time it is especially difficult for her to remember the poem about Father William. On the left below, we can see the poem as Alice should have recited it; on the right is the poem as it comes out of her mouth:

Figure 11.15 "'Who are you?' said the Caterpillar." (Source: Oittinen 2017–20).

"You are old, Father William," the young man cried.

"The few locks which are left you are grey;

You are hale, Father William, a hearty old man.

Now tell me the reason I pray."

(Father William by Southey)

"You are old, Father William," the young man said,

"And your hair has become very white,

And yet you incessantly stand on your head—

Do you think, at your age, it is right?"

(Father William by Carroll)

Figure 11.16 Father William. (Source: Carroll 1865).

Carroll's depiction of Father William and his son (Figure 11.16) is one of the most hilarious in the whole book. The carnivalized poem, originally by Robert Southey, is ridiculing the reverent Father William and his son. Carroll has depicted the father as an old fool standing on his head and the crazy son as pulling his hair and falling over his chair. While, as usual, Carroll does not show any visual background, the characters and the illustrated poem itself are full of carnivalized laughter. I found Carroll's image quite appealing and wanted to underscore its carnivalesque nature even more by placing the characters in a nonsensical world, where everything is upside down. In other words, my Father William (Figure 11.17) is carnivalized as a complete lunatic, turning summersaults down the hill.

In this example Carroll is also visually satirizing old people and old age. Similarly, I have taken the characters' carnivalization to the extreme: the original cheerfulness has turned into madness. Throughout the book, Carroll's Alice sincerely tries to meet adult expectations and be a good girl. In those situations, such as the scene described above, she worries about following the instructions she has received from older people, and asks herself: Is it safe to drink? Is it safe to eat? Will it make me bigger or smaller? In the Figures 11.18 and 11.19, Alice is again full of curiosity as she is mentally debating two possible options: should she follow the rules and regulations or not?

Figure 11.17 Father William. (Source: Oittinen 2017–20).

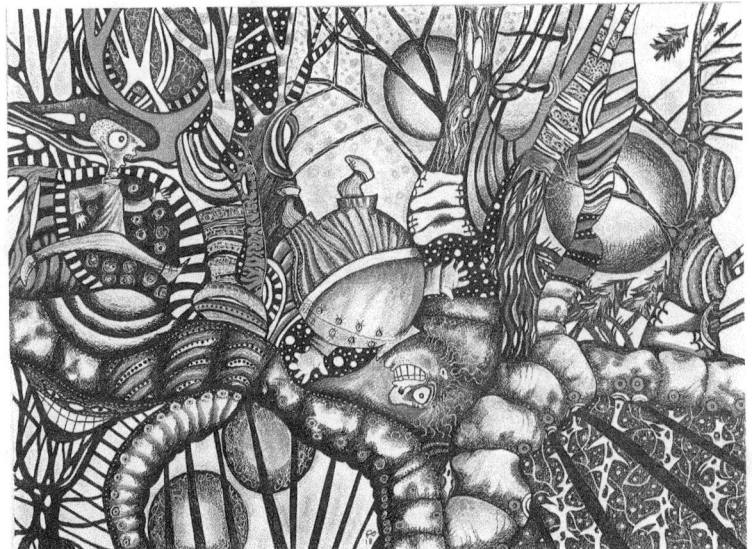

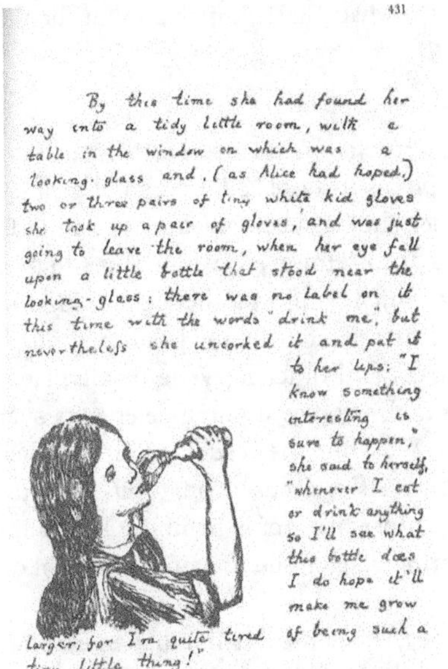

431

By this time she had found her way into a tidy little room, with a table in the window on which was a looking-glass and, (as Alice had hoped,) two or three pairs of tiny white kid gloves she took up a pair of gloves, and was just going to leave the room, when her eye fell upon a little bottle that stood near the looking-glass; there was no label on it this time with the words "drink me", but nevertheless she uncorked it and put it to her lips: "I know something interesting is sure to happen," she said to herself, "whenever I eat or drink anything so I'll see what this bottle does I do hope it'll make me grow larger, for I'm quite tired of being such a tiny little thing!"

It did so indeed, and much sooner,

Figure 11.18 "… so I'll see what this bottle does." (Source: Carroll 1865).

Figure 11.19 "The top of what? The stalk of what?" thought Alice. (Source: Oittinen 2017–20).

In my visual interpretation (Figure 11.19), Alice is wondering which of the mushroom pieces to taste. Being a good girl, again, Alice tries to remember the advice she has been given by the adult Caterpillar: beware of what you eat and drink. However, even in this situation, Alice is hesitant and not at all sure which would be the right thing to do: How can one be a good child? At first glance, the image's background looks decorative, filled with candy trees and other fairytale details. However, upon closer inspection we begin also to see ominous elements such as bones, skulls and severed hands. Yet while the reader might feel the pangs of perilous foreboding, Alice herself is focused on what is in front of her and is completely oblivious to what looms behind. Once more, the situation is heteroglot: by ignoring danger, she remains in control of what will happen to her next.

In the next scene, Alice's head is in a bad spot, and she is pondering whether she should "bite off a little bit of the top of the mushroom."[43] In the end, she succeeds in her efforts and exclaims: "Come,' my head's free at last!"[44] In Carroll's visual interpretations (Figures 11.20 and

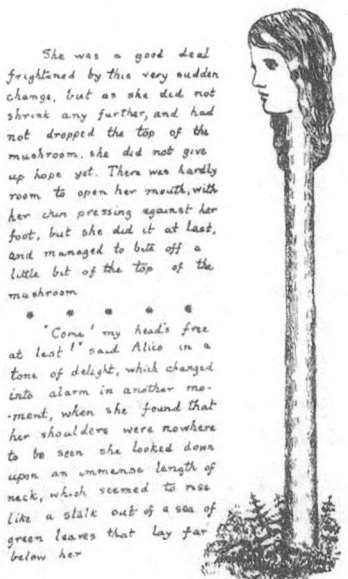

Figure 11.20 "'Come! my head's free at last!' said Alice in a tone of delight, which changed into alarm in another moment, when she found that her shoulders were nowhere to be seen …" (Source: Carroll 1865).

11.21), we can see that Alice's neck has grown significantly. There is also something menacing about her own appearance, which is also felt in my illustration of Alice in this state (Figure 11.22). Her curved bent neck seems to ensnare the bird she is conversing with, and yet it is the girl who turns out to be under attack: "a sharp hiss made her draw back: a large pigeon had flown into her face"[45] In my version of the same episode, we see Alice's (Figure 11.22) long neck tied in several knots and wrapping around a fir tree. It sways precariously in the air while she tries to defend herself against the angry screaming pigeon. Unable to shoo away her attacker (her hands are way down below), she has no way to protect herself from its sharp beak. Here the wrath of the little bird is, once more, exaggerated and carnivalized to the point of ridiculousness. By comparing the two images presenting Alice's long, pliable neck, we can see that Carroll's Alice still looks worried whereas my Alice is already relieved.

"What can all that green stuff be?" said Alice, "and where have my shoulders got to? And oh! my poor hands! how is it I can't see you?" She was moving them about as she spoke, but no result seemed to follow, except a little rustling among the leaves. Then she tried to bring her head down to her hands, and was delighted to find that her neck would bend about easily in every direction, like a serpent. She had just succeeded in bending it down in a beautiful zig-zag, and was going to dive in among the leaves, which she found to be the tops of the trees of the wood she had been wandering in, when a sharp hiss made her draw back: a large pigeon had flown into her face, and was violently beating her with its wings. "Serpent!" screamed the pigeon. "I'm not a serpent!" said Alice indignantly, "let me alone!"

Figure 11.21 "... was going to dive in among the leaves ... when a sharp hiss made her draw back: a large pigeon had flown into her face, and was violently beating her with its wings. 'Serpent!' screamed the pigeon." (Source: Carroll 1865).

Figure 11.22 "'Serpent!' screamed the pigeon." (Source: Oittinen 2017–20).

In the Figures 11.23, 11.24, and 11.25, Alice has metamorphosed into a giant. In Carroll's interpretation (Figure 11.23), Alice is crammed inside the White Rabbit's house. She feels angry and disgusted, as she is not only uncomfortable but even in pain if we are to judge by the way her hands are clutching at her dress. Upon a closer look, she seems even passive and surrendering.

In my illustration of the same scene (Figure 11.24), Alice runs forward happily, completely unconstrained by the house enclosing her. The doors

Figure 11.23 Big Alice in the White Rabbit's house. (Source: Carroll 1865)

Figure 11.24 Alice escaping from the White Rabbit's house. (Source: Oittinen 2020, forthcoming).

Figure 11.25 Alice's monstruous feet. (Source: Oittinen 2017–20).

flying around her as well as the windows and trees in the background are all tiny compared with the girl—even tiny Bill the lizard, kicked out of the chimney, is soaring through the air. In this scene, Alice has freed herself from all existing rules and regulations. In my other illustration (Figure 11.25) of a similar moment, Alice is so huge one can only see her monstruous feet, which appear to be kicking everybody and everything else away. Yet the menacing potential of the image (she could trample over the world around her) melts away once we discover that some of the creatures in the background are laughing. This laughter suggests the atmosphere of a carnival, in which many participate voluntarily and with great joy.

In the following examples (Figures 11.26 and 11.27), the mood of the two images is significantly different: in the scene depicted by Carroll (Figure 11.26), the crowd is surrounding Bill the Lizard, feeling sorry for the poor creature who has been kicked through the chimney by the very big Alice. Bill's friends in this image draw close to him in order to offer some comfort.

In my image (Figure 11.27), the situation has changed and the crowd has become noisier. No longer worried for their lives, they are now frowning and showing their teeth to Alice. Even Bill is unhappy. Yet again, when we take another look at the characters in my intervisualization, they seem moody,

Figure 11.26 Poor Bill the Lizard. (Source: Carroll 1865).

Figure 11.27 The mischievous crowd and Bill the Lizard. (Source: Oittinen 2017–20).

474

executions which the Queen had ordered.

They very soon came upon a Gryphon, which lay fast asleep in the sun: (if you don't know what a Gryphon is, look at the picture): "up, lazy thing!" said the Queen, "and take this young lady to see the Mock Turtle, and to  hear its history. I must go back and see after some executions I ordered," and she walked off, leaving Alice with the Gryphon. Alice did not quite like the look of the creature, but on the whole she thought it quite as safe to stay as to go after that savage Queen: so she waited.

The Gryphon sat up and rubbed its eyes: then it watched the Queen till she was out of sight: then it chuckled. "What fun!" said the Gryphon, half to itself, half to Alice.

"What *is* the fun?" said Alice.

"Why, *she*," said the Gryphon; "it's all her fancy, that: they never executes nobody, you know: come on!"

Figure 11.28 The Gryphon. (Source: Carroll 1865).

Figure 11.29 The Gryphon. (Source: Oittinen 2017–20).

mischievous, and far too serious. Eventually, they too become carnivalized and reveal themselves to be laughable fools.

In general, in Carroll's story, there are many characters which are so terrifying that they turn—through carnivalization—into their opposites. Among those nasty and grotesque creatures is my favorite the Gryphon.

As depicted by Carroll (Figure 11.28), the Gryphon constantly exerts power over its pal, the theatrical, pitiful Mock Turtle. At first Alice can only see the creature as a bully, but when it behaves so badly and seems so terrible it crosses over into the ridiculous, loses its authority altogether, and becomes fully carnivalized. According to Carroll's accompanying text, Alice announces that she has never in her life been ordered as much as by the Gryphon. This caricature of an adult who tries to teach her about the songs, dances, and the school of the sea turns out to be nothing but a grumpy, funny old thing (Figure 11.29). The roles are thus reversed, and Alice appears to be the only adult in the situation. Carroll's illustrations fail to capture that aspect of his story.

In Figure 11.30, of the dancing Mockturtle and the Gryphon again, Carroll has depicted Alice as small and distant. The contrast in the sizes of the participants in the scene create an ominous effect, giving

Many Faces of Alice in Carnival 237

Figure 11.30 The Gryphon, the Mockturtle, and Alice 1. (Source: Carroll 1865).

the reader the impression that Alice has no power whatsoever. There is once again the clear feel of danger. In my illustration (Figure 11.31), the Gryphon and the Mockturtle are having a heated conversation, while the smiling Alice is sitting cozily nearby with the March Hare.[46] There are many other creatures in the image's background, such as the worried mice, clock-eating fishes, and crying birds, which add to the feeling of danger encoded in the scene. Yet, again, despite everything, Alice seems to be having a good time.

In this Figure 11.32, we can see Carroll's Alice meeting with the Gryphon and the Mock Turtle once more. Scared and serious, she is standing between the two, unsure about what to do. In my depiction of the scene (Figure 11.33), there are severed hands and feet and other frightening items, which suggest inherent risk. On the other hand, my Alice is self-assured and dancing, and her smile and closed eyes imply that the situation is not as grave as it seems:

Yet perhaps the ultimate symbol of authority in the novel is represented by the character of the Red Queen, with whom Alice has to interact on several occasions. For example, Alice meets her when she is trying to play croquet. In Carroll's visual interpretation of this moment (Figure 11.34), Alice is

Figure 11.31 The Gryphon, the Mockturtle, and Alice 2. (Source: Oittinen 2017–20).

Figure 11.32 The Gryphon, the Mockturtle, and Alice 3 (Source: Carroll 1865).

Many Faces of Alice in Carnival 239

Figure 11.33 The Gryphon, the Mockturtle, and Alice 4 (Source: Oittinen 2017–20).

Figure 11.34 "The chief difficulty which Alice found at first was to manage her ostrich ..." (Source: Carroll 1865). In later versions illustrated by Tenniel, the bird is verbally and visually—a flamingo.

Figure 11.35 "The chief difficulty which Alice found at first was to manage her ostrich …" (Source: Oittinen 2017–20) (My image shows a flamingo. See Figure 11.34.).

Figure 11.36 The embarrassed, smiling Queen (Source: Carroll 1865).

Figure 11.37 "'Nonsense!' cried Alice, so loudly that everybody jumped," the idea of having the sentence first!'" (Source: Oittinen 2017–20).

standing by herself, with no Queen around, focusing on the flamingo, which she finds hard to handle.[47]

In my image (Figure 11.35), the Queen is there and looks as if she is about to attack the girl. The exaggerated figure of the looming adult once again becomes too terrible to believe in. In the end, Alice tries to make some sense of the situation by engaging the Queen in a conversation. Rather than appearing worried or scared, the child seems just angry.

When the Queen appears again later in the story, her authority seems unquestionable, yet Alice refuses to accept the older woman's superior position, and invalidates her commands and executions behind her back. Toward the very end of the novel, Carroll's Queen turns up again only to lose her power completely through Alice's disobedience. In the following image (Figure 13.36), the Queen is ordering the soldiers to cut off the heads of anyone resisting her. However, here Carroll himself has made his visual Queen the very opposite of herself—she looks far too embarrassed and smiling, which makes it hard to believe in her nasty character:

Figure 11.38 "'I won't', said Alice, 'you're nothing but a pack of cards! Who cares for you?'" (Source: Oittinen 2017–20).

At the trial at the end, my Alice (Figure 11.37) gets upset, grows much bigger and creates quite a commotion by crying "Nonsense!" Everybody leaps to their feet, trying to escape the wrath of the newly huge Alice, who seems to grow even stronger. Thus, at the closing of the book, Alice has become the true and only adult in the whole story: she has turned into an infuriated giant (Figure 11.38). Alice joins the flamingo and hedgehog and they fly up back into the frame story, away from the parallel world and the fierce Queen who has been reduced to a silly, screaming witch with no authority whatsoever.

5. Conclusion

In any situation where we combine words and images, such as the illustrations of Alice, they interact and influence each other and new meanings arise. A new illustration gives a new life to the verbal text, every time different. In this chapter, I explored the following questions concerning illustrating Alice: How do Bakhtin's views about carnival, heteroglossia, and dialogism reveal themselves in my material? How have Bakhtin's ideas helped me understand the differences between Carroll's original visual interpretations and my own? What is the role that binary oppositions play in the construction of meaning? How do authoritarian and internally persuasive worlds interact? How do the parallel worlds of the real and the imaginary intersect and influence Alice's character? How is the child's rebellion against authority represented in words and images?

Every time Alice and the Underground creatures meet, there is a profound shift in meaning and a new sense of understanding the world. While Carroll's visual story is somber and dark, his verbal text is full of laughter and carnivalistic twists. In my intervisual translation of Carroll's visual story of Alice, the protagonist is transformed from a serious character into a lively girl with a unique sense of humor, which leads to new interpretations of the original text as well. This is always the case with heteroglot interactions: any small change in detail in a dialogic situation results in the revitalization of the event and the birth of new meaningful potentialities.

In my set of visualizations, I wanted to capture the multiplicity of Alice's existence and convey the carnivalesque nature of the world around her. Whether big or small, faced by threatening beings or ridiculous creatures, in my interpretation Alice is never afraid, and neither is the careful reader who is capable of interpreting properly the visual signs of carnivalesque mirth surrounding the girl. Meaning is always created anew, as author, artist, and reader collaborate to produce new interpretations of the presented events. Even though Lewis Carroll can no longer speak for himself, we can enter an imaginary dialogue with his words and images, ask questions, and draw our own conclusions, as Alice would do. It was surprising for me to see how much Carroll's illustrations have affected my visual solutions. My original idea, which emerged over four years ago, was to get further away from Carroll's illustrations, and yet, it is impossible to ignore the fact that his illustrations have had a great influence not only on my images but also on the way I see the world.

Alice's story is also a social satire, where the protagonist laughs at various institutions of power, such as the school and the church. Just as Bakhtin would have it, here, too, anything pretentious or arrogant is ridiculed and discarded as insignificant. My illustration strives to encode visually this carnivalesque victory over established powers of authority to the best of my artistic abilities. The task is not easy; it requires both introspection and serious research into Victorian social structures. Whether insightful or not, my interpretation cannot last for too long; I, too, must abdicate my crown and allow the chain of signification to move forward to/through others. Illustrating—or intersemiotic translation or intervisual translation—is part of an ever-changing carnivalesque situation where the crown of interpretation is always in motion, passing from a pauper/child/clown to a queen/adult/authority and back again, ad infinitum.

Yet it is important to remember that the laughter depicted by Bakhtin is not malevolent or spiteful but a way of being happy and benevolent, without any fear. In a similar way, Carroll's satire is not negative but a way to defeat the fear of the original text, which I have tried to represent visually through my work. My newest set of visualizations of *Alice's Adventures in Wonderland* is only one among countless numbers of versions and possible answers to questions posed by the original story. This dialogue will continue, uninterrupted, for many more years to come, giving us all—readers, artists, translators—the opportunity to enrich our own and each other's understanding of the source, and change it and ourselves as a result.

Acknowledgement

I am grateful to Adjunct Professor, Eliisa Pitkäsalo, PhD, a fine Finnish scholar and a dear friend, for lending me her eyes and ears. Thank you!

Notes

1. Lewis Carroll, *The Complete Works by Lewis Carroll with Illustrations by John Tenniel*, ill. John Tenniel (New York: Barnes & Noble, 1994), 21. For Carroll's manuscript, see [Mikhail M. Bakhtin] Mihail Bahtin, *Lewis Carroll. The Complete Illustrated Works*, ed. Edward Giuliano, ill. John Tenniel, Henry Holiday, Arthur B. Frost, Lewis Carroll, Harry Furniss, and E. Gertrude Thomson (London: Leopard, 1995).
2. Lewis Carroll, *Alice's Adventures under Ground. A Christmas Gift to a Dear Child in Memory of a Summer Day.* Manuscript ill. Lewis Carroll (New York: Dover Publications, 1965) [1865; the first unpublished version in 1864].
3. Roman Jakobson, "On Linguistic Aspects of Translation," in *On Translation*, ed. Reuben A. Brower (New York: Oxford University Press, 1966), 232–9, 233; Riitta Oittinen, Anne Ketola, and Melissa Garavini, *Translating Picturebooks. Revoicing the Verbal, the Visual, and the Aural for a Child Audience* (New York: Routledge, 2018), 129–30, 135–7.
4. Mikhail M. Bakhtin, *Rabelais and His World*, trans. Hélène Iswolsky (Bloomington: Indiana University Press, 1984), 5, 7–9, 11, 84.

5. Caryl Emerson, one of the first translators of Bakhtin's books, uses the term "decrowning," which I adopt here as well. See Mikhail M. Bakhtin, *Problems of Dostoevsky's Poetics*, trans. and ed. Caryl Emerson (Minneapolis: University of Minnesota Press, 1987), 124–6. Hélène Iswolsky translates the term as "uncrowning." See Bakhtin, *Rabelais and His World*, 235.
6. Simon Dentith, *Bakhtinian Thought. An Introductory Reader. Critical Readers in Theory and Practice* (London: Routledge, 1995), 65.
7. See Riitta Oittinen, *Translating for Children*, ill. Riitta Oittinen, cover art Riitta Oittinen(Oxfordshire: Taylor & Francis, 2000); Riitta Oittinen, "On Translating Picturebooks," in *Perspectives Journal: Studies in Translation, Theory and Practice* 9, no. 2 (2001): 109–25; Riitta Oittinen, *Kuvakirja kääntäjän kädessä* (Picturebook in the Hand of a Translator), ill. Riitta Oittinen, cover art Riitta Oittinen (Helsinki: Lasten Keskus, 2004); Riitta Oittinen, "Audiences and Influences: Multisensory Translations of Picturebooks," in *Whose Story? Translating the Verbal and the Visual in Literature for Young Audiences*, ed. Maria González Davies and Riitta Oittinen (Newcastle: Cambridge Scholars Publishing, 2008), 3–16; Riitta Oittinen, "From Thumbelina to Winnie-the-Pooh: Pictures, Words and Sounds in Translation," *The Verbal, the Visual, and the Translator. Meta Special Issue*, ed. Klaus Kaindl and Riitta Oittinen 53, no. 1 (2008): 76–89; Riitta Oittinen, "The Visual Carnival of the Finnish Monkerias," in *A Jabberwocky Companion*, ed. Anna Kérchy, Kit Kelen, and Björn Sundmark, ill. Riitta Oittinen et al., (Portlaoise: Evertype, 2021); Riitta Oittinen and Tiina Tuominen, *Olennaisen äärellä. Johdatus audiovisuaaliseen kääntämiseen* (On the Edge of the Essential. Introduction to Audiovisual Translation), ill. Riitta Oittinen, cover art Riitta Oittinen (Tampere: Tampere University Press, 2007); Riitta Oittinen, Anne Ketola, and Melissa Garavini, *Translating Picturebooks. Revoicing the Verbal, the Visual, and the Aural for a Child Audience*, ill. Riitta Oittinen (New York: Routledge, 2018).
8. Bakhtin, *Rabelais and His World*, 3, 66, 67, 33, 180, 512.
9. Ibid., 94.
10. Ibid., 299.
11. Ibid., 5, 7–9, 11, 19–20, 24–5, 84.
12. See Gary Saul Morson and Caryl Emerson, *Creation of a Prosaics* (Stanford: Stanford University Press, 1990), 130–3.
13. Mikhail M. Bakhtin, *The Dialogic Imagination: Four Essays*, ed. Michael Holquist, trans. Caryl Emerson and Michael Holquist (Austin: University of Texas Press, 1981).
14. Bakhtin, *Dialogic Imagination*, Glossary.
15. Ibid., 447.
16. Ibid., 131–3, emphasis in original.
17. Ibid., 428.

18. Uri Shulevitz, *Writing with Pictures. How to Write and Illustrate Children's Books*, ill. Uri Shulevitz (New York: Watson-Guptill, 1985), 16, 51; Riitta Oittinen *Translating for Children*, 106; Riitta Oittinen et al., *Translating Picturebooks*, 15–21.
19. Louise M. Rosenblatt, *The Reader, the Text, the Poem. The Transactional Theory of the Literary Work* (Carbondale: Southern Illinois University Press, 1978), 12–14.
20. Mihail Bahtin [Bakhtin], *Kirjallisuuden ja estetiikan ongelmia* (Problems of Literature and Aesthetics), trans. Kerttu Kyhälä-Juntunen and Veikko Airola (The Soviet Union: Publishing House Progress, 1979), 417.
21. Bakhtin, *Dialogic Imagination*, 280.
22. Riitta Oittinen, *Kääntäjän karnevaali* (Translator's Carnival), ill. Riitta Oittinen et al. (Tampere: Tampere University Press, 1995), 69.
23. Bakhtin, *Dialogic Imagination*, 22–3.
24. Bakhtin, *Problems of Dostoevsky's Poetics*, 124.
25. According to Jon Lindseth and Markus Lång, eds., *Alice in a World of Wonderlands: Translations of Alice's Adventures in Wonderland in 150 Languages to Celebrate the 150th Anniversary of the Original Publication* (New Castle: Oak Knoll Press, 2015), Carroll's *Alice's Adventures in Wonderland* has been translated into around 150 languages. Also see Lång's reedited offprint published in 2015. According to Victor Fet's email message on December 10, 2020, today there are already at least 180 translations of the novel into many different languages.
26. There is some variation in the capitalizations of the titles of Carroll's books. I have used the titles as used in Carroll, *The Complete Works by Lewis Carroll with Illustrations by John Tenniel*.
27. Illustrated by Carroll and published posthumously.
28. There is also *The Nursery "Alice"* which is not mentioned by Weaver. It was directed for smaller children and illustrated by John Tenniel. See Warren Weaver, *Alice in Many Tongues. The Translations of Alice in Wonderland* (Madison: University of Wisconsin Press, 1964), 18–19; also see Riitta Oittinen, *I Am Me—I Am Other: On the Dialogics of Translating for Children*. Published PhD dissertation, ill. Riitta Oittinen (Tampere: Tampere University Press), 195.
29. See Anna Kérchy's illuminating *Alice in Transmedia Wonderland. Curiouser and Curiouser. New Forms of a Children's Classic* (Jefferson, NC: McFarland, 2016), where she deals with different Alice versions and rewritings, such as the Girlish Fantasy Alice and the Erotic Alice, 125–65. Also see Martin Gardner, *The Annotated Alice. Alice's Adventures in Wonderland* and *Through the Looking-Glass and What Alice Found There* by Lewis Carroll, ill. John Tenniel (Harmondsworth, Middlesex: Penguin, 1970); Zongxin Feng, "Translation and Reconstruction of a Wonderland: Alice's Adventures in China," *Budapest: Neohelicon* 36 (2009): 237–51; Mark M. Hennelly, "Alice's

Adventures at the Carnival," in *Victorian Literature and Culture* 37, no. 1 (2009): 103–28.
30. Bakhtin, *Problems of Dostoevsky's Poetics*, 124–6.
31. Carroll, *Alice's Adventures under Ground*, : page numbering ambiguous.
32. As to Carroll's verbal Alice, the verbal texts in the two versions, one with Carroll's illustration and the other one with Tenniel's, are quite close to each other and the main differences lie in changes concerning articles, prepositions, or sentence structures; some poems have also been changed and three chapters added to the later version to be illustrated by Tenniel. In other words, the first story of Alice, *Alice's Adventures under Ground*, was a work in progress and did not include three chapters that were to be added to the first full version of the book illustrated by Tenniel: "Pig and Pepper," "A Mad Tea-Party," and "The Caucus Race." See the introduction to Bahtin, *Lewis Carroll. The Complete Illustrated Works*, xiii. Yet Alice's character is very similar in both texts.
33. [Mikhail M. Bakhtin] Mihail Bahtin, *Dostojevskin poetiikan ongelmia* [Problems of Dostoevsky's Poetics], trans. Paula Nieminen and Tapani Laine (Finland: Kustannus Oy Orient Express, 1991), 186–7.
34. Carroll himself never published any illustration of the Cheshire-Cat. It was John Tenniel that created the first visual image of the cat in print.
35. [Mikhail M. Bakhtin] Mihail Bahtin, *Alice's Adventures in Wonderland*, ill. by Riitta Oittinen (2017–20).
36. There are four Finnish full translations of *Alice's Adventures in Wonderland*: the first in 1906 by Anni Swan; the second in 1972 by Kirsi Kunnas and Eeva-Liisa Manner; the third in 1995 by Alice Martin; the fourth in 2000 by Tuomas Nevanlinna. See Markus Lång, ed., *Alice in a World of a Finnish Wonderland Enhanced* (Helsinki: BoD—Books on Demand, 2015).
37. See *The Complete Works by Lewis Carroll with Illustrations by John Tenniel* and Carroll, *Through the Looking-Glass and What Alice Found There*, ill. John Tenniel (New York: Barnes & Noble, 1994), 44–5.
38. Bakhtin, *Rabelais and His World*, 24.
39. Riitta Oittinen, *Liisa, Liisa ja Alice* [Liisa, Liisa and Alice] (Tampere: Tampere University Press, 1997).
40. Bakhtin, *Rabelais and His World*, 11–12.
41. Riitta Oittinen in Joanna Dybiec-Gajer, Riitta Oittinen, and Małgorzata Kodura, *Negotiating Translation and Transcreation of Children's Literature. From Alice to the Moomins*, ed. Joanna Dybiec-Gajer, Riitta Oittinen, and Małgorzata Kodura, ill. Riitta Oittinen (New Frontiers in Translation Studies. Singapore: Springer, 2020), 13–37.
42. Bakhtin, *Rabelais and His World*, 19–20, 24–5; Riitta Oittinen, *Translating for Children*, ill. Riitta Oittinen (Oxfordshire: Taylor & Francis, 2000), 56–7.
43. Carroll 1864: page numbering ambiguous.
44. Ibid.

45. Ibid., 33/63. There is some variation in the page numberings of Carroll's original: the pages are numbered in two different ways, probably first by Carroll and later by someone else. Some of the numberings are ambiguous.
46. The March Hare appears for the first time, verbally and visually, in the version Tenniel has depicted. Here I have borrowed the character from my illustration of *Through the Looking-Glass and What Alice Found There* (2018–21).
47. Originally, Carroll depicted the bird as an ostrich. In later versions, the bird is a flamingo both verbally and visually. In my illustration, I followed Carroll's later decision to draw the bird as a flamingo.

Bibliography

[Bakhtin, Mikhail M.] Bahtin, Mihail. *The Dialogic Imagination: Four Essays* (*Voprosy literatury i estetiki*). Edited by Michael Holquist. Translated by Caryl Emerson and Michael Holquist. Austin: University of Texas Press, 1990.

[Bakhtin, Mikhail M.] Bahtin, Mihail. *Dostojevskin poetiikan ongelmia* (*Problemy poetiki Dostojevskogo*). Translated by Paula Nieminen and Tapani Laine. Finland: Kustannus Oy Orient Express, 1991.

[Bakhtin, Mikhail M.] Bahtin, Mihail. *Kirjallisuuden ja estetiikan ongelmia* (Problems of Literature and Aesthetics). Translated by Kerttu Kyhälä-Juntunen and Veikko Airola. The Soviet Union: Publishing House Progress, 1979.

[Bakhtin, Mikhail M.] Bahtin, Mihail. *Problems of Dostoevsky's Poetics* (*Problemy poetiki Dostojevskogo*). Translated and Edited by Caryl Emerson. Minneapolis: University of Minnesota Press, 1987.

[Bakhtin, Mikhail M.] Bahtin, Mihail. *Rabelais and His World* (*Tvorchestvo Fransua Rable*). Translated by Hélène Iswolsky. Bloomington: Indiana University Press, 1984.

Carroll, Lewis. *Liisan seikkailut ihmemaassa* (*Alice's Adventures in Wonderland*). Illustrated by John Tenniel. Translated by Anni Swan. Porvoo: WSOY, 1906.

[Carroll, Lewis]. *Alicen seikkailut ihmemaassa* [*Alice's Adventures in Wonderland*]. Illustrated by John Tenniel. Translated into Finnish by Alice Martin. Porvoo: WSOY, 1995.

[Carroll, Lewis]. *Alice's Adventures in Wonderland*. Illustrated by Riitta Oittinen, 2017–2020.

[Carroll, Lewis] *Alice's Adventures under Ground. A Christmas Gift to a Dear Child in Memory of a Summer Day*. Manuscript illustrated by Lewis Carroll. New York: Dover Publications, Inc., 1965 [1865; the first unpublished version in 1864].

[Carroll, Lewis]. *The Complete Works by Lewis Carroll with Illustrations by John Tenniel*. Illustrated by John Tenniel. The United States of America: Barnes & Noble, Inc., 1994 [1865].

[Carroll, Lewis] *Lewis Carroll. The Complete Illustrated Works*. Illustrated by John Tenniel, Henry Holiday, Arthur B. Frost, Lewis Carroll, Harry Furniss, and E. Gertrude Thomson. Edited by Edward Giuliano. London: Leopard, 1995 [1865].

[Carroll, Lewis]. *Liisa ihmemaassa* [*Alice's Adventures in Wonderland*]. Illustrated by Helen Oxenbury. Translated by Tuomas Nevanlinna. Helsinki: Otava 2000.

[Carroll, Lewis]. *Liisan seikkailut ihmemaassa ja Liisan seikkailut peilimaailmassa*. [*Alice's Adventures in Wonderland and Through the Looking-Glass and What Alice Found There*]. Illustrated by John Tenniel. Translated into Finnish by Kirsi Kunnas and Eeva-Liisa Manner. Jyväskylä: Gummerus, 1974.

[Carroll, Lewis] *The Nursery "Alice."* Adapted by Lewis Carroll. Illustrated by John Tenniel. Cover art by E. Gertrude Thomson. London: Macmillan and Co., 1965 [1890].

[Carroll, Lewis]. *Through the Looking-Glass and What Alice Found There*. Illustrated by John Tenniel. USA: Barnes and Noble Inc., 1994 [1871].

[Carroll, Lewis]. *Through the Looking-Glass and What Alice Found There*. Illustrated by Riitta Oittinen, 2017–2021.

Dentith, Simon. *Bakhtinian Thought. An Introductory Reader. Critical Readers in Theory and Practice*. London: Routledge, 1995.

Dybiec-Gajer, Joanna, Riitta Oittinen, and Małgorzata Kodura. *Negotiating Translation and Transcreation of Children's Literature. From Alice to the Moomins*. Edited by Joanna Dybiec-Gajer, Riitta Oittinen, and Małgorzata Kodura. Illustrated by Riitta Oittinen. New Frontiers in Translation Studies. Singapore: Springer, 2020.

Feng, Zongxin. "Translation and Reconstruction of a Wonderland: Alice's Adventures in China." *Budapest: Neohelicon* 36 (2009): 237–51.

Fet, Victor. Email message to Riitta Oittinen, December 10, 2020.

Gardner, Martin. *The Annotated Alice. Alice's Adventures in Wonderland and Through the Looking-Glass and What Alice Found There* by Lewis Carroll. Illustrated by John Tenniel. Harmondsworth: Penguin, 1970.

Hennelly, Mark M. "Alice's Adventures at the Carnival." *Victorian Literature and Culture* 37, no. 1 (2009): 103–28.

Jakobson, Roman. "On Linguistic Aspects of Translation." In *On Translation*. Edited by Reuben A. Brower, 232–9. New York: Oxford University Press, 1966.

Kérchy, Anna. *Alice in Transmedia Wonderland. Curiouser and Curiouser. New Forms of a Children's Classic*. Jefferson, NC: McFarland Publishers, 2016.

Lång, Markus, ed. *Alice in a World of a Finnish Wonderland Enhanced*. Helsinki: BoD—Books on Demand, 2015.

Lindseth, Jon, and Markus Lång. *Alice in a World of Wonderlands: Translations of Alice's Adventures in Wonderland in 150 Languages to Celebrate the 150th Anniversary of the Original Publication*. Edited by Jon Lindseth and Markus Lång. New Castle: Oak Knoll Press, 2015.

Morson, Gary Saul, and Caryl Emerson. *Creation of a Prosaics*. Stanford: Stanford University Press, 1990.

Oittinen, Riitta. "Audiences and Influences: Multisensory Translations of Picturebooks." In *Whose Story? Translating the Verbal and the Visual in Literature for Young Audiences*. Edited by Maria González Davies and Riitta Oittinen, 3–16. Newcastle: Cambridge Scholars Publishing, 2008.

Oittinen, Riitta. "From Thumbelina to Winnie-the-Pooh: Pictures, Words and Sounds in Translation." *The Verbal, the Visual, and the Translator. Meta Special Issue*. Edited by Klaus Kaindl and Riitta Oittinen 53, no. 1 (2008): 76–89.

Oittinen, Riitta. "I Am Me—I Am Other: On the Dialogics of Translating for Children." Published PhD dissertation, Illustrated by Riitta Oittinen, Tampere, Tampere University Press, 1993.

Oittinen, Riitta. *Kääntäjän karnevaali* (Translator's Carnival). Illustrated by Riitta Oittinen et al. Tampere: Tampere University Press, 1995.

Oittinen, Riitta. *Kuvakirja kääntäjän kädessä* (Picturebook in the Hand of a Translator). Illustrated by Riitta Oittinen. Cover art by Riitta Oittinen. Helsinki: Lasten Keskus, 2004.

Oittinen, Riitta *Liisa, Liisa ja Alice* [Liisa, Liisa and Alice] 1997. Illustrated by Riitta Oittinen. Cover art by Riitta Oittinen Tampere: Tampere University Press.

Oittinen, Riitta. "On Translating Picturebooks." *Perspectives Journal: Studies in Translation, Theory and Practice* 9, no. 2 (2001): 109–25.

Oittinen, Riitta. *Translating for Children*. Illustrated by Riitta Oittinen. Cover art by Riitta Oittinen. New York: Garland Publishing, 2000.

Oittinen, Riitta. "The Visual Carnival of the Finnish Monkerias." In *A Jabberwocky Companion*. Edited by Anna Kérchy, Kit Kelen, and Björn Sundmark. Illustrated by Riitta Oittinen et al. Portlaoise: Evertype, 2021.

Oittinen, Riitta, Anne Ketola, and Melissa Garavini. *Translating Picturebooks. Revoicing the Verbal, the Visual, and the Aural for a Child Audience*. Illustrated by Riitta Oittinen et al. New York: Routledge, 2018.

Oittinen, Riitta, and Tiina Tuominen. *Olennaisen äärellä. Johdatus audiovisuaaliseen kääntämiseen* (On the Edge of the Essential. Introduction to Audiovisual Translation). Illustrated by Riitta Oittinen. Tampere: Tampere University Press, 2007.

Rosenblatt, Louise M. *The Reader, the Text, the Poem. The Transactional Theory of the Literary Work*. Carbondale: Southern Illinois University Press, 1978.

Shulevitz, Uri. *Writing with Pictures. How to Write and Illustrate Children's Books.* Illustrated by Uri Shulevitz. New York: Watson-Guptill Publications, 1985.

Southey, Robert "The Old Man's Comforts and How He Gained Them." http://old poetry.com/opoem/8045. Accessed November 20, 2021

Weaver, Warren. *Alice in Many Tongues. The Translations of Alice in Wonderland.* Madison: University of Wisconsin Press, 1964.

12

Juvenile *Quixotes* in Eighteenth-Century England

Scott Pollard

For this essay, I feel like I am threading a needle. Cervantes and British literature scholars have written extensively about the extraordinary influence *Don Quixote* has had on English literature, drama, culture, publishing, and politics, beginning not long after the publication of the first volume of *Don Quixote* in 1605 and extending into the twenty-first century, but peaking in the eighteenth. Interest in *Quixote* was part of a larger fascination with Spanish culture and literature—*Pax Hispanica*—at a time when Spain was the most powerful country in Europe.[1] In 1605, diplomats brought volume 1 back to England, and at the same time it was bought with funds provided by Shakespeare's patron, the Earl of Southampton, for Oxford's Bodleian Library.[2] While Shakespeare's connection to *Don Quixote* is the best-known early example of the novel's presence in England because of the lost play *Cardenio* (1613) that he coauthored with John Fletcher, many others appropriated the novel through their work before Thomas Shelton's 1612 translation of volume 1.[3]

After Shelton's translation and the 1620 translation of volume 2 (anonymous, misattributed to Shelton), from the late seventeenth into the eighteenth century, there were six more translations: John Phillips (1687), Pierre Motteaux (1700), John Stevens (1700), Charles Jarvis (1742), Tobias Smollett (1755), and George Kelly (1769). While the seventeenth-century appearance of *Don Quixote* had its most profound effect on English drama, the proliferation of translations coincided with, and perhaps even spurred, the advent of the eighteenth-century English novel, a coincidence well explored by scholars.[4] As Susan Staves claims, "No national literature assimilated the idea of Don Quixote more thoroughly than the English."[5] The cultural power of *Don Quixote* in England was such that it garnered its own term, Quixotism, which April Alliston describes as "an imbalance of reading, an over-identification insufficiently tempered by judgments of probability."[6] Pedro Javier Pardo notes that what happens in England with *Don Quixote* is an example of a "reproductive reception, that is, the reproduction of a work in a foreign language through translation, adaptation, commentary, or even edition in the original language" that becomes a "productive reception … of works inspired, derived, influenced or modelled on *Don Quixote*, and, more specifically, the process of imitation and rewriting of the novel that will turn it into a myth."[7] Pardo's insights into *Don Quixote*'s British receptions mirror David Brewer's concept of "imaginative expansion" in *The Afterlife of Character, 1726–1825* "as an umbrella term for an array of reading practices in eighteenth-century Britain by which characters in broadly successful texts were treated as if they were fundamentally incomplete and the common property of all."[8] Finally, to move the novel beyond the Spanish-English cultural circuit, in *Atlas of the European Novel, 1800–1900* Franco Moretti uses the idea of translation waves to broadly track *Don Quixote*'s dissemination across the globe, while in "Quixotism as Global Heuristic: Atlantic and Pacific Diasporas," Aaron Hanlon, building on Moretti, explores more particularly how Quixotism moves beyond Spain and England to become a worldwide literary trope: "when Quixote becomes 'globalized,' he also becomes deracinated … [and he] does this work of cultural translation between the local and the global more prominently than most characters in eighteenth-century fiction."[9] In *The Dialogic Imagination*, Bakhtin provides a theoretical umbrella for all of these scholarly insights through the concept of re-accentuation:

> When this is done, the list of all subsequent re-accentuations of images in a given novel—say, the image of Don Quixote—takes on an enormous heuristic significance, deepening and broadening our artistic and ideological understanding of them. For, we repeat, great novelistic images continue to grow and develop even after the moment of their creation; they are capable of being creatively transformed in different eras, far distant from the day and hour of their original birth.[10]

Bakhtin references *Don Quixote* repeatedly as he theorizes re-accentuation, putting Cervantes at the structural core of his idea. In the quotation above, his final summation of the significance of re-accentuation, Bakhtin invokes Cervantes as key exemplar in the global development of the novel as an evolving and adaptive cultural force, a truth that forecast the discoveries of subsequent scholarship.

As the above quick scholarly review clearly demonstrates, Don Quixote's disseminatory path has been well documented. The work's route through England, in particular, seems to have been exhaustively recorded. Two scholars who take up Quixotism—Aaron Hanlon and Amelia Dale—invoke

David Brewer's concept of "inexhaustibility" from *The Afterlife of Character, 1726-1825*, to explain the persistence of literary characters like Don Quixote who had transcended their origins and "were both fundamentally inexhaustible and available to all."[11] And here is the eye of the needle for me: although so much has been done to chart and explore Quixotic discourses in and through Britain, the uses of Don Quixote as a children's text at the very beginnings of British children's literature has not yet been investigated much at all. I heed Bakhtin's cautionary words: "Individual languages, their roles and their actual historical meaning are fully disclosed only within the totality of an era's heteroglossia."[12] I am not claiming that studying British juvenile Quixotes will complete our understanding of the era's Quixotic heteroglossia, but only that this essay will explore another gloss, another manifestation, of a powerful cultural import.

In his article on late seventeenth-century British abridgements of *Quixote*, Gregory Baum observes that the proliferation of versions of *Don Quixote*—translations, adaptations, and abridgements—rendered the content of Cervantes's novel unstable and changeable.[13] Such instability created fertile and exploitable sources for production and reproduction in the cultural marketplace, which in the eighteenth century was marked by intense creative, demographic, and economic ferment.[14] If this burgeoning capitalist economy seems a bit chaotic as businesses, writers, and creative artists sought to make a profit out of whatever material they could get their hands on, scholars like James Raven and the other contributors to *Books and Their Readers in Eighteenth-Century England: New Essays* demonstrate a more orderly exploitation. For the British *Quixotes* in particular, through the seventeenth, eighteenth, and into the nineteenth century, scholars identify an epistemological arc that reflects historical changes in the conceptions of the self, agency, and society as Britain moves from the Enlightenment to Romanticism. For Susan Staves, Quixote begins as "a buffoon, a madman" to become "an idealistic and noble hero."[15] For Pedro Javier Pardo, "Quixote Figures" arc from the "Comic to the Serious" in three stages: "Ridiculous," "Admirable," and "Romantic."[16] Pardo's categories reflect Bakhtin's discussion of the conditions for re-accentuation: "In an era when the dialogue of languages has experienced great change, the language of an image begins to sound in a different way, or is bathed in a different light, or is perceived against a different dialogizing background."[17] In addition to securing its place in the cultural market place for adults, *Don Quixote* "sound[s] in a different way" when it is also imbedded in the beginnings of British children's literature, when the printer John Newbery inaugurated the children's book trade in 1744 with *A Pretty Little Pocket-Book*.[18] Although John Newbery does not publish a children's *Quixote* before he dies, his nephew and successor, Francis

Newbery, and two other competitors do publish three juvenile editions of *Don Quixote*: Woodgate (1768), Turpin (1776), and F. Newbery (1778),[19] which began a tradition of juvenile *Quixote* adaptations in English that extends to the present.[20]

Through these three early adaptations, my essay will analyze how the embedded potentialities of Don Quixote, as articulated by Staves and Prado, manifested the initial characteristics of eighteenth-century children's literature. In one of the earliest scholarly books on children's literature, *Children's Books in England*, F. J. Harvey Darton offers the classic definition of children's literature: "Printed works produced ostensibly to give children spontaneous pleasure, and not primarily to teach them, nor solely to make them good, nor to keep them profitably quiet."[21] This idea of children's literature tied to a child's pleasure comes directly from John Newbery, the first children's bookseller, who founded his company in 1744. As Jackie C. Horne points out in *History and the Construction of the Child in Early British Children's Literature*, in the early part of the century the purpose of juvenile literature was seen as fundamentally didactic with a preceptive and "moral purpose" to train literate children to private and public virtue,[22] reflecting "the truism of eighteenth-century humanist teaching: that effective representations of the ideal would provide the sharpest spur to readerly emulation."[23] In *Engines of Instruction, Mischief, and Magic: Children's Literature in England from Its Beginning to 1839*, Mary V. Jackson similarly identifies the ideological function of children's books: "They were tools for social, moral, religious, and political conditioning."[24] But with John Newbery, that ideological function shifts from simple social conditioning to something much more dynamic. Jackson categorizes Newbery as an Enlightenment figure, inspired by John Locke, "who championed the interests of those at the lower end of the scale"[25] and whose vision of childhood took "the Enlightenment concept of tabula rasa and the means of acquiring knowledge and values ..., and follow[ed] them to their logical conclusion." For Jackson, "Newbery arrived unwittingly at a brand of ardent nationalism as a revolutionary in its threat to oligarchy as any hatched in the American colonies or France, though devoid of malice or even envy, so sure was he of the inevitably and benign efficacy of it.[26] Newbery and the cohort of similar children's publishers took advantage of the rising literacy of the middle class to market their secular vision of entertainment and instruction, a pedagogy meant to empower and create the intellectual and imaginative conditions for upward mobility. This view then fed into the Romantic, Rousseauian view of childhood, when "in many ways childhood was the best time of life ... [and] a child should have the right to be a child ... [and] to be happy."[27] After Newbery's death, his ideas and those of the Romantic child continue to dominate the book trade during what

Jackson labels as the "Transition Period" (1768–88),[28] after which and into the nineteenth century children's publishing was dominated by a resurgent didacticism that focused on faith, obedience, and an immobilizing rigid class hierarchy. The three adaptations of Don Quixote were published during the period of the empowered and liberated child, and they sometimes do and sometimes do not reflect its values, collectively representing what Bakhtin would call "a microcosm of heteroglossia."[29]

To understand better these early adaptations of *Don Quixote* in British children's literature, we must first look at the history of chivalric romances in Britain and their connection to children. Jackson notes that the genre of chivalric romance came to England with William the Conqueror. Like *Don Quixote*'s arrival in England in the seventeenth century, the chivalric tradition also came from the continent, just centuries earlier. With the coincidence of Caxton's printing press and the turn of British culture inward and away from France in the fifteenth century, the initial publications of chivalric romances (e.g., *Roland* and *Parcifal*) were anglicized and translated from their French and continental sources for the literate aristocracy. As time went on, and literacy moved down the social scale, cheaper and abridged versions of these books—chapbooks—were printed to satisfy not only an adult reading public but "the ardor of the young and lowly for these marvelous tales and audacious adventures."[30] Darton quotes Richard Steele describing his eight-year-old godson from an article in *The Tatler* (1709):

> I found him very much turned his studies for about a twelve-month past, into the lives and adventures of Don Bellianis of Greece, Guy of Warwick, the seven champions, and other historians of that age ... He would tell you the mismanagements of John Hickathrift, find fault with the passionate temper of Bevis of Southampton, and loved Saint George for being the champion of England; and by this means had his thoughts insensibly molded into the notions of discretion, virtue, and honor.[31]

Steele's description of his godson's fascination with chivalric romances mirrors Cervantes's own description of Quixote's obsession at the very beginning of volume 1, revealing the imaginative kinship between the child fan and the famous fictional adult fan of chivalric romance. In the beginning of the eighteenth century, chivalric romances function as a means to resistant readings for children, a counter-discourse to the current didactic pedagogy, forerunner to Newbery's idea of the independent child reader, and predictor of *Don Quixote* as children's literature.

The end of the above Steele quotation—"by this means had his thoughts insensibly molded into the notions of discretion, virtue, and honor"—is particularly interesting because of its connection to the phenomenon of Quixotism. For Steele's godson, the chivalric histories he has read produce the value set he uses to assess and interact with the world. Like Quixote, they form the lens through which he looks at the world. In *The Practice of Quixotism*, Scott Paul Gordon notes the importance of genre in grounding what he calls the "Quixote trope" in eighteenth-century Britain: "The persistent description of quixotes as those who elevate their private and individual mental creations ignores—or deliberately mistakes—the fact that quixote's vision derives from a shared way of seeing: a genre."[32] For Gordon, this trope is negatively charged, because it is used to depict "another's deluded perceptions that implies the objectivity of one's own—precisely to dismiss others' beliefs."[33] But unlike adults, for children, particularly framed by either Newbery's Enlightenment understanding or that of the Romantic child, chivalric romance is positively charged because it enables independence and autonomy, a means of avoiding the stultifying effects of a conventional education. In *The Age of Reasons*, Wendy Motooka identifies "the central trope of *Don Quixote*" as "the act of self-authorization, disguised as deference to established rules."[34] Steele's godson authorized himself—what he learned and the values he held—through the chivalric romances he read. His choices are not shared or guided by others—that is, the adult world which would teach him—but by his own agency and the reading he prefers. Motooka speaks of the eighteenth century as containing an Age of Reason and an Age of Sentiment. The former represents the conventional Enlightenment understanding of reason as objective and universal, while the latter focuses on how "experience and the empirical method are the means through which the individual acquires" reason.[35] The latter is grounded in the individual's subjectivity, represents a universalism from the inside out, and produces a rationality that is particular to the individual and may not be shared by others.[36] In other words, sentimentalism describes Quixote and Quixotism, Steele's godson's autodidacticism and reading habits, and the autonomous child reader, first as conceived by the Newberyes and then by Rousseau and the Romantics. The remainder of this essay will explore how the three adaptations of *Don Quixote*—"translating [the novel] from one accentual register to another"[37]—enable the independent, literate child.

All three adaptations focus primarily on the stories of Don Quixote and Sancho, reducing the number and length, or leaving out completely the many interpolated tales, like that of Marcela and Grisostomo from volume 1, as well as those that relegate Don Quixote and Sancho to a secondary role, like Camacho's wedding from volume 2. Also, without the meta-commentary that regularly calls attention to the nature of text and narrative, like the appearance of volume 1 in volume 2, the resultant streamlined narratives read much more like straightforward, linear romances than the original, with its distracted and distracting shifts in perspective, narrative voice, and story. I am not claiming that these adaptations just simplify *Don Quixote* for a young audience to make the narrative easier to follow, because what remains is complex and labyrinthine, just like much of the historical canon of children's literature.[38] Rather, like Steele's godson's love of chivalric romance, which links him imaginatively and intellectually to Don Quixote's own obsession, these adaptations (and those after them as well) assume that temperamental linkage. Moreover, the child reader's direct connection to Don Quixote suggests other possibilities. Rather than simply reading about the distant adventures of epic chivalric heroes, Don Quixote uses chivalric romances as the "seemingly established rules"[39] to extemporize chivalric adventures in the ordinary world. In the early eighteenth century, with its focus on prescriptive moral education, Don Quixote could not function as a model of appropriate, ethical behavior. But after Newbery and Rousseau and the shift in the conception of the child as a more autonomous thinking and feeling subject (rather than a subject which simply behaves or misbehaves), Don Quixote can function as a model to engage sentimentally—that is, subjectively—with the world and make sense of experience. The results are messier but empowering for the child as self-sufficient agent. This does not mean that the child can act without consequence, just as Don Quixote does not act without consequence. As Horne notes about John Newbery, who, although opposed to the "morally focused writings" of early eighteenth-century didactic works for children, still adhered "to the key Enlightenment belief in the power of literary exemplars to teach morality."[40] The conception of the child has changed, and as a result the means of teaching the child morality changes.

Given Cervantes's intent in the original novel to indict the genre of chivalric romance, it is not surprising that Cervantes makes Don Quixote suffer so violently for his mania. Volume I is marked by all the painful indignities that Quixote suffers, but he survives to the end because of the power of the mania that keeps him moving toward another adventure. Chivalric romance empowers his imagination to improvise adventures out of what is in front of him, and Cervantes fights back with an extraordinary force that cannot quite defeat Quixote in the end. In volume II, Cervantes does not exercise as much violence against Quixote, but instead he ups the ante and steals away from Quixote the narrative control over his own fantasy and reassigns it to other characters (Sancho, Samson Carrasco, the Duke and Duchess). Rather than physical pain, Quixote's loss of imaginary power over his own destiny is what finally does him in, and in the end he subsides into normality and dies. Cervantes exhausts Don Quixote's chivalric being. Physically, intellectually, and emotionally, the author knocks the stuffing out of his main character. If Cervantes were successful, no one would have ever taken up Don Quixote's story again, but the subsequent history of world literature and culture show otherwise, because as Bakhtin puts it, "The historical life of classic works is in fact the uninterrupted process of their social and ideological re-accentuation."[41]

To return to Darton, how does *Don Quixote* become children's literature—"ostensibly to give children spontaneous pleasure, and not primarily to teach them, nor solely to make them good"[42]—that is, meant to give pleasure and yet still have a moral, instructive function? To counter Cervantine exhaustion, how do these children's versions of *Don Quixote* inspire physical, imaginative, and emotional pleasure without the tragedy of an exhausted self? The best answer to these questions may be in the "Preface to the Reader" section of the Woodgate edition:

> I might, no doubt, very well have spared the Reader so much Trouble as to peruse a Preface to recommend this so well known, and everywhere approved History to your favourable Acceptance, which in all likelihood, as it never did it never will miss of due Praise amongst all Conditions of People, not only in our but in other Nations, gaining universal Applause ... It contains a variety of delightful Passages, in which, for the most Part, the conceited knight and his comical Squire had a finger; centering however, in moral Solidity, by exposing Folly, that Men might learn from it.[43]

Claiming the story's popularity, universality, and moral purpose, the preface advances a thesis that bridges pleasure and education, making it a perfect example of the children's books of its era. These books are not about the Cervantine gutting of a character or genre—with its resulting violent consequences—but about the joy of reading and instruction. If Cervantes had realized his overt purpose for *Don Quixote*, we would not have the extraordinary spread of the novel across time and across the world, but Cervantes's intentions failed, and instead the novel, figure, and story are adapted, reworked, and re-acculturated again and again and again. The remainder of this essay will look particularly at how these three adaptations of *Don Quixote* de-escalate the violence of the original to create a safer world where Don Quixote can extemporize his adventures and achieve a fuller and freer agency than in Cervantes's original.

The shortest of the three, the Turpin (103 pages, 1776), begins to set expectations with the title page, which claims that the book was "translated by the order of the Emperor of Lilliput, for the amusement of his merry little subjects," and that "The whimsies of our Mad-brain Knight, /and Sancho's Humour, will delight: / Their entertaining Rambles read, / And you will laugh your fill indeed."[44] Although the book frames Quixote as mad, it does not dwell on his mental state once he begins to travel and have adventures. There is no constant drumbeat of madness, as there is in the original from the narrator and the other characters. No one attempts to take away his agency, as so many characters try and succeed in doing in the original. In this version, as the focalizer for the child reader, Don Quixote has an agency that is free and clear: he can do what he wants with few restrictions, few telling him what he can and cannot do, whereas the original features a constant chorus of characters trying to influence Quixote's decisions and actions. If the Turpin makes Quixote the ideal protagonist for a child audience, it also, once the action starts, de-escalates, and diffuses conflict and its effects. At home at the beginning, Don Quixote's first battle is with spiders in his cellar: "He took up his sword, and began to cut about him, to kill, or drive away, the many Regiments of Spiders that had taken possession of his armour."[45] In the first inn scene, the carriers whom Quixote fells are made right with "wine poured down their throats," and when the guests shower Quixote with stones, "the beaver of his helmet secured him from the danger of the stones."[46] In the windmill scene, Quixote's fall is broken by being tossed in a pond, from which he is rescued by Rocinante: "up went man and horse, and being quite canted over they were thrown into a great pond, and lucky it was so, for had they been thrown from such a great height on the ground, they must certainly be dashed to pieces. Don Quixote, nearly drowned, was brought out by his trusty Rocinante."[47] In the aftermath of Quixote's battle with the sheep, the Turpin avoids the scene of mutual vomiting between Quixote and Sancho, but does focus on Quixote's concern for the loss of his teeth. In the encounter with the penitents, Quixote is the cause for the priest's broken leg, but the priest does not excommunicate him. Quixote does not strike Sancho at the end of the fulling mill scene, as in the original, raising the tension between them; instead, Sancho's laughter simply diffuses the tension and the scene ends without any lingering psychological damage. When Quixote and Sancho encounter the galley slaves, there are no stories from the prisoners, nor interpretive commentary, and Quixote offers no philosophical discussion about human freedom before instigating the release of the men; unlike the original, Quixote is not beaten up by the ungrateful people he helps liberate, not punished for his "good" deed. Instead, they simply humor him: "Don Quixote then calling the Thieves about him, commanded them to present themselves before the Princess Dulcinea del Toboso; which, on their promising to do so, he sent them away."[48]

The Turpin adaptation does not expunge all the violence—Quixote still loses a part of his ear to the Biscayan, he still kills sheep—but simplifies and reduces it, making the adventures and their ensuing conflicts less consequential and easier to navigate through to other adventures, other chivalric interactions with the world, which might be best characterized as sentimental play. At the end of the Turpin, Quixote becomes ill and then recovers both his physical and mental well-being, after which he returns home where he lives out the rest of his life as a responsible citizen:

> On the morrow, having taken leave of the Duke and Duchess, who made them handsome presents, they [Sancho and Don Quixote] set off on their journey home, where they arrived to the great comfort of their families, where Don Quixote peaceably spent the rest of his days on his little estate, and Sancho was appointed governor over a large herd of goats. [49]

Quixote never loses agency. He returns home on his own. He does not have to be tricked, bargained with, coerced, and caged, as he is at the end of volume I of the original, and he does not have his agency subtly or violently taken from him, as Sancho and Samson Carasco respectively do in volume II. In the Turpin, Quixote can have his fun, put childish things away (I Corinthians 13), and then return home to live his life as a productive adult. He represents the autonomous Enlightenment child who is free to read and make sense of the world through the knowledge he possesses, and he represents the Rousseauian child inhabiting a playful space protected from the responsibilities of the adult world, until the time comes to take up those responsibilities of his own accord and not because a cabal of conscientious adults conspire to make him behave, as in the original.

The Woodgate *Don Quixote* (1768, 118 pages) is slightly longer than the Turpin, and its editor's decisions make it distinct from the Turpin in a variety of ways. Like the Turpin, the Woodgate highlights Quixote's whimsies, but unlike the Turpin, which essentially ignores Quixote's madness after the initial framing of the tale, the Woodgate focuses more on his madness and, as a result, less on his adventures. Most tellingly, the Woodgate maintains the barber and priest's retrieval plot from volume I, along with all the interpolated stories (Cardenio and Lucinda, Fernando and Dorotea, The Captive, Doña Clara) adjunct to it. These stories shift the overall narrative focus away from Don Quixote, weakening his role as focalizer for the reader, as well as making the novel seem as much about bringing Quixote back home as it is about Quixote himself. Oddly, the material included from volume II weakens the retrieval narrative, because it reduces Samson Carrasco's role to an incidental one. He is not introduced as a character before the third sally, and when he appears as the Knight of the Woods/Mirror, it is only after Quixote defeats him that we learn of his part in the retrieval plot:

> But the Knight of the Glass's squire, seeing his master in that desperate plight, came running without his great nose, and, falling at his feet, implored him to spare his life, for all had been but a frolick, they both being sent by the curate and barber, his neighbors, to encounter him and his squire, and all they would have done, had they conquered, would have been no more than to have enjoyned them to return to their habitations.[50]

This is the one incident of the retrieval plot in volume II. Samson Carrasco disappears and does not reappear at the end of the book as the Knight of the White Moon to defeat Don Quixote and demand that he returns home. Moreover, while Quixote's imaginative power in volume 1 is compromised by the space given to the retrieval narrative and interpolated tales, Quixote seems to have more imaginative freedom in volume II, because neither Sancho nor the Duke and Duchess exert much power over him, as they do in the original. In terms of agency, the Woodgate Quixote is something of a mixed bag, following Cervantes' lead in volume I of introducing much competition for Quixote's imaginative dominance but breaking with Cervantes' heavy-handedness in volume II by restoring some agency to Quixote by severely reducing the subplots and the influence of secondary characters. Nonetheless, given that this adaptation challenges Quixote's imaginative and intellectual autonomy beginning in volume I, this Quixote serves less effectively as mirror to the empowered child as understood by Newbery or Rousseau.

In terms of violence, the Woodgate has also mitigated it some. In the windmill scene, Quixote's fall is broken by a pond, and at the end of the fulling mill scene Sancho's laughter diffuses the tension between them, so Quixote does not strike Sancho. The return home in the cart at the end of volume I features none of the violent incidents of the original. But, as in the Turpin, there is still violence: Quixote and Sancho are still beaten by the Yanguesans, Quixote is beaten by a crazed Cardenio, and knight and squire are stampeded by bulls near the end of the book. Despite the mitigation of violence earlier in the book, the denouement is instigated by violence. First, the injuries incurred from the bulls (rather than defeat by the Knight of the White Moon) send Don Quixote and Sancho back home. Second, once home, Quixote suffers a violent nightmare—not in the original—the trauma of which restores his sanity and precipitates his death:

> In his sleep he dreamed he was in hell, saw the infernal furies tossing to and fro, on fiery forks, the many authors of books, containing the feats of knights-errant, laughing at their piteous cries, and upbraiding them as egregious sinners, in filling the world with so many lyes and fables, that never had being but in their whimsical brains, created to seduce people to folly and imposture: others he saw hanged up by the heels on burning rocks, and smoked by old stump-footed devils, stub-horned, and crooked nosed: The fuel was rolls of the manuscripts.[51]

The Woodgate ends with a traumatizing, punitive moral deterrent that restores Quixote's sanity and social responsibility (he dictates his will), but sends him into a death spiral. To return to the issue of agency, while this adaptation seems to afford Quixote a modicum of greater agency in volume II, it takes it away at the end, leaving Quixote desperately trying to assert some kind of normality and be right with the world before he dies. This adaptation is much more in line with the Cervantine original, or the heavy-handed moralizing children's texts of the early eighteenth century—when the figure of *Don Quixote* was initially judged "a buffoon, a madman" and not to be taken as a moral or behavioral exemplar—rather than one that would promote the Rousseauian child or what was becoming the Romantic vision of Don Quixote, "an idealistic and noble hero,"[52] a Byronic hero standing against society for the strength and integrity of his personal vision.

The F. Newbery *Quixote* (1778, 263 pages) is by far the longest of the three adaptations and, thus, contains the most material from the original. As such, it seems more like the Woodgate than the Turpin, because it includes the retrieval narratives of volumes I and II, as well as most of the interpolated tales. Like the Woodgate, Quixote's madness is kept in focus throughout the book, his adventures arc is interrupted and diluted by other narrative threads, and he loses imaginative control. Unlike the Woodgate, which downplays the retrieval narrative from volume II and restores some autonomy to the Quixote character before the end, the F. Newbery maintains the retrieval plot, and Quixote returns home not by his own choice, but because he is fooled and defeated by Samson Carrasco masquerading as the Knight of the White Moon.

Like both the Turpin and Woodgate, while there is still much violence, it is mitigated regularly throughout the book. Notably, though, in the Newbery the violence is often mitigated through Quixote's own reasonableness. The penitent with the broken leg whom Quixote interviews does not excommunicate the knight, and in the subsequent conversation, Quixote attempts to explain his actions and mistakes, offers help, and then asks for pardon: "Don Quixote called Sancho, and with his assistance disengaged the licentiate; he then gave him the torch, and bid him follow his comrades and beg their pardon in his name for the injury he could not avoid doing them."[53] And even when Quixote suffers violence, he is sometimes willing to learn from the experience. After being stoned by the galley slaves, Quixote reflects on his choices: "had I believed you [Sancho], I might have prevented this trouble, but as it is done, I must have patience, and take warning."[54] In the original, the conversations between Don Quixote and Sancho are obviously a fundamental part of the novel, but those interactions are often the two of them talking past one another, or Quixote asserting verbal authority over Sancho. In this adaptation, the two often function as reasonable interlocutors, with Sancho leading Don Quixote, if retroactively, to reason. In the "Parliament of Death" scene, Quixote lets Sancho reason him out of taking revenge on the actors by using Quixote chivalric frame of reference to steer him clear of violence:

> It is mere madness, Sir, to attempt such an exercise; but if this consideration does not prevail with you to be quiet, be assured that all those who stand there, though there appear to be princes, kings, and emperors, there is not one knight errant. Now indeed, said Don Quixote, you have hit the point Sancho, I neither can nor ought to draw my sword against any who are not dubbed knights.[55]

Here is an example of eighteenth-century reason, not universal, but personal and sentimental. Using Quixote's core set of values, Sancho helps Quixote navigate the world rationally rather than ideologically.

Sancho's function as rational interlocutor may be most obvious after Don Quixote is defeated by Samson Carrasco and forced to return home. In the original, Quixote melodramatically wants Carrasco to finish the job and kill him, tragically ending his chivalric arc; however in the Newbery, Quixote isn't suicidal, and Sancho helps him reason his way back home. Responding to Quixote's immediate obsessing over his loss and despairing over the damage to his identity, Sancho responds:

> No more, quoth Sancho, Sir, today for you, and tomorrow for me: and as for these matters of encounters and bangs, never trouble your head about them—He that falls today, may rise to-morrow—I mean by giving way to despondency, you prejudice your health, and prevent the recovery of fresh spirits, for fresh encounters."[56]

Traveling back home when Quixote once more falls into despondency, Sancho responds, "It is as much the part of a valiant mind, dear Sir, to be patient under misfortune, as to rejoice in prosperity." Sancho functions as a chivalric psychologist, trying to keep Don Quixote engaged and moving forward in the world, and Quixote appreciates his insights: "You are much of a philosopher, Sancho, said Don Quixote, and talk very discretely." It should be noted that after this exchange, Quixote voluntarily gives up his armor—"hang up my armor for a trophy"[57]—and is ready to move on back home. One night on the return journey, when Quixote slips back into his former way of thinking and asks Sancho to whip himself to speed Dulcinea's disenchantment, Sancho deceptively obliges him by whipping a nearby tree, an act that produces a compassionate response in Quixote: "Heaven forbid, friend Sancho, that for my pleasure you should lose that life, upon which depends the maintenance of your wife and children! Let Dulcinea wait a better opportunity."[58]

This rational, centering conversation allows Quixote to return home imagining a pastoral future and without the fear and foreboding of the original when he sees signs of death on entering the village. Instead, they enter the village and are welcomed with love and forbearance; the villagers are willing to play along with his vision of a pastoral future, since they have him home and can now minister to his needs. Moreover, Quixote himself reintegrates into the community when he says to the housekeeper, "assure yourselves, that whether I am a knight errant, or a wandering shepherd, I will not fail to provide for you."[59] In the final chapter, Quixote becomes ill, awakes from a deep sleep, recovers his sanity joyfully, dictates his will—responsibly disbursing his effects to family and friends—and then dies "a natural death."[60] Chronologically, it is not clear whether this chapter follows immediately after the previous chapter, although there are textual hints that it could be interpreted as doing so. Chronologically squishy, so to speak, this ending has neither the dark and absolutely disapproving finality of the Woodgate, nor the open-ended future of the Turpin. Rather, it begins with a meditation, which frames Quixote's death:

> As all human things, especially the lives of men, are transitory, incessantly declining from their beginning, till they arrive at their final period: and as that of Don Quixote had no peculiar privilege from heaven to exempt it from the common fate, his end and dissolution came when he least thought of it.[61]

The chapter ends with an elegy by Samson Carrasco, whose final couplet is: "His days of life tho' madness stain'd, / In death his sober senses he retain'd."[62] What we have here, then, is final chapter that begins by asserting Quixote's common humanity, and ends with a verse that acknowledges, but does not condemn the problem with Quixote's choices while recognizing his redemption in death. We are given the continuity of life into death, and we see Don Quixote, as well as his family and the villagers, reasoning along that continuity, with neither a sense of punishment, nor morbid fascination. The liberality of this adaptation's ending is amazing for its scope and complexity, and what it expects its readers to process and reason through. This is neither a happy, nor tragic ending, and the morality is not black and white, but nuanced and capacious, far more so than Cervantes's ending of volume II, which leaves no doubt about Cervantes' condemnation of Quixote's adventurism and finishes with the sting of the village forgetting their benefactor.

The eighteenth century in Britain was an amazing period of cultural ferment and rising literacy, linked with a burgeoning economy searching for material from which to produce profit. Cervantes's *Don Quixote* was one of the sources that this cultural industry took up, translated, adapted, and reworked for a vast variety of divergent uses, one of which was in the new genre of children's literature. Scholars like Javier Pardo, J.A. G. Ardilla, Susan Staves, Wendy Motooka, and Scott Paul Gordon have extensively tracked, identified, and categorized the arrival of Cervantes's *Don Quixote* in England and its fulsome dissemination throughout the culture, while scholars like Harvey Darton, Mary V. Jackson, and Jacqueline Horne have tracked, identified, and categorized the arcs childhood, childhood education, and children's literature. These two scholarly threads intersect with the Woodgate, Turpin, and F. Newbery adaptations of *Don Quixote*.

Moreover, these adaptations are fascinating because they condense in a ten-year period so many of the intellectual, philosophical, aesthetic, and educational trends that these scholars delineate. They reflect the diffuse and diverse uses of Don Quixote throughout the century, and each is geared for a different audience with distinct beliefs and expectations. The Woodgate is essentially a moral tale treating Don Quixote as a buffoon whose bad behavior must ultimately be severely punished: it functions as a guide for what not to do and what not to become. The Turpin seems the Woodgate's opposite, an adventure tale whose protagonist is free to explore his imagination and follow his own pleasure with few consequences and whose nonnormative behavior is simply resolved into conventional adult behavior at the end of the book: this Quixote stands in for the Rousseauian child whose world affords him much freedom, and where adulthood and death are far off. The F. Newbery is much thornier, neither simply moralizing nor forbearing, but much more realistic about how Quixote pursues his journey, for he is introduced to a world that is openly out of step with and antagonistic to his values, and he must work to problem solve his way through it, which he does until the antagonistic counternarrative defeats him. This defeat is not a sign of ethical errancy, though—a moral judgment—but a turning point in the narrative to get him back home where he can reintegrate, first as Don Quixote and then as Alonso Quesada. This is an Enlightenment Don Quixote who acts upon his knowledge and values, and although he faces many obstacles in the world that world does not, in the end, condemn him for what he thinks and does, but helps him find a path forward to think beyond his narcissism, feel compassion for others, and have a more humane understanding of the world before he dies. Again, Bakhtin offers a way to theorize this transformation:

> Thanks to the intentional potential embedded in them [classic works], such works have proved capable of uncovering in each era and against ever new dialogizing backgrounds ever newer aspects of meaning; their semantic content literally continues to grow, to further create out of itself ... capable of being creatively transformed in different eras, far distant from the day and hour of their original birth.[63]

The F. Newbery begins with a world that is morally black and white, but ends with one that is tolerant, sentimental, Rousseauian, and Romantic: Don Quixote has changed, and so has the world around him. As the collected essays in the recent volume, *The Poetics of Re-accentuation: Don Quixote in Film, Theater, and Modern Literature*, show, Don Quixote is perpetually becoming. He is the perfect sign for Derridean *différance*, never finished and always changing. The eighteenth-century British children's adaptations are essentially more examples, once again ad infinitum, of the power of Quixotic *différance*.

Notes

1. J. A. G. Ardila, "The Influence and Reception of Cervantes in Britain, 1607–2005," in *The Cervantean Heritage: Reception and Influence of Cervantes in Britain,* ed. J. A. G. Ardila (London: Legenda, 2009), 3.
2. Ibid., 4; Pedro Javier Pardo, "*Don Quixote* in Great Britain," in *Don Quixote around the Globe,* ed. Slav N. Gratchev and Howard Mancing (Newark, DE: Juan de La Cuesta, 2020), 21.
3. Playwrights like Francis Beaumont, George Wilkins, Thomas Middleton, and Ben Jonson. For a lengthier discussion of the early presence of *Don Quixote* in England, please see José Manuel Barrio Marco's "La proyección artística y literaria de Cervantes y *Don Quijote* en la Inglaterra del siglo

XVII: los cauces de recepción en el contexto político y cultural de la época," in *La Huella De Cervantes Y Del Quijote En La Cultura Anglosajona*, ed. José M. Barrio and María José Crespo Allué (Valladolid: Universidad de Valladolid, 2007), 19–72.
4. A small exemplary sample: Ardila, *The Cervantean Heritage*; José M. Barrio and María José Crespo Allué, *La Huella De Cervantes Y Del Quijote En La Cultura Anglosajona* (Valladolid: Universidad de Valladolid, 2007); Aaron R. Hanlon, "Quixotism as Global Heuristic: Atlantic and Pacific Diasporas," *Studies in Eighteenth-Century Culture* 46 (2017): 49–62; Howard Mancing, *The Cervantes Encyclopedia* (Westport, CT: Greenwood Press, 2004); Franco Moretti, *Atlas of the European Novel, 1800–1900* (New York: Verso, 1998); Jed Rasula, "When Exception Is the Rule: *Don Quixote* as Incitement to Literature," in *Comparative Literature* 51, no. 2 (Spring 1999): 123–51; Ilan Stavans, *Quixote: The Novel and the World* (New York: Norton, 2015); Susan Staves, "Don Quixote in Eighteenth Century England," in *Comparative Literature* 24, no. 3 (Summer 1972): 193–215.
5. Staves, "Don Quixote in Eighteenth Century England," 193.
6. April Alliston, "Female Quixotism and the Novel: Character and Plausibility, Honesty and Fidelity," *Eighteenth Century* 52, no. 3–4 (Fall/Winter 2011): 253.
7. Pardo, "*Don Quixote* in Great Britain," 22.
8. David A. Brewer, *The Afterlife of Character, 1726–1825* (Philadelphia: University of Pennsylvania Press), 22.
9. Hanlon, "Quixotism as Global Heuristic, 49.
10. Mikhail M. Bakhtin, *The Dialogic Imagination: Four Essays*, ed. Michael Holquist and Caryl Emerson. (Austin: University of Texas Press, 1984), 422.
11. Brewer, *Afterlife of Character*, 21.
12. Bakhtin, *Dialogic Imagination*, 412.
13. Gregory Baum, "Windmills and Water: The Narrative Instability and *Don Quixote* in England," in *A Novel without Boundaries: Sensing* Don Quixote *400 Years Later*, ed. Carmen Garcia de la Rasill and Jorge Abril-Sànchez (Newark, DE: Juan de la Cuesta, 2016), 133.
14. James Raven notes, "During the eighteenth century the pace of most book trades development was startling, even in comparison with many other eighteenth-century domestic industries. After vigorous growth from the late 1690s, publication rates mushroomed between the late 1740s and the end of the century." James Raven, "The Book Trades," in *Books and Their Readers in Eighteenth-Century England: New Essays*, ed. Isabel Rivers (New York: Continuum, 2000), 2.
15. Staves, "Don Quixote in Eighteenth Century England," 193.
16. Pardo, "*Don Quixote* in Great Britain," 24–32.
17. Bakhtin, *Dialogic Imagination*, 420.
18. F. J. Harvey Darton, *Children's Books in England*, 2nd edition (Cambridge: Cambridge University Press, 1958 [1932]), 122.

19. These three texts are from the microfiche collection of the Opie Collection of Children's Literature (Weston Library, Bodleian Libraries, University of Oxford). Two have a very small number of missing pages—Newbery (pp. 208–19, the end of chapter XXXI, all of XXXII, the beginning of XXXIII), Woodgate (pp. 34–39, middle of chapter IV)—not enough to affect the argument of this essay.
20. Please see Velma Bourgeois Richmond's *Don Quixote as Children's Literature: A Tradition in English Words and Pictures* (Jefferson, NC: MacFarland, 2018), an extended annotated bibliography.
21. Darton, *Children's Books in England*, 1.
22. Jackie C. Horne, *History and the Construction of the Child in Early British Children's Literature* (Burlington, VT: Ashgate, 2011), 1–2.
23. Ibid., 12.
24. Mary V. Jackson, *Engines of Instruction, Mischief, and Magic: Children's Literature in England from Its Beginning to 1839* (Lincoln, NE: University Press of Nebraska, 1989), 16.
25. Ibid., 105.
26. Ibid., 84–5.
27. Horne, *History and the Construction of the Child in Early British Children's Literature*, 11.
28. Jackson, *Engines of Instruction, Mischief, and Magic*, 111–28.
29. Bakhtin, *Dialogic Imagination*, 411.
30. Ibid., 38.
31. Darton, *Children's Books in England*, 33.
32. Scott Paul Gordon, *The Practice of Quixotism: Postmodern Theory and Eighteenth-Century Women's Writing* (New York: Palgrave Macmillan, 2006), 1, 32–3.
33. Ibid., 1.
34. Wendy Motooka, *The Age of Reasons: Quixotism, Sentimentalism and Political Economy in Eighteenth-Century Britain* (New York: Routledge, 1998), 1.
35. Ibid., 2.
36. Ibid., 4.
37. Bakhtin, *Dialogic Imagination*, 411.
38. Although common assumptions about children's stories are that they are simple, simply written, and didactic, they are just as often complex and expect readers to be perceptive and capable of making nuanced judgments about what they read. In his article, "Pleasures and Genre: Speculations on the Characteristics of Children's Fiction" (*Children's Literature* 28 [2000]: 1–14), Perry Nodelman describes this tension on p. 1: "First, ... At least in comparison to many adult literary texts, they [children's books] are short, simple, often didactic in intention, and clearly positive in their outlook on life—optimistic, with happy endings. But second, as the extensive critical discussion of many of these texts implies, their apparent

simplicity contains depths, often surprisingly pessimistic qualifications of the apparent optimism, dangerously and delightfully counterproductive possibilities that oppose and undermine the apparent messages. These texts can be easily and effortlessly heard or read, but once read, they continue to develop significance, importance, complexity, to echo ever outward and inward." The three adaptations of *Don Quixote* effectively embody this tension between the simple and complex, optimistic and pessimistic, and my analysis of the three books will be grounded in the assumption of that tension.

39. Motooka, *Age of Reasons*, 1.
40. Horne, *History and the Construction of the Child in Early British Children's Literature*, 2.
41. Bakhtin, *Dialogic Imagination*, 421.
42. Darton, *Children's Books in England*, 1.
43. Miguel de Cervantes Saavedra, *The Much-Esteemed History of the Ever-Famous Knight Don Quixote De La Mancha: Containing His Many Wonderful Adventures and Atchievements, Very Pleasant and Diverting. with the Comical Humours of Sancho Pancha, His Remarkable 'squire, Etc.: Being an Entire History of All the Memorable Transactions Recorded of Them* (London: H. Woodgate and S. Brooks, 1768), 3–4.
44. Miguel de Cervantes Saavedra, *The Entertaining History of That Famous Knight, Don Quixote De La Mancha: With the Humours of His Comical Squire Sancho Pancha* (London: H. Turpin, at no. 104, St. John's-street, West Smithfield …, and sold by S. Bladon, no. 16, and J. Bew, no 28, in Paternoster-Row, 1776), n.p.
45. Ibid., 5.
46. Ibid. 17.
47. Ibid., 34–5.
48. Ibid., 70.
49. Ibid., 103.
50. Saavedra, *The Much-Esteemed History of the Ever-Famous Knight Don Quixote De La Mancha*, 92.
51. Ibid., 117.
52. Staves, "Don Quixote in Eighteenth Century England," 193.
53. Miguel de Cervantes Saavedra, *The Life and Exploits of the Ingenious Gentleman Don Quixote, De La Mancha: With the Humorous Conceits of His Facetious Squire Sancho Panca* (London: F. Newbery, the corner of St. Paul's Church-yard, 1778), 36.
54. Ibid., 48.
55. Ibid., 147.
56. Ibid., 250.
57. Ibid., 251.
58. Ibid, 256.
59. Ibid., 259.

60. Ibid., 263.
61. Ibid., 260.
62. Ibid., 263.
63. Bakhtin, *Dialogic Imagination*, 421–2.

Bibliography

Alliston, April. "Female Quixotism and the Novel: Character and Plausibility, Honesty and Fidelity." *Eighteenth Century* 52, no. 3–4 (Fall/Winter 2011): 249–69.

Ardila, J. A. G. "The Influence and Reception of Cervantes in Britain, 1607–2005." In *The Cervantean Heritage: Reception and Influence of Cervantes in Britain*. Edited by J. A. G. Ardila, 3–31. London: Legenda, 2009.

Bakhtin, Mikhail M. *The Dialogic Imagination: Four Essays*. Edited by Michael Holquist. Translated by Caryl Emerson and Michael Holquist. Austin: University of Texas Press, 1981.

Barrio Marco, José Manuel. "La proyección artística y literaria de Cervantes y *Don Quijote* en la Inglaterra del siglo XVII: los cauces de recepción en el contexto político y cultural de la época." In *La Huella De Cervantes Y Del Quijote En La Cultura Anglosajona*. Edited by José M. Barrio and María José Crespo Allué, 19–72. Valladolid: Universidad de Valladolid, 2007.

Baum, Gregory. "Windmills and Water: The Narrative Instability and *Don Quixote* in England." In *A Novel without Boundaries: Sensing Don Quixote 400 Years Later*. Edited by Carmen Garcia de la Raslll and Jorge Abril-Sànchez, 133–50. Newark, DE: Juan de la Cuesta, 2016.

Brewer, David A. *The Afterlife of Character, 1726–1825*. Philadelphia: University of Pennsylvania Press, 2005.

Cervantes Saavedra, Miguel de. *The Entertaining History of That Famous Knight, Don Quixote De La Mancha: With the Humours of His Comical Squire Sancho Pancha*. London: H. Turpin (at no. 104, St. John's-street, West Smithfield …, and sold by S. Bladon, no. 16, and J. Bew, no. 28, in Pater-noster-Row), 1776.

Cervantes Saavedra, Miguel de. *The Life and Exploits of the Ingenious Gentleman Don Quixote, De La Mancha: With the Humorous Conceits of His Facetious Squire Sancho Panca*. London: F. Newbery (the corner of St. Paul's Churchyard), 1778.

Cervantes Saavedra, Miguel de. *The Much-Esteemed History of the Ever-Famous Knight Don Quixote De La Mancha: Containing His Many Wonderful Adventures and Achievements, Very Pleasant and Diverting. with the Comical Humours of Sancho Pancha, His Remarkable 'squire, Etc.: Being an Entire History of All the Memorable Transactions Recorded of Them*. London: H. Woodgate and S. Brooks, 1768.

Dale, Amelia. *The Printed Reader: Gender, Quixotism, and Textual Bodies in Eighteenth-Century Britain*. Lewisburg, PA: Bucknell University Press, 2019.

Darton, F. J. Harvey. *Children's Books in England*. 2nd edition. Cambridge: Cambridge University Press, 1958 [1932].

Gordon, Scott Paul. *The Practice of Quixotism: Postmodern Theory and Eighteenth-Century Women's Writing*. New York: Palgrave Macmillan, 2006.

Gratchev, Vlatcheslav, and Howard Mancing, eds. *The Poetics of Re-accentuation: Don Quixote in Film, Theater, and Modern Literature*. Lewisburg, PA: Bucknell University Press, 2017.

Hanlon, Aaron R. "Quixotism as Global Heuristic: Atlantic and Pacific Diasporas." *Studies in Eighteenth-Century Culture* 46 (2017): 49–62.

Horne, Jackie C. *History and the Construction of the Child in Early British Children's Literature*. Burlington, VT: Ashgate, 2011.

Jackson, Mary V. *Engines of Instruction, Mischief, and Magic: Children's Literature in England from Its Beginning to 1839*. Lincoln: University Press of Nebraska, 1989.

Motooka, Wendy. *The Age of Reasons: Quixotism, Sentimentalism and Political Economy in Eighteenth-Century Britain*. New York: Routledge, 1998.

Nodelman, Perry. "Pleasures and Genre: Speculations on the Characteristics of Children's Fiction." *Children's Literature* 28 (2000): 1–14

Pardo, Pedro Javier. "*Don Quixote* in Great Britain." In *Don Quixote around the Globe*. Edited by Slav N. Gratchev and Howard Mancing, 21–51. Newark, DE: Juan de La Cuesta, 2020.

Raven, James. "The Book Trades." In *Books and their Readers in Eighteenth-Century England: New Essays*. Edited by Isabel Rivers, 1–34. New York: Continuum, 2000.

Richmond, Velma Bourgeois. *Don Quixote as Children's Literature: A Tradition in English Words and Pictures*. Jefferson, NC: MacFarland, 2018.

Staves, Susan. "Don Quixote in Eighteenth Century England." *Comparative Literature* 24, no. 3 (Summer 1972): 193–215.

Afterword: Translating (with) Bakhtin

Galin Tihanov

It is a great privilege to be writing a brief afterword to this wide-ranging, learned, and insightful collection of essays on Bakhtin and translation. The editors and the authors of the individual chapters have reflected on translation from a multitude of helpful perspectives; crucially, they have done so by interrogating Bakhtin's legacy, including his key concepts: dialogue, heteroglossia, polyphony, all of them closely related to current conversations on the nature and role of translation. What I wish to do here is to continue the important work of the scholars who have contributed to this stimulating collection by offering some further considerations on the potential Bakhtin's work holds for rethinking the relationship between translation and a notion of literary tradition that is not necessarily confined to the compelling canon of (Western) modernity.

1

We need a wider theory of translation which comprehends translation both more globally and more historically. Let me begin with a brief historical excursus. Translation, in the modern sense in which we understand the term, is a fairly recent phenomenon. Its emergence is concomitant with the rising sense of intellectual property—and of the significance originality and imagination play in literature and in scholarship—that appears in the late eighteenth century. Before that, translation lives other lives: those of imitation, transposition, rendition, emulation, and recreation of the text. This is true of the West, as much as it is true of the wider cultural region formed by the Middle East, the Caucasus, Central Asia, and the Indian Subcontinent. In the European context, we are aware of poetic contests that sought to emulate rhetorically examples of Greek and Roman poetry; these competitions were forms of translation; the resulting texts do not insist on originality, nor—importantly—do they insist on complete faithfulness. They present a mode of creativity that is beyond the—at the time still constraining—binary expectations of either originality or loyalty. For centuries on end, helping oneself to someone else's plot or figure of speech, or range of similes, or metaphors, often suitably updated, was a way of ferrying an earlier discourse into a new zone of contemporaneity. This wider meaning of "translation" which highlights both the passive following and the cocreative departure from the example continues—at least to some extent—to be constitutive of our seemingly more advanced, but perhaps also more one-sided understanding of translation today. As late as the twentieth century, we can still observe this mode of consciously unfaithful translation in what, in the German tradition, is known as *Nachdichtung*, the making of poetry following another text, a process grounded in a deliberate refusal of copying or rendering that text with precision. Of course, there lurks behind all this the question of the canon, for it is the assumption of the rhetorical force and beauty of the canonical text that often enables these acts of permissible transgression. In Central Asia and Persia, as well as in the Arab-speaking world, for a very long time the practice of translation remains alien to our *modern* notion of it. When Nizami, in the second half of the twelfth century, creates his five epic poems in Persian, all through to the eighteenth century we have nothing but forms of rendition that are based on emulation, adaptation, and conversation with the canonical pieces—but not on the literal reproduction our norms of translation would require. This emulation through conversation with the source text is a genre of its own at the time, known as *nazire*: a work in its own right that responds to an earlier work by plunging today's reader into uncertainty as to where the line between translation, re-creation, and original writing is to be drawn—if such a line exists at all before the late eighteenth century.[1] I would thus venture a hypothesis: for as long as the canon—based on the certainty flowing from adherence to a combination of rhythm, plot, composition, and rhetorical figures—remains in place, there is no imperative for literal repetition or exactitude. It is with the shift toward originality, the premium value placed on novelty, and the sense of property that emerges as a by-product of this shift late in the eighteenth and in the first half of the nineteenth century that tradition is put under strain and ceases to be self-evident (in Europe, the practice of translation as identifying "ownership" begins gradually and tentatively already in the sixteenth century). We know that it is precisely at that time—late in the eighteenth and early in the nineteenth century—that the European canon of "great literature" is constructed, in which Shakespeare takes his pride of place. But no longer as the borrower of circulating plots, but rather as the originally irregular, chaotic, and disorderly potent genius that the German Romantics saw in him. Similarly, Calderón is unearthed from oblivion. But not the Calderón who was stealing plots, lifting in one of his plays an entire act from Tirso de Molina. Rather, it is his Baroque vacillation between dream and reality, the quality of unfolding, to invoke Deleuze, that underwrite his place in this new canon which reshuffles the previous order and signals the virtues of instability, not least the unmooring of literature from a long-standing pool of recurring plots, meters, compositional patterns, and rhetorical devices.

This is when translation as we know it becomes important, fitting into a new situation in which novelty and originality require to be captured with reliable precision of nuance. What is more, this is a process that—historically speaking—seems to me to be nothing but the culmination and the logical end to the protracted transition from powerful cosmopolitan koines—Greek, Latin, Persian, Sanskrit—to a multitude of (national) vernaculars, each of which insists on its own inimitable vocabulary, sensitivity, and plasticity, in the way advocated by the many supporters of a presumably organic bond between language and thinking, from Humboldt to Georgii Gachev. Although this is true of the translation of profane rather than sacred texts (the history of the translation of the Bible would reveal other patterns and trends), what I am contending here holds true for the way not just *literary* texts have been treated until the early nineteenth century. The translation of philosophical and political texts would be marked by the same relaxed interpretation of fidelity, by cocreation and adaptation, sometimes amounting to cowriting. One of my favorite examples is the first German translation of Edmund Burke's "Reflections on the Revolution in France" by that inveterate Conservative Friedrich Gentz. Gentz published his translation of Burke's important book in 1793, only three years after its appearance. The translation is marred not just by inaccuracies, but by numerous insertions of Gentz's own thoughts and interpretations of Burke's work.[2] By our standards today, this is not a reliable translation, and yet it is this translation that penetrated German and Austrian conservative debates and participated in them for more than a century and a half until a new German edition was published not long before the eventful 1968 that eventually signaled the less than conventional ways in which Gentz approached his task as translator.[3] The moral of the story here is one we may wish to keep in mind: the texture of ideas is discursive, and translations—even before the time our stricter notions of loyalty to the source text were introduced—have always been very much part of this texture. Once a translation begins its circulation, it begins its work through this discursive universe, of which it becomes inseparable. The effects of a translation, once planted in the discursive body of culture, cannot be undone; the clock can never be turned back completely.

2

Beginning with a celebration of Dostoevsky as a unique and inimitable writer of singular achievement, Mikhail Bakhtin, as I have argued elsewhere,[4] ended up in the 1930s (in his essays on the novel) and in 1963 (in the reworked version of his Dostoevsky book) focusing on the impersonal memory of genre, leaving little room for creativity as such and examining instead the inherent laws of poetics (note the change in the title of the 1963 book *Problemy poetiki Dostoevskogo*). Bakhtin's entire work and intellectual agenda, indeed the most important questions he sought to answer, are shaped by his resistance to traditionally conceived, stable subjectivity: from the question of the body (which we gradually cease to possess and be in control of, as the book on Rabelais maintains) to the question of language (which, as the essays on the novel would have it, reaches us through established generic patterns and is never quite our own—as it has always already been in someone else's mouth). The fortunes of the novel embody this rejection of classical subjectivity in full measure: the individual writer is virtually irrelevant; he or she is no more than an instrument through which the genre materializes itself, no more than a mouthpiece that enunciates the calls of generic memory. Bakhtin, in other words, despite his apparent attraction to canonical figures such as Goethe, Dostoevsky, and Rabelais, would ideally have liked to be able to write a history of literature without names. (The formula, "history without names," was, of course, derived from the work of art historian Heinrich Wölfflin and had drawn approval from the Russian formalist Boris Eikhenbaum and also from Pavel Medvedev, who, together with Matvei Kagan, was the most important transmitter of art-historical and art-theoretical knowledge in the Bakhtin Circle.) Bakhtin's trajectory is thus the trajectory of a thinker who returns from a more modern notion of individual originality and creativity to the notion of a nameless tradition, in which stable discursive formations recur and suck in, in a manner that is as fascinating as it is irresistible, the work of individual writers who are deprived of their individualities to become servants of tradition. Of course, Bakhtin remains modern as he performs this move, for tradition to him is not a soothing force; it is disruptive in the way the archaic is both disruptive, but also enduringly constitutive, of the modern.

Bakhtin, then, is a thinker who de-emphasizes originality and property, those underlying features attached to our modern understanding of literature and its translation. If a pun be allowed, he retranslates literature away from individual endeavor, toward the work of anonymous verbal masses that support the typomachia of dialogue and monologue, of the centripetal and the centrifugal.

This transformation which subjects the term to inner growth (sometimes at the expense of exactitude), a transformation whereby the term expands its scope of relevance to the point of turning into a broader metaphor, is the most important feature informing Bakhtin's prose, the hallmark of his writings, especially those of the 1930s. It is this transformative energy that sets him apart from his likely, or even demonstrable, antecedents hailing from various specializations, be they linguistic, sociological, theological, or art historical for that matter. It is not difficult, for example, to demonstrate how several of Bakhtin's concepts—architectonics, space, gothic realism— were derived, at least to a significant degree, from the German art-historical tradition. This, however, would tell us very little about the significant transformation of these concepts when thrown into the melting pot of Bakhtin's argumentation. Bakhtin's originality as thinker is actually the originality of the great synthesizer who took at liberty from various specialized discourses—linguistics, art history, theology—and then reshaped, extended, and augmented the scope of the respective concepts.

Bakhtin is thus a thinker who handles language in a way that protects him from falling prey to terminological fetishism. His often-metaphoric employment of terminology from different domains of knowledge gives volume and breadth to his writing and propels it into a quality that cannot be matched by a translation that shies away from preserving this potential metaphoricity.

Of course, the case for translating—and interpreting—Bakhtin with due sensitivity for his capacious and often unfixed terminology should not be pushed too far. The early Bakhtin, for example, was serious about phenomenology, as not only *Towards a Phenomenology of the Act*, *Author and Hero in Aesthetic Activity* but also "The Problem of Content, Material, and Form in Verbal Art" abundantly demonstrate. As late as the early 1940s, in a fragment titled "Towards the Philosophical Foundations of the Humanities" ["K filosofskim osnovam gumanitarnykh nauk"], in which he takes his leave from phenomenology, Bakhtin confronts his readers with a piece of philosophical prose that poses multiple challenges:

Проблема понимания. Понимание как видение смысла, но не феноменальное, а видение живого смысла переживания и выражения, видение внутренне осмысленного, так сказать, самоосмысленного явления.

Выражение как осмысленная материя или материализованный смысл, элемент свободы, пронизавший необходимость. Внешняя и *внутренняя* плоть для милования. Различные пласты души в разной мере поддаются овнешнению. Неовнешняемое художественное ядро души (я для себя). Встречная активность познаваемого предмета.⁵

Clearly Bakhtin here activates a vocabulary that is as recognizably Hegelian ("an element of freedom that had shot through necessity"; "externalization" = "Entäußerung"), as it is Platonic and phenomenological ("видение смысла"), even as he rejects the phenomenological perspective. A translator will have no choice but to heed these fixed layers of terminology. Yet even here the fragment carries an almost untranslatable potentiality inscribed in the noun "милова́ние," to be rendered most certainly as "caressing," but to a reader of Russian, if read out with a different accentuation ("mílovanie" instead of "milovánie"), also triggering associations with "forgiveness" and "absolution." This example is only one illustration of the rewarding, perhaps also daunting, task of translating Bakhtin's philosophical prose at the confluence of equivalences shaped by, and indicative of, different philosophical and cultural traditions.

Bakhtin's work can infuse trust in the eventual returns of meaning, celebrated for its ability to cross borders, to exude invigorating and challenging multiplicity, and to resist monopolizing appropriation. Ferrying a thinker across time and language, translation is the platform that can transform these returns into departures.

Notes

1. On *nazire* in the context of translations-responses to Nizami's five poems, see, above all, G. Aliev, *Temy i siuzhety Nizami v literaturakh narodov Vostoka* (Moscow: Nauka, 1985).
2. For a recent study of this translation, see Jonathan Green, "Friedrich Gentz's Translation of Burke's *Reflections*," *Historical Journal* 57, no. 3 (2014): 639–59.
3. Edmund Burke, *Betrachtungen über die französische Revolution* (Frankfurt am Main: Suhrkamp, 1967).
4. See chapter 3 in Galin Tihanov, *The Birth and Death of Literary Theory: Regimes of Relevance in Russia and Beyond* (Stanford: Stanford University Press, 2019).
5. Mikhail M. Bakhtin, "K filosofksim osnovam gumanitarnykh nauk," *Sobranie sochinenii* (Moscow: Russkie slovari 5, 1996), 9.

Bibliography

Aliev, G. *Temy i siuzhety Nizami v literaturakh narodov Vostoka.* Moscow: Nauka, 1985.

Bakhtin, Mikhail M. "K filosofksim osnovam gumanitarnykh nauk." In *Sobranie sochinenii.* Moscow: Russkie slovari 5, 1996.

Burke, Edmund. *Betrachtungen über die französische Revolution.* Frankfurt am Main: Suhrkamp, 1967.

Green, Jonathan. "Friedrich Gentz's Translation of Burke's *Reflections*," *Historical Journal* 57, no. 3 (2014): 639–59.

Tihanov, Galin. *The Birth and Death of Literary Theory: Regimes of Relevance in Russia and Beyond.* Stanford: Stanford University Press, 2019.

Index

Note: Because Mikhail Bakhtin is mentioned so frequently throughout, the Index contains no separate entry for him.

Austin, Jane 104
Author and Hero in Aesthetic Activity 283

Babel, Isaac 88
Bakhtinian theory 0 57
Bakhtin circle 73
Beatus Ille 189–97, 199, 201–3
Bleakhause 11
Borges, Jorge 170
Bridget Jones's Diary 104, 105
Brothers Karamazov 11
Byron, Goerge Gordon 116, 117

Caiston, Nick 132–40, 142
Calderon 280, 281
Carlson, Marvin 63
Carroll, Lewis 147–51, 155, 171, 172, 212, 214–17, 219–20, 227, 248
Cervantes 171, 257
Chan, Leo 67
China men 63
Colombian Spanish 51
CyraCom 46–8, 50

Demurova, Nina 147
Dialogic Imagination 45, 48, 59, 258
Diary of a Writer for 1873 80
Don Quijote 11, 171, 257–70
Dostoevsky, Fyodor 282
Dubliners 14–17, 19, 28, 31, 34
Duvakin, Victor 113, 114, 116, 121–2

Eco, Umberto 161, 164, 165
Eikhenbaum, Boris 282
Emerson Caril 58

Evgeniy Onegin 86

First Stylistic Line 11
From the Prehistory of Novelistic Discourse 57

Gente di Dublino 16
German Romantics 280
Gils, David 49–50
Goethe, Johann 116–17, 121
Gogol, Nikolay 45
Golden Age (Spain) 135, 190
Gone with the Wind 93, 95, 97, 100, 103, 105, 106
Grossman, Edith 197–200, 202–3
Guillén, Jorge 168–9

Hardy, Thomas 81
Heteroglassia 10, 11, 46
Holquist, Michael 48
Hunting of the Snark 147–8, 152, 155

Joyce, James 14–15, 17, 21

Kagan, Matvey 282
Kingston, Maxine 60–4, 66

Little Dorrit 11

Magrelli, Valerio 163
Medvedev, Pavel 282
Mendoza, Eduardo 129–30, 132, 136, 141
Mitchell, Margaret 93–4, 101, 105
Molina, Muñoz 189–90, 192, 194–8, 200, 201, 203

Nabokov, Vladimir 86
Newberry, Fillip 268, 272
Nietzsche, Friedrich 80

Ortega y Gasset, Jose 140
Otherness 10

Pasternak, Boris 116–17, 121
Poe, Edgar 147
Popper, Amalia 16
Portrait of the Artist as a Young Man 17
Problems of Dostoevsky's Poetics 282
Pushkin, Alexander 166, 168

Rabelais and His World 210
re-accentuation 10, 12
Retranslation Hypothesis 35, 36
Rilke, Rainer Maria 86

Second Stylistic Line 11
Sinyavsky, Andrei 113
Synaeathesia 177

Tihanov, Galin 121
Tirso de Molina 281
Toward a Phenomenology of the Act 283
Twain, Mark 81, 83

Ulysses 11, 15, 16, 19
Unamuno, Miguel de 140
Uncle Charles Principle 30

Veniti, Lawrence 201
Victoria parody 149
Voloshinov, Valentin 163

William the Conqueror 261
Woman Warrier, The 60

Zhukovsky, Vasily 116, 117

www.ingramcontent.com/pod-product-compliance
Lightning Source LLC
Chambersburg PA
CBHW052154300426
44115CB00011B/1661